CHARACTER IS BEAUTY
REDEFINING
YORUBA CULTURE
& IDENTITY
(IWALEWA-HAUS, 1981-1996)

CHARACTER IS BEAUTY
REDEFINING
YORUBA CULTURE
& IDENTITY

(IWALEWA-HAUS, 1981-1996)

EDITED BY
WOLE OGUNDELE,
OLU OBAFEMI,
and
FEMI ABODUNRIN

Africa World Press, Inc.

P.O. Box 1892

Trenton, NJ 08607

P.O. Box 48

Asmara, ERITREA

Africa World Press, Inc.

| P.O. Box 1892 | P.O. Box 48 |
| Trenton, NJ 08607 | Asmara, ERITREA |

Cover Artwork: Georgina Beier
Cover and Book Design: Jonathan Gullery

Library of Congress Cataloging-in-Publication Data

Character is beauty: redefining Yoruba culture and identity--Iwalewa
-Haus, 1981-1996 / edited by Olu Obafemi, Wole Ogundele & Femi
Abodunrin.
    p. cm.
  Includes bibliographical references and index.
  ISBN 0-86543-623-1 (hc.). — ISBN 0-86543-624-X (pbk.)
    1. Yoruba (African people) 2. Arts, Yoruba. 3. IWALEWA-Haus
(Bayreuth, Germany) I. Obafemi, Olu. 1945- . II. Ogundele,
Wole. III. Abodunrin, Femi.
DT515.45.Y67C47 1998
305.896'333--dc21   98-37142
                      CIP

Contents

IV. Art

V. Yoruba Society

VI. Music

VII. Colonialism

A straight tree is the pride of the forest.
A fast deer is the pride of the bush..
Ìwò`rí wò`túrá

INTRODUCTION

The rise of Africa (and other third world continents) into cultural prominence in the second half of this century especially presented problems to Western universities. When the academic war over whether they were worth according serious scholarly interest was won, the problem of how to fit them into the traditional departments arose. Most universities in America that had serious interests in studying Africa and its history(ies), cultures, and traditional systems solved this by simply creating one kind of institute or another. Thus, although not fully admitted into the prestigious departments, some space at the fringe had been created, where these exotic disciplines could be indulged in by those who were interested, without compromising the intellectual integrity of the older, more solid Eurocentric ones.

Thus, although nobody now questions the intellectual worth of studying African History, Literature, Language(s) or Art, African Studies remains on the fringes—in Institutes, Programs, Centers—of most American universities. Where they are incorporated into the mainstream departments, they become a part of global or semi-global studies, like Post-Colonial Literatures or Cultural Studies.

Reluctantly, European universities followed the American lead in establishing their own institutes and centers. Where departments are created, all of black Africa, and all the disciplines, are crammed together into one. It was in this kind of prevalent thinking that Iwalewa-Haus, University of Bayreuth, was founded in 1981. Long in gestation, the original idea was in fact to create a museum-cum-gallery in which traditional as well as contemporary African arts would be periodically mounted. It is, however, a mark of the sincerity of those who originated the idea, and of their desire to do things differently, that they listened to the man whom they had in mind to start the house, and that his own ideas prevailed. Given the nature of the fact that German universities are part of the general state establishment, that they were even ready to consider him at all shows their spirit of adventure.

For Ulli Beier, the founding director of Iwalewa-Haus, and its director for all but five years of the house's existence to date, is an unconventional scholar and an anti-establishment man. These facts will prove important for the activities of the house, and for the contents and purpose of this book. Universities generally are not involved in the practical business of cultural productions or promotion: they prefer to have experts who merely want to study, analyze and (nowadays) theorize them. Even when they set up institutes of cultural studies, it is still more of the same thing, save for the occasional invitation of artists to perform--as reinforcement of what is being studied. Where that university (and its center for African Studies) is far away from the society and culture it studies, the problems are compounded.

Ulli Beier is an unconventional scholar in the sense that, rather than make himself an "expert" in African or Indian or South Pacific Studies, he has preferred to be closely involved in the lives of the societies he has been in, to be a part of their cultural lives and, where possible, to participate in their artistic productions. Thus, when he agreed to be director of Iwalewa-Haus, it was on condition that the house would not just exhibit cultural/artistic artefacts from third-world societies (a practice which often has the unintended consequence of assimilation into Western intellectual traditions and views), but would actively participate in the revitalization and continuation of the different cultural/artistic lives of those societies. Although at home in most parts of the third world, Ulli Beier's "home" is Nigeria—specifically, Yorubaland. He came into that society in 1950 and stayed there uninterruptedly till 1966. His activities in those sixteen years are known worldwide and need not be repeated here. What needs to be pointed out here, rather, is that in his active connection with that society, its people, and its cultural and artistic activities over the past forty years can be read the fortunes and misfortunes that have visited that society from the colonial era to the present post-colonial period. He came to that society when it was on the threshold of mass-scale transformation from a traditional to a marginally modern society; he was pivotal to its artistic-literary renaissance that started in the 1950s and peaked so abruptly in the 1970s; and he has been witness to the crises of cultural and political identities that have beset it since the early 1980s.

In the small, in-house publication outfit of Iwalewa-Haus can be found a record of this history. The house publishes on almost every third-world culture and society but, precisely because of Ulli Beier's special connection with Yoruba society and people, its collection and publications on that society are unique: numerous interviews with Wole Soyinka and other Yoruba scholars on Yoruba music, art, philosophy, religion, etc.; autobiographical documents and interviews with virtually all members of the Osogbo Art Movement; books, memoirs, and interviews on the Duro Ladipo theater by other members of the company; Ulli and Georgina Beier's own memoirs and reflections on that theater and the Art Movement; pictures, music recordings, films, and original documents dating from the 1950s and earlier. All these in addition to the fact that the house has been actively promoting all aspects of Yoruba theatrical performances and artistic practices where they still exist, or reviving and supporting them where they have been in danger of dying. It is out of these unrivalled publications of Iwalewa-Haus that we have selected these papers, interviews, and monographs for publication. They have been selected not just for their uniqueness, but for some other major reasons. As said earlier, Iwalewa-Haus's publishing outfit is in-house—very small and with very limited distribution facilities; we have therefore thought to make a selection of them available to a wider audience. Secondly, most of the publications are inevitably in English and, therefore, unavailable to the vast German audience; so why not make them available to a wider English-speaking audience? And especially to the Yoruba English-reading public? Thirdly, and most important of all, we think that as most of the papers deal with the past and present states of Yoruba society and culture, the connected themes of past glory, (brief) renaissance, and present crises can be coherently put together. This third reason means that the motivation to assemble the papers which make up this book is more than the merely academic. In the tradition of Ulli Beier himself and Iwalewa-Haus, it aims to directly intervene and provoke debate, followed by a determination to do something. The book is, therefore, specifically addressed to the Yoruba English-reading/speaking audience. To the extent that all (black) African societies face the same kind of crises that the Yoruba people face, it is of course also addressed to them. All African societies had their political identities and futures determined for them on maps in Berlin in 1884-1885. All have since then been existing precariously in the cusp between technologized modernity and traditional ways. Thus, although this collection is specifically on Yoruba society, its broad concerns apply to most African societies. It remains to say a few introductory words about the different sections.

I. Crisis of Yoruba Culture

A dialogic, reflexive debate which is nostalgic and passionate is palpable in these exchanges, which collectively address the issue of the crisis of Yoruba culture in contemporary times. The leading discussion between Ulli Beier and Wole Soyinka recalls the peace, the serenity, the integrity and the dynamism of the cultural and theatrical praxis in Ibadan a decade before and shortly after independence. The Yoruba Travelling Theater, the Atilogwu of the Igbo, the Agbor dancers, etc., assembled with the dynamic grandeur of traditional authority to produce a vibrant socio-cosmic culture in Nigeria.

The true essence of nationalism, race/ethnic personality, and the anticipation of a euphoric, abundance-promised independence soon began to fade as the para-bourgeois elite confiscated the hegemony of neo-colonial African states. Both the intellectual elite and the essential adjuncts of indigenous culture were immediately grounded. The travesty and mimicry of the present icon and symbol of traditional authority, the now very untraditional traditional rulers, is the most violent testimony to the anomic state in which the essential Yoruba culture has fallen. A chaotic and hypocritical relationship exists between traditional oligarchy and modern dictatorship in Nigeria today. In the Soyinka-Beier exchange, the tangle between the Oni of Ife and the Emir of Kano on the one hand, and the Buhari/Idiagbon Administration (1983-1985) on the other is seen as the turning point; but the post-independence roots go back to the days of "the penny-a-year oba." Material greed and the need for stereotypic rubber-stamping of illegitimate rulership have produced a leprous embrace between erstwhile custodians of the people's political self-regulation and the new, cynical appropriators and manipulators of power, be they civilian or military.

II. Theater

The fundamental concern about the on-going vulgarization of the ethos of Yoruba social and cultural life is manifested most in the performative arts. This section therefore concerns the history, development and character of contemporary Yoruba theater from its beginnings through the triumphant phase of the Yoruba Travelling Theater, to the present phase of "decline" into cheap, cash-driven video productions. Excerpts from Ulli Beier's comprehensive account of the making of Duro Ladipo's theater titled "The Return of Sango" give a foretaste of the essential attributes of Yoruba theater in all its manifestations. The link between the indigenous theatrical modes exemplified in the Alarinjo masque-dramaturgy and the folk operatic theater has been explored in the other essays. The major apprehension here is that aesthetic and political relevance are being sacrificed on the altar of commodification and political expediency, re-enacting the essential crisis in Yoruba and the Nigerian cultures and society.

III. Yoruba Religion, Arts & Aesthetics

This section focuses on the concept of aesthetics in Yoruba art—both from the viewpoint of the artists (as here exemplified by Roland Abiodun, Twins Seven-Seven and Georgina Beier) and from the cosmo-cultural world view of the Yoruba. The main point being made here is that aesthetics, or the concept of beauty, is contextual. Its main attributes and ingredients are: character-cultivation and enduring values (Ìwà-Le`wà); meaning-generation; and painstakingness (Ìfarabalè`, which is also Ìwàpè`lé`). All yield wholesomeness, completeness, and fulfillment. The concept of beauty (aesthetics) among the Yoruba transcends both the formalist/structuralist principles, it also lies outside the confines of physicality (shape, form, color) to embrace content, meaning social function, and relevance. Beauty is therefore permanence of value as derived from both the physical state and the spiritual/metaphysical significance. This position is fully and manifestly explored in the discussion between Ulli Beier and Roland Abiodun under the title "Yoruba Aesthetic." It is also in this context that the revelation of the emergence and discovery of Twins Seven-Seven from the stature of a salesman/dancer/medicine vendor to the status of an accomplished artist comes into bold relief. Twins Seven-Seven is not an academically cultivated artist, and for this he is ranged with the equivocal reception of Amos Tutuola in English literature parlance, as partly analyzed in Georgina Beier's essay "To Organise is to Destroy: The Oshogbo Art School." In the various discussions on Yoruba arts and aesthetics, the meanings of certain key Yoruba terms, indispensable to any discussion of Yoruba aesthetic practices, are grappled with, perhaps for the first time. This has enabled the discussants to look at Yoruba arts from inside rather than analyze them with Western concepts as has always been the academic practice.

IV. Multicultural Music

"Yoruba society is certainly the most tolerant society that I know," Ulli Beier has often said. Then, to support this assertion, he would often ask, rhetorically: "Otherwise, how could they have 401 gods?" Wole Soyinka, too, often said that, to his knowledge, Africans are the only people who have never waged religious wars. To be tolerant is to be multicultural, to allow that other people have their own "gods" and must worship them their own way—that even when you have the same gods, you can still worship them differently. Hence the Yoruba saying: Bi o ti wu eni la nse imole eni (Let me practice my Islam the way I know best). To recognize difference and make allowance for it is to have innate strength and resilience, even though one may not realize it. Yoruba religion and culture have shown both strength and resilience, especially in the black diaspora. In the area of music, these same qualities are currently being proved again by the activities of Iwalewa-Haus: in Tunji Akanmu Beier, whose magnificent edifice of multicultural music was built on the foundation of dundun and bata, and in groups like OKUTA PERCUSSION and BASSAMA. Tolerance and multiculturalism have always been the "survival genius" of Yoruba society.

V. Colonialism

The story of colonialism in Africa is one whose conclusion is still far into the future, for, as most observers have perceived, barely five years into the "independence decade" (the 1960s), it did not—and could not—end with flag independence. In this section, Wole Soyinka, Ulli Beier, and the philosopher Sophie Oluwole, provide new perspectives on its education aspect. "Education would lead to liberation" was the doctrine and indeed the University College, Ibadan, was established in 1948 as part of the long-term preparation for political independence. But it was "Western Education," not "African education." The ironies and ambiguities inherent in that defining and delimiting difference have since ramified, not diminished. In Sophie Oluwole's struggle to establish a discipline called African philosophy, we are reminded again that education in Africa must be "African," to be enriched and not displaced by "Western Education."

Preface

Olu Obafemi
Forty Years In African Art And Life: Reflections on Ulli Beier

Variously defined as a Border Operator (John Thomson), a literary entre-peneur (Peter Benson), a spokesman (Owomoyela), etc, Ulli Beier's most enduring artistic and cultural creations include ODU, a Journal of Yoruba Culture (founded 1954), BLACK ORPHEUS (Founded 1957), MBARI PUB-LICATIONS, the MBARI CLUB in lbadan, MBARI MBAYO in Oshogbo, INTRODUCTION TO AFRICAN LITERATURE (1967), and IWALEWA-Haus in Bayreuth, Germany. Ulli Beier's versatile creative activity brought to the limelight great African writers like Gabriel Okara, Wole Soyinka, Christopher Okigbo, J.P. Clark, Dennis Brutus, Alex la Guma, Ama Ata Aidoo, and Kofi Awoonor, all of whose works he first published. He opened links with Francophone literature and philosophy by translating writers like Sedar Senghor, Aimé Césaire and Rabearivelo. He promoted theater artists like E.K. Ogunmola and Duro Ladipo and visual artists like Twins Seven-Seven (Taiwo Olaniyi), Demas Nwoko, and Uche Okeke.

Ulli Beier was born in Germany in 1922, in Glowitz (now Poland). He studied archeology before the second imperialist war interrupted his study and his life, having been held in a British detention camp for six years (1940-1946). He took his BA degree in the detention camp and went on to get an honours degree in literature as a self-taught external student of the University of London. He spent several years teaching handicapped children in London before his appointment to the University College lbadan in 1950. He came to Nigeria with Susanne Wenger, the Austrian artist, who later became deeply involved in Yoruba religion and is famous for her artistic work in the Oshun grove of Oshogbo. While many saw him as a personalizer or personifier of African (especially Yoruba) culture, Ulli Beier saw himself as no more than a catalyst of the Nigerian total experience. Whether from extreme modesty or in an attempt to identify himself totally as a Yoruba, he assumed many pseudonyms during his years in Nigeria, for example Sangodare Akanji, Omidiji Aragbabalu, and the controversial Obotunde Ijimere.

O: It is widely acknowledged that you are one of the few individuals who made a tremendous impact on the development of African literature, art, and culture in general. To clarify the nature of these contributions I would like to ask you a few questions. First of all: what do you consider your main contribution, which achievement are you most fond of?

U: I can't really answer that, because I did not go to Nigeria to make "a contribution." You should read my recent essay "In a Colonial University" (Iwalewa 1993). That describes in some detail how I came to Nigeria almost by accident and how I got involved in various activities gradually, simply in response to certain situations. Originally I had no other aim in mind except to teach English literature. But I soon found out that my students couldn't relate to what I said: It seemed like an alien subject. To make it more meaningful I tried to find out what African literature there was that I could refer to.

My colleagues assured me that there was no such thing! I found their lack of curiosity difficult to understand. Of course, the great upsurge of Nigerian literature had not happened in 1950 but there were some great writers in the francophone countries. So I translated Senghor, Césaire, Rabearivelo, and Diop and introduced them into my classes.

One of the most exciting discoveries I made were S.A. Babalola's translations of Ijala—they opened up a whole new world for me. I suddenly realized what wealth of poetry was to be discovered in the Yoruba language: what wit and what wisdom and what powerful images. Without knowing it at the time, my life had taken a decisive turn. Once you read Ijala you get drawn into a whole new life style.

As early as 1952 I held an Extra Mural Weekend School in Abeokuta called "African Poetry." It was a rather wild mixture of material that we looked at. It was not a highly organized course. But I think it made a point: it demonstrated the fact that literature was not some strange English invention, something one had to learn in order to pass one's school certificate or to become part of the new elite. It showed the students that they had their own tradition of classical literature, which was as rich as that of any nation, and it put English literature in its proper place. English literature was no longer the expression of a superior culture that was to be imposed on Nigerians in order to replace their own culture. It was merely another form of expression that could offer one a widening of the horizon, a further window onto the world. I suppose I am still doing the same thing now, forty years later. When I put on an annual concert of African music in the Bayreuth Opera House I am trying to say to the German audience: "With due respect to Bach, Mozart, and Beethoven, there are other classical music traditions, different, but as complex and intense and rewarding as your own. And you must listen to a Dundun orchestra or to Igbo xylophones with as much concentration as you do to a Beethoven string quartet."

The wonderful thing about living in a new country, in a new culture, is that you make discoveries every day. My first years in Nigeria were full of surprises. Life could never become a routine. You develop a heightened sense of awareness.

Strangely enough, many of my colleagues at the University tried to shut themselves off from the experience. They created a ghetto around themselves. They saw their task as a civilizing mission: a Nigerian elite had to be created, fit to rule Nigeria because they had absorbed enough British values. The British recognized no other values in life than their own.

I was lucky, because after one frustrating year in the English Department I could switch over to the Department of Extra-Mural Studies, which was headed by that dynamic and inspiring Ghanaian Robert Gardiner. Here I had motivated colleagues like Gerald Moore (and later even Ezekiel Mphahlele!) and, above all, I was independent of the London University syllabus. It was not the University of Ibadan let alone the University of London!) who determined what was to be studied, but the students themselves. If I could also persuade them to study African Literature or African Art or even to found a Theater Company, the University could not stop us.

Robert Gardiner gave me that freedom and he also gave me the inspiration. Gardiner used the Extra-Mural Department to raise all those issues that the University, in its ivory-tower seclusion, would ignore.

He saw literature not as an academic subject, not as a specialization in "Eng.Lit.," but as a way of understanding other people, their problems, their philosophies, and their cultures. He was a highly political man; and in many of our literature courses, we used literature to discuss other issues. My own contribution to the Extra-Mural Department were the cultural seminars. The pioneering venture was called "West African Culture." It was held on the University campus in the summer of 1953.

We went on with a course on Yoruba culture, which took place in Ede in 1954. This time we were on much more solid ground: the lecturers included three Obas - the Oni of Ife, Timi Laoye, and the Ogoga of Ikere. There were also S.A. Babalolo, E.L. Lasebikan, and the philosopher T.S. Sowande. It was this course that inspired the creation of ODU.

All these people were not only highly knowledgeable about their culture, they were passionate about it. I dreamt in those days of the possibility of revising the entire structure of education in Yorubaland. That all these committed people could give an entirely new slant to the educational system the British had planted in Nigeria. But up till today Nigerian schools and universities still propagate to a large extent colonial ideas. Isn't that right?

O: Yes, it is, in a way.

U: I am sorry I have been rather long-winded in trying to explain how I got involved. The only real quality I brought to these experiences was, perhaps, flexibility.

O: Thank you very much. This is an aspect of your contribution about which not much has been recorded. Now, in an attempt to quantify your contribution, you have been described in various ways as a border operator, a spokesman of African literature. And because of your organizational ability and your success in raising funds for various activities you were seen as a literary entrepreneur. An important area which I would like you to touch upon is the foundation of BLACK ORPHEUS, which, I think, has done a lot to bring scholars and writers together. What was your motivation in starting BLACK ORPHEUS and in what direction did you steer the magazine?

U: Well, it was quite simple, really. I had been interested in African literature for a while and I was teaching it, but I had never thought of a magazine. Then in 1956 in Paris I attended the first Pan-African Conference of African Writers and Artists organized by Présence Africaine. It was a very exciting conference, a highpowered affair, which was taken very seriously by the French media. Picasso himself designed the poster! It was not treated like a fringe event. It was amazing for me to see how vital the literary movement was in the Caribbean and in the French African territories.

The highlight of the conference was the clash between Richard Wright and Aimé Césaire. Richard Wright had been to Ghana at the invitation of Victor Padmore, Nkrumah's West Indian adviser. He had gone with the illusion of "coming home," like so many other Afro-Americans. But Ghana bewildered him and he could not see any merit in Ghanaian culture at all. In his book "Black Power," which he published later, he describes Ghana as a place riddled with "superstition." So he stood up there on the rostrum and proclaimed: "Thank you white man for destroying our culture!" He felt that Africa had to be totally modernized, that it had to be "militarized" and that in the process of doing this it had to strip itself of its "dark" past.

It pained me deeply to hear him speak like that, because I had been an admirer of his writings for years; I had used books like "Black Boy" and "Native Son" in my classes. Césaire's response was passionate and inspiring. He had no difficulty in carrying the bulk of the audience with him.It was at this moment that the idea of BLACK ORPHEUS was born. I wanted Nigerians to have access to this dynamic world. I wanted my students to share the excitement I had felt in Paris. I was helped by meeting Janheinz Jahn for the first time. Of course, we had corresponded for the last three years. He had published his anthology of African poetry in German as early as 1954, when African literature was virtually unknown in Germany. In the process of compiling his "Schwarzer Orpheus" he had corresponded for years with people all over Africa, including myself. I had helped him to get some material from Nigeria, which included works by Mabel Imoukhuede, Denis Osadebey, and even some Ijala poems in S.A. Babalola's translations.

Jahn had, at the time the largest existing archive on African literature and he was a very useful and energetic partner. Once we had made up our minds to start a journal, we wasted no time. The Literature Bureau of the Ministry of Education in Ibadan was sympathetic. They were already publishing ODU and were happy with its success. So by September 1957 our first issue appeared, with poems by S.A. Babalola, Leopold Sedar Senghor, and Gabriel Okara, with an article on Amos Tutuola and a report on the Présence Africaine conference in Paris.

BLACK ORPHEUS was not a big commercial enterprise. The magazine was almost hand- made. There was no staff, only voluntary work. The covers were screen-printed. The edition did not exceed fifteen hundred. Yet its influence was disproportionately high. In Germany Jahn found a friendly bookseller who took a hundred copies which found their way into the hands of writers and scholars. In Holland a passionate journalist called van Brassem personally distributed another hundred copies. One of these reached the artist Ru van Rossem, who later became involved in the Mbari Clubs and ran graphic art workshops there. In South Africa the magazine had to be smuggled in and it was sold illegally, under the counter, by Vanguard Bookshop in Johannesburg. The bookshop owner took considerable risk doing so!

BLACK ORPHEUS had no ideology. What we wanted to do was to provide a platform for writers. Our criterion was quality. We also wanted to acquaint Nigerian or Ghanaian writers with the literary activities that went on in French-speaking Africa. At a later stage we even introduced North African Writers. We also kept the bridges open to the past: each issue of BLACK ORPHEUS contained some translations of traditional poetry.

O: So the awareness that something existed before was there.

U: Of course. We wanted to remind people that all African cultures had lyrical, epical, and dramatic forms, that all this new literature was not happening in a vacuum. And it was not like being a literary archeologist! In the Nigeria of the 1950s and 60s everything was happening at the same time! While some people were writing political poems for the West African Pilot and while Wole Soyinka was performing his first great plays, the hunters were still singing their Ijala, the Shango priests were still chanting Shango Pipe, and the oracle priests were still reciting their Odu. You did not have to go out of your way to find these things: simply by sitting on my verandah on Ibokun Road in Oshogbo I would hear the mother of twins improvising her songs in praise of Ibeji, I would hear the rara chanting of the bride on her way to her husband's house, I would hear the oriki of all the major orisha! It was all very much alive and I felt it would be very wrong to pretend it was a thing of the past, with no relevance to the present. In those days even political campaigns were fought with the help of dundun drummers and oriki-chanters!

O: Thank you. Peter Benson wrote a book on the history of BLACK ORPHEUS and TRANSITION and he had very many things to say on BLACK ORPHEUS, on your role in it.

U: Yes, but he never bothered to interview me. In fact, I never met him. But that's only by the way.

O: His contribution was good. It wasn't negative in any way, because he attributed BLACK ORPHEUS solely to you. But what interests me in his account is that he claims that aesthetically you were leaning towards surrealism and that politically you loved the ideology of negritude, though later on perhaps you shifted your position.

U: No, no, that is completely incorrect. You can only publish the literature that exists! In 1957 there was no Wole Soyinka and there was no Christopher Okigbo. The first issue of BLACK ORPHEUS featured Gabriel Okara—hardly a negritude writer. The first four issues may have had a predominance of French African, Carribbean, and Black American writing, but that was simply because anglophone writing in Africa appeared on the scene slightly later. I met Wole Soyinka in London in 1958. A Nigerian BBC producer had shown me three of his poems: "The Immigrant," "The Other Immigrant," and "My Next Door Neighbour." I was quite excited by these and rang him to make an appointment. He came to meet me at Gallery One in Soho, where Susanne Wenger was holding her first London exhibition. I published the poems in our next issue, Nr. 5, which appeared in May 1959. But anyway, who published Wole's first plays?

O: It was you, I think. The THREE PLAYS.

U: That's right. I created MBARI PUBLICATIONS and we published Wole's first three plays, J.P.'s SONG OF A GOAT, Okigbo's first two volumes of poetry, J.P.'s first volume of poetry, and Alex La Guma's novel A WALK IN THE NIGHT which I had to smuggle out of South Africa. We published Mphalele's stories and Denis Brutus' first volume of poetry (while he was in jail) and Kofi Awoonor's first poems and Lenrie Peters from Sierra Leone. We published Ama Ata Aidoo's first short story in BLACK ORPHEUS. So what do you mean by saying I was a surrealist and a negritude partisan? Where were Heinemann and Longmans in those days? Where were the American publishers? They wouldn't touch it. As far as I can remember I only published one surrealist story; that was BECAUSE OF THE KING OF FRANCE by Adrienne Comelle. She was a black American writer, married to a sociologist called Kennedy who was working in Ibadan. One day he came to me and said that his wife wrote stories, but was too shy to show them to anybody. Could I give her an opinion? I fell in love with that story and published it at once. And if I didn't publish any more surrealist stories, it was because I didn't come across any others that I thought were good, that's all. Adrienne Cornelle, by the way, went on to become a famous playwright in New York!

When I look back at my years with BLACK ORPHEUS now, I can't see any really good writer today whom I missed out on or whom I didn't do justice to. Or can you think of anybody whom I should have published and didn't? There are, I must admit, a few things here and there, that I wish I hadn't published, though not many. Sometimes you feel you want to encourage somebody. You want to be kind. But as an editor one should never do that. One has to be ruthlessly honest with people. I remember I rejected J.P.'s first short story, a very sentimental piece about a white "palm oil ruffian" who exploited African women. It was badly written. He was furious with me at that time, even though I spent one afternoon trying to explain to him what I thought was wrong with it. But today, I am sure, he will be glad it wasn't published; because he went on to write so much better things. So you see: BLACK ORPHEUS did not so much reflect on my personal preferences, but it reflected my judgement of what was good in African literature at that time. By and large, I think, I fully stand by my judgement, even today.

O: Thank you very much. I don't think Peter Benson meant it negatively. But there is another thing people have been accusing you of. They said that you tried to dominate the critical voice of BLACK ORPHEUS, and that is why you used so many pseudonyms.

U: You seem to forget, that there weren't any literary critics around in those days. Most creative writers don't really like to tear each other's work apart. And the Ireles and Nwogas appeared a little later on the scene. I used whom I could: Gerald Moore contributed heavily, so did J.A. Ramsaran. Later on Ezekiel Mphalele and Ronald Dathorne shouldered much of the burden. I could persuade some people to contribute an occasional review. Cyprian Ekwensi, for example, or Dennis Duerden or Geombeyl Adali Mortty. As BLACK ORPHEUS became internationally known I could persuade famous people like Martin Esslin or Paul Theroux to write for it.

But in the early days I had to play the donkey. It became a similar issue, when we started the MBARI CLUB in Ibadan. No Nigerian newspaper at the time had an arts page or a feuilleton. I went from editor to editor asking them to report on MBARI exhibitions and concerts and plays, but they kept saying that they had no one to do it. They invited me to write for them myself. I did so for the first few weeks and I did go around and found people who organized reviews columns or whole pages for local papers.

As for pseudonyms: Sangodare Akanji or Omidiji Aragbabalu are not my pseudonyms, they are my oriki—given to me by the Shango priests of Oshogbo and the Erinle priests of Ilobu respectively. Maybe you didn't know it, but Wole also used a pseudonym in BLACK ORPHEUS—though he did not indulge in it as often as I did.

O: There was a feeling that BO concentrated heavily on poetry and fiction but neglected the performing arts. Why so little drama?

U: A magazine can absorb a poem and a short story easily, but the reproduction of a complete play would burst its frame. That's why we published plays in MBARI PUBLICATIONS: Wole's plays, Duro's plays, and J.P.'s plays.

O: There was this tremendous impact you had on artists like Twins Seven-Seven and Demas Nwoko. A lot has been said about the workshops you ran in Oshogbo. . . .

U: I am glad you mention this, because there has been a lot of myth-making around these workshops. But let's talk about Demas first. Demas Nwoko was trained in Zaria, at the Nigerian College of Arts, Science and Technology. He was the leader in the revolt against the British art education system that was foisted on the students. Quite early on he evolved a very personal style of painting. Later he became a successful stage designer, and finally a brilliant, self-trained architect: I think he is by far the most interesting architect operating in Nigeria! I had nothing to do with his brilliant career at all, except that I have always admired his work. We were co-founders of MBARI Ibadan and I exhibited his work, but that was all.

A lot of nonsense has been written about the Oshogbo art workshops. I am not an artist. I have never painted a picture in my life and I could not run an art workshop. Yet people who knew better, because they were actually there, like Michael Crowder and Frank Willett, have described me as running the Oshogbo art workshops. This simply is not true. The first two workshops in 1962 and 1963 were run by Denis Williams, a West Indian painter and scholar whom I invited to Oshogbo. His workshops created a lot of life and activity, but they did not produce any professional artists, because they lasted only five days and Denis being very busy in Ibadan on his research could not do any follow up-work, as we had hoped. In 1963, however, Georgina Beier arrived in Oshogbo and she opened a studio in which Rufus Ogundele and Jacob Afolabi could work. It was then only that these two artists developed the confidence and they started to become professional artists. Then, in 1964, Georgina ran the famous workshop from which Muraina Oyelami, Twins Seven-Seven, Bisi Fabunmi and Tijani Mayakiri emerged. Until we left Nigeria in December 1966 all these artists, and some like Samuel Ojo, who joined the group later, were working in our house or in a studio we had opened for them in the Ataoja's palace. I arranged exhibitons for the artists. I created galleries for them. I wrote about them ... but I never taught them.

But all this has been described in detail in the publication "Thirty Years of Oshogbo Art" which was published by IWALEWA-HAUS in 1992. We don't really have to go into this again.

O: Thank you. This is the kind of clarification I thought was necessary for historical purpose. So you didn't teach art, but is it true that you taught creative writing in New Guinea?

U: Yes, I did run a creative writing class in Papua New Guinea, though at first rather reluctantly. I went to PNG because the newly founded University was looking for someone to teach "New Literature from Developing Nations." In other words: the kind of thing that I had been doing for the last fifteen years on the fringe of the University of Ibadan and almost against the University's wishes, I could now set up as the official literature course. I found that very tempting.

The University Of Papua New Guinea was in those early years the best university I have ever been in. It was independent of any Australian institution. It had a highly motivated staff—mostly Australians—and it had only 350 students at that time. I knew virtually every one of them.

I compiled a literature course consisting of a study of PNG oral traditions, African, Indian, and Australian literature in English, Modern World Literature. English classics were merely brought in as optional subjects in the final year.

The only problem was that literature was a "half-unit" that had to be combined with another language half-unit. My best students hated the language courses and so I was in danger of losing them. The only way to keep them was to offer an alternative "half-unit" and this is how I came to teach "Creative Writing," with some trepidation. Because basically I believed that it could not be done.

O: Yes, nobody can teach the art of creativity.

U: I made the course by invitation only. During the first year students could submit their writing to me—stories, poetry, drama, whatever they wished. But at this stage they received no credit for it all. Out of these I would select about half a dozen with whom I thought I could work and they could then drop the language part and take creative writing.

But it is a nerve-wracking experience for the teacher. When somebody submits to you a piece of writing, it's often very easy to improve it. But that's pointless unless you are quite sure what the student really wanted to do. Otherwise you are merely impeding his natural development. Teaching is not a matter of showing somebody some useful tricks, but of getting to know the student, of understanding him and giving him the confidence to be himself. It is a very delicate thing: the chemistry has to be right between the teacher and the student, you have to divest yourself of the image of authority.

Georgina has this sensitivity in the highest degree, that's why some of the greatest artists in New Guinea and in Nigeria emerged from her studio. But I think we are drifting. Let's get back to Nigeria.

O: Yes, we must talk about Duro Ladipo. Because people are intrigued about what kind of relationship you had with Duro Ladipo, to the effect that people think you have actually shaped his theater. It was even said that the impact was so much that you were indispensible to him and that he could hardly stand on his own feet after you left for New Guinea.

U: Surely, you know perfectly well, that this is nonsense. We left Oshogbo in December 1966. My working association with Duro had lasted five years. But as you know, he went on producing new plays and performing round the world for another decade. He survived the years of the civil war, when touring was difficult. He performed in Switzerland, in Yugoslavia, in France, Iran, and Brazil. He made two tours of the United States. What more do you want a man to do, to prove that he can stand on his own feet by himself.

Most of what was written about the relationship between Duro and myself was pure speculation. The authors never consulted either him or me. In fact, with all the stuff that has been written about this, only one person ever came to interview me—that was a black American who wrote a thesis on Duro for some American university. I never saw what he wrote, though. There appeared to be two opinions, both equally absurd. Those who wanted to denigrate Duro (because they were partisans of Ogunde) claimed that Duro was no real artist at all, because all his plays had been concocted by a white man. Those who tried, like Yemi Ogunbiyi, to rehabilitate Duro, then went on to say that I had nothing to do with it whatsoever.

The relationship between Duro and me is difficult to describe, like all human relationships. We were friends, long before I knew he could compose music and long before he ever attempted to write a play. After he returned from the North in 1958 and opened the Popular Bar in Oshogbo, we saw each other almost daily. We drank beer together, we talked, we argued. We went to the Oshun festival together or we shared the ram with a Muslim friend during the Ileya festival.

The most important thing I did for him was to stand by him during his confrontation with the Anglican Church. The church fathers had created a tremendous row, because he had brought "pagan" drums into the church during his Easter Cantata in 1961. It was hard for him, because his father was a catechist and I think he never forgave Duro.

I opened a new circuit for Duro by taking him to Segun Olusola of WNTV and by arranging a performance of his Christmas Cantata at MBARI Ibadan. The MBARI CLUB in Ibadan inspired him and he was determined to have something like that in Oshogbo too. It was not easy to raise money for this, but we managed to create MBARI-MBAYO on a grant of £200. Of course I discussed his plays with him, just as he discussed other things with me—politics or family matters. It seems absurd, but, at that stage, I knew more about Yoruba history and religion than he did. But then he had been through an Anglican Mission school while I had had the benefit of the friendship of Timi Laoye of Ede who took great pains to open my eyes to the culture he loved so much. From him I first learned about the wisdom, the humour, the energy, and, above all, the tolerance of Yoruba culture. It is this tolerance, this openness of Yoruba culture that explains in the end my whole existence in Yorubaland. They made me part of it. Very soon I felt much more at home with the Shango worshippers of Ede or Oshogbo than with most of my colleagues at the university. I was no stranger in Oshogbo or Ede or Ilobu.

Let me tell you a little anecdote. In 1960 I took Langston Hughes, the black American poet, around Oshogbo, and everywhere we went the children shouted: "Oyinbo! " But they were referring to him and not to me, because by then I was Sangodare Akanji to them.

When people are trying to assess my "role" in Nigeria, they are forgetting that I did not go to "study" a culture. I was neither a historian nor an anthropologist. I just became part of it all, because I responded to what I saw and to what I met; and because people treated me like another human being, not like a European or a colonialist or a scholar. You said you wanted to assess my "contribution" to Nigerian culture and particularly to Yoruba culture. I must have made some impact, simply because I was there, because I was enthusiastic about their culture and because I could see certain aspects of their life-style with completely fresh eyes, while they were simply taking it for granted.

But let me tell you one thing: I took far more from Yoruba culture than I put back into it. What I learned from priests and kings and artists and friends about life and its meaning and ultimately also about myself—my limitations and my talents—was enormous. Whatever I have become in life, I owe to Nigeria. And people like Timi Laoye and Duro Ladipo and the Iya Shango in Ilobu—to name a very few—had a lot to do with it.

To describe the relationship between Duro and me is the subject matter of a book. I have just written it, a book in which I want to pay homage to his genius. I think you will have to wait for it. Hopefully it will appear in Spring 1994.

But one thing I might say: if you remember what I just said about teaching creative writing—that there has to be this empathy, this wavelength between the teacher and the student—with Duro I had this wavelength as never before. And we were both students and teachers of each other, you might say; we stimulated each other, to the extent that I, who had never thought of myself as a playwright, began to write plays for his theater.

O: What kind of plays? Obotunde Ijimere's plays?

U: Well, it started when Duro had to do a monthly TV play (at some stage even a weekly one) to keep alive. It is almost impossible for anybody to be that productive without wearing himself out. So I helped him out with ideas and sometimes sketched out a suggestion. These were bread-and-butter-plays, mind you, without any great artistic pretensions. One idea that came to me was to adapt an eighteenth-century German play by Lessing about the competition of the three "great" religions: Christianity, Islam and Judaism. It was set in Jerusalem of the thirteenth-century and it preached a spirit of tolerance and mutual respect. It was easy to adapt into an Oshogbo setting: the competitors were Christianity, Islam, and Oshun worship and the play pleaded for the recognition of Yoruba religion as a philosophy of life of equal value.

The Ijimere plays arose out of a translation exercise. Duro had never realy written his plays down. The songs were memorized by the actors and the dialogue was improvised. But when a German TV team filmed a complete version of OBA KOSO for ZDF, we had to produce a complete German text for the subtitles. It was only then that Duro made a complete written version of the play and we sat down and produced an English version, which was later turned into German. We enjoyed ourselves so much doing this, that we went on to translate OBA MORO and OBA WAJA as well. These three English versions were published by MBARI PUBLICATIONS. It was immediately after that, that I wrote the first three Ijimere plays: "The Imprisonment of Obatala," "Everyman," and "Woyengi."

Working with Duro had produced a certain mood. I enjoyed this game wit language and I just carried on. "Everyman" and "Woyengi" were written very specifically for the theater—I even had specific actors in my mind. "The Imprisonment of Obatala" was different—here I just got carried away by language.

Now you want to know why I chose a pseudonym and why I chose such a crazy one. Ijimere really was a pseudonym, unlike Sangodare or Omidiji. I chose a pseudonym, because I felt that, though I might have written some plays, this didn't tum me into a professional playwright. I didn't believe that I had any major contribution to make in this field.

It is difficult to remember your feelings after so many years, but it is a little bit like this: you write some plays in a kind of daze. You realize it is working with Duro that has put you into that mood. You look at these manuscripts and you think: Have I really done this? So you invent some fictitious character. It's a joke you share with those to whom you offer the plays. It's also like a masquerade: everybody knows there is a man underneath the cloth, but we also know that the man gets transformed into something else while he is wearing it. Now it was not much of a secret at the time, because Duro knew and so did the whole company in Oshogbo, Wole knew and all my friends at lbadan.

O: You said Wole Soyinka knew; but Oyekan Owomoyela published a book in America and in this particular essay he said Soyinka gave "The Imprisonment of Obatala" the kind of perception which shows that it was a true self apprehension of the Yoruba world view, because the writer was Yoruba.

U: Is Mr. Owomoyela trying to say that only a Yoruba can comprehend the Yoruba world view? And does he really think Wole is that narrow-minded? Wole compared my play with the Brazilian play "Oxala" which deals with the same myth. But the myth and its interpretation had changed in the diaspora, acquiring new and different meanings. Whereas my own version was based on what I had learned in the very heart of Yorubaland. So quite naturally it was closer to the way Wole himself perceived it. The Yoruba world-view is very flexible. After all, nothing is written. There are no rigid commandments, as in the Bible. The gods have to be re-interpreted all the time through their priests, and they have to be brought to life through the worshippers when they go into trance.

So the image of the god changes, to the extent that the cult itself may split. This is particulary prominent in the Obatala cult, where you have Ogiyan, Ajagemo, Orisanla, and so many variants of the basic concept. So my version, although quite a personal one, is legitimate; and the Brazilian one is also legitimate. Wole Soyinka's Ogun is something quite different from the Ogun I have encountered in Ire Ekiti, but Yoruba religion is not dogmatic—that is it's greatness. It is this flexibility also which made it possible for Susanne Wenger to play the role she did. She could not have done that in many other cultures. But I think we are deviating from the theme.

O: But why the choice of Obotunde Ijimere with all its bizarre connotations?

U: Well, Ijimere is my favorite monkey. I knew these creatures well. They are dignified and wise. In Yoruba tradition they are sometimes referred to as Babalawos. I like the way they look you boldly in the face.

The idea of Obotunde is not as strange as you think. There are many such stories linked to Egungun and Oro. But I don't want to drift off into mythology again. The name was a joke: it was bandied around casually between Duro and me and some other friends and then suddenly it stuck. It was also a way of signalling immediately that this was a pseudonym.

O: We will have to talk about IWALEWA-HAUS; without that the story would not be complete. I know that it's attached to the University of Bayreuth. I know that it's a kind of multipurpose institute. But it also represents a kind of continuity for you...doesn't it?

U: That is correct. I was not at all interested in a job in Bayreuth. I had no desire to live in Europe again. I had been away for too long and I felt that if I couldn't live in Nigeria, Australia was far freer, far more relaxed than Europe.

But this job, when the concept finally evolved after lengthy correspondences with the Vice Chancellor, was very tempting. I rejected the intitial proposal of a museum outright. That's not my kind of job. Its too dead. But when they agreed that IWALEWA should not only be a museum of contemporary art from Africa and other non-Western countries, that it would also be an art gallery with constantly changing exhibitions, that we could have artists-in-residence, that we could make African food, then I felt I had to take the job, because it gave me the opportunity to combine all my past experiences from Nigeria, India, Papua New Guinea, and Australia into one organic whole.

I saw lots of possibilities: possibilities of providing new opportunities for my artist and musician friends from all those countries. People like Obiora Udechukwu, Muraina Oyelami, Middle Art, Rufus Ogundele from Nigeria or Kauage from Papua New Guinea, to mention a few, could find the peace here to work away from home pressures and everyday harassments. They could exhibit here and mostly we had the opportunity to arrange further shows for them in other cities. So IWALEWA-HAUS could open up new horizons for them in Europe, while their prolonged presence in Bayreuth gave us the opportunity to work on their biographies or to have discussions with them on their aesthetic concepts. Artists-in-residence have the opportunity to meet German artists here, but they also have the opportunity to meet each other: Obiora Udechukwu, for example, first met Muraina Oyelami in IWALEWA-HAUS!

From a certain point of view I find our work in music even more important. Because an artist works in isolation. He can show his completed work to others and discuss it with them. But while he is creating he must lock himself in. Music, on the other hand, is a social art form. It's a joint effort of several people. Therefore it allows you all kinds of possibilities for intercultural experimentation.

When I was working with Duro we brought the Agbor dancers to participate in the original performance of MOREMI. So we had dundun and bata
drummers as well as Igbo slit gongs and calabash horns. In the final scene
Duro managed to combine all these instruments into one spectacular orches-
tral sound. I was hoping then, that this successful experiment would lead to
a whole new development. Imagine the kind of orchestra a composer could
create, if he combined instruments from all over Nigeria: the trumpets of the
North with the xylophones of the Plateau, the slit gongs of the East, the talking drums of the West, and so on. But it never happend. Soon after the performance of MOREMI the civil war came and made such interaction
impossible, and later on no one seemed very interested.

In Bayreuth I was able to pick up this idea again. Here we could bring
together African or Indian musicians with great Jazz performers. More important still: we could bring together musicians from, say, Africa, India, and
Indonesia to work together and create an entirely new music. I think I can say
without exaggeration that in what is sometimes grandiloquently called "World
Music" we, at IWALEWA-HAUS, have played a leading part.

You see, we are a very small institution. I have only got one colleague, a
half-time secretary, and a tiny vote. There are other institutions in this country who have the money to fly in a xylophone orchestra of 18 Chopi musicians or the Kathakali Theater from Kerala with a cast of forty. We couldn't
compete with that, nor is it our priority. We are neither an ethnographic institute, trying to show people the "authentic" cultures of other continents, nor
are we a concert agency. This is a place that likes to stimulate creativity. We
are a new kind of MBARI. I believe very strongly, like the Owerri Igbos
believe, who build the Mbari mud monuments, that without creativity a community is doomed. And there is another big lesson we learn from the builders
of MBARI houses: it's the process of creation that is important—not the finished object. It is not the function of the artist to create museum pieces that
last a thousand years. It is his function to constantly renew the creative
process, to rethink the culture. To adapt, to modify, to transform. And so in
this ever-changing world, African cultures must transform themselves constantly by interacting with the other cultures of this world. This interaction
takes place right here at IWALEWA-HAUS and that we make such encounters possible, that is our major contribution. Groups like OKUTA PERCUS-
SION and BASSAMA were created here. It is here that we created the concept
of KARNATIC BACH, that we got a jazz giant like Bill Cobham to play with
an Alarinjo Masquerade from Erin-Oshun in Nigeria!

O: I see. You feel we can't keep cultures separated and isolated.

U: How could we? Our politics and our economics are totally interwined.
Nobody can pretend to be independent. Shouldn't we then also explore the

positive side of this situation? After all, it depends on us how we handle this. If we remain passive, we shall become a global coca-cola culture. But if we become aware and active, this meeting and confrontation and overlapping of cultures can lead to a tremendous enrichment. And there is also a very political element in what we do at IWALEWA-HAUS. We are living here in a country—and in a continent!—that sees a very strong resurgence of fascism and racism. Europeans feel more and more threatened by foreigners. Of course there have been speeches and marches and demonstrations against this hostility to foreigners. But when you stage concerts with a German, an Indian, and an African musician playing harmoniously together and when people see that the music they perform is greater than the sum of the individual parts that have gone into it, then you have made a very important point in the minds of people without having used any political rhetoric at all.

O: This is important: a syncretic development of the world.

U: Another thing we try to do is to break down peoples' compartmentalized thinking. In Germany people distinguish between E-Musik and U-Musik. E-Musik means "emste Musik"—serious music, by which they mean "classical" European music. U-Musik is "Unterhaltungsmusik," that is, entertainment music. Radio and TV programs and concert programs and performance venues are all classified according to these categories. In practice this means that even the most complex African or Indian music is usually relegated to a Jazz club or even to a rock cellar.

I make a point of putting on an African or Indian concert in the Bayreuth Opera house once a year, if I can afford it. I need a lot of sponsorship to do this, because the Opera House is tremendously expensive and it only seats 500 people. But it is the most beautiful theater in Europe (built, 1748) and it is a very prestigious venue. And when someone goes there to listen to a Yoruba dundun orchestra he will realize that this is classical music in its own right and that you have to concentrate on it as much as you do on a Beethoven string quartet.

Our first concert of this type in 1984 caused a scandal. It was considered a kind of sacrilege. We called it "Classical African and Indian Drum Music" and it featured amongst others Muraina Oyelami, Lamidi Ayankunle, Tunji Beier, T.A.S. Mani, Shashi Kumar, and Ramamani. In the meantime people have accepted these concerts here as a normal annual event.

O: I gather that IWALEWA-HAUS has had a great deal of success in Germany and beyond, and that you get a great deal of support from the City of Bayreuth itself. But what is your relationship to the University? How do you relate to the faculties and the research program?

U: I have always existed on the fringe of universities. By and large universities are happy to have one department or institute that can do things that the university itself finds hard to do. At Ibadan the Extra-Mural Department played such a role. The university itself was a colonial ivory tower, but Robert Gardiner's Extra-Mural Department stood in the midst of life! We were part of the culture and the politics of the country. Some people within the university resented this, but there were always those who were glad of having that extra dimension. Similarly the Institute of African Studies at the University of Ife could fulfil all kinds of cultural functions: we staged arts festivals, we ran a professional theater company, we created a pottery museum, we ran a kind of Mbari club, Ori[7]-Olokun. Of course, there we had a Vice Chancellor who gave us tremendous support: Dr. Oluwasami.

In Bayreuth we are in a similar position: IWALEWA-HAUS is on the fringe of the University. The University, by and large, is aware of the benefits it derives from the house: IWALEWA forms a link between the University and the town; it provides a stimulating setting for seminars and conferences. It establishes an international network for the University and it does all these wonderful things that universities cannot normally do, like staging concerts, organizing exhibitions, and so on. But while the University welcomes these activities it sometimes finds them difficult to handle, administratively.

There are always those who think that what we are doing is not respectable or "academic," but I have lived with that kind of thing all my life. Those who opposed my early efforts on behalf of African literature in the University of Ibadan most strongly, were those who later made their career as "experts" on African literature.

When IWALEWA-HAUS opened in 1981, nobody in this country took contemporary African art seriously. Now museums and galleries are falling over backwards to promote African artists. The most prestigious German art magazine, KUNST FORUM, published a special issue on contemporary African art called "AFRIKA IWALEWA."

O: This must be rather gratifying for you.

U: In a way, it is. On the other hand, maybe it's time for me to leave and do something else.

O: What will you do when you leave Bayreuth?

U: I haven't got a clue. But if I get a chance, I'll sit down in a Nigerian village and write.

O: Just one more question: I find that both your first wife and your present wife and your children are all artists. Is this fortuitous or by design?

U: Nobody "designs" his life like that. You certainly can't design what your children may become. There is a cultural element here. I grew up with art. My father was a musician. He was a medical doctor, but like many physicians in Berlin in the twenties and thirties he was also a musician, a highly gifted one at that. Chamber music was performed in our house once or twice a week and I met many artists and musicians in our home. So it became a normal condition of existence for me.

Susanne Wenger was an established artist when she came to Nigeria - she was about thirty five years old at that time. The way in which Nigeria affected her life is another big story, and it has been told many times.

Georgina came to Nigeria when she was twenty one. She was painting pictures, but she never referred to herself as an artist in those days. She hated the self-conscious association which the term carried in England. Like myself, her life was formed by Nigeria. We both became what we are through the Nigerian experience, because we laid ourselves open to it. Her contribution to the cultural development of Nigeria was more important than mine, but it has never been fully recognized, because she has never held big posts in academic institutions and because she does not write about what she does. Many young artists in Nigeria owe their career and their livelihood to her and the process is still going on. For the last few years she has held an annual workshop at the Nike Center, and with stunning success. Georgina is a very powerful artist in her own right, but she has always devoted more time to teaching and promotion of others than to furthering her own career.

My older son, Tokunbo, lives in Sydney and he is an electronics engineer, though with particular interest in sound recording. His personality was strongly influenced by his early years in Papua New Guinea. My younger son, Tunji, is a musician. I knew he was going to be a musician when he was 18 months old: the great dundun player Ayansola performed in our house in Ife. In a culture of musicians he towered like a giant above the rest. I could see then that the child would never forget this experience.

But as we left Ife when he was only four years old, he had to wait until he was ten, before his wish to learn Yoruba drumming would be fulfilled. Then Muraina Oyelami came to Sydney and taught him the gudugudu. After two weeks the two performed in public at the Festival of Sydney. When Muraina returned to Nigeria, Tunji followed him to Nigeria for three months further training. We had no hesitation to let him go by himself. Among his other teachers were Lamidi Ayankunle and Ademola Onibonokuta. By the time he was twelve he performed with the Oyelami Performing Group at the Singapore arts festival. Later he studied South Indian percussion in Bangalore.

Since then he has formed several intercultural groups. The most established and successful among them is OKUTA PERCUSSION, in which Rabiu Ayandokun from Erin-Oshun, Ron Reeves from Australia and Tunji Beier create an entirely new music out of Yoruba, South Indian, and Indonesian percussion. Here we have the kind of cross-cultural interaction that I have always dreamed of, and in the success of Tunji I see a kind of fulfillment of my own life's work.

1.

THE CRISIS OF YORUBA CULTURE

The Crisis of Yoruba culture
A Conversation between Wole Soyinka and Ulli Beier

U: There was a short time in Nigerian history, between Independence and the first military coup, in which we lived through a period of great optimism. Financially the people of Nigeria were relatively well off, and they assumed that with independence things were going to improve steadily. In the West people believed in the benefits of universal free primary education. They were proud of being the "First in Africa" to have set up a television station. The University of Ibadan was functioning and had a good reputation.

Night life was boisterous; people could afford to go out, drink beer, and listen to really good bands. Even in Oshogbo, which then had 120.000 inhabitants, one could hear three or four bands at weekends. The Yoruba Travelling Theater was booming. A decade after Independence, 'Biodun Jeyifo counted about a hundred Yoruba theater companies, all managing to survive somehow off their performances. People actually preferred the theater to the movies; but then those were the days of Ogunde, Ogunmola, Duro Ladipo, and the Orisun players. Where in the world could you find a comparable constellation?

W: There was ferment!

U: There was no official planning. Little government interference. It was a natural growth. If you now think back to this period, how do you view it with hind sight? Why does it appear to us now as a "golden age," rather than a mere beginning?

W: My immediate reaction is: if only we had known what we had then! And how fragile it could become. Not that it was fragile, but how fragile it could become under the buffeting of the rapidly changing political and economic situation. We took our values for granted then.

Let's talk about, well, let me not call it "family values," because in America that has become almost a dirty word. Let's just say: "family sense." So, first of all: at the core of Yoruba society there was this family sense. It was something that extended beyond the borders of Nigeria. Remember, when I was travelling around in a landrover, doing research into West-African theater. To Togo, to Ghana, to the Ivory Coast. It never failed to strike me, this sense of Yoruba existence and solidarity, of self-cogni-tion.

U: So you found it even in Abidjan? In Treicheville?

W: It was incredible. Yes, even in Treicheville people would ask about their cousins at home, as if they just lived a mile or two away. There was this kind of—I hate to call it Pan- Yoruba feeling, because then you think imme-diately of an artificial creation. It was the recognition of something that had obviously existed for hundreds and hundreds of years and which had survived the imposition of colonial boundaries. So that took a buffeting first of all, as the sense of the independent nation grew more and more rigid.

Ghana, for instance, began to take the lead in a particular direction, becoming ideologically hermetic. We use ideology here in a loose sense, but Ghana identified itself out of the West African community.

U: Starting with the break-up of West African Airways. . . .

W: The Bank of West Africa. . . .

U: The West African Cocoa Marketing Board. All these institutions became national.

W: So I think that within Nigeria the Yoruba sense of belonging became stronger, first of all. At the time the Yoruba within Nigeria, including even immediate neighbors in Dahomey, had a sense of themselves as a distinct entity. This attitude was shared also by most other communities in Nigeria. In Lagos the Igbo community met weekly, had their cultural societies who contributed money towards the higher education of some of their children and supported all kinds of community projects. They organized the Atilogu dancers and they rehearsed strictly. The same thing with the Agbor[6] dancers and the Itsekiri dancers. In the South at least, there was hardly any commu-nity that did not identify itself through such cultural groups. This was carried, of course, into politics. The Action Group was based undoubtedly on the Egbe Omo Oduduwa, and it was founded as the political wing of that cultural organization in order to rival the NCNC, which was based on the Igbo State Union. You know very well how all these different groups had a competition of self-cognizing, shall we say "nation states," within Nigeria. That rivalry was very palpable, no question at all. You could touch it, you could feel it.

U: And if you think of some of the politicians, like Akintola; his use of the Yoruba lan-guage. . . .

W: O yes, even the worst of Akintola's enemies had to admit that this was an exemplar of Yoruba linguistic acrobatics! And the fight between him and Awolowo—at the begin-ning—was like a fight within the family.

4

U: People took pride in their language then. And another thing was that the Obas...

W: Ooooooooh yes!

U: .... were still proper Obas. They were Christians and some were Muslims, but they took their office extremely seriously. If you think of someone like Timi Laoye of Ede, Oba Adenle the Ataoja of Oshogbo, they were wise men, tolerant and true peace makers. And Moses Oyinlola, the Olokuku of Okuku, I have not seen a man anywhere in the world of whom one could have said so convincingly "every inch a king." And the Oni of Ife then: a man of the world, a diplomat, a politician and a businessman, but a man of great stature and dignity.

W: Yes. The Obas were not beggars and they were not cultural relics. They were authen-tic spiritual leaders. The occasional fight for succession was conducted very tersely, in a very tough manner; occasionally also using some people's political clout. But there was no betrayal to external sources of the institution of kingship. There was no chea-pening of it. On the other hand, the Ooni of Ife today is an embarrassment.

U: I don't know whether you have come across this French picture book on African kings. It shows royal figures from Ghana or the Cameroons, even those extravagant figures from the Nigerian Delta who sport European top hats. But they carry it off with panache! The only one who is an embarrassment in this book is the Oni of Ife. He had himself photographed, slouching on a sofa, like an Odalisque.

W: I may never have told you this, but during the coronation of the Oni I saved that in-stitution from a serious embarrassment. Elufowoju, who was the photographer of the African Studies Institute at Ife, took the official photographs for the occasion. One day, when I was sitting in my office, a bunch of postcards arrived. Elufowoju had sent them, in case I wanted to send them to some of my friends. I looked at this picture and nearly fainted with embarrassment. You have to see it! It was a composite photograph. There was the crown, which was photographed separately and the Ooni was looking at it with his mouth wide open, like óbè re ! It was like Ojú ò rólárí ! He was salivating at the crown! I said to Elufowoju: What is this? Is there a war going on between you and the Ooni? He said no, I took several pictures and the Ooni himself se-lected this one. He said that the Ooni had ordered a vast quantity of them and that he had already sent out some of them. So I sent my staff out, you know, the acting company, especially those who were from Ife; I sent them round the town to all the shops to collect whatever they could find of these pictures. And I asked Elufowoju to let me have all those he had left in his office. And I said: I will compensate you by giving you some other work. But this one, forget you ever did it! Just bring me the negative. Then I went to the Ooni and said: "By the way, I have seized all those post-cards." He said: "Ah, didn't you like it? I thought it was rather good." I told him: "If I wanted to construct an image of ojú ò rólárí—that's exactly what I would do." I said: "You are salivating and panting looking at the crown."

U: If you think of his predecessor. When you entered his palace you knew you were in the presence of an Ooni. He had a position even beyond the confines of his sacred of-fice. He knew how to combine his traditional duties of an Ooni with those of a minister of state. Yet he was totally accessible. He would receive you at any time. He knew that an Oba must be available for his people and for strangers. Unlike this present Ooni. I once accompanied the Timi of Ede, who is a close friend of his and a business associate. But even he was kept waiting endlessly.

W: And another thing. Let's spend a little more time on the Ooni, because he is the symbol of everything that happened to the Yoruba people during the last two or three decades. Remember, some years ago, during the regime of Buhari, the Ooni of Ife and the Emir of Kano, Bayero, went to Jerusalem together. That was before we established formal relationships with Israel. They were received very well there, by the government and by the Prime Minister himself. Of course, when they came back, Buhari was furious! Never mind that some months later they started negotiations with Israel. But at the time they had to make a gesture and so they restricted the movements of the Emir and the Ooni. The governors were ordered to issue restriction orders: they had to remain confined to their towns for six months. I know that Buhari visited the Emir of Kano. I don't know what he said, but I am quite sure that he apologized and explained that for political reasons this had to be done. And the Governor of Oyo also visited the Ooni and explained that it was an unpleasant duty he had to perform, but that as a Yoruba son he had to pay due respect to the Ooni. In any case the restriction was administered very leniently. The Governor knew very well that the Ooni went to parties in Lagos, but he never said anything.

But the moment the six months' restriction was lifted, the Ooni gathered his chiefs and went to Oyo to thank the Governor. It was a day of shame for the entire Yoruba na-tion. O.K., you have to accept the fact that they are pow-erful enough to force the re-striction on you. You bear that humiliation with dignity. You don't say a word. You just sit there. A true Oba would even have refused to travel immediately after the lif-ting of the ban. He would have con-sidered it cheap to jump into a car at once. But the Ooni went to this Governor and said: "I have come to thank you for lifting the restric-tion. It has been a good lesson and I have brought my chiefs along, because I want them to see that they are subject to discipline also. So when I tell them that they must have discipline, they will know what I mean." It was shameful! Photographs, the lot. And this Governor, who at the time wasn't even a Yoruba, repeating those cliché phrases: "we want our Obas to be respected," and so on.

I went to the Ooni yet again and said: "Did you really have to do that? What was the point? What did you think you would gain?" And he said: "But you heard what I said. It was for my chiefs, I wanted them to understand"; and he went on and on and on. But of course it was a lie. All he wanted to do is look for some contracts. . . .

The man who is occupying the most important throne in Yorubaland is unfortunately also the man who has presided over the demise of Yoruba self-worth. He has been parading himself all over the world, even campaigning for Sanni Abacha. He goes to America and says: "Look, I am the leader of the Yoruba people and I tell you that this is our position: we are in full support of the head of state."

U: He seems to be the symbol of the Yoruba malaise. Other Obas also give way to these immense political pressures. And many attach even more importance to their business deals than to their royal functions. But all the other Obas now have retained some dignity, even when they are forced to compromise.

W: He is the saka jojo of Yoruba Obas. You may not know that expression. When I was a child the old silent films were introduced to Nigeria: Charlie Chaplin, Buster Keaton and so many other comedians. We were inspired by those films to produce our own shadow plays. We made cut-out figures from cardboard and moved them in front of a lantern. So if I call him saka jojo. I mean a cardboard piece of humanity clowning. . . making movements across the wall.

There is something else I want to say about this Yoruba crisis: the figure of Awolowo, his activity, his position in those years. It is true that some people declared he was nothing but a tribalist who cared for nobody but the Yorubas. But even some Igbos compared him favourably to Zik. The parameter is Awolowo's pride of race, which was something Zik never had. Zik was a compromiser. In fact he compared himself once to a beautiful bride, who was being courted by all those political parties. Can you imagine Awolowo sitting on the fence like that? It was something even the Sardauna of Sokoto once acknowledged. He said that he would never forgive Awolowo, because Awolowo made him get up from his exalted throne and campaign like a commoner; because during the first post-Independence election in Nigeria, Awolowo had made inroads into the North, by allying himself to NEPU, while Azikiwe had a kind of pact with the Sardauna, that they would not campaign in each other's region.

U: But let us go back to the 60s now and talk about the events of which you said before: "I wish we had known then what we had!" It was a period of intense theater activity and one of the big events of the period was a kind of festival you staged in Ibadan, in which you brought Ogunmola, Ogunde, Duro Ladipo, and the Orisun players all toge-ther into one big event. What was the motivation behind this theater summit?

W: The idea was very simple. You remember I had been travelling all over West Africa and had seen the various travelling theaters, like the "Trios" in Ghana, and I was im-pressed by the movements across the borders of many of these companies. I would ar-rive in Abidjan and find Ogunde performing. I would arrive in Ghana and meet a group from Abidjan. So I had the idea of organizing a big festival of all these various groups, but of course, that was far too ambitious; and it was not easy to arrange eit-her, because they were travelling theaters in the real sense of the word. I thought of this as a pilot festival, which would allow people to enjoy the richness and the variety of travelling theater in the Westem Region, because the West was easily the rich-est region in that kind of activity.

U: How would you assess these three companies? How would you describe each com-pany's specific contribution?

W: Duro Ladipo was obviously the tragic genius. His plays were densely poetic. He re-ally explored the origins of his people.

U: Before Duro the popular Yoruba theater always treated babalawos or orisa-priests as comical figures or even as despicable ones. In Ogunde's plays it was always the school teacher type who was flaunted as the progressive hero. Duro was the first to restore the balance. He gave Yoruba culture back its dignity.

W: He made his audience understand the role of an orisa-priest in the community. Ogun-mola was of course the great comedian. I don't think that he ever denigrated traditio-nal aspects of Yoruba culture. . . .

U: No, he just left it out.

W: On the other hand, for Duro every single aspect of Yoruba life formed part of the—I won't say jigsaw—but the composition of Yoruba soci-ety. And the thing about Duro -he didn't just play the role, he was inducted into the rite of Shango, so that when he entered the stage, he was virtually in a state of possession.

U: And he had this enormous presence.

W: Yes, and is it not interesting: Duro died during the dry season, in Mach. And in Ibadan—only in Ibadan—there was the most unbelievable thun-derstorm the night he died. And everybody remarked: Shango has passed. It was remarkable, the storm discharged itself that night and there was no more. It was really interesting. . . .

U: I remember one night we met in Lagos and I took you to see a per-formance of "Love of Money." It was a very long time ago, because it was the first time you actually saw Ogunmola perform. And I remember how excited you were, particularly by the scene with the wedding preparations. Ogunmola created the impression of a bustling house-hold of fifty or a hundred people, all milling around, doing different jobs, carrying things here and there and getting into each other's way. Yet all he had at his disposal to achieve that effect was an empty stage, no backdrop, no props and just two actors—himself and his wife—to suggest a crowd.

W: Yes, that is what attracted me to his theater: the real innovation and the economy with which the effects were produced. And that is what I wanted my own actors to absorb: the seamlessness of it. That the theater is a seamless continuum and, in terms of inno-vative devices, there isn't really such a thing as Yoruba theater or European theater. And, of course, we were also aiming at this economy of expression and at creating a travelling theater. So it was a tremendous experience. And I remember that organizing this little festival took so much of my energy and so much tension, too, that I under-rehearsed my own team. We performed both "Brother Jero" and "The Lion and the Je-wel." "Brother Jero" was O.K., but I realised on the night of "The Lion and the Je-wel" that it was horribly under-rehearsed. Nevertheless, it was certainly one of the great theatrical heights of that period.

U: What do you think about Ogunde's contribution to the theater scene? Of course he was the initiator of the whole movement!

W: Well, one thing about Ogunde, his plays deepened towards the end. He became more and more aware of the possibilities of the Yoruba tradition. I never found that he suc-ceeded in integrating his theater. In other words, he took elements of the traditional theater and planted them in his normal dialogue theater. As you know, he began with a kind of Vaudeville tradition and only later began to bring in Egungun, the Orisa and he went deeper into the liturgy and dramatic incantations. . . .

U: His weakness, as far as I am concerned, was that he was not really an actor.

W: No, never! It was always Hubert Ogunde's personality on stage, no matter what he was doing. Whether it was a role from history, from mythology, whether he was a politician or a victim of British colonial rule—it was always Hubert Ogunde. He had the least expressive face of all of them. He had a handsome face and a handsome fi-gure. . . .

U: There was a bit of vanity about it too. . . .

W: Absolutely! The cock of the roost with all his harem around him acting on stage! And yet, he gave an entirely new dimension to the theater scene in Nigeria.

U: When did you actually found the Orisun players?

W: O.K. Now when I arrived back in Nigeria, the first thing I did was "A Dance of the Forest." And I first of all wanted to set a standard, a high standard of professionalism from the word Go. So that the young actors I would later train would understand from the very beginning that this was the standard that we wanted to take on tour. So in spite of these immense logistical problems of dealing with a cast that was partly living in Lagos and partly in Ibadan and all of whom had senior positions as teachers, public servants, broadcasters, or oil company executives, we staged this play with senior people like Yemi Lijadu, Olga Adeniyi-Jones, Patrick Ozieh, Segun Olusola, Ralph Opara, Francesca Pereira. I had to take advantage of the Independence celebrations to get letters which released them for rehearsals. It was sheer opportunism. It was a chance once in a lifetime; and I said, let's take advantage of this now and do some-thing big with a high level of professionality and then start training a new generation. The young actors, Femi Euba, Sola Rhodes, were already inside, understudying. Jimmy Solanke and Tunji Oyelana came a little later. And I told Yemi Lijadu and the rest: we want to bring up this new generation and you will be the Baba Sale and the Iya Sale— the fathers and mothers behind the scene. It's amazing how they actually understood and played that role. And then later, when I came to extract Orisun Theater from the parent body, they were the ones who were handling publicity, selling tic-kets, while Orisun could devote themselves purely to their artistic responsibilities.

And again, they were able to work in tandem with the 1960 Masks. While the 1960 Masks were able to handle a play like "Dear Parent and Ogre" by Sarif Easmon, the Orisun Players went on to do political sketches. . . .

U: "Before the Black Out". . . .

W: By this time Akintola had gone wild. I actually had to train my actors in self-defense on stage, because Akintola and Fani-Kayode sent thugs to break up our performances. They also sent the attorney general to our performance, to see whether they could charge us.

U: For sedition?

W: Oh yes, sedition was very popular then. Remember Sam Aluko, who had been char-ged. But when they had their caucus meeting, they decided, they didn't have a strong case in court so they would rather break up our performances with thugs. That's why I called my boys together and trained them in self-defense.

U: Orisun was much more than a theater company.

W: O absolutely. It was a family. Apart from the politics.

U: It was also a total way of life. . . .

W: Completely. Those boys, Jimmy Solanke, Tunji Oyelana, Yomi Obileye, Yewande Akinbo ... it was a commune. Whatever we had, we shared.

You remember we took over that house in Agodi, the one you engineered as a "Headquarters for Black Or-pheus." They lived there. The ones who had no homes. And they cooked there. And whatever food I could get I brought into the house. There was no replication of that period! And the real tragedy is, you know, there is no possible replication! What is left is the reality of some-thing valuable, which still exists in the careers of Tunji Oyelana, Yewande ... and any time I have a production, anywhere I can, I call them, rely on them. They form the core of the new company and they immediately help to form a community. In fact, I recently had an "Orisun" production in London.

U: You can actually say that of all the companies who were active in the sixties: they had a total commitment to this new way of life. If you think of Duro's company, many of them came from routine jobs: shop assistant, petrol station attendant, pools manager, where they had earned more than in the theater. They didn't really have any career opportunities—not in the the-ater either, as far as they could see—but they saw a new meaning to their lives when they joined the company and that became more important to them than money.

W: Tunji Oyelana had been the private secretary to an Oba, but he just turned his back on that kind of life. Orisun became a microcosm of Yoruba life, extended family Yoruba principles. And of course, it wasn't just Yoruba people in my kind of company.

U: No. It was a remarkable time from that point of view. As you pointed out before: Yorubas, Igbos, Efiks, all put a lot of effort into maintaining and projecting a separate cultural identity within the larger nation state, but there was also a genuine faith in Nigeria and many organizations cut right across these groupings. After all, we also had Mbari!

W: Thank you. Mbari, which cut across the languages and also across the different arts. In Mbari we had the painters, the poets, the musicians, and the actors. And once people came into that kind of community, they simply absorbed the principles. And as I said earlier: none of us at that time knew what a great thing we had, because we could not imagine what a terrible level of national disintegration we could reach.

U: For a while, I think, Mbari was a worthwhile institution.

W: Oh yes, it was terrific!

U: Of course, we did use outside funds, but it was not really very much.

W: Considering the achievements, Mbari was a shoestring operation. And comparing it to art institutions in Europe and America. I know what kind of budgets they consume.

U: You know when the idea of a Mbari first occurred in my mind? I had sent "A Dance of the Forest" to the Nigeria Council, suggesting it as the offi-cial play for the inde-pendence celebrations. The secretary returned it to me

11

with the commentary: "We can't make heads or tales of this." Then I thought, if this is the official Nigerian body making decisions on cultural matters, then we must create an independent organization in which a few like-minded young artists can have the freedom to pursue their own aims.

W: Well, the timing was perfect, if you remember. I was looking for premises to start an arts club and you arrived from Paris. You had made contact with that foundation and you said: "Look, give me a proposal quickly. Can you and Chris Okigbo and J.P. Clark get together?" So things just came together at a propitious moment.

But there is something else I want to mention that was very important at the time. The Cooperatives in the West. I have never before or since seen an organ that operated at state level—and we are talking of a state with a population of at least 20 million—that led to a movement which kept its roots firmly in the community. Remember the Co-op in Ibadan. That was the most prominent. But there were branches of that Coop ever-ywhere, where the farmers and the craftsmen brought their goods and the Coop paid them generous prices. The leather workers, the carvers, but mostly it was food. I am not talking of cocoa now. That was a thing of its own. I am talking of the petty pro-ducers, who brought their goods to the Co-op and were paid immediately. And they could actually see what was needed, what was moving. I cannot remember any com-plaint about it. There was never any scandal about the running of it. And it integrated the peasantry, the smallest tier of productivity in the entire Western region, with the highest level of distribution in the state.

These cooperatives were the symbols of the cohesion of society, because when you have productivity organized on that level, in such a way as not to alienate the people—that is a real testimony to the family feeling within the community. And when that goes, something really serious has happened to the community itself. Under Akintola the cooperatives began to decline, because that is when the government began to dip its hand into the purse. The farmers weren't paid any more and they stopped bringing their goods. One after the other, the Coop shops disappeared, until in the end the one at the center of lbadan also closed. First the goods became fewer, less varied, until finally it was turned into just another shop. It was like a symbol of the disintegration of our society.

U: And this happened at a time when the region was pretty well off. There was no finan-cial crisis. In fact, even junior clerks, primary school teachers, and farmers were living comfortably. So it was really a wilful destruction.

But let us retum to Mbari for a moment. Two of the absolute highlights for me were the first perfomances of "Brother Jero" and "Song of a Goat."

"Brother Jero" with Yemi Lijadu as Jeroboam and Ralph Opara as Chume. That was a performance bristling with energy and wit and irony. One of the greatest theater performances I can remember anywhere. J.P's "Song of a Goat" was something else again. It was no longer a performance, it became a ritual and a distinctly uncanny experience. Francesca Pereira went into something like a trance.

W: O yes. That was an incredible experience. I think we were all a little bit possessed that night. Certainly Segun Olusola was sufficiently terrified during the crucial moment of the ritual. . . .

U: When you actually sacrificed a goat on stage.

W: You remember that Segun Olusola played the part of Tonye, the young man who cuc-kolded his senior brother. And you know he was to escape through the window. We made use of the library window, which adjoined the stage. I played Zifa, the senior brother, and when I was charging him, instead of just escaping, he began to barricade himself in. He put chairs and tables against the window. And when I tried to get in and couldn't, I got wild. I smashed the window down. And at the other end of the library there was a door. That narrow door that led onto the street. And as I climbed through the window I saw Segun standing there with his hand on the door and the next thing, he was running up the hill towards that church ... you know St. Emanuel's Church. I saw his fat bottom waddling and disappear over the horizon and at that moment I came to myself. Later I said to Segun: "What happened?" And he said: "I took one look at your eyes and I decided I wasn't staying around that night! This was no play acting. "

U: Well, it started off as play alright, but it was the spilling of the goat's blood that got into Francesca's head.

W: Yes, she was the first to get wild and that affected everybody else.

U: I believe that this kind of thing could only have happened at Mbari. On a proper stage the artificiality of the situation, the presence of technicians and stage hands would have kept everything within prescribed limits. To me it was the informality of Mbari that was its great asset and that made such extraordinary experiences possible. I guess after the civil war it was not possible to resurrect this any more.

W: There was an irony about the loyalty during the war. Somebody like Dapo Adelugba, who became a senior director of the Orisun players, he arranged with television to have a weekly play to keep the company alive. First of all its impossible. You can't have enough material for a half-hour play every week. And the kind of rehearsal time you get ... so the standard really went down. And when I came out of prison and took one look at it, I was appalled and immediately terminated the whole thing. Better to have no theater, than to have a theater at that level. The ensemble playing had disintegrated and even the core members had lost their standard. And Wale Ogunyemi tur-ned out plays at an appalling rate.

U: The civil war destroyed a lot of things. The artists and writers of Mbari dispersed in different directions, had different loyalties, found themselves suddenly on opposing sides. It was not so easy to restore the same kind of trust after the war. But Mbari itself began to disintegrate before the civil war.

Personally I lost interest in it, when they decided not to renew the lease of the original premises, but to move to the Central Hotel. I thought it was too big, too ugly, and it had the wrong atmosphere. I conceded the point that one could build a proper stage and that Demas Nwoko could make good use of such a stage. But it was expensive. It took up virtually the club's entire grant, and with it one also bought a lot of useless space. All those hotel rooms.

Besides it was a nouveau-riche concrete monster. I couldn't see how the atmosphere of Mbari could be recreated. So even though Chris Okigbo tried to offer me the chairmanship of the new club, at least for the first year, I decided to leave and concentrate more on Oshogbo.

W: It had become a committee thing then. You could never recreate that atmosphere: the combination of that old Lebanese man and his own enclave there and then being si-tuated in the middle of the market. It was right in the heart of throbbing Yoruba life. They didn't see what they were losing. The size was totally irrelevant. The very ma-keshift quality of the original Mbari was a challenge. And it didn't alienate anybody. Moving into the Central alienated a lot of people.

U: "Threshold fear." In the old Mbari everybody could feel at home. There was no class or clique that dominated the place.

W: You had students, you had the peace corps. You had crooks, you had con men, you had pickpockets. I described a scene in "Ibadan" when a whole lot of con men cheated women who had come to do their shopping in Ibadan. They came from Ondo or Ekiti or even further afield. The crooks came with lucky dips. You were supposed to bring one Naira and pick up your luck in a box. Of course it wasn't the dip itself that was the business. It was very good psychology. They would watch those women who had come from the interior, having collected money from their fellow traders to do their Christmas shopping or Ramadan shopping. They would watch and assess which of them had money. Suddenly they would cause a commotion and snatch her purse. And it was through our own self policing that we were finally able to invite the police to come and arrest them. They were heavy thugs. They were difficult to tackle on ones own. And of course they had friends in the police also. But eventually we were able to break up that ring, and one of their leaders became a very good friend of mine.

U: I gather it was the Orisun boys who broke up the ring. They were a wonderful link between Mbari and the wider public. It was they, also, I feel, who spread the popula-rity of the Mbari shirt. In the fifties Adire was worn exclusively by women. And even when we started wearing it as shirts, it did not catch the imagination of a wider pu-blic. It was only when the staff of Mbari, like Ademola, the Alake's grandson, started wearing them, and above all the Orisun players, that you began to see people hawking Adire shirts on the street: young boys with long poles and twenty, thirty shirts of dif-ferent sizes hanging from them.

W: A whole culture developed. You could go to East Africa or South Africa at the time and see the Mbari shirt. You remember Herb Shaw? The American who taught drama in East Africa? I think it was in Makerere. He was the one who spread the Mbari shirt in East Africa.

U: Now we have said that the civil war destroyed many things in Nigeria and caused some irreparable damage to the different cultures. But in some sense the country emerged from it intact. In fact, there was a kind of high spirit. Think of the University of Ife under the leadership of Dr. Oluwasami. It was highly motivated.

W: There was some optimism because there was the feeling: O yes, we can overcome even a civil war.

U: A sense of indestructability of Nigeria. It was exhilarating to visit the University of Nsukka after the war. It was a tremendously inspiring place when the students first went there, cleaned the place up, and more or less twisted the government's arm to re-open the university.

W: A determination to rebuild.

U: Remember the "Ant Hill," the Uli art movement. The place was bursting with creati-vity.

W: It was still the Mbari spirit that carried on. They had been involved in it and set up their own centers. All that was encouraging, but the economic productivity had gone to pots. War had become a business. You remember the famous cheeroots, the cigars that used to be manufactured behind Bamgbose Street in Lagos? We used to go there and purchase them for about 10 shillings a hundred. I went there when I came out of detention and I found the shop closed down. Why? The woman had become a trader supplying materials to the army during the war: food, clothing, blankets—she had be-come an army contractor.

Before the war there had been this little industry. She personally super-vised it and she did very well on it. But the war was much more profitable than that. And she didn't just go there and make big money and keep the lit-tle cheeroot factory on the side. No. She stopped it completely. And that was true of many small scale industries. When the war was over they never went back to it. They now began to chase contracts. Their whole life was entirely commercialized. They took up more and more contracts with the corresponding bribery. The famous 10 percent became institutionalized.

U: It became a hell of a lot more than 10 percent.

W: Thank you. It went to 15, 20, 25 percent. And they became agents rather than producers. And to make things worse: if the economy had remained at that level, some of them might have returned to their former trade. But then the oil money came. That finished off the entire productive responsibility.

Remember the Ikorodu ceramic factory? Never mind what you thought of the quality of design at the time. But things were being produced there that were put to immediate use in the country and it cut out some of the imports. But that just disappeared. Let's not talk about Abuja. The war industry, followed by oil, totally distorted our lives.

U: It also meant that the states just relied on their share of federal oil money, which was enough to keep them going. They allowed their small industries and even their agri-culture to go to ruin. In the late seventies Nigeria even began to import palm oil. The West was particularly affected. Land became an object of speculation. Whole villages lost their land, selling under presume or seduced by their own greed. In the Oshogbo area you can't see a yam field anymore. The yam people eat comes from the Midwest or from the North.

With this new commercialism other things started to happen. Money began to play an ever- increasing part in the installation of Obas, with the result that Obas in turn have to become businessmen. One of their lucrative businesses nowadays is to sell chieftaincy titles ...

W: To all and sundry!

U: The popular currency for a chieftaincy title is a V-Boot. Another alarming symptom of the disintegration of Yoruba society is the language itself. If you listen to a Lagos area boy or a taxi driver, the language has become hard. The rhythm has gone, the tone levels have been flattened, the text interspersed with English words and uttered at tremendous speed.

W: Even the language of music doesn't sound like it anymore. The lyrics have gone. It is linked thoroughly to commercialism. A new phase of praise-singing has developed, different from the spontaneous praise-singing we used to know in the night clubs of the sixties, which was bestowed on you the moment you appeared on stage, the mo-ment you entered the bar. The singer did not really expect any reward, it was part-and-parcel of the performance. Maybe you put a few token coins on his forehead or you bought a couple of drinks for the band. But now: what it means is that the singer takes the same Agbada of praise-singing - he takes it off you when he's finished with you and puts it on the next person. No inventiveness, just using the same sequence of praises for each individual.

U: This has been triggered off by this obnoxious "spraying."

W: Thank you, I was coming to that.

U: Lavishing money over the performer has nothing to do with the quality of the perfor-mance nor with the personality of the singer. It is a form of self-display of the nou-veau-riche: "I can spray more than you!"

W: Why should the singer waste his creative energy, when all the man wanted to hear was his name interpolated into the same formulistic singing.

U: I remember how well-informed the old juju bands were about people's lives. Black Morocco would refer to recent events in your life. He certainly knew one's oriki. He would know who your recent girl friend was.

W: That's right and his praises would be specific to her: the texture, the complexion, her specific variety of beauty as opposed to the last one. But now it is standard. They will sing about anybody you bring in as long as she is a sprayer. She can be as thin as a rake, if the praise they used last had to do with a real market-mammy type, they would just repeat the same phrases and there would be no shame in it, no sense of impropriety. And she would be basking in it, all that matters is that her name is mentioned. It doesn't matter what accolades; whatever they used over and over again, for the opposition, for the enemy. And from there music moved into the sanctimonious. It's almost as if to compensate for this worship of money and of status. It is very dif-ficult to analyze the relationship, or what stimulated what, but I have observed that the music now also indulges in fulsome prayers to God, the standard invocations to hope and good luck. These have now become the centerpiece of the new social music repeated ad nauseam and inflated in its worth. In other words you can have that thin phrase repeated with the most unctuous kind of voice. A new religiosity has been born through new social music whose literacy is of the lowest—in fact which has no imagi-nation whatsoever. So you can have a whole thing lasting for 15 minutes - in fact lon-ger, LP length, consisting of nothing but: "May my head not encounter evil on the way." And that will be repeated throughout in a more and more unctuous manner. No more imagination, no more creativity. And then a combination of that with all the new technical effects.

Compare that with the beautiful music of Tunde Nightingale, Black Morocco, Orlando Owo with his beautiful husky voice. Compare the original juju music with the social music of today and you can see the collapse of the group personality, the total social decay.

U: One problem is, the public no longer demands the imagination and creativity we have known. Another fact is the political hopelessness and frustration. People have lost their faith and their sense of belonging. So they just play along with whatever corrupt government is in power and try to get out of it what they can for themselves. They become Muslims and go to Abuja to look for contracts.

W: Yes that's another phenomenon. Changing your name so you can be associated with the feudal power.

U: That amounts to a deliberate negation of your own identity. The question is, with political power permanently concentrated in the North and with the money monopolies centered more and more in the North, what chances has Yoruba culture got to survive? And more seriously: how much do Yoruba care about their culture and their identity nowadays?

W: Now here we come to the positive side, or the negative one; I don't know what to say, it depends on whether you look as it as a Nigerian nationalist or a Yoruba nationalist.

The reverse process has begun. There is now a feeling of self-disgust by the younger generation and in that I include the forty, forty-five years olds, who looked at the entire phenomenon and said: wait a minute, we are Yoruba people and that bastardization of our existence, the lowering of the quality of life from our original existence, the humiliation of our people by those traitors who go begging cap in hand, betraying the political cause for their own profit: "we will not stand for it any longer." There is a swell of reaction against it. It is exemplified in the most frightening way in the kind of experience we encounter today, when we try to mobilize political opposition to the dictatorship, and our people say clearly to us: Listen, we are ready for struggle, but we are not willing to struggle for a Nigerian nation. There is only one nation we are willing to recognize and that is the Oduduwa nation.

In the States alone there are at least four Yoruba movements that I know: Egbe Omo Oduduwa, Yoruba Progressive Union, Oduduwa Nation. . . and one of them was so blatantly Yoruba that I had to say to them: Listen, at this stage at least this is a national struggle. If you want to become affiliated to NALICON (the "National Liberation Council") you have to change your name. I cannot accept a sectional-based organization. You know what they did? They went and had a meeting and they came back and said to me: "O.K., we've changed our name. We are now "Action Group for Democracy"

U: Very clever.

W: Look, I roared with laughter. I thought it was one up on me. I had no choice but to register the organization. I thought it was so witty and at the same time is showed such a resolve. They got back to me within ten minutes and said: "Action Group for Democracy, any objections?" I was defeated on this one. Some of them were collec-ting money and not only in America. Even before I left Nigeria, there was a group -professionals, doctors, engineers, pharmacists, journalists between the ages of 25 to 45, some of whom have researched the resources that exist in the Yoruba part of the country. I was impressed by their industry. They had identified the minerals that could be explored. On one occasion they invited me and said: we have always admired you and we will always give you support. But today we have not invited you to talk about how to terminate this dictatorship. We have made up our mind. We have not invited you to ask your opinion. We want to tell you what we want to do and we want to ask you whether you can help us. · They said, we have examined our history, we have looked at the treachery of our leaders. We have asked you because you are not one of the traitors. But we feel that you are wasting your energy, and we do not want to be wasted. You have described your generation as the wasted generation. We are determined not to waste ourselves and we are sure that you are wasting yourself because you continue to believe in a certain chimera called "Nigeria." We don't. This is our program. It dovetails with yours, fine. But this is the platform on which we stand. We want nothing less than a Yoruba state. Our minds are made up. Howe-ver long it takes, we cannot lose this vision. We do not believe in Nigeria. And they showed me why the Yoruba nation should stand alone.

I just sat amazed, while I was being lectured for over an hour. And they said: O.K. this is our program. How can you help us—if want to. And that movement is gaining ground all the time.

U: An interesting rider on this: a few years ago I met a Yoruba Oba, a man of rare inte-grity. He told me that a certain mineral had been found on his territory. But he said: "I have no intention to do anything about it. Because if I do, some Northerner will get the contract. Maybe some businessman from Lagos will get the subcontract. But this town will get nothing out of it. All that will happen is that they will destroy our envi-ronment. Let it stay there."

W: That's right. That is the mood right now. That is precisely the kind of language those young men are using. And even in the recent constitutional agenda—even some of the women amongst them—they say: We only went there to let them know we want a Yoruba state.

There are similar movements in different areas. And what we are witnessing is a phase of "To your tents Israel!" That is the expresssion we use when we want to translate the Yoruba expression Let each person cling to his mother's breasts. It is essentially the political expression of this sense of race humiliation.

U: It is a potentially dangerous situation. Who could have thought ten years ago that we could witness the rise of violent Hindu chauvinism in India. The Yoruba people cer-tainly must reassert their cultural identity but we must hope that they will not lose sight of the essential values of their culture in the process.

But when you think of the sixties, which we have been talking about as if they are the golden age in the history of Nigeria, I am sure that most people, certainly the intellectuals, accepted the concept of Nigeria.

W: We certainly tried to make it work.

U: There was a lot of good will. People thought, we'll give this a go! But somehow these so-called leaders had frittered it away. They have sold out this idealism. Nigeria has just become the personal property of a few. In the sixties I was amazed by people's optimism. But they said to me, look, with the spread of modem education we shall see the rise of a new elite in the North. A new generation will think more like us. They will be less conservative, more liberal, more open to the world and we will grow together. You may remember that in the last numbers of "Black Orpheus" I published quite a few stories from North Africa. I tried to encourage this optimism by showing people that there was this other, liberal and open-minded aspect of Islam. And up to a point I think you can say its happening. Look at the last election. There was a definite breaking down of cultural and religious borders.

W: I was coming to that. Yes.

U: The Emir of Kano. He is a modem statesman. Nobody could accuse him of being a mediaeval potentate. Some change has actually taken place, but these people are not having the say in the North.

W: Absolutely not. Its that clique. And I emphasize it in my forthcoming book. But to come back to the election. I have videos of Abiola's campaign. I have not seen such ecstasy on the faces of people. Not since the time of Awolowo. You want to see those videos. You want to compare them to that of Tofa, campaigning in the same state, in his own state. And you will see that on the one hand there is total absolute rapture at the reception of this man. On the other side: duty and support, but nothing compared to Abiola. All that bullshit that Northerners weren't ready for a Yoruba. It was explo-ded totally.

U: I suppose it is the frustration over the annulment of this election that has produced those extreme Yoruba nationalists.

W: Precisely. Their feeling is: If the nation went this far, and if there is a self-interested clique so determined, ruthless, and unpatriotic as to actually fritter away this galvani-zing moment of the national feeling and the nation's will—well, in that case, let's not wa-ste any more energy on an ideal that those who are in a position of power are willing to nullify. Its incalculable what June 12th has done.

U: But let me come to a last issue. Because, whatever happens politically, supposing even that the political problems can be resolved one way or the other, there still remains a cultural problem; because for several decades Yoruba children have been educated away from their culture at school. They have been educated to actually despise their history, their religion. We have seen sparks of cultural revival in the sixties: Duro Ladipo and your own activities have jerked people out of this complacency and made them rethink their history and gave them a new awareness. Nevertheless we are faced today by a profiteering class of Yoruba entrepreneurs who are only too willing to ex-ploit their own people, so that political autonomy in itself is not the answer. There is a cultural vacuum.

I met a new generation of Yoruba academics who come to me and say: I missed out on this important period of our history. I was too young to experience the ferment of the sixties. I have never seen a Duro Ladipo performance. I never knew the Mbari Club. There is a deep sense of loss, of being cheated out of one's heritage, to the extent that I find myself playing the role of an "informant," an eye witness, to this younger generation.

W: Yes, and we did not even touch on the role played by foreign interests. What I call the "Walkman Culture." When I was running the cultural center at the University of Ife, you remember we ran a bar in the foyer of the theater and we had the rotunda. I made a rule that there should be no foreign pop music played in the foyer of the theater. I said: the students have their own club. Let them play what they want there, whatever is to their own taste. But I run this place. This is Ife. This is an Ife cultural center. I will not have this kind of pop music played here. We played Juju musicians like Orlando Owo, we played music from the East, that wonderful singer Njemanze, we played Professor Majority. And I said, if any students bring in records of rock or pop, I'll get them smashed. I said this is an opportunity for all you students who come here to know that there is an alternative. This is an option. This is the purpose of this place. But it is interesting, they kept bringing their pop music and it was not until I actually grabbed a pop record and smashed it, that the barman understood I was serious about this.

Unfortunately for them, this was the one place on the campus where they could relax. It was the one place where the toilets worked, where they could get cheap snacks, see some shows and get reduced tickets. Whereas they were charging high prices in their own club. They were fleecing one another. Some of them gradually got interested in the music I played in the center. But it is tragic that a whole generation had been lost to their own popular music. They said, what sort of music is this, this is square stuff. I said: "Your father is square."

U: But this is something that went wrong very early on. Do you remember the "Universal Free Education Scheme" introduced by S.O. Awokoya in the then Western Region of Nigeria in 1956? He was one of my best friends, but I quarreled with him continuously over that issue. People in those days had a blind faith in that magic thing called "education," that was supposed to solve all the problems of society. Nobody thought of what the purpose of education was. What are we educating our children to become? What will they learn about their own society? Their history? The philosophy of the Yoruba?

Where will their identity lie, when they have passed through that edu-cation? Will they have learned anything at all about the other cultural groups in Nigeria with whom they will have to cooperate in forming a nation?

If the education is merely job-orientated, if all it does is to enable you to earn more money than those who did not go through that system successfully, are you not training a class of egotistical exploiters? If you don't know what the impact of this type of education will be on society, why simply more of the same?

Nobody, literally nobody, would listen to me then. Only in the seventies Babs Fafunwa started his experiment in Yoruba education at Ife. In six selected schools he introduced Yoruba as the language of instruction, right through Primary School from Class I to Class VI. He argued correctly that to impose English as a language of instruction too early would alienate them from their society and that it was not even an efficient way of teaching them English. He carried out this experiment with great enthusiasm and with considerable success, but of course nothing came out of it in the end. It was never adopted as a general policy of education.

W: Yes, and what did he do to himself? After he became Federal Minister of Education he declared publicly that he must no longer be called Babs Fafunwa, that he was now Aliu Fafunwa.

U: Was that the price he paid for becoming a minister?

W: That's right. When a senior person gives an example like that, of opportunism, which denies your own origin, how can people then take his project of promoting the Yoruba language seriously? It affects it, whether you like it or not. You cannot objectivize what you are doing and separate yourself from it by example. You are going the way of all others, to be acceptable to a section of the country that happens to be distributing the goodies at the moment. You abandon a name by which you have been known for decades—Babs for Babatunde—and you publish it in all the papers that you want to be called Aliu.

U: You know last night Al Imfeld said something to me that is quite relevant to this is-sue. You know that Al Imfeld is a cousin of the famous rebel Catholic theologian Hans Küng.

W: O really? I didn't know that.

U: He told me that he said to Hans Küng: all your ecumenical meetings and get-togethers and conferences and services. I do appreciate that you want to break down the differences between the different churches and you are stretching out a hand towards Judaism and Islam, but at no time ever has any of you considered African religion as a religion. Now if you look at the Yoruba people themselves, all these younger people we have talked about, who have developed a new pride in Yoruba language and history and identity. When it comes to religion. . . .

W: They shy away.

U: Yes. And it amounts to a form of schizophrenia. If you are really going to have this Yoruba revival that you are talking about—regardless of which political framework it will take place in—sooner or later they will have to face the issue of Yoruba religion squarely. And I am not thinking of the Yoruba theologians, like Dr. Idowu, who pick elements from Yoruba religion and create some kind of construction that will make it look "kosher" from a Christian point of view. And all those elements that do not fit the Christian world view will be declared a subsequent degeneration of the original "true" essence of Yoruba religion. That doesn't help.

What has to be done is to show that Yoruba religion had some universal human values which are as valid today as they were a hundred years ago and that there were elements of this religion that were superior to the so-called "universal" religions. For example, its tolerance. But apart from you, nobody has stood up and said this.

W: Well I have met some people of my own persuasion. You know at Houston Texas they have this huge festival every year which features one country. And this year it was the whole of West Africa. And there was a Yoruba there who stood up and said: You cannot simply seperate Yoruba religion from the Yoruba world view and from all what you call Yoruba civilization.

U: It has been a taboo subject.

W: Yes, and you know, I take every opportunity to push it. And I say: Look you people with your big, so-called universal religions. All you have is a history of blood-thirstiness. I said: You cannot find a single example of any Yoruba religion waging a war on its own behalf. There is no Orisha community that has gone aggressively proseletyzing. In spite of this total lack of aggressiveness it penetrated and infiltrated other religions and has created whole new viable systems of values in Cuba and Brazil.

There is at least one lesson to the world which divides itself into two or three religions to the neglect of every other viable system of values. I do agree, of course, that there has been a lot of superficial, sometimes ambiguous flirtation with African values, particularly in America, like the Kwanza. They have set up their own Black New Year Festival and it has become a big thing, thoroughly commercialized like Christmas. They send out Kwanza cards and they have a festival—rather like Harvest. They start preparing long in advance, they have write ups, they light candles and they wear Akwete cloth.

U: That reminds me of Mr. Amu. Do you remember that charming musician in Accra who performed baroque music on atentebem flutes? For his daughter's wedding he invented an "African wedding cake." It was made of Fufu . You cut it with a knife and it contained pepper stew. But what was the point?

W: Precisely. Because there is already a traditional form of wedding in that kind of so-ciety. So why use the cake symbolism? But you are right about the reluctance of Afri-can Americans to focus on a recognizable and still existing (it doesn't have to be Yoruba) symbol, saying: this has a meaning for a contemporary black person in Ame-rica. They don't do that. They substitute.

U: But there are many things that you could use. Many Yoruba rituals have a universal meaning—they cut across all cultural boundaries. Tunji was very lucky, because when he was born in Papua New Guinea there was a Yoruba doctor, one Doctor Lucas who was there on a WHO mission. And he held a proper Yoruba naming ceremony for him, with pepper and honey and all the rest of it. And for us it was a great deal more meaningful than baptism and it had an equally powerful appeal for all the New Gui-nean friends who were present.

One thing which everybody loved: instead of the parents dictatorially imposing a name on the child, every friend could confer his own chosen name on the child. So you teach the child from the beginning that he will be different things to different people in life, and that he is part of a larger community; that his parents are not the only ones who take responsibility for him and that his own responsibilities extend far beyond his nuclear family.

W: And we don't need a priest to do it. Anybody can do it, and you can use whatever foodstuff is available. You can adapt to circumstances and even add new meanings. Because the symbolism is the earthing of the child.

U: And giving him a taste of what life has in store for him.

W: Giving him a little bit of bitter and a little bit of sweet. Even I myself have performed many naming ceremonies. In fact right now Olaokun, my son, is waiting for me to come and name his newborn child. So he is also an example of this kind of sensibility. Even though he grew up in England and married a white girl. But the passion with which he has integrated himself into that society, both politically and culturally, is amazing. So you see evidence of that phenomenon all around.

U: But how will these values be imparted to a new generation? I find that my Nigerian friends in Germany face this problem. Their children grow up in an alien environ-ment. It is natural for them to come home and expect to be served by their parents, because that's what the children in their environment do. It takes a huge effort to te-ach them elementary rules of Yoruba behavior, politeness, and respect under the cir-cumstances. How much more difficult to impart essential values? How will children growing up in exile retain the subtleties of their language? How will they understand what orisa is or ori? And is a child in Lagos not as alienated from its culture as a Yoruba child growing up in America or Europe? Do we need to create institutions? Some new form of school?

W: Something like this has been undertaken by a group in California. They call themsel-ves the "League of Patriotic Nigerians." I went to give them a lecture to help them with their fund raising. They actually want to raise a structure which they call Nige-rian House, because they are acutely aware of the loss of this culture to their children. They have been exiled for a long time. They teach their children Yoruba at home, or Igbo, as the case may be, but they want to institutionalize this. They are going to make it open to Americans, too. So this is a tendency, and I doubt if it is going to be short-lived, because there is a real need. And part of it arises from the fact that many children have been growing up accepting American values unques-tioningly and some parents have become so upset with it that they swore they would not let their children lose their culture. So I think all is not lost.

U: Sometimes one wants to despair. But the Yoruba people have demon-strated a remar-kable sense of survival throughout their history. So that gives one hope that they will survive even this latest and most dangerous crisis.

The Osun Grove of Oshogbo: Symbol of the Crisis of Yoruba Culture Conversations between Susanne Wenger and Ulli Beier

In the past all Yoruba towns had their sacred groves, in which the most important rituals and sacrifices were carried out. The Egungun Masqueraders, the Oro Society and the major Orisa all occupied their own sacred area. The shrines were modest low mud buildings, which blended perfectly into the environment. Thick mud pillars supported the extended roofs of the shrines, creating a wide shady area under which the worshippers could sit, while the senior priests officiated inside. The roofs were of thatch and some maintenance work on roofs and walls had to be carried out annually. The total area of sacred forest amounted to a kind of game reserve, because it was forbidden to hunt, fish, or fell trees in the area.

When I first saw the Osun grove in Oshogbo in 1951 it had already been decimated by the expanding town. Oshogbo then had 120,000 inhabitants, which made it one of the largest Yoruba towns after Ibadan and Ogbomosho. A vast area of forest between the palace and the present grove had already been eroded to make room for housing. A motor road had been built through the entire length of the grove from North to South, to connect the town with a farm settlement that had been established by the Department of Agriculture. Most of the forest to the West of this road had been cut down to make room for a teak plantation that was managed by the Department of Forestry. The reduction of the forest area, the noise of the road, and disregard for the hunting taboo had virtually eliminated the animal population of the forest.

The annual Osun festival was still attended by very large crowds, but most of those who came to the ceremony were not Osun worshippers, but citizens who were celebrating the foundation of their town. The first Ataoja of Oshogbo had migrated from the town of Ibokun after a chieftaincy dispute. After moving for a long time through the forest with his followers he finally decided to build his palace at the site of the present Osun shrine. The goddess Osun, however, emerged from the river and warned him that this was her sacred grove, that he should build his palace further up on the hill. The Ataoja made a pact with Osun: he promised to protect her forest, while she promised to protect his town. During the invasion of Yoruba country by the Fulani armies the goddess indeed intervened; twice the cavalry from the North was defeated outside the city walls.

The Ataoja, on the other hand were not quite as successful in protecting the grove and there is a serious danger at the moment that they might lose the battle all together.

Not only has the forest been reduced, but the festival itself has changed its character. The main ritual had been a procession to the river by the Oba followed by his chiefs and the townspeople. At the shrine a sacrifice would be offered, whereupon the Oba would proceed to the river to feed the fish. It is said that a large fish used to emerge from the river, blowing water into his hands. In this way the goddess expressed her satisfaction through her messenger.

Nowadays the king drives to the river by car. A huge tent is erected near the river bank, where the Oba feasts the dignitaries of the town. Beer flows lavishly, praise singers sing the oba's oriki (rather than those of the goddess), and a motley crowd of entertainers sing, drum, and dance for the illustrious guests in the hope of picking up some largesse. The Osun ritual has been totally marginalized and the festival has been reduced to a fun fair. It is safe to say, however, that without Susanne Wenger's intervention in the early nineteen sixties, the grove might no longer exist today.

Susanne Wenger came to Nigeria in December 1950. After a strenuous trip to Jebba and Bida at Easter 1951 she broke down with tuberculosis. She had contracted the disease in Vienna many years earlier, but it had been dormant. She was bedridden for nine months but was finally cured, when Prof. Lorenzo Turner (an African American guest professor at the University of Ibadan) procured the new wonderdrug Streptomycin for her, which was as yet unavailable in Britain, but which had just appeared on the market in America. In retrospect she was to interpret this illness as her "initiation disease," a kind of shamanic preparation for her initiation into the Obatala cult.

In Ede, where she moved immediately after her recovery, she met the Ajagemo, an important priest of Obatala who initiated her into the cult. Whereas in ancient times initiates were physically removed from contact with society by being kept in a cloister for several years, Susanne Wenger went into a spiritual withdrawal. For virtually a decade she withdrew from most social contact, and struggled to find some equilibrium between the powerful symbolism of Yoruba religion and the vast cultural baggage she brought with her from Europe. (She was thirty-seven years old when she entered this new world.)

It was shortly after she had emerged from this self-imposed seclusion that she was approached by the priests of Osun in Oshogbo. The main shrine by the river was collapsing, and the community of worshippers had become so small that they could not raise the money to pay for the labor to repair it. Susanne Wenger employed two bricklayers called Oyewale and Lani, who repaired the shrine and then re-erected the wall that was shielding the inner sanctuary of the forest from casual visitors.

Only gradually did some artistic work appear, when Oyewale and Lani spontaneously added some relief figures to the wall.

As a next step, Susanne Wenger now proceeded to re-erect the shrine at Idi baba—a site on Ibokun Road, where the Osun festival ends with a final sacrifice. So far the work had been paid for from my salary. Now I apealed to the Cultural Attaché of the German Embassy who—surprisingly—organized a subsidy of £70 without batting an eyelid. (Those were the days when foreign embassies competed with each other in giving "aid.") Here Susanne Wenger worked on an empty site. There was no trace of the original shrine, apart from some peregun trees. She was free to invent, therefore, her own shrine and she placed a number of cement figures between the trees outside it.

From here she moved back into the grove itself and for nearly a quarter of a century she erected shrines and giant sculptures on ancient sites where the original sacred buildings had long collapsed and been turned back to the earth.

Her work became increasingly personal as the years went by. Her shrines imposed an entirely new aesthetic on the grove. Here buildings were large and complex—half building, half sculpture—and they became more and more expressionist as she went on. Her sculptures became monumental, no longer harmonizing with the trees, but competing with them.

Some people have accused her of imposing herself on a foreign environment, of treating the sacred Osun grove like a personal art gallery, and reinterpreting Yoruba religion in a manner that bears little resemblance to its original spirit.

To this reproach one can answer that Yoruba religion is not dogmatic, that it allows for a wide variety of interpretations and that the multiplicity of orisa is probably the result of cults bursting with new ideas and gradually breaking up into two or three separate but related religious groups. In the sixties the Osun worshippers were such a tiny minority within the town of Oshogbo that they could hardly reject such a powerful ally who had turned up in their midst like a deus ex machina. It is fairly certain that without Susanne Wenger's activities the grove would have become the victim of timber merchants, real estate agents, and developers long ago. But her activities attracted worldwide attention. Numerous television programs featured her and her shrines in Britain, Germany, Sweden, Austria, and the US. Innumerable articles were written about her. Most of them ill-informed and many sensational, but it all helped to make people Nigeria feel that something important was going on here, that should not be interfered with.

Apart from the trivialized annual Osun festival, less and less worship went into the grove, but Susanne Wenger feels that art can be a substitute for ritual. She has succeeded to stop further inroads into the grove; the department of Antiquities declared it to be a National Monument and actually pays for a couple of guards to patrol the groves and act as guides.

But in spite of such official sanction, there has been no lack of hostility. The shrine at Idi Baba was destroyed three times, the Obatala shrine at Obatata was demolished by fanatical Muslims once. A cement sculpture on the King's Market had to be removed by order of the Ataoja because it displayed a male genital, which offended many Muslims. Susanne Wenger's plea of artistic license did not make any sense in this context. Nevertheless she has become an institution, an integral part of Oshogbo, that even her enemies have come to accept. Her work in the Osun grove has attracted numerous visitors from all over the world: African Americans who try to trace their roots, young Greens and environmentalists from Europe, art lovers from everywhere, and an increasing number of curious Nigerians.

The eighty-one year old artist still works two days of the week on a huge sculpture by the river and her indefatigable struggle for the preservation of the grove has achieved, in the eyes of many, heroic proportions.

Since the preceding interview was recorded, however, she appears to be losing the battle. A totally new threat has developed.

In 1993 Governor Adeleke of Osun State, without consulting Susanne Wenger or even the Ataoja, commissioned a heavy iron gate to be placed at the entrance to Ojubo Oshogbo. The gate is competently welded by an academically trained Nigerian artist. It might look quite splendid as the entrance to one of the nouveau riche mansions that business men and politicians are fond of building for themselves these days. But it is deeply disturbing in the atmosphere of the Osun grove. The very material is hostile to Osun. The heavy, fortress-like feeling is alien to the forest and it jars with the lightness of Susanne Wenger's tortoise gate, which it now hides from view. Whether one likes Susanne Wenger's works or not, they have long become an integral part of the Osun grove. They have become part of Yoruba history. The iron gate seems like a symbol of the new Nigerian commercialism and it is an eyesore in this context. But while the Ataoja, the Oshogbo Union, the Rotary Club of Oshogbo, and the combined artists of Oshogbo have protested against it, no action has been taken to shift it.

Worse still, a large cement platform has been constructed, where the

Ataoja will sit in future, when he is feasting his guests during the Osun festival. There has been talk of coca-cola kiosks to cater for tourists. With that sacrilege, the defilement of the sacred site will be complete.

The growing insensitivity of the Oshogbo people towards the Osun grove and its deeper meaning has become a symbol of the crisis of identity that has afflicted the Yoruba nation. The failure of the people of Oshogbo to keep the first Ataoja's pact with Osun has resulted in a process of self-destruction that is eating away their soul.

(ULLI BEIER)

The Sacred Grove of Sun: Uli Beier Talks to Susanne Wegner

U: Oshogbo is the only town in central Yorubaland that still has its sacred grove intact. This is largely due to your own effort and inspiration. Can we assume that not too long ago every Yoruba town had such a grove?

S: Oh yes. Every town had its sacred grove and today you have a situation where somewhere, in the midst of busy traffic, there is some last sacred site left, some tiny enclave; and when the only surviving old man dies who still carries out a ritual there—then that's the end of it.

In Oshogbo the big mosque is built on the site that was once occupied by the sacred grove of Sonponna. Originally the forest stretched from the King's Market right down to the river. In the meantime the town has spread out more and more and what we are left with today is only a fraction of the forest.

U: I suspect that the mosque was purposefully erected on the site to demonstrate the victory of the new religion.

S: That's the same in Europe, where the church is right in the center of the town surrounded by the cemetery. That was probably an ancient site too. But sometimes these ideas continue to exist behind the Christian or Muslim faCade. Because a living religion is a dimension of reality, and reality is not subject to fashions. Franz Werfel knew that very well. In his book on St. Bernadette he says that Bernadette was an ancient goddess who had to be sanctified by the Catholic Church. Of course she is still that goddess, but also the Virgin Mary. Intelligent ethnologists are discovering more archaic realities of religion that exist everywhere in the world. Namely, that in every culture there must be human beings who are capable of transcending the conventional boundaries of normal life—the Shamans. Yoruba Olorisa, the strong ones amongst them, are Shamans. Of course the circumstances of life and the culture produce different variants of this phenomenon in different parts of the world. But the basic principles are everywhere the same, for instance the "initiation sickness"! The body must be subjected to heavy punishment, before it can undertake the journeys into another sphere.

U: Initiation sickness: is that a disease that is caused by initiation, or is the illness a precondition to initiation?

S: Initiation sickness usually comes like a thunderbolt. It is the god's message to the chosen one.

U: For example smallpox, which is sent by Sonponna?

S: Yes, or a disturbance of the mind that could take years. But when the culture is intact, the state of mind is being contained and channeled into a specific direction.

Yoruba culture is spiritually very refined and they know how to direct the evolution of a human being without destruction. The babalawo, the oracle priest, is the visible symbol of this refinement. He is at the center of this directed development. It is the coolest form of priesthood. He has to be both, cool and bold.

He must constantly be able to transport himself out of his normal consciousness. After all, the patient—the human being who asks his advice—is not allowed to reveal to him the history of his problem, -otherwise he might just as well consult the head of his family. The babalawo must be capable of understanding the problem on a different spiritual plane.

U: You mean not rationally.

S: I would like to put it like this: a human being cannot live without intellect, but he can live without meta-intellect. It simply means that he has no spiritual commitments and is satisfied to cope with his daily existence. But when a human being takes over the priesthood he needs intuition—he must achieve the breakthrough into spheres of human individuality that otherwise remain fallow. Aristotle has expressed that in his own way: "Clairvoyance is a quality of the human soul."

U: And the priests must develop this quality and refine it?

S: Yes. But, as you know, I do not believe that our perception applies only to human beings. I have made my experiences with trees and animals. Perhaps that is why I have become so totally involved with Yoruba, because they have always understood that you might, in certain circumstances, need a tree to reach understanding. Only a tree can reach such depth in the exploration of total reality. It is surely not an accident that Araba, the highest title of a babalawo, is also the name of a tree.

U: Let us return to our original theme. The sacred grove is not just a geographical location in which one builds a series of shrines. It has its own religious significance. It is not a mere backdrop for human ritual activities, it contributes actively towards these rituals.

S: The forest is the origin. The primary world, the totality of life into which man penetrates like a robber. A Yoruba is what you might call an "intellectual robber." He possesses great spiritual boldness. The initiated priest, who has penetrated the magic world of the forest, has developed such distinctive intellectual and spiritual qualities that the normal social situation can no longer contain them. He can live more comfortably with gods and spirits. That is the kind of "solitude" that is meaningful. Solitude in which a human being is isolating himself in a numb state of mind is merely a failed attempt to penetrate this world—you have seen it yourself often enough. Somewhere in the forest an old woman is sitting in front of a shrine, completely relaxed, a completely harmonious human being, because she lives on intimate terms with those things that normal human beings fear; she eats with them, she bathes with them, she sleeps with them.

U: Surely this is a very unusual destiny, which the chosen one will not accept without a struggle. Because every human being will want to follow his normal instinct, which is to merge into society without any friction.

S: Exactly, and this is why he has to go through the initiation sickness. First comes predestination. He is born to fulfill this task. When he becomes aware of this, he resists, because he wants to satisfy his normal desire for happiness. Then he gives in, gradually. . . . Today the initiations are not as difficult as before. Ritual has taken over control; the gesture, the ritual gesture, what Thomas Merton called "the liturgic self." The action in itself produces an effect, so do the earth and the shrine, because all these materials are also orisa and they evoke a kind of wisdom in the human being, which then forms his life. In Christianity also human beings submit to ritual, because they realize that they contain truths. The sanctimonious lowering of the eyelids was once a genuine form of internalizing. But when you live these things without understanding them, then it becomes sanctimoniousness.

"The one and only saving church" is a form of arrogance, though it probably arose from the need of a total identification with a symbol, which every religion needs to survive.

U: The arrogance of Christianity surely arises also from its attitude to nature. Man as the crowning of creation, no longer the younger brother of the tree. Man as the "owner" of earth, river, and tree. No longer an integral part of the environment.

S: When the balance is wrong, the religion becomes an instrument of power. An institution in which one can have a career.

U: Can you define the role of tree and animal in Yoruba religion more closely? Could one say, if we look at it from a modern point of view that the sacred groves of the Yoruba have preempted our concept of conservation?

S: The idea that certain trees and certain animals ought to be protected has always existed. Just as you are not allowed to hunt, fish, or cut trees in the Osun grove, so it was also in all other sacred groves. And after all, this is my own legitimation, when I try to preserve this place. But a situation has arisen when people can destroy my shrines with impunity, as you have seen yourself, when it is possible that the little shrine at Idi Baba is being destroyed three times and there is no authority to which I can turn to complain, then it becomes very difficult. In Europe I could have redress because of the Greens; but here we have not reached that point.

U: It is a matter of bridging a time gap. That is quite clear to me. Maybe it is only a matter of a few years before the new environmental consciousness that is growing all over the world will take root in Nigeria.

But what was that ancient form of awareness? What was this religious form of environmentalism? Can you define that?

S: Through his unusual abilities, his privileged position in the universe, man disturbs the balance of nature: It is the task of the Ifa Oba Oracle to constantly restore this balance. It may actually be true (and not just a cranky idea of mine) that in the hierarchy between God and man, the tree is older, therefore more important. In earlier times human beings knew this and gave the tree his due respect. Today they kill the tree, not only because of greed but also because of their stupidity. For example they burnt the root of a large tree at Lakokan, because it was growing across the path. They were too lazy to step over it, but the tree did not survive it.

U: One can say that when Yoruba religion was still intact it taught man a certain humility towards the tree, and that was one of its great qualities.

S: That is correct. But there is something else. Man's life is accompanied by a continuous, uninterrupted ritual, which begins before his birth and continues after his death and which is to enable him to fulfill his metaphysical life.

We now are embittered about man and what he is doing to the world. But let us not forget that man is something very special. We should not forget, that even these horrendous things, like gene-manipulation, are merely perversions of man's magnificent qualities. Man is an ambassador. There is no doubt about it. One can say that as a religious being man has the possibility to integrate the wisdom of the tree into his life; whereas the tree probably does not have the possibility of integrating the human being.

U: Can you elaborate on your provocative statement that gene-manipulation is merely a perversion of man's positive qualities?

S: That is Esu.

U: Esu? What do you mean by that?

S: Esu is small when you think of him as big; he is big when you think of him as small. Therein lies the possibility of the all-embracing.

U: Are you referring to the possibilities of metamorphosis? The eternally changing forms of life? Or to the coexistence and the inherent truth of opposites?

S: All that. But above all this human penetration into secrets of nature. That is why Ogboni is so important to me, because in this so-called "earth-cult" it is taken for granted that the earth is not just the soil in which the farmer plants and harvests his crops, it is also the soil in which we plant and harvest in a metaphysical sense. The Ogbonis know that matter is a dimension of the spirit. The gene-manipulators know that too. But now the human will is no longer subjugated to the sacred sphere of existence, it merely serves money and power. In such a situation it can easily happen that the basic substance of life is being attacked and destroyed. This decision, which happens in the very center of existence is taken by Esu. There are three roads emanating from him. He is the gate-keeper. But one road always remained taboo. There was always a secret that man took care not to discover. The Yoruba have two terms for what we, simplistically, call "secret." In the Ifa Oracle, Awo is that which is hidden, but which the Babalawo learns to see through his ritual. But when the Ogboni processions proceed through the town at night, a priest walks ahead with his brass staff and cries: Asiri - that refers to the things we will not try to know. Olodumare, the highest being, remains protected in Yoruba religion by this Asiri. We describe vaguely with oriki, but there is no ritual.

U: On certain roads one does not walk. Man refrains from certain actions. But if the power of money has replaced all other cultural values during the last two or three decades and man knows no limits, then the logging of a sacred grove becomes a symbol for a dying culture.

S: Of course. Just think of St. Boniface (the Apostle of the Germans). He felled the holy oak tree, the symbol of the gods, with his axe. That was also gene- manipulation.

U: But who will understand this symbolism here?

S: This is the terrible aspect of evolution. That you always come too late. It was my idea, to bring the two sides closer together.

U: To keep the ancient wisdom alive long enough until one can reach very similar conclusions with the findings of a modern age?

S: Yes. I have the oriki Labosunde. That is the oriki of the Ogboni priest who carried the edan fearlessly into the enemy camp in order to stop the fratricidal war. I met his grandson in Ibadan. He was immensely old and he had tied a tortoise to his leg, because he had some unfinished business in life. He chained himself symbolically to the earth. Sometimes I feel like this tortoise or like a chained slave who has to complete this work at the river. But who understands that here? The only one who really understands the issue is Adebisi.

U: On the other hand there are certain people in Europe who understand.

S: That's why I am in contact with Europe. There are actually people in

Europe who try to save a tiny bit of riverbank under even more difficult circumstances. Somehow they get access to a piece of land, where they break up all the cement that turns the river into a canal. Such people are my allies today. And when they replant the regained riverbank it might even happen that a few animals return to the site that had disappeared long ago.

U: This is the kind of success that you are having here too.

S: Yes, as people have been telling me here: don't worry, if the forest is left in peace for a while, then the animals return—they come out of the earth. And indeed, I sometimes see a little crocodile now, that lives very close to my working place by the river.

U: Yesterday morning we sat by the river and literally saw hundreds of small monkeys. If you consider that about ten years ago the monkeys had almost totally disappeared, because they had been hunted systematically, then this represents a considerable success.

S: I am not surprised, when I see the monkeys having babies. They seem to have them all the time. But I only ask myself: where do they go? Because I have been living many years by the river, but I have never seen a dead monkey.

U: In any case the forest is full of monkeys and here and there the antelopes also reappear; and it happens very rarely now that somebody goes to hunt in the forest. Between the teak plantation and the Lakokan shrine a few farms have disappeared and the government has actually started some reafforestation, however timidly. There are always people in high offices who support you in your work. And there is something else one should not forget: in what other country on earth would one allow an artist to work undisturbed for thirty years in a sacred forest? After all, you are not doing a restoration job. You are creating something completely new. The old orisa priests may accept that without any queries because Yoruba religion has always been capable of absorbing new ideas and integrating them. They know that orisa can be interpreted in different ways. And, after all, the multiplicity of orisa has arisen partly because one took symbols from other cultures and allotted them a place within one's own cosmology. It is far more surprising that even bureaucrats and politicians have never stopped your activities, which must be rather incomprehensible to them at times.

S: Yes, it is true. Nobody interferes. They allow me to continue pottering around with my sculpture by the river. That is the energy source, with which I can recharge myself. I have creative peace.

The Age of Miracles: Crises in Contemporary Yoruba Society Conversations between Ulli Beier and Wole Ogundele

U. What was the thing that excited you about Death and the King's Horseman? What do you see in it, and how do you interpret it? I also think that it is Soyinka's most important play, easily.

W. First of all the sheer poetry - Elesin Oba's poetry. The first part of the play is a combination of so many things. I cannot read it without hearing the Yoruba version at the back of my mind. Then, of course, the entire subject, the theme of it. I also see it as a very ambivalent play: there is celebration in it, but also an angry lament. After my first reading of the play, I went back to listening to Yoruba oral poetry with a different ear. It also induces in me that sense of irreparable loss.

U. What do you see as the particular beauty of Yoruba poetry as such? What do you see in it? I can read it, at least in English, again and again I can listen to Soyinka read it. Even the translations I made with Bakare Gbadamosi which Soyinka is now reading. I can hear iruki Sango a thousand times, I cannot get tired—why is this? What particular quality that Yoruba poetry has that is to me special. What would you say it is?

W. First, I would say its just the sound! That would be for any language but. . . .

U. Yoruba is poetic even if it doesn't try to be poetic, just because of the sound itself. It is losing that quality. If you hear a Lagos taxi driver, you'll see that something has happened to the language—they speak it too fast, they slur over vowels virtually, they flatten the tone. The tone intervals become smaller. The language is harsh and even brutal, reflecting what they've become. If you hear somebody like Muraina—he can still have this certain ponderousness. . . .

W. The full articulation!

U. Full articulation! He can say, I want to eat pounded yam, it still sounds like poetry. It has that ring to it—that sonorous kind of quality. He just does, even in his ordinary speech. But most people now mix it with too many English words. There is at least one element which we can see which is inimitable: the sound. I don't think any European language can come close to it, simply because of the structure of the language—we have too many consonants. This is why in Germany or England we will consider Italian the most suitable language for singing because it has less consonants and more strong vowels. But in Yoruba, of course, more because every syllable ends in a vowel! The other thing is that the tonal structure in itself gives it a melody and rhythm. What else do you see?

W. Also the ease with which Yoruba poetry can just go into the metaphysical realm, and make it so real.

U. I think you're very right—the ease with which it can just step into the metaphysical world and come back again. For somebody brought up on European poetry, one thing which is so exciting about Yoruba poetry is that it is not "precious."

W. There is no artifice!

U. It is direct. The poet doesn't take himself as seriously—he's not any special person.

W. He may be a seer or a prophet, but he is very down-to-earth!

U. Basically, what is great about Yoruba society is that it is classless, really. That is to say that, in spite of the fact that you have all these, hierarchy doesn't mean that anybody is better than any other person.

W. The artistic productions that are available to the king are also available to the ordinary person. Also, I remember Biodun Jeyifo telling me that you made an observation which until then hadn't even occurred to him as a Yoruba scholar—which is that you noticed, especially in the 50s, that most of the profound babalawo that you met were poor.

U. Oh yes! Absolutely.

W. Therefore the tradition of the creative life being its own reward is not entirely foreign to us.

U. The Yoruba poet was unpretentious as a person. The poet, as you pointed out, had access to the metaphysical, but hasn't everybody got it in the culture? So, being a priest is a career in that sense.

W. Even those born into it, into the family of chanters or priests, didn't have special privileges conferred on them.

U. So what I like about it is a certain simplicity of tone in spite of all that. There is no pretense, there is no arrogance, no elitism, and all these things which we associate with the poet in our society.

W. Unfortunately we are now also imbibing that idea of the poet as a special person in our society. It is paradoxical really: when the (oral) poet had concrete and immediate functions, he was not special; now that the (literary) poet's role is marginal, that he writes in a language other than the people's, we are all conferring on him a special status.

U. It is sick. This is the sickness of our society. What was so refreshing to me living among the Yoruba was there was none of that at all. Whoever and whatever genius you are, even a carver—somebody like Bamigboye— you simply lived like an ordinary person.

W. In those days, whenever somebody died, it was a particular age grade that buried him or her. It wasn't something you did in a hurry, got paid and left. The grave digging would start at about 9 p.m. and go on until the small hours of the morning. And there was a lot of poetry—funeral funeral dirges were chanted throughout. Digging the grave was a ritual on its own, and any member of the age-grade participating in the digging would simply burst into these dirges.

U. I have even seen in Ekiti—you know, when the corpse is finally laid down and earth is thrown on it, you have to stamp it down. The people stamping it were dancing to some rhythm, and somebody was actually beating a drum to it—it became a dance. Poetry was part of everyday world, it accompanied every aspect of life. There were occasions when everyone becomes a poet, as you say. For example, when there is a sudden death, say, of a small child. I've experienced this in Osogbo—the mother would run out of the house in the middle of the night, and she will find a form, a poetic form to announce her grief, and to express it. This is quite unbelievable, because you can't really have that in any European culture. When we are hit like that we become dumb actually. We're lucky if we can cry, but we have no language at that point. There is a quotation from the German classical poet Goethe which says that "when man is struck dumb by his grief, it is the poet only who has the gift of expressing what he suffers." In fact this is not so in Yoruba culture. Here in Europe, the poet has become some specialist, and we the rest are the unpoetic lot. Whereas in Yoruba everybody could find in the right moment the words. A form has been created by the culture and it was available to everyone. And basically, I know that at Sango festival, it was just some of the ordinary women worshippers who would sing the oriki, and two or three of them throwing the thing back and forth. That was the normal thing which I've seen. If it is Ijala, it is the hunters. The other thing is that even when the thing is so powerful, so serious, and often so metaphysical, at the same time there is always this humor in it. We have particularly the romantic poets, and according to this tradition poetry is supposed to be lofty. It cannot be about ordinary things, always sublime. It lacks directness, and it lacks punch therefore. If you have a humorous poem, it has to be a category—humorous poetry—which is considered to be a cheaper muse.

W. No, not in Yoruba poetry. Again, here is where the younger contemporary Nigerian poets and critics do not know their traditions. Even in times of grave political crisis, the oral poet never lost his sense of humor. Now, we think that the only kind of literature worth writing and reading is the one that deals with the weighty political problems, and in an attitude of unrelieved seriousness, which is also unrelieved tediousness. I remember that when Niyi Osundare published his very lyrical volume, Moonsongs, some Nigerian reviewers accused him of abandoning the cause, of "fiddling while Rome burnt," so to speak. I also remember an Ugandan student not being happy with Soyinka's A Play of Giants because it turned what was a real-life tragedy into a comedy! In any single oral poem, no matter how short, the elements of seriousness and humor are present, the one enhancing the impact of the other.

U. One thing is that Yoruba understand that life is not like that, -they see that life is not as simplified, the way we try to present it in literature. They are too realistic for that. There is also psychology in it—it would be unbearable to live only on the lofty zone! And this gives room for personal contributions, for improvisations both in art and in daily life.

W. People revel in iyato - difference! Olabiyi Yai has worked around that area—that in fact the principle of aesthetics lies in the variation. Monotony—No! A new musician first pays homage to his mentor and/or predecessors, then announces his own iyato!

U. It goes through everything. The priest personifying Obatala or Sango will do it differently from his counterpart in the next village or even his predecessor in his shrine. Because through him, through his mind, through his brain, otherwise he would deny an important aspect of life.

We were going to talk about Death and the King's Horseman, the material of which I always thought symbolizes the ethnocentric approach of any colonial power, basically any European action. The D.O. in this case was clearly thinking that he was acting on humanitarian grounds. He really was trying to save somebody's life. In many other cases you could say that the interference in the other culture was deliberate with ulterior or selfish motives, but in this case that is not even the case. The D.O. had no means of actually understanding, but he can be blamed because there is the inherent arrogance of not bothering to be informed, this is what I can't understand. This seems to inform the entire relationship between colonial powers and the colonized—this is how I saw the entire story. Wole Soyinka in fact, in his forward said that he didn't see it as a conflict of culture, and when you wrote your article about it you saw other things as well—may be you should quickly explain that.

W. Apart from the Duro Ladipo play, the comedian Baba Sala also had a version of it. The main point of his own version, since it was in comic form, was how the prince—the Aremo—instead of Olokun Esin, seized the opportunity of his impending death to wallow in an orgy of food, drink, and sex.

Then of course, he refused to die. When I wrote my paper I had that also at the back of my mind. Basically, I was looking at the play in terms of what has happened to the culture at this particular point in time, especially from the end of the civil war to the present moment. I was then interpreting it both historically and ahistorically. The play, in my view had a relevance that transcended the specific historical event, and Elesin Oba represents something that has happened to that culture. When I then looked at Soyinka's play, I saw it partly as a question of leadership in Africa, most especially Nigeria. What kind of leadership have we had since colonialism, and how have our leaders both at the national and sub-national levels behaved and fared?

U.   If we take the Elesin Oba as a symbol for that, you have to interpret the play to mean that he has in fact failed. You can say that anybody who was violently taken off a trance to which he has been building up all his entire life, you cannot really expect him to repeat the act—I don't think it is possible. He could have committed suicide the way the son did.

W.   Yes, the purity of the act was lost.

U.   You can't blame him for that. On the other hand, Wole seems to, and I don't know if you see it like that, he seems to indicate he is not to blame, because the incident with the bride indicates the act was already not pure.

W.   I think that the center of the play is not his failure to die, but the taking of the bride. It is the turning point, and the irony is that it is an unnecessary act. Here is a man who is renouncing the world and leaving it with a lot of bluster and heroism, but who gets diverted. He makes us believe that he is going to die, but really his mind is still in this world. It is a fatal diversion, and that diversion represents the corruption of leadership in Africa, from the colonial period to the present—the failure to recognize the historic responsibility thrust on them. It also so happens that the obscenity which overtook Nigeria started during that civil war. We know how certain leaders abandoned all kinds of caution. Suddenly there was access to a lot of money, and some people have given the explanation that the Yoruba were now virtually in control of the nation, especially the economy. The feeling in the country, which is of course superficial, was that the Yoruba people were totally given to hedonism. Elesin Oba also personifies this, once the spiritual aspect has been diverted, any casual observer of the Yoruba social ethos would come to the same conclusion—that any excuse would do to have an all-night party once it's Saturday. Elesin probably meant well when he started out, but he overestimated his own powers, or rather, preferred not to contemplate his own weaknesses and doubts—the basic human instinct to cling to life, the converse of which is that though it may be good in the world of the ancestors, but we don't know that for certain; and therefore there is really no enthusiasm to go. Whereas the impression that Elesin has given all along is that he is very enthusiastic to go. Among the ironic complexities of the play is that it is also evocative of another aspect of Yoruba philosophy: that after all is said and done, this life is good. One should maximize his potentialities in life, but when it is time to go you should go resolutely.

U.   There are some old priests who had medicine buried somewhere and when they feel it is time to go, they just send their sons to go and dig it out and destroy it—the moment that happens, he dies. That is one way of ritualizing it. So in some sense the play is also basically about corruption, a problem with the culture altogether. One other problem may be that, once the community is already divided, then it is already hard on the individual who has to carry its burden. The very fact that the Iyalode is also conniving in this—she should have been the one to stand up and put an end to it. But how different the attitude was to death is in an account by somebody who observed a human sacrifice in Abeokuta. I cannot remember who the victim was, but again he was dressed ceremonially, and was carried triumphantly through the streets. What he felt about, nobody knew, but what is interesting is that the women rushed forward to touch him—to pray that he would be reborn to them! They felt that this thing was ennobling this person to the degree you want him to be reborn to you. So there is something different here. Maybe in places like Benin and Dahomey, where corpses were piled up, it became a bit perverse, but this was a different matter. Here human sacrifice occurred in very extreme situations, and it meant something totally different.

W.   One has also heard of people who died willingly on behalf of their community—even Ifa priests! These are the aspects that are lost, and without dwelling on it Soyinka manages to convey either the decline or the gradual loss of this spirituality. What has come to the surface is the exploitation which the leaders themselves might not have been aware of: that while they're claiming to still have that spiritual aspect they really do not have it and they know it. Many critics have seen only that celebratory thing, in spite of Soyinka's preface. Whereas everyone sort of admires Iyalode as spokesperson for Yoruba culture, I cannot truly sympathize with her—she concedes to Elesin-Oba too easily. Because the whole thing backfires proves that she was wrong all along. She makes very great speeches at the end, but it's rather too late. I also find that in every Soyinka play in one form or the other there is always a generational conflict. In several plays the older generation either wins or there is a kind of mutual destruction, but in Death and the King's Horseman the young man at least gets some kind of victory.

U.   I think you may be right in saying that the play expresses his disappointment or even anger with the culture—his disillusionment with the failure of the culture.

W.   That is where the play (and others) speaks to me personally. Having grown away from the culture through formal education and through physical distance, I didn't identify very much with Yoruba. And then, coming back to Ibadan and reading about what had happened (not in any systematic manner!) in the 50s and 60s—a kind of renaissance at least at the artistic level, and after people like Ulli Beier did what they did and left—what further things have we done? Has there been a general awareness caused by the activities of these people and the events of those decades—an awareness beyond academic circles and universities that we must keep the momentum?

U. There was at the time, in Duro's time, changes of attitude through Duro's activities. When we started Mbari Club, it had a certain attraction particularly for the ordinary people. But when we first had Oba Koso in 1962 there was very strong opposition from the churches—Bishop Philips was denouncing and condemning it in public. The Mbari Boys, as they were called, were abused as Olorishas![1] But there came a time when Bishop Philips came and attended plays in Mbari! So, somehow, in his own lifetime, Duro won that battle on the local level. In Osogbo, he became highly respected. The problems here were mainly at the national level because politicians didn't really understand him—but they did not really understand anybody, so you can't really count that. Disappointing was the fact that for a long long time he was really blocked at the University of Ibadan. On the popular level Duro really established a new awakening. The whole Osogbo artist thing was only perhaps possible because these things had gone before, in the sense that you can't just pick somebody out of a crowd and turn him into an artist. There are some people who look at these experiments and see Seven-Seven, Muraina, and Rufus Ogundele and say, oh well, all Africans are born artists. That is just not true. It's a difficult process to become an artist. Something had happened and that is that there are a lot of young people who had actually joined the theater earning less money than they did before. Muraina earned less money in the theater company than as a petrol-station attendant opposite. Tijani Mayakiri earned less money. There was a crowd of young people who had recognized that there is something else in life than to survive or to become rich. That was the achievement of the new company—Duro's achievement. This was a new attitude, awareness of the richness of the culture.

W. We can say that what happened was a kind of cultural revolution.

U. It was, because it was against the establishment. It was really a large thing. It started with the Extramural Studies opposing the university syllabus, with Robert Gardiner saying we have to relate to what happens in this country. That was one basis of it, the next was the Ibadan Mbari Club. There we tried to say we have to become independent of this government patronage because we are too far from them in thinking. And then the Osogbo thing, everything then integrated. Wole was quite instrumental in bringing all the theater companies together at one stage—Ogunde, Duro, and Ogunmola. Why did it not continue? It did not continue for a number of reasons. But before the civil war something happened to the Mbari Club in Ibadan. There was definitely an awareness being created by all these things, no doubt. It went beyond university circles. Just a little example: Wole and I were using Adire shirts—I was probably the first person ever who made a shirt out of Adire, because any Nigerian would have said this is a woman's thing—which became known as the Mbari shirt. I did it because I liked it and not out of any revolutionary motive at the time. It was not until we had a cleaner who was called Smith for one reason or the other (he was a Yoruba). When he started wearing Adire shirts, then suddenly we had little boys carrying Adire shirts of various sizes around. Then it became a fashion. This is one minor way in which an awareness was created.

W. I think that the momentum was lost was also because dispersed and fragmented among so many travelling theater groups that mushroomed. It became purely a bread-and-butter thing and only accidentally artistic or cultural.

U. I got very upset going to see the plays of Moses Olaiya, I found it very crude, if you compare it to Ogunmola's acting. I went to one of his plays in which a cripple or a dwarf was used as a comic figure! That to me was something very, very un-Yoruba, and I found it disgusting. One of the things I had always admired about this culture was the way any deformity was treated with total respect, in the same ways as lunacy was treated with total respect! A lunatic in the early days in Osogbo would walk around unmolested—nobody would jeer at them. Even if they kept throwing their clothes away people kept giving them. When I saw Olaiya's play, to me that was an indication that something terrible had happened to the society. The change which people like Moses Olaiya brought had its roots in the 1940s and early 1950s: the starting-off point of the Yoruba theater was to always ridicule tradition. The hero would be the very school teacher which Wole lampooned in Lakunle. Every babalawo was a figure of fun, which I always find very painful, very offensive. First we had Oba Moro (by Duro Ladipo), and Onibonokuta was playing the priest who is sent to investigate the site when the demons were coming, and he is making his merindinlogun. There he played it initially in that style, and I knew about his father. So I asked him, do you feel your father was a character like that? You're now representing your father in this play—this is what I said to him—then he started to think. People were in two minds, you see. It was actually a revolution to play a babalawo or an Obatala priest on stage with dignity.

44

W. Would you think then that it is the persistent influence of the Church, and possibly Islam too? These were two institutions that saw no good in these people.

U. There came a time when the established churches - the Catholic Fathers used to come to attend Duro's plays. The ones from Inisha came— they were the usual white Fathers who moved in groups of three, and they always came from different countries. They were very nice, very intelligent people. They always came to Mbari, and even at one stage the Osogbo artists did chasubles* for Father Mark, who later became an anthropologist. So, these were quite enlightened people, quite interested in the culture. It was the Aladuras who became much more aggressive, not even so much the real Aladuras that people like I.K. Dairo went to. You now have these mushroom churches, they come up and they're really businesses—nasty businesses. These are the sort of people who are usually antagonistic.

W. One of the good things that the travelling theater did was to bring a lot of traditional poetry to the foreground, even though several of them did it "to death," so to speak. They were more interested in its supposed concrete magic powers than in its intellectual or aesthetic qualities.

U. The theater has been killed by the film. I think Ogunde killed his own theater.

W. He did. And now you can hardly find a theater going, it's all on video. Now you have so-called communication companies in Lagos who just churn out these videos. Okay, some of them deal with contemporary urban problems, but basically what they're just doing is exploiting what they think tradition was to titillate people.

U. There is one other factor that has changed drastically—that is the quality of the

Obas. In my time we had Timi Laoye of Ede, Oba Adenle of Osogbo, Aderemi—the Ooni of Ife whom I saw regularly and he was always good company. Timi Laoye was an exceptional figure—he really also created a renaissance in his own town by simply reviving the whole thing, and so did Adenle. In Okuku there was an Oba who spoke no word of English at all, who was a giant. He could just say something and people knew this has to be done, because he had such authority—not that he had any legal power! We had these Obas and that gave the whole thing a very different setting. Now, if you look at the successors of these people, that core of the culture has been taken out, the quality of the Obas is no longer there. You've probably heard the story of Alafin Aole—he was made to commit suicide. Before he committed suicide he broke a pot and shot an arrow in all the four cardinal points; then he uttered very, very dire curses on the people. It's almost like his curses have come true. It is quite an ominous thing and somebody should write a

45

play about it. It always disturbs me. He was already a very disturbing character—he was a slave dealer in Apomu. The Oba of Apomu had him arrested and beat him or something like that. Later on he became the Alafin, and you know that during the installation of the Alafin people ask him what do you want, which town do you want to conquer. He said that he wanted the head of the Oba of Apomu—he was in fact shielded by the Ooni. The Alafin threatened to destroy Apomu, until the Oba agreed to die. He killed himself, and they sent his head to the Alafin. This happened then, which is already the core something that happened to the culture, to my mind. It's not entirely new, but it was balanced before by other things.

W. I always thought that the fact that the Yoruba people were their own worst enemies was because the civil war—the Yoruba civil war—was interrupted. Perhaps if it had been fought to a natural conclusion, as civil wars in other places were, a new political unity might have emerged. Going back even further as you've just done makes it even more interesting. Now, although Yoruba culture like most African cultures have been praised for the respect and reverence that they give to children—the younger generation; but the way I read the role of the younger generation in Death and the King's Horseman, concerning Olunde and the young lady, is that overall they're not given much say. It looks to me as if Olunde's spirituality is on the whole wasted. Even in the plot of the play, his role is recognized as serving a useful purpose in redeeming the honor and integrity of the kingdom, but it really does not lead anywhere. Reading your interview with Soyinka, I can see the concept of the abami-omo, that is going to be, hopefully, the product of Elesin's union with the young lady. But that seems to me a never-never future, something remote and just a possibility. Historically, when the British helped to destroy the established political order, if one wants to be unkind, you could say that the political upstarts who would be of the younger generation—they were the pushy and the grabby people, and this is represented in the political parties that sprang up in the South. It was like a deliberate plan to destroy whatever remained of the old order, and on balance it made a mess of the whole thing.

U. It destroyed the balance—I think that is very true. They rejected the old order. They felt the Obas to be rivals. It happened everywhere, look at Nkrumah's fight with the Ashantehene.

W. Does this not then say that somehow some continuity is needed? While on the one hand there is a need to modernize, it seems to me as if people did not give thought to the idea that tradition itself can be modernized rather than modernization meaning rejection of tradition, and wholesale importation of Western values and ways?

U. You should not forget that in fact tradition in Africa has always modernized itself for centuries. They adapted in many things—you'll find for example that the Oba's crown is made out of colored beads which were brought by the Portuguese in the seventeenth century. You will find that Egbas and Ekitis were using dundun drums which were brought from Oyo, whereas the Oyos themselves could have got the dundun drums from whoever. In a simpler form that drum exists throughout the sub--Saharan belt. In some sense, to me the great strength of the culture in the past had been this ability to absorb. If you look at an Epa mask, you will see that the actual mask is a highly abstracted image—it's almost totally geometrical. Whereas the figure on top invariably is much more naturalistic, so you can have two styles in the same carving. The same carving embodies two traditions—there is an overlaying of traditions and this has been in Yoruba country for a long time. The multiplicity of Orisa is the same thing—that you absorb what was there before, you don't wipe it out but you let it run parallel. You can say that the civilization or movement that the AG represented were the first people who refused to do that. They were the first people who didn't understand the historical process of evolution, that the Yorubas have evolved, and they were the ones who were rejecting it. The fight against the Alaafin is the culmination of that.

W. May be the Action Group might have carried things too far, but I tend to see that there is a subconscious rebellion of the youth and that it goes back a long way. The culture on the whole recognizes the youth but it insists that you must take your place in the queue, from where you move up. Therefore the infusion of young blood into the system was not very much there. When the AG reacted it was a subconscious reaction against this age-old hierarchical thing in itself. Of course, the whole thing was first helped by colonialism and then the new political context of the country, and education and all that. I have the feeling that the youth have an ambiguous position in the culture as such, and this might be contributing to the present crisis that the culture is experiencing. Again, Olunde in Death and the King's Horseman seems to me to epitomize that contradiction. Here is somebody who definitely has the spirituality that his father has lost—he's very much in touch with the well-spring of the culture. But in redeeming whatever honor and integrity of the culture, he becomes a sacrificial lamb.

U. But what choice does he have—what should he have done?

W. Given the nature of the play, I don't think he has a choice. Basically, the play is not his.

U. Regardless of the intention of the playwright, if you look at the historical situation, you will see that the son is perhaps even more committed to the idea than the father, or to the ideal: what option has he got to assert that idea now, and is there anything he can do that is not going to be in vain?

W. To answer that question, one has to look at this play in the context of other Soyinka plays. Consistently, and I have in mind Camwood on the Leaves, here is a play in which the young man openly rebels against the father, and that freedom is achieved at a very high and rather unpalatable cost. It looks to me as if Soyinka is saying that for this culture to revitalize itself, for new energy to be infused in it, some parricide is necessary, -looking at it at a mythical, symbolic level. In a way, Olunde has contributed immensely to Elesin's suicide, by shaming him, and by displacing him in fact.

U. One of the disturbing things about the play and about the reality behind the play is that Olunde does the redeeming act, but at the same time it doesn't achieve anything in concrete terms. The sacrifice he brings is not the equivalent of what the father should have done. You can say it is in vain, but I don't think it is a meaningless thing to do. Think back to Soyinka's own action just preceding the civil war—if you want to be rational about it, you can say it is just a stupid thing—obviously without any chance of success, and ultimately he went to jail. On the other hand, for somebody like me living in a kind of exile in New Guinea, and hearing all these horrendous stories on the radio, for me, his sacrifice was not in vain, it kept my hope in Nigeria alive. The kind of things he did again and again made me feel that this is not the full side of the story—there are people with integrity and they're willing to put their head on the block. You need some of these people, and I'm sure there must have been many Nigerians for whom the symbolism of his act has meaning. In that sense Olunde's act also had meaning.

W. It seems to me that Soyinka is always hinting at the fact that one particular threshold must be crossed before we can achieve full liberation that will also be a revitalization of the society. Paradoxically, in death, Elesin by committing this act cleared the way for a self-renewal by the culture—in the sense that with Olunde's and the Elesin's death that particular practice for which Elesin stands can no longer continue. Iyaloja seems to hint at the fact that we now have to make a new beginning, a beginning which the child in the girl's womb represents, but that child will come into the world without the glorious anachronism that Elesin represents, but with the spiritual force of conviction which Olunde possesses.

U. If you see it like that then you could, theoretically, justify the AG for trying to do just that. Theoretically, you could say that they said all right the time is over for the Obas, the Chiefs and so on, it's now the time of another age-group to take over the leadership, because these people are not capable of understanding the new realities. But why did they make such a mess of it culturally and in every respect?

W. Their error was to think that you could build the new structure on borrowed foundations, that you have to have modernity whole from the West rather than modernizing tradition.

U.   Again, very much what you said that people felt, that in order to become modernized they would have to give up everything—it's like a conversion. If you're going to become a Christian or Muslim, you've got to destroy your idols. I went to Nigeria in 1950, I was 28 years old, and I had not actually found my own identity at the point. It was my experience of Yoruba culture that made it possible for me to find out who I am, and what I want from life. I learnt a lot from that culture, -I absorbed a lot of values from that culture, and it influenced my life totally. But, it doesn't mean that I have become a convert—it just meant that whatever I had before that other thing also began to fall into place—in other words, in experiencing Yoruba culture I understood my own culture better. That is the only way you can benefit, otherwise you become an indiscriminate lover of blacks, -there are these ridiculous people all over the world. It was quite an organic process, without my planing to have it like that. But it seems to me that the Yorubas and most Africans missed out on that process, because they had gone through a school system that made them reject—that says you should be ashamed of yourself. The fact that something has to change, or an institution has to be abolished—maybe we shouldn't even have an Oba anymore—I don't know, but may be Yoruba society is even better without an Oba at the moment—I am beginning to think. But this doesn't mean that you despise the institution of the Obaship—you're only saying that we ought to change the system, and that is different.

W.   Then you're being selective, which is different from wholesale rejection.

U.   Which is what happened very, very heavily, and that is where the whole process failed. The AG being in a responsible position carries a lot of blame. There were no theoreticians in the group—Biobaku was the only one who had something to say for the culture; but really, to the extent of drawing any lessons from it, it remained academic. I feel that was where there was a big failure, and the Egbe Omo Oduduwa didn't do what it pretended to do. You can almost say that Awo was cynical—he made use of the Obas, at the same time he destroyed them, by destroying their status.

W.   It's strange that as rational and sober as he was, Awo had that inexplicable blind-spot—his total disregard of his cultural heritage, which is very un-Yoruba.

U.   Do you know that he wrote with pride in his book AWO, that his father was one of the first set of Christians in Ikene, and he describes with pride how his father went with some other people and destroyed the Sonponna shrine. He even claims that the Yorubas were dirty—that they didn't wash properly before they became Christians. Akintola, tragically, was quite different. He spoke very good Yoruba. He was a great admirer of Duro Ladipo, unfortunately for Duro. There is no reason why a Yoruba shouldn't become a Christian or a Moslem, except that in traditional Yoruba societies there was tolerance. For a little while in the 1950s, you could still find that the Christians and Muslims even fitted in. But a moment came when the Xtians and Muslims became totally intolerant, and thereby destroyed the system.

W. What I cannot understand and what is going on now is that the economic and political situation has driven people back into tradition—more people now consult Ifa priests and so on because of their anxieties. At the same time the churches and mosques have grown. The nativist churches promise instant cures, instant miracles, to any and all problems, but when they don't deliver, people return to traditional ways. Also, the churches and mosques are more dead-against tradition than they've always been. It is as if people are living three or four different lives and refusing to relate all to one another.

U. There are people who go to a babalawo at night, then to the alufaa and then to the aladura.

W. And when they go to the babalawo at night, they have more faith in him than when they go to church on Sunday or to the mosque on Friday. But why is it that when the churches and mosques wage their wars against the babalawo why are all these people unable to stop it, especially as they know that many of these pastors and Imams also consult the babalawo? So they integrate them at the level of personal live, but at the public level, you must keep up appearances.

U. You end up with a schizophrenic society.

W. That is my reading of the situation. I also think that we should talk about the language question, which has political overtones which are possibly dangerous. Perhaps another way by which there is a crisis in the culture and by which that crisis can be resolved positively is via the language question. As we remarked earlier on, the Yoruba language now is a far cry from the language you met—it has lost its expressiveness, and that ability to say whatever anybody wanted to say in it. What you find operating within the context of Nigeria are children growing up who don't know Yoruba very well, but who also don't know English very well. I know many so-called middle--class families now, who punish their children for speaking Yoruba. They think a child should start speaking English from the word go. At another level, when you tell the Professors of Yoruba and other culture scholars that our language is under threat, they retort that Yoruba literature is alive and well. I'm never satisfied with that: -literature may be central to the growth of language, but in a contemporary world such as we have now, that is not enough. In fact, the literature itself can become irrelevant if the use of language in other areas of human activity are not growing along with the literature—in science, medicine, even in ordinary discourse, political, social or whatever. I would like to hear your opinion about this.

U. I think you're right. For example, who reads Yoruba poetry? It used to be something you hear all the time, you're surrounded with it. Daily life is poetry all the time, just like language is poetry and music. But nowadays, there are some odd people who read a book of Yoruba poetry—it's not the same thing! There is no occasion when it is made public. When I went to Brazil, you go to the market, and there will be a corner where somebody will be selling books—he has written some poetry, and he stands there declaiming it and selling it! Even in big cities like Rio de Janeiro, you find the night porter at the big hotel who when there is nothing to do sits there reading poetry. This can only happen through a more civilized form of Yoruba conversation, which can only be encouraged in the family. One thing that you intellectuals should be doing is really to support, encourage, and give prestige to things like the alarinjo theaters. In that kind of context, you get a lot of poetry. How many people in the University of Ife or Ibadan in the years that you've been there when they had a family festivity on which they spent a lot of money, invited an alarinjo group to entertain their guests? Have you ever experienced that? The thing to do is to give it the prestige it needs. These things don't cost much money, and really it is lack of interest. We did all the time when I was at Ife. In the eyes of many of these people it hasn't got prestige. The Ife campus then had a vibrant cultural life. Of course, the economic situation wasn't as bad, but even now I still think its possible. If Nike Davies can do, surely a university can, if they want to. Its like everything—you don't support your own cause. What used to be an everyday thing has now become a luxury item, but let it at least survive as a luxury item. The Japanese have indigo textile, and there are certain craftsmen who still know this craft very well, and they're declared by the Emperor to be a living national treasure. Who has ever done that to any Nigerian thing? It is the materialism or whatever it is that has happened has created this thing, plus the poverty whereby people now fight for survival—they can only think about food. There is, of course, also an international conspiracy about traditional cultures, if you like. There was a program on television last night on the IMF—the program was entitled "With Poverty We Could Live"—but now you take the basis for our existence. And this is true, because everywhere there is a big IMF scheme—it is the poor people who get hit worst. One woman interpreted SAP to mean Sapping of African Peoples!

W. This keeps taking me back to the language question. English was forced on us because of colonialism, but then we also on our own enthusiastically embraced English even when we could have made a choice, when we had alternatives. This enthusiastic acceptance of English can be seen as an index of the rejection of all things African. I say this even within the context of the larger polity of Nigeria with 250 languages, three being major.

U. You have to see the political problem, and that is you cannot easily have a national language in Nigeria.

W. But we don't need to have one national language—other countries have done it and are doing it.

U. Okay, Switzerland.

W. Maybe I'm being romantic about the importance of language; I think if we could come by some political arrangement whereby we say, we will retain English at some level. Then, it is not just a question of let each child learn one or two other languages, but let Yoruba speaking-peoples use Yoruba, Hausa-peoples use Hausa, etc. If we begin to think and do things and conduct political/intellectual activities in these languages, don't you think there could be a turn-around?

U. But there is also work involved, and also a fanaticism involved. Through the political events in Europe, when the Jewish immigration to Palestine occurred, some people said it is no good for us to speak German here. The one language that could have easily become the lingua franca because many people, the less-educated Jews from the whole of Eastern and Central Europe knew it, and that is Yiddish, which is a form of medieval German if you like. They all knew this language and it would have been easy to make this the lingua franca. But some people said, this is not dignified, unless we speak Hebrew. Hebrew was the language of the Bible, and people had to sit down and invent the vocabulary for Physics—for anything, and then they went and forced people to speak it. It's possible. You find that now perhaps some of the people who are developing a very strong modern Yoruba identity are people living in exile. Because they live in exile and they have to explain themselves, they develop within themselves a concept of what Yoruba is, and the interesting thing of course, is that among all the African cultures, Yoruba must be the one that has the greatest adherents among non-Yorubas. Look at Robert Farris Thomson—he believes in it, he feels it, and he lives it. There are several people like that. What I'm trying to say is that of course, there are people who study this and that but it doesn't mean anything. But there are lots of people who have deep feelings for Yoruba particularly—I mean Verger! The way I see it at the moment, Yoruba religion in some form or the other has some bigger chance of survival in Brazil and Cuba rather than in Nigeria!

W. I once had a white-American student who offered to take me to a babalawo in New York—he believed in it.

U. Some of the people who come from the US to the Osun festival used to come from Puerto Rico originally—there is a whole Orisa scene there. But there is also the other side, a lack of confidence, cultural confidence. It is what makes Lucas say we come from Egypt, or Biobaku say we come from Meroe—all these borrowed glory. Now the Black Americans say Islam, because these are the people who nearly conquered Europe. Then it becomes a big militant, foul thing. It is really a lie.

W. In the context of Nigeria, it is part of the crisis in Yoruba culture: people are thinking in terms of their economic survival within Nigeria and any amount or kind of surrender that would ensure that is willingly made.

U. What is it that makes it possible—when before we had said that the babalawo was a poor man, the Oba wasn't rich—why now is this greed? It can only be because, over the last generation at least, they have abandoned the values of the culture, they have abandoned the religion, the political system; and this business of deference to elders simplifies etiquette, because everybody knows exactly where he stands. You do what is expected of you, and it is not humiliating for you to do it. It actually takes a certain egotistical competitiveness out of the society, because it gives everybody his place, and everybody his dignity also—even the small child!

W. The position of Western culture, western education, western junk and languages is just assumed to be natural. The natural conclusion would be that it is because we are operating within the socio-political context of Nigeria—my fear is that if it should ever come and we have a Yoruba nation, people would say lets continue with English.

U. The really serious question to ask is: Will it at this stage serve any serious purpose? Will there be a Yoruba cultural revival? Or, as this Sudanese friend of mine said, will there be anybody who will be able to talk reasonably about these things? Because, let's face it, there has been a century of systematic brainwashing—it hadn't affected many people at first but increasingly more. Europeans up till today cannot see the guilt they have in all this. It's not so much that they exploited the countries, but what they've done to their minds. They in fact feel that they have given you all these opportunities.

W. There is also the feeling that if you borrow from your neighbor, it's an admission of inferiority, and then finally, there is a lack of imagination.

U. This is what they do, and this is my whole complaint—cultural interchange is always between the people and the colonial power; between Senegal and France, Nigeria and Britain, Papua New Guinea and Australia. These things have happened in the past and why not now? For example, the Timi of Ede did a very wonderful experiment, one day he said to me the Yoruba word for organ is duru, how come they call it duru? It can only be that there must have been some instrument that reminded them of the sound, and therefore he said, I'm going to set out to find out this duru. He wrote to all the Obas he knew, and finally from Ogbomoso the Soun sent him two musicians who played duru. What duru is is very, very interesting. It's basically something like an enormous goje, almost 1 meter high and it had a huge gourd at the bottom—it was the size of coral from Guinea. It had three strings, and these three strings probably needed a bow, and at the top there was also a piece of metal with rings, so that anytime the thing is shaking it made another extra noise. There were two apiti players—when they played this together, the apiti drummers were playing by hand, and the duru players were also hitting their thing as if it was a drum. I think they got this instrument from further North, and having to play with Yoruba drums they could not accept because the sound was too soft. So they started to adapt it and treated it like a drum, so there was something like that happening. At Mbari, the Timi used to bring them.

W. Again it's a whole diversion from our internal resources that colonialism caused. I don't think it's just that the Yoruba don't find anything good from their neighbors. It is that the Western world is the successful world and that is the only place where anything is now worth borrowing. Then there is the mistake that appearance corresponds to the inner reality of the culture, which, in the present situation of general confusion many Africans also substitute for the real thing. To use the popular artists as example once again, its not difficult for any of them to learn a few oriki of egungun or whatever orisa and then use them side by side with chants from the Quran in fuji music, then they're hailed as promoters of Yoruba culture. The parallel of it is the mistaken belief by government, both federal and state, that a festival of Arts essentially is just the dancing—that's all there is to African culture.

U. Basically, what we've said throughout this discussion is that no one has looked at the content of education, and that is one of the first things that should be done. Here and there reforms have been made, like in your literature thing, people said we call it literatures and African literature would be the core of the thing; -that is a very good step in the right direction. But because it was an isolated thing, just one department took a stand, but the university wasn't sufficiently behind it. I don't know what you can do—first of all the thinking should be done which hasn't really been done: what kind of education do we want for our people, ideally. Of course, you're right in saying that the first thing to reestablish is the language to the place it belongs. Secondly, there was Oduduwa, but Oduduwa becomes meaningless the moment you do not give the Oba his authority—it worked through the Oba. The other thing to my mind is the Ogboni society, because it was trans-tribal. You could go to anywhere in Yoruba country, if you were an Ogboni, and give your signs, and you have to be admitted—it rose above all other divisions. For example, when Owu was besieged, the Olowu had one of his wives who was the daughter of the king of Ede—when it was seen that the town could not last for much longer, they took the edan of the Onile—smuggle it to the king of Ede, and deposit it at the Ogboni house. I still saw it there! Again that is something that is gone. Finally, there is the Ifa oracle which is universal in Yoruba, but once again it has become corrupt.

2.
THEATER

The Return of Shango: The Theater of Duro Lapido
Uli Beier

One of the major problems facing any Yoruba theater group was how to keep a good actress. Most parents did not consider acting a respectable profession for girls, insisting rather that they get married. Even rebellious young women would want to get married sooner or later, thus putting an end to their careers. Hubert Ogunde, the most successful of all Yoruba playwrights, solved the problem by marrying all the actresses. Duro was not rich enough to do so, yet there was one girl he simply had to marry. She was irreplaceable. Abiodun was an Ekiti girl with an unusually expressive voice and a powerful stage presence. Small, strikingly beautiful, with very large eyes, she brought a new dimension to the performance by introducing her Ekiti style of singing with its ancient harmonies. She alone could match Duro's towering stage presence.

Duro was nervous of confronting her parents. He had never been to Epe Ekiti and he was uncertain of local costume. He knew that very traditional people were bound to have strong reservations about their daughter marrying an actor. He could not count on support from his father, with whom relations had remained strained. So he asked us to accompany him to Ekiti, to act as surrogate parents and help to convince Abiodun's parents that Duro's theater was a respectable venture and that being an actress needn't be an undignified career for their daughter.

The visit was unforgettable, because it coincided with the Egungun festival. The ancestral masks were covered with raffia, with legs partly exposed. The mask consisted of a flat piece of wood, sitting horizontally on top of the head, painted in red, ochre, and white lime, with tiny white eyes as the only actual feature. These masks did not have the wild fierceness of some Egungun I had seen in Oshogbo or Ede, but they were even more mysterious—part animal, part human spirits.

Our meeting with Abiodun's parents made us feel like diplomats. However, we were warmly received and we seemed to strike the right note. Duro and Abiodun got married and before long she was the main asset in the company, not only his star actress but a composer and a true partner to Duro for the rest of his life.

Duro was now ready for his greatest challenge: the production of Oba Koso. From Johnson's History of the Yoruba, Duro selected the story of Shango for the first anniversary of Mbari Mbayo in March 1963. The ancient myth has all the makings of a tragedy of Shakespearean proportions:

Shango is a fierce warrior king whose only ambition is to enlarge his empire. But his people suffer from constant wars. They have lost so many of their sons on the battlefield that they lack the manpower to look after their farms. A delegation of elders implores the king to stop warring. Shango is finally persuaded by his wife Oya to recall his generals. But he realizes that he has lost control over them. They have become so powerful that they act like kings in their own right. He tries to play them off one against the other, but Gbonka kills Timi in a duel and then openly defies the king. The people of Oyo are frightened and side with the rebel. Shango is forced into exile. Accompanied only by his loyal wife Oya, he heads for Tapa, his mother's country. When Oya abandons him as well, he commits suicide. Shango's friends come to bury him, but are told that he has ascended to heaven. He answers their prayer with thunder and lightning. Defiantly they sing "Oba Koso" (the king did not hang).

This is the synopsis which resulted from Duro's perusal of Johnson's text. He had set himself a daunting task: he was going to portray the metamorphosis of a king into a god. His Anglican education had taught him nothing about the world of the orisha. He had never attended an ebo of Shango, he had never been inside a Shango shrine, he didn't know Shango's oriki. During the following weeks I introduced him to Shango priests in Oshogbo, Ede, and Otan Aiyegbaju. Timi Laoye of Ede was particularly helpful. Shango was his personal orisha and to him he had dedicated a spectacular shrine with twenty-one magnificent carvings.

When we sat together at dusk, Duro would ask me why a European like myself had become so friendly with the Shango worshippers and what had attracted me to them initially. The decision to produce Oba Koso challenged Duro's entire education. The play became the turning point in his life. The first performance, in March 1963, coincided with the Mbari Mbayo anniversary and had the impact of an explosion. The audience was stunned—overwhelmed. They had never seen anything remotely comparable on a Yoruba stage: the fierce entrances of Duro, the moving, plaintive voice of Oya, the wild, yet disciplined dancing of Gbonka and Timi, the incantations in the witches' scene, the thundering interventions of the bata drums.

I remember the excitement of the audience on that occasion distinctly; yet looking at the photographs of early performances it all looks rather bleak. The costumes were still rather simple, there were no painted backdrops.

The play failed in one crucial respect, and this troubled Duro deeply. When Sango hanged himself, the audience burst into uncontrollable laughter. Yet Duro had found a simple and effective way to solve that difficult moment: Shango placed the noose round his neck, pulled it upwards and roared. The stage was plunged in darkness. When the lights went on, Oya was seen mourning her husband. Considering the little technical means at his disposal, it was the most economical and discreet way of suggesting a suicide. But the audience was not moved. In our first post-mortem about the play we tried to analyze what had gone wrong. Duro suggested rewriting Oya's farewell song, first shocking the audience with an even more abrupt suicide and then drowning immediately the king's scream of despair in salvoes of bata drumming. All these were very sound dramatic considerations. I suggested that perhaps something far more fundamental was at fault. Throughout, Shango had been portrayed as a ruthless tyrant, so that his ostracism had come almost as a relief. Therefore his suffering was not cathartic and his deification unconvincing.

Duro decided to go through his text all over again and change the mood of the music, wherever Shango's oriki spoke of his generosity and his humor, in order to emphasize these qualities in his character. As time went by he began to identify more and more with the personality of Shango. He did away with the melodramatic gestures he had borrowed from the routine performances of other travelling theaters and toned down his movements and facial expressions to a minimum.

The play evolved over a period of three years. Duro as well as his wife Abiodun and his two main actors, Tijani Mayakiri (Timi) and Ademola Onibonokuta (Gbonka), worked constantly on their parts and introduced a variety of new musical effects into the play. The most striking were Gbonka's incantations in the witches' forest, Timi's song on arriving in Ede, and Oya's lament on the death of her husband. Timi and Gbonka developed their costumes, constantly adding bits and pieces until they became truly magical garments with a mysterious power of their own.

Oba Koso reached its first peak at the Berlin Festival in 1964 with a tightly knit performance that swept the stage with a blaze of color. It happened again in the palace of the Alaafin of Oyo, where the descendants of the three protagonists, Shango, Timi, and Gbonka, actually sat in the audience!

The play continued to evolve over the next fourteen years, until Duro's death, and its impact was not lessened even after the lead parts were taken by new actors. However, the performance in Bahia, Brazil, in 1969 was the most gratifying to Duro. A large section of the audience was composed of Yoruba descendants, and many were olorisha . The emotion aroused by this performance was so powerful that Duro sat down that night and wrote me a long, moving letter—the only letter he ever wrote to me in his whole life.

When the first press reviews of Oba Koso started to appear, the dignitaries of the Anglican Church accused Duro of being a worshipper of idols. At that time it was not uncommon for people to shout olorisha, which was intended as a term of abuse, at the Mbari Mbayo actors. To begin with, Duro had perceived Shango merely as a historical figure, as an ancient hero who had been destroyed by the ingratitude of his people. But the more he tried to understand the personality of the god, the more time he spent with Shango priests in Oshogbo, the more he began to identify with his role.

The actors of Mbari Mbayo were often associated in the mind of the audience and of their fellow actors with one particular role—so much so that Mayakiri came to be called Timi, and Onibonokuta Gbonka. The identification of the latter with his part went so far that he began to challenge Duro's authority within the company on the grounds that, hadn't he, Gbonka, driven Shango out of Oyo? So how could he now be expected to take orders from him? The more Duro became known to the public as Shango, the more he worried. Was he really allowed to do such a thing or was he an impostor who was breaking a dangerous taboo? His roaring, fire-spitting entrances had become truly powerful, but the more he convinced his audience, the more anxious he became.

One day, as he was cycling from Ilobu to Oshogbo, he was attacked by a swarm of bees which settled on his head. Later he was found unconscious and taken to the hospital. To Duro it was a clear sign that he had offended Shango. Accordingly, he went to the shrine to make a sacrifice and ask the orisha's permission to represent him on stage.

From that day on, Duro would sacrifice a cock to Shango before every performance of Oba Koso, and it was now that his performances achieved both the stature and the power that made him famous all over the world. He had shed all the clichés that informed the Yoruba travelling theater and his performance had become concise and austere. His stage presence was so enormous that he could dispense with every superfluous gesture.

I was convinced that, had he been born half a century earlier, he would have been a powerful Shango priest and probably even a baba elegun [2]. The personality of the orisha was perfectly congenial to his own. In September 1964, when the company was to perform in Berlin, sacrificing became a problem. How to avoid the gutter press headlines: "Nigerian troupe performs pagan rites" or "African actors indulge in primitive sacrifice"? Fortunately the company was not housed in a hotel, but in a hostel out of town. A friendly German woman, Karla Aimes, who had been assigned as an attendant to the company, managed, with the help of a Turkish restaurant owner, to secure a live cockerel which she smuggled into the camp.

A year later we ran into the same problem in Liverpool, at the start of the Commonwealth Festival. This time Georgina made discreet inquiries and was advised to ask at the central bus station. The conductor said: "You Jewish, luv?"

"No. . . ."

"Muslim?"

"No, Shango. . . ."

"Oh, another one of 'em. Take the 93 bus and tell them to let you off at the chicken farm."

When Duro died unexpectedly in 1978, the press carried banner headlines reporting loud thunder at the time of his demise, right in the middle of the dry season, so that people felt they had lost more than a playwright and an actor. By the time he died, Duro had become a living legend, a last resurrection of Shango.

Border Crossings

Duro will always be remembered as the playwright whose insight into Yoruba history and religion caused a whole generation to perceive their tradition in a different light. Although for years he had to suffer the taunts of "olorisha" and "idol worshipper," by the time he died he had become a veritable hero. When people called him Shango, it was in terms of the highest respect. It would be wrong, however, to think of Duro as a narrow traditionalist let alone a conservative. He had learnt to enjoy the splendor, the intrigue and the wisdom of Yoruba culture, but his mind was wide open to other ideas, from all over the world. He had a healthy curiosity, was a lateral thinker, and was prepared to use any material for his plays, from whatever source, if it fired his imagination.

He would use biblical material as easily as Johnson's History of the Yoruba; he incorporated material from other Nigerian cultures; he even tried his hand at European plots. He was always curious about theater in Europe and asked me to tell him about German plays. In the days when he had to come up with a new TV play every week, he actually adapted the plot of an eighteenth-century German play Nathan der Weise by Gotthold Ephraim Lessing:

Nathan der Weise is set in Jerusalem during the crusades. Each of the three religions, Christianity, Islam and Judaism claims that it alone is in possession of the truth. The wise old Jew Nathan settles the argument with a parable: Once upon a time a man had a magic ring which enabled its owner to distinguish the truth. He had three sons whom he loved equally and he could not make up his mind which one of them should inherit the ring. In the end he had two copies made; they were so perfect that he himself could no longer tell the original. He then asked his sons to pick one ring each and told them: the only way people will ever know which of you is in possession of the original ring is through your way of life; go out into the world and vie with each other in truthfulness.

The theme of this play could easily be related to Nigeria in the 1960s: Nathan der Weise became a babalawo and Judaism was replaced by traditional Yoruba religion. The play offered Duro the opportunity to ask his audiences to see orisha-worship as a religion on a par with Christianity and Islam—a very bold statement indeed in those days.

The following year Duro went as far as producing a radio play by Friedrich Durremnatt, in Yoruba, for WNBS. I had prepared for him an English text of Der Doppelganger which he translated into Yoruba. The play was then produced with the help of Segun Olusola. This remarkable experiment took place years before Theater Express[4] began to adapt Durrenmatt and Chekov for the stage.

In 1964, for the second anniversary of Mbari Mbayo, Duro chose a play in which he actually had to portray an European. Oba Waja was based on an historical incident that took place in Oyo in 1947:

When the Alain of Oyo died in that year, the Elesin, commander of the king's horsemen, was to die after him, according to ancient custom. As Alafin could not be expected to cross the river into the land of the dead by himself and it was the Elesin's duty to lead him. The Elesin had prepared for this event all his life. Once the fateful day arrived, he would dress up like a king, dance through the town with drummers and be paid the highest respect. Towards evening he would return home, look at the setting sun and die—not through poison, but by an act of will. In 1947 this age-old custom was broken by the British District Officer who regarded it as barbaric and who let it be known that suicide was an offence under British law.

He had the Elesin arrested during his trance-like dance, after which it became emotionally impossible for the commander of the King's horsemen to renew the feat. Elesin's son, who had heard the news of the Alafin's death rushed home from the Gold Coast to bury his father and was so horrified to meet him alive that he committed suicide on the spot.

This remarkable story was told to me by Pierre Verger[5] , who had researched it in Oyo. He had even corresponded with the District Officer, who had confirmed the event. Around 1961 I gave a summary of the episode to Wole Soyinka, suggesting he use it for a play. Wole was interested, but was kept busy by other projects for many more years. Therefore in 1964 I gave the synopsis to Duro, who produced Oba Waja. Only ten years later did Wole eventually write Death and the King's Horseman, which many people consider his greatest play.

With Oba Waja Duro attempted something quite difficult—he presented a historical event seen through the opposing views of two cultures. He tackled the issue of colonialism and its disastrous impact on Yoruba culture. His portrayal of a British officer could not, of course, match his numinous personification of the Thunder God, but he gave a plausible performance. Oba Waja lacks the subtleties and ironies of the King's Horseman, but in parts has great lyrical beauty.

A far more successful "intercultural" play was Moremi, which Duro presented on the occasion of the fourth Mbari Mbayo anniversary in 1966. For Moremi he had returned once more to Johnson's History of the Yoruba as source material and he used it in a particularly interesting way:

> The story deals with the conflict between the first Yoruba settlers in Ife and the Aboriginals whom the Yoruba referred to as Igbos— that is the `Forest people´. The Igbos, who lived scattered in small villages in the forest, attacked the markets of Ife sporadically and abducted Yoruba women. The Yoruba did not know how to meet this challenge because the raids were led by ancestral masquerades and the newcomers did not know how to confront the ancestral spirits of the land on which they hoped to prosper. Moremi, an exceptionally beautiful wife of the Oni of Ife, prayed to the river goddess Esinminrin for help. In return she promised to offer any sacrifice the goddess would demand.

Esinminrin advised her to allow herself to be taken prisoner by the Igbos. The King of the Igbos would marry her because of her beauty; thus she would be able to learn their secret.

Moremi followed her advice and learned the magic formulas with which to neutralise the supernatural powers. She fled home and with their help the Igbos were defeated. The Oni of Ife did not kill their king, nor did he want to destroy his enemies. On the contrary, he asked the Igbos to settle within the walls of his town and gave their king a Yoruba chieftaincy title in order to integrate his people fully. The river goddess Esinminrin asked Moremi to

65

sacrifice Oluorogbo, her only son. But the child ascended to heaven and is still worshipped in one of Ife's major shrines today.

Duro Ladipo took the bold step of inviting a group of dancers from Agbor[6] to participate in the play. The Agbor dancers had been frequent visitors to the Mbari Clubs, both in Ibadan and Oshogbo. I had been introduced to them in the late fifties by Mr. S. S. Allanah, my colleague in the Department of Extra Mural Studies, who was stationed in Agbor . They had impressed Yoruba audiences with their intensely energetic and acrobatic dancing. By using them to represent the Igbos, Duro was juxtaposing two completely diverse styles of dancing and singing. He also had two different sets of instruments: Bata, Dundun and Igbin drums at the court of the Oni of Ife and slit gongs and calabash horns at the court of the king of the Igbos. In the final scene of the reconciliation between the two groups all the instruments played together—all following a simple basic beat that Rufus Ogundele hammered out on a bass bongo. The sound was spectacular and it opened new vistas, with Nigerian orchestras made up of talking drums, slit gongs and xylophones, flutes, horns, and trumpets. I had a vision of an orchestra more complex and more colorful than a European symphony orchestra, but of course Duro could never have afforded such a venture. The Agbor dancers were a luxury he could permit himself only once. In subsequent performances he had to produce the play without them, and it lost its most important dimension.

Those first performances of Moremi, however, were as grand as the best performances of Oba Koso. The music was breathtaking in its variety, contrast, and novelty. Jire, who played the part of Moremi while Abiodun Ladipo was pregnant, surprised the company by the strength and integrity of her performance. Nobody had suspected that an actress who so far had served only as a chorus girl could give such a powerful performance. Alake Ajibola acted the River Goddess with subtlety and Tijani Mayakiri was a convincing Babalawo. Muraina Oyelami played a dignified Igbo king. The backdrops by Georgina Beier[3] used different types of appliqué: Dutch prints for the Igbo palace; adire for the river, etc. Moremi was one of the most striking successes of Duro's career. The play had an important political dimension in 1966. After the years of tension between ethnic groups that had led to the first military coup in January 1966, Duro Ladipo produced a play about what we have since come to call multiculturalism!

In 1972 Duro crossed cultural boundaries yet again, transporting an Ijaw creation story into a Yoruba play. The myth "Woyengi" was first published by Gabriel Okara in Black Orpheus No.2. For the 1972 Ife Arts Festival Duro produced the play Oluweri, working mainly from Ijimere's play Woyengi.

The Ijaws believe that before coming into this world people kneel before the creator goddess Woyengi and choose the sort of life they want to lead on earth. There were two women who desired to come to earth together; one asked to be granted many childen, the other, magical powers. Both wishes were granted—but sometime later the magician and healer became jealous of her friend who had so many children. She decided to challenge the creator goddess and force her to change her fate.

On her way to heaven she overcame all obstacles and defeated all the gate keepers with her magical powers. But in her pride she had forgotten that it was Woyengi who had given her those powers, and that Woyengi could also take them away.

These Ijaw concepts coincide with the Yoruba notion of Orí—the personal destiny which a human being brings down from heaven and which he must live out on earth as best as he can. Oluweri provided splendid roles for both Abiodun Ladipo as the magician and Idowu Ladipo as the mother; it even provided roles for half a dozen of Duro's children! For Duro, Oluweri was a particularly meaningful theme: ever since the first performance of Oba Koso Duro was convinced that he was fulfilling the destiny he had carried down from heaven and for the rest of his life he acted with the conviction and unwavering strength of a man who knows that he is following his ori

Theater and Politics

Hubert Ogunde was at his best when he treated political issues. When he dealt with politics, his theater assumed a larger dimension. In his "bread and butter" plays he merely tried to please the audience, while with his political plays he challenged them.

Duro Ladipo also challenged his audience, but he was not interested in topical themes. He never joined a political party or supported any particular politician. He saw himself as a philosopher. He tried to make people aware of their history and culture. He thought of the values that he was trying to project in his plays as timeless.

But if Duro was not interested in politicians, politicians were interested in him. The more successful he became as a playwright, the more difficult it became for him to extricate himself from local politics. The years 1962-66 were the most crucial in his artistic career: he established himself as a playwright and a director with a distinct style, he made his first tours overseas and he wrote his greatest plays: Oba Koso and Moremi. Yet they were also years of intense political unrest in Westem Nigeria. 1962, the year of the inauguration of the Mbari Mbayo Club in Oshogbo and of the historic performance of Oba Moro, was also the year in which a state of emergency was declared in Westem Nigeria.

Chief Obafemi Awolowo, leader of the Action Group, whose stronghold was Western Nigeria, had resigned the premiership of the Western Region in order to become leader of the opposition in the Federal Parliament. The premiership of the Western Region of Nigeria then passed on to his Deputy, Chief S.L. Akintola. Awolowo created alliances with minority groups in both Northern and Eastern Nigeria, and thus challenged the political status quo. He pronounced a new political philosophy which he called "democratic socialism" which alienated some of the influential businessmen in his own party. His deputy and other members of the Action Group disagreed with what they thought a politics of confrontation. They argued that it would condemn them to remain forever in opposition. Chief Akintola argued that the Action Group should develop friendly relations with the North and then join a grand national coalition, that they might "get their share of the national cake."

In the Action Group conference of 1962, however, the bulk of the party stood solidly behind Chief Awolowo. The rift between the two factions grew and it was finally exploited by the politicians of the North. A violent confrontation occurred between the two factions during a session of the Western House of Assembly. According to newspaper reports a Member of the House flung a chair up into the air, jumped onto a table, and shouted: "There is fire on the mountain!" Miraculously, the Federal Government was fully prepared for the crisis. Police moved immediately into Western House and arrested all the members. A state of emergency was declared and Dr. Majekodunmi, Federal Minister of Health, was appointed administrator of the West. Both government and opposition politicians were ordered to retire to their residence and not to venture beyond a radius of two miles.

Gradually the ban was lifted from members of the Akintola faction and from the NCNC opposition party. The really staunch Action Group supporters remained under house arrest, were then accused of plotting to overthrow the Federal Government, and eventually were charged with treason. In the ensuing trial Chief Obafemi Awolowo received a ten-year sentence, while twenty of his supporters were given shorter terms.

In the meantime Chief Akintola had formed a new party, the NNDP, consisting of his faction within the Action Group and of a group of carpet-crossers from the opposition party, the NCNC. Together they set up an interim government in the Western House of Assembly.

In the Federal elections of 1964 the NNDP went into open alliance with the Northern NPC, while the Action Group and the NCNC teamed up to form the UPGA (the United Progressive Grand Alliance). The UPGA candidates were being harassed to such an extent in the North and the West that they finally decided to boycott the election. The predictable result was a landslide victory for the NPC-NNDP alliance. Thus the NNDP established a power base in the Federal Government.

It was not until October 1965 that Chief Akintola finally decided to face the electorate in the Western Region. In spite of the heavy patronage dispensed by the provisional government, the people of the Western Region had remained loyal to the Action Group. They voted heavily against the NNDP, but to save his position Chief Akintola decided to rig the elections. The fraud was blatant: in some cases the election results were simply reversed in the official announcement.

But the people were not fooled, however, and refused to accept the so-called official results. The next few months saw a farmers' revolt in Western Nigeria. Successful NNDP candidates were driven out of their towns. Often their cars and their houses were set on fire. To prevent them from returning, the farmers set up roadblocks on all major highways. Armed with dane guns[8] and cutlasses, they checked all cars but behaved in a disciplined manner.

Unfortunately, groups of thugs exploited the situation of civil unrest and set up their own roadblocks. They would pour petrol over a car, light a match, and threaten to burn the owner alive in his vehicle unless he handed over all his money. The riot police that was moved into the region was powerless to deal with such massive disorders. Even Yoruba Obas who had openly supported the NNDP were harassed by their people. Some were driven out of town and their palaces burnt down.

Officially the Federal Government never acknowledged that there had been a breakdown of law and order in the West. Before the Commonwealth Prime Mnisters' Conference in Lagos, the Nigerian Prime Mnister Abubakar Tafawa Balewa asserted in a public statement that there was no breakdown of law and order in the West. To prove him wrong the rioters thought up a gruesome device: they threw a dead body on the tarmac just as the Canadian Prime Minister was getting out of his plane. As he descended the gangway he stepped onto the corpse.

In December 1965, armored cars were stationed at the disused airport outside Oshogbo. From time to time they would drive down the main streets in a show of strength. Periodically the vehicles stopped; the soldiers jumped down and used clubs to chase people into their houses. Nobody was really hurt, but the people felt provoked and threatened. The rumor circulated that the Federal Government had a secret plan to send in tanks and "flatten" six Yoruba towns. The people of Oshogbo were convinced they were among the towns to be victimized. It is not surprising therefore that the coup staged by young army majors in January 1966 was greeted with jubilation in the West. People danced in the streets, total strangers embraced each other, and Action Group supporters went around systematically burning down the houses of NNDP politicians. In Oshogbo these punitive expeditions were carried out with restraint: no one was killed or even hurt. A house that caught fire accidentally was rebuilt by the Action Group. But once again the thugs exploited the absence of the political force: they threatened to burn down people's houses in order to extort money from the owners. They settled personal scores and in some cases other people's scores—for a fee.

It was against this political backdrop that Duro Ladipo had to develop his theater. These were restless times and travelling was dangerous. The political parties employed strong men to guard their meetings as well as act as bodyguards, but these "party hooligans" as they were called, soon became uncontrollable. They fought gang wars and carried out private vendettas.

Duro Ladipo tried to steer clear of politics and politicians. Like all artists who are politically naive, he thought that he could go about his business without getting involved. But things were not that simple. His rivals tried to label him an NNDP supporter, it seemed an easy way to arrest his meteoric career. In reality it was the NNDP who tried to use Duro for its own purpose.

Chief Obafemi Awolowo, leader of the Action Group, was a Methodist and a puritan. He never attended any of Duro's performances. He probably disapproved of theatrical performances altogether and would certainly have frowned upon a "pagan" play such as Oba Koso.

Chief S. L. Akintola, on the other hand, was known to be a passionate lover of Yoruba language and culture. When he made a speech, even his political opponents would praise his knowledge of "deep" Yoruba and would go on quoting his proverbial expressions for weeks on end. On several occasions he praised Duro Ladipo in his speeches and told people to go and see Oba Koso if they wanted to hear good Yoruba. It is likely that at this time he spoke without ulterior motives.

But when Hubert Ogunde caused so much political damage to the NNDP with his play Yoruba Ronu, some party officials had the idea of organizing a play that would be an answer to it. One evening, soon after Duro Ladipo's return from Berlin in October 1964, a black limousine drove up to his house. An elegantly dressed gentleman stepped out and handed Duro a script. It was a play in praise of the NNDP and Duro was made the following offer: he was to go on tour with this play for the two months preceding the federal elections. There were to be two TV performances and he would be paid a lump sum of four thousand pounds. In those days it was a huge sum for Duro Ladipo.

Duro did not know how to extricate himself from this dangerous situation and pleaded for time. When I returned from Germany two weeks later, I found him in a state of great anxiety. He knew that if he refused, he might well be mugged by NNDP thugs. His cousin, the popular musician I. K. Dairo, had only recently been waylaid and severely beaten because he had composed a song in praise of Awolowo. If, on the other hand, he did perform the play, the Action Group would surely take revenge on him.

Asked for advice, I told Duro that since his life was in danger in either case, he might just as well do what he thought was right—in other words, refuse to perform the propaganda play. He would then have to deal with the threat. I thought he had only two options: he could either send his actors home, tell the NNDP they had gone on strike, and lie low until after the election, or else exploit the popularity he had gained from his Berlin tour, step up his publicity, perform in important venues, and be in the public eye as much as possible. It was to be hoped that in the latter case the NNDP, having already lost face through the banning of Ogunde, might consider a move against Duro counter-productive.

Duro boldly decided to choose the second option. But the pressures from party officials mounted and so did their no-longer-veiled threats. In the end I went to Ogbomosho to see the Premier in his private residence. Chief Akintola had always been a very accessible politician, but at this stage he had so many enemies that he had begun to barricade himself in his house. He received me nevertheless. I argued diplomatically that Duro Ladipo should not be wasted on such a task—that, whereas any one of two dozen theater companies might produce the political script, only one person in Nigeria could achieve the greatness of Oba Koso. I told him that Duro was being harassed and threatened and that if anything happened to him, I would make sure that the whole world knew about it. The Premier listened politely, appeared genuinely shocked, and promised to put a stop to the harassment at once. He kept his word and, from then on, the black limousines stayed away.

In 1965 the political situation became tenser and Duro's problems grew. When the Federal Government of Nigeria was selecting a Yoruba opera company for the Commonwealth Festival, Oba Koso was finally selected after much wrangling amongst officials. Many actors in Kola Ogunmola's company openly accused Duro of having used his political connections in the NNDP.

But it was Duro's friends rather than his enemies who did him the most damage. The Oba of Otan Aiyegbaju, a town some 30 kilometers north of Oshogbo, was a close friend of his at the time. The two men had gone to school together, and now Duro tried to involve his friend in the activities of the Mbari Mbayo Club and invited him as a guest of honor to a number of functions. Gilbert Fawole II was a highly intelligent man and made good speeches, lending dignity to every occasion. It was not difficult for Duro to persuade him to preserve the beautiful old palace of Otan Aiyegbaju and to build his modern "upstair" in one of the back courtyards. What was more, the Oba invited the Oshogbo artists to decorate his palace. There was an aluminum relief door by Ashiru Olatunde, murals by Georgina Beier and Bisi

Fabunmi, and cement balustrades by Adebisi Akanji. When the work was nearly finished a group of elders came to greet the artists. To our surprise, they said: "We have come to greet you for your work. We have not come to greet the Oba." It now became clear that the people of Otan Aiyegbaju were reject- ing their king because he was a supporter of the NNDP, whereas they them- selves were all loyal to the Action Group.

When the Oba invited Duro to give a "Command Performance" of Oba Koso in the palace, it turned out that the audience consisted of Mrs. Akintola and a group of high- ranking NNDP politicians and officials. Duro was thus being used for political purposes, in the way many artists, who lived under the illusion that they could keep their art separate from politics, have been exploited the world over. The politicians chatted loudly throughout the play, paying little attention to the stage, while their bodyguards, taking their cue from their masters, drank noisily in the background. Georgina and I left the performance ostentatiously in protest, but Duro could not risk a head-on con- frontation by breaking off the performance. After this incident, in the eyes of many people Duro became associated with the NNDP.

In November 1965 the people of Otan Aiyegbaju openly revolted against their Oba, claiming that he had helped to rig the elections to the Western Region House of Parliament. Gilbert Fawole had to flee to Oshogbo, but as a gesture of spite he burnt his own palace before he left. The works of the Oshogbo artists were largely destroyed.

When the riot police tried to reinstate the Oba, the farmers fired on them with their dane guns. When the police returned a few days later, with rein- forcements, to attack the town, the inhabitants fled to their farms. For two months Otan Aiyegbaju remained a ghost town. The inhabitants did not return until the military coup of 15 January 1966. In December 1965 the situation in Western Nigeria became unbearably tense. The roadblocks that had been set up everywhere by the farmers made it virtually impossible for Duro to go on tour.

Duro was now preparing Moremi for the 1966 Mbari Mbayo anniversary. The political situation gave it a new dimension not originally intended. The play is about warfare and reconciliation, it is about the integration of two dif- ferent cultures and presents the ancient city of Ife as a multicultural society. At a time when the Government of the Western Region was conducting a hate campaign against the Igbo people (of Eastern Nigeria), Duro Ladipo brought a group of Igbo dancers from Agbor to Oshogbo to participate in his play. Some NNDP politicians saw this as a provocation. Duro received threaten- ing letters. The "unpolitical" artist was once again at the center of controversy, but this time the threat was coming from the other side.

When the majors staged their coup on January 15th 1966 Georgina and I happened to be in Offa[10] on a short holiday. When we returned to Oshogbo a few days later the town was in a state of euphoric chaos. People were jubilating because the regime they hated had been overthrown. They had taken their revenge on those politicians who had supported the government, their houses were burnt to the ground. Even the Ataoja of Oshogbo was threatened by hooligans and only the timely intervention of senior citizens prevented the latter from burning down the palace. The police kept to their barracks and this allowed the thugs to roam around the town and extort money from people whom they accused—rightly or wrongly—of being NNDP members. Some unscrupulous businessmen hired thugs to destroy the shops of their rivals. Duro too was victimized.

When I went to the house I found the whole family sitting in the front room in a state of terror. For the last few days gangs of thugs, led by actors from rival theater companies, had threatened to burn Duro's house. His play having been selected for the Commonwealth Festival in Britain was cited as "evidence" of his allegiance to the NNDP. Each time he was obliged to buy them off with sums of money, yet the thugs kept coming back with increased demands.

My instinct told me that as long as Duro was hiding in his house, the public would judge him to be guilty. I took him out immediately, so that he could show his face and confront his critics. We went to the post office, we went to the market, we went to eat in a public restaurant. We went to visit friends and rivals and politicians. We saw the head of the local Action Group and asked him to intervene. The latter was a highly responsible person and he used his influence immediately.

Within a couple of weeks Oshogbo returned to normal. The soldiers appeared on the scene and order was restored. The public was quick to forget the smear campaign against Duro, and when the fourth anniversary celebrations were held at Mbari Mbayo in March, Duro was once again the beloved playwright who drew the crowds.

The Nigerian civil war severely restricted Duro's travelling and nearly ruined him financially. But he survived all hardships and went on to give highly successful performances in Switzerland, France, Iran, Brazil, and the United States. Towards the end of his career he distanced himself from politics the way he had always wanted to. The politicians left him alone, but it meant that they also ignored him. In spite of all his achievements and in spite of the fact that he had done more for the reputation of Nigeria abroad than most other artists, Duro was not invited to participate in the World Festival of Black Arts which the Nigerian government hosted in Lagos in 1977.

Notes

1. olorishas: Worshippers or priests of an orisha.
2. baba elegun: The Shango priest who is possessed by his god during the annual festival and in a trance demonstrates his superhuman strength in a theatrical performance.
3. Georgina Beier: English artist, who ran the Oshogbo art workshops and was stage designer to Duro's company.
4. Theater Express was a company founded by Segun Olusola in 1966. It consisted of three actors who performed in English. I adapted Chekov's "The Proposal" and Durrenmatt's "Abendstunde im Spatherbst."
5. Pierre Verger: distinguished photographer and scholar of Yoruba culture. Author of Les Dieux d'Afrique etc.
6. Agbor: a town in present day Delta State of Nigeria; it was part of Western region in the early 1960s.
7. Ori: head. But refers more to the individual's essence, fate, origin, and fortune.
8. dane guns: guns made by local blacksmiths. They use flint and pellets.
9. "deep Yoruba": generally perceived to be idiomatic, proverbial and allusive. Different from conversational Yoruba and therefore not easily understood.
10. Offa: a town about 100 kilometers north of Oshogbo.

The Yoruba Operatic[1] Theater:
A World in Search of Harmony and Social
Order: Lapido, Ogunde and Olaiya
Olu Obafemi

Introduction

The Yoruba operatic theater (variously named Yoruba Folk Opera, Yoruba Popular Opera, Yoruba Travelling Theater) ranges widely between the *serious* historical-mythological dramas of the late Duro Ladipo, through Hubert Ogunde's political satires and morality plays, the late Kola Ogunmola's comic fantasies, and the comedy theater of Moses Olaiya (alias Baba Sala) and his Alawada Group. This kind of theater which includes numerous practitioners like Adeyemi Afolayan (Ade Love), the late Funmilayo Ranco (a female theater practitioner), and Lere Paimo (formerly in the late Ladipo's company), dates from 1944 with the establishment of Ogunde's theater company.

The history of the origin of the Yoruba "folk opera" has been treated by earlier critics and theater historians and need not be restated here.[2] What must be mentioned, however obvious it appears, is the dual heritage which this theater shares with Nigerian drama in English. This dual heritage is seen in the integration of the themes, materials, and form of traditional drama with additional elements adopted from western dramatic experience. The works of the practitioners of this theater are products of both the colonial experience, (through education and the Christian religion), and the practitioners' own cultural background. Similarly, the popular nature of their theater facilitates the rooting of their dramaturgy in the oral tradition of their people. What results is the synthesis of cultures in their dramatic works.

The works and lives of these practitioners reflect this dual heritage. Chief Ogunde, the rightly acclaimed patron of Yoruba theater, is, for example, an initiate of the cults of *Osugbo* and *Egungun* even though his father was a Baptist clergyman. The two shaping forces on his work are thus the "pagan" and the "Christian": these influences are reflected in the synthetic process of his theater. Ogunde freely mixes Jazz, African rhumba, and the Yoruba *gangan* (talking drum) in the same dramatic experience. Also, culture conflict supplies the themes of some of his operas, as in *God and Africa*[3]. But in this theater, more than in the Nigerian drama in English, the dominant influence is the traditional festival and other verbal and performed arts of the Yoruba. It is important here to identify and briefly describe the elements of oral traditional performance which supply the main ingredients for the contemporary theater in Nigeria, and more directly the "folk opera," which maintains a close relationship with traditional drama. The three main constituents of oral performance are oral literature (poetry and folktales), music, and dance. The important point to note is that these three elements are interrelated and they are all realized, basically, in performance. For instance, poetry is actualized in performance via songs, chants, music, and recitative forms. The two main aspects of poetry that will feature significantly in this study are the esoteric and the popular. The esoteric will comprise such forms as the *Ifá*, an oracular literature associated with Orunmila, the Yoruba god of divination. *Ifá* divination poetry exists in various principal figures called *Odu*, which are articulated by *Ifá* priests called *Babalawo* to obtain divine messages. Other forms of oracular poetry include *Ofò*: incantation, the poetry used in casting magical spells. More popular elements of performed poetry found in the operatic theater include the panegyric poetry called *Oriki* (praise poems). An example is *Sango Pipe*, the praise songs specially reserved for eulogizing *Sango*, the Yoruba god of thunder, lightning, and retributive justice. This form comes commonly through *Rárà* (a slow chant dedicated to Sango). All these elements of poetry, cultic and mundane, feature very prominently in most of the works treated in this study.

Much of this poetry is either sung or chanted to music and drums. For instance, *Sango Pipe* is chanted to *Bata* drum, a large slit drum reserved for praising and humoring Sango. Other drums utilized by these practitioners for rhythm and meaning include *Gangan* (also called *Dundun*)—a talking drum specially used for intellectual articulation, what one can describe as a pristine form of speech-making which has survived till today. Other forms of drums which are used to entertain as well as make dramatic statements include *Igbin*, a large slit drum with a very heavy rhythm. But besides drums, there are other musical instruments employed in this kind of theater to achieve linguistic as well as dramatic effects. For instance, *Toromagbe*, a kind of flute used for hypnotic effect, is often used to give potency to incantation and magic. *Agogo* (clinking metallic objects) also come in handy for providing musical entertainment and articulating certain messages in traditional as well as in contemporary theater. All these theatrical elements forming part of oral performance indicate the heavy reliance of the contemporary theater in Nigeria on oral literature through oral performance. Adedeji also points out the influence of the *Alarinjo*, a professional oral theater, on Ogunde's theater. He finds that the nature and purpose of the Ogunde theater strikingly relate to that of the Alarinjo. In conformity with the practice of the traditional theater as a lineage profession (Ogunde casts members of his family in his productions).[4]

Elsewhere, Adedeji points out as further evidence of the dominance of oral tradition in Yoruba theater the use of the presentation formula of most traditional verbal arts, especially the *Ijuba* (Supplication or Pledge) as Opening Glee or Entrance-Song. This theatrical device was initiated into the Yoruba theater by Esa Ogbin, the primordial masque-dramaturge, in homage to the Ologbin of Ogbin, the father of traditional theater.[5] Most practitioners of this theater employ this introductory formula, in different ways, in their work. Actually, Ebun Clark's assertion that Ladipo's reduced popularity among Yoruba audiences is attributable to his refusal to use the opening glee, a convention familiar to and demanded by these audiences, is only partly true. Ladipo, unlike Ogunde, built the opening glee into the body of his plays as a part of structure and meaning rather than treating it as a conventional ornament. In fact, Ladipo's reliance on tradition for theatrical expression is the most profound of all the theater practitioners using this mode.

Other distinguishing features of the Yoruba (operatic) theater, apart from its use of music and dance for rhythm and meaning, include its heavy reliance on improvisation and an active involvement of the audience in the process of performance. The usually large audiences of this theater are greatly involved in the performances as they are vocal, enthusiastic, and alive. They provide endings to communally owned and indigenous traditional sayings and proverbs, take up choruses of chants, and punctuate "stories with exclamations, or interjections and approbation"[6] to give life to the theater. As an itinerant theater, the Yoruba "folk opera" is rarely in a scripted form. Only a few of these plays are written: Duro Ladipo's plays and Ogunmola's *The Palm Wine Drinkard* are among the few.[7]

Because this theater covers a wide area of human experience, I have chosen a play each from the works of the three major exponents of this theater—Ladipo, Ogunde, and Olaiya—to examine the relationship between statement and structure, the common matrix being the practitioner's commitment, like the traditional performing artist, to the community in its search for harmony and truth within its physical and cosmological boundary. The subject of this theater[8] ranges between the ritual dramatization of the history, myth, and legends of the community (Ladipo's special area), the employment of satire to expose anti-social behavior in the community (Ogunde), and the use of slapstick (in traditional Yoruba, this is *Efe*) for theatrical purposes to entertain as well as to ridicule contemporary social ills (Olaiya in all his plays). This broad categorization does not lose sight of areas of overlap in these works, nor does it overlook the entertainment role of the theater as well as its function as an instrument of moral instruction.[9] *Oba Ko So, Strike and Hunger*, and *Tokunbo* we select from the works of Ladipo, Ogunde, and Olaiya, respectively, and in a representative manner, to establish that Yoruba drama as an art form concerns itself with the achievement of socio-cosmic harmony. This claim holds for the other vernacular dramas in Nigeria.

I
The World in Search of Harmony: Duro Ladipo's *Oba Ko So*

Many critics have dealt with the themes of Duro Ladipo's plays. But very few critics have concerned themselves with the relationship between form and meaning in his drama. Whereas most of the critics have identified elements of cultural awareness in his plays, they have not related form to theme in a way that testifies to Ladipo's competence in handling his material. The most relevant contributions to this study are from Wole Soyinka and Robert Amstrong. Both identify the tragic potential in Ladipo's drama. Soyinka's evaluation of theater as "one of the earliest arenas in which man has attempted to come to terms with the spatial phenomenon of his being" is similar to the proposition in this essay which holds that Nigerian drama in its various forms and shades is preoccupied with man's perennial search for coherence and social growth. Soyinka asserts that *Oba Ko So* is a tragic unfolding of Sango's reign and posthumous deification as a "spiritual consolidation of the race, through immersion with the poetry of origin,"[10] but he does not establish any enduring principle for evaluating the drama.

Robert Armstrong employs his mythoform theory[11] to establish the cross-cultural validity of the tragic form through the example of Sophocles' *Oedipus Rex* and Ladipo's *Oba Waja*. The mythoform theory, according to Armstrong, "incarnates the very conditions of man's consciousness" which are culturally viable in general and specific ways. He acknowledges that, in *Oba Waja*, the people of Oyo's upbraiding of Ojurongbe, the commander of the king's horse (*Elesin Oba*), for shirking his traditional duty of accompanying the king to the unknown, and his son Dawudu's performance of that function by dying wilfully, are cathartic in the Aristotelian sense:

Dawudu brings victory for the mythoform while Ojurongbe's

apostasy suffers defeat. Dawudu's death itself is a victory for him as a good citizen of Oyo, while Ojurongbe's death, I suspect, brings minor satisfaction to the view. Expressed in the alternative terms, we can say that the ending of the work releases us from pity through Ojurongbe's death and from the terror which was evoked by the suspension of the normal order of the suasion over the culture through the sacrifice of Dawudu.[12]

While this assertion that Ojurongbe's "role-bungling" is a threat to the community's sense of security, hence giving rise to fear and terror which Dawudu's death removes, is accurate, one finds Armstrong's employment of Aristotle's theory to establish the universality of the tragic notion untenable as it is not textually vindicated. For instance, while *Oedipus Rex* is a tragedy of character, *Oba Waja* is not. It is not appropriate to refer to either Ojurongbe or Dawudu as the tragic hero in the drama. A drama such as *Oba Waja*, centered not on heroism but on social order, does not require a tragic hero. Hence, a more reliable critical mode must be employed to appreciate such religio-historical dramas that abound in Nigerian "folk opera." The absence of such a mode, coupled with a rigid adherence to Aristotle's *Poetics*, has led critics like Ogunba and Adedeji, in otherwise insightful essays, to castigate Ladipo for a lack of profundity and an inability to achieve depth of characterization in *Oba Ko So*. Conceding historical accuracy and plausibility, Oyin Ogunba finds Ladipo lacking insight into motivation of action in human behaviour and sympathetic self-identification which an artist should have in abundance.[13]

Ogunba also finds *Oba Ko So* "disorganized" and "unimpressive" in .the way the author creates Sango whose deification, in the context of the play, he asserts, is undeserved. Joel Adedeji writes the play off as no more than a "dramatized chronicle, weak in structure, and lacking in character."[14]

This essay intends to make clear the difference between such *ritual drama*[15] as *Oba Ko So* and the secular drama to which Aristotle's principles may apply. While one does not subscribe dogmatically to the mythic-ritual origin of drama, one is aware that some dramas, like most of Ladipo's, are ritualistic in content and form, and the critical principles employed to understand such dramas differ from those applied to purely secular dramas.

Oba Ko So does not, for instance, rely heavily on probes to the psychological depths of individuals like Sango. It is concerned with a more basic and total spiritual atmosphere of the collective consciousness of the people of Oyo. H.D.F. Kitto has usefully described the nature of religious drama:

It is a form of drama which uses naturalism, but can and frequently does set it at defiance: that can draw on character
sharply, but does not exist in order to study or display character: it can indeed almost dispense with character drawing.
The individual, so to speak grows in his creator's hands.[16]

The central concern of *Oba Ko So* is not necessarily Oba Sango but
humanity. The play, in conformity with the nature of the Yoruba opera (which
strives to project community-sense and spirit, the folk-will), shows the people's
search for physical and psychological fulfilment. In fact, in the Yoruba cosmogony which Ladipo mirrors in this play, the stature and the existence of the
gods is determined by the people. The enhancement of *Alafin* Sango's stature
through deification that is celebrated in the play is for socio-cosmic order, rather
than being a response to the achievement of the king as a human being. That is
why, in spite of his human weaknesses, which culminate in his destruction of his
own people, he is still being worshipped today as a god and remembered as a king.
A similar example of veneration not based on individual achievement is the continued worship of Obatala, the Yoruba god of creation, throughout Yorubaland.
Obatala was defeated in his primordial battle with Oduduwa over the founding
of Ile-Ife. The battle was repeated with the same result in the later struggle
between their sons, Obalufon Alayemore (Obatala's son) and Oranmiyan
(Oduduwa's son). Yet Obatala is still today known as the arch-divinity of the
Yoruba pantheon,[17] the same way Sango remains the god of lightning and retributive justice.

Oba Ko So, therefore, is not simply the tragedy of *Alafin* Sango, nor of
his war generals. It is not just the drama of a tyrannical king who discards the
advice of his people against military exploits, exiling himself at the point of
revolt. It is, essentially, a ritual dramatization of an aspect of the origin myth of
the Yoruba: Sango's founding of Oyo. In this drama, the individual, king or subject, submerges his individualism on behalf of the community, what Soyinka aptly
describes as "loss of individuation."[18] Significantly, Ladipo's statement in this
play is the explication through theater of one of the ways the Yorubas achieve
coherence in their universe. He reveals the attainment of harmony after conflict,
chaos, and revolt.

The legend which supplies the plot of the play is the story of Sango as
the first king of Oyo and the events that lead to his becoming a god. It is presented
through episodes, one relating to the other in the manner of a ritual celebration,
brought to a pulsating climax in music, song, drumming, dance and the poetic
chants of incantations and praises. The action shifts from Oyo—founded by
Sango and now in a state of an uneasy peace—to Ede, a newly established kingdom and a threat to Oyo. There are eight episodes in the play, each complete in

itself, but integral to the whole.

Within the first episode of the play, all the elements are exposed. The conflicts are introduced and they create a dramatic suspense and tension which is not fully resolved until the climax of the play in the seventh and eighth episodes when *Oba* Sango hangs himself and is deified. The first episode also brings out the elements of structure and theme, showing how they relate in the play.

The language of *Oba Ko So* is essentially the language of worship and it operates on two levels: the cultic and the ordinary. The cultic language is used by the devotee-performers like Gbonka and Timi while the ordinary citizens of Oyo, the participating audience who use the ordinary language, act as chorus. Oral Yoruba literature is the main source of the language in the play. The two generals use the poetic language of *Ifá* literature, basically the *Ofò* (incantation), while *Oriki* (praise chant) is the dominant language common to the generality of the people. This is evident from the opening scene. Amidst *bata* drumming, dancing and singing, *Iwarefa*, the court poet and minstrel, evokes Sango through his *Oriki*, equating him with death (*Iku*), and establishes his super-human attributes, echoed antiphonally by the Oloris:

Iwarefa:	Ikuoooooo
	Iku baba-yeye, alase ekeji orisa?
Oloris:	Kabiyesi.
Iwarefa:	Alagbara lori awon olori kunkun
	Ijangbon lori alaigbonran
	Inaju ekun ti deru bode
	(*Oba Ko So*, p. 2)
Iwarefa:	O Great death.
	Death, Supreme, Father-Mother,
	next to God in command.
Oloris:	Your Majesty.
Iwarefa:	Subduer of the recalcitrant
	Who out-troubles the troublesome.
	The leopard's frightful gaze that
	scares the hunter.

This aura of the supernatural woven around Sango is continuously repeated in the play until he is eventually deified at the end.

One obvious reason for the popularity of the Yoruba opera with the Yoruba audience is the use of the indigenous language. Apart from the fact that it is familiar to the people, it helps the dramatist to elicit audience-participation more effectively than Nigerian drama in English. And this is an important aspect of the drama. Both Sango and Gbonka make effective use of the phone-antiphonal device to involve the Oyo people in the confrontation between the two, and Ladipo achieves dramatic effect through this. A Yoruba audience inevitably joins, through the collective unconscious, in this call-and-response exercise between Sango and Gbonka and the Oyo people:

Sango:	Gbonka o momo te o!
	Moni yio momo te o!
	Eni to ba f'oju di Sango
Ara Oyo:	Yio te. (p. 50)
San go:	Gbonka will be humiliated, I say!
	I say he will be humiliated!
	Whoever despises Sango
Oyo People:	Will be humiliated.

In all his plays, as this treatment of *Oba Ko So* has shown, Ladipo's artistic purpose is the unraveling of man's universe in the idiom of his daily and historical experience as a way of "preserving peace and accord within the comunity" as Ola Rotimi once put it.[19] This central theme thrives on the cultural adjuncts of myth, legend, and the lore of the community. Ladipo employs dance, music, mimes, chants, and other verbal arts to achieve rapport between performance and audience—audience participation. This he achieves by using the dramatic tools familiar to the audience. Aesthetics and message are handled effectively through the use of consciously repeated episodes, actions, language and rhythm. Anthony Graham-White made a similar observation of Ladipo's use of repetition and parallelism:

> The repetitions, parallelisms, and elaborate images are far more than stylistic embellishment; the weaving of verbal patterns and the embroidery of particular moments gives a movement to the play.[20]

The limitations in Ladipo's work are not significantly different from those in the works of other practitioners of this theater, which will be examined later in this section. In spite of his incessant recourse to historical themes dramatized through traditional techniques, Ladipo has been accused of being intellectually indoctrinated (I suppose by Ulli Beier), and also accused of departing from the popular structural convention of the Yoruba opera. This convention, the Opening glee, Opera proper, and the Closing glee, adhered to by Ogunde and Ogunmola, has been given as a strong reason why Ogunde's theater enjoys a greater popularity than Ladipo's. Proposing this thesis, Ebun Clark regards Ladipo's departure as tantamount to a failure to identify with the form of the traditional Yoruba theater: a break with the age-old tradition of the Yoruba theater which uses a "multi unit structure" beginning and ending with song and dance:

> A theater that uses Yoruba material but breaks away from the established programme structure will not show an inter-relation of content with form but a dissociation of content from form. Conversely, a theater that uses Yoruba material classical or modern, and also uses the accepted programme structure will show a complete fusion of content with form.[21]

I am not concerned here with the debate on the degree of the popularity of these theater practitioners which, after all, is a factor of taste and time. Ogunde and Ladipo had different approaches to their work, and each attained his height at different periods. Ogunde dominated the Nigerian theatrical scene in the forties, fifties, and sixties. Ladipo, whose theater dates from the early sixties, reached the height of dramatic fulfilment in the late years of that decade and on into the early seventies until he died in 1978. Ebun Clark must have directed her focus onto the external structure of the Yoruba opera rather than the internal logic of the theater. What we propose here is the closeness between the statement and aesthetics in Ladipo's plays, demonstrating his success in using myth, ritual, and history through theater to appeal to the sensibility and perception of his audience on the vision of socio-cosmic harmony.

II
Ogunde's *Strike and Hunger*

From the historical and mythological world of Ladipo's *Oba Ko So* one turns to Ogunde's commentary on contemporary Nigerian society. *Strike and Hunger* has been chosen from Ogunde's opus as an example of plays committed to the nationalist struggle as well as of political satire in post-independence Nigeria.[22] The cultural consciousness and political nationalisn that began to spread through Nigeria immediately after the Second World War permeated all human endeavors, and Ogunde's theater was deeply committed to the nationalists' cause. Ladipo's theater developed after Independence in 1960 when the use of history and oral tradition in theatrical presentations received wide national acclaim.

This investigation of *Strike and Hunger* centers on the topicality of the play and the dramatic technique, both of which are inspired by the traditional travelling theater. In examining the social statement in relation to the art-form in Ogunde's plays, it is essential to observe the syncretic aesthetics that shape his work. Ogunde once talked of the inevitability of 'pagan' and 'church' influences on him. These influences blend first as conflict:

> Here I was, a youth versed, as I could claim to be then, in juju music and used to the altar of the Ifa priest. I had eaten fowls and sheep slaughtered in pagan festivals and enjoyed them full. Then I was in a church, singing songs of praise to God and denouncing the jujuman and his ways.[23]

then as syncretic imagination:

> I began to see that I could blend the charms and splendour of the church house and the colourful solemnity of the altar and use them to good advantage.[24]

The main concern of this study is with *Strike and Hunger*—Ogunde exposes tyranny which foreign domination constituted in colonial Nigeria. It was this situation that led to the 1945 Workers Strike. In this topical play, Ogunde reveals his role as a guardian of society's conscience, a role which he inherits from the traditional artist, especially the Alarinjo Masque-dramaturge. The artist in traditional society saw himself as the instrument of folkwill. This tradition is inherited by the contemporary artist in his own society. The structure of the play is influenced by the traditional travelling theater with its "multi-unit structure," (an opening glee, the play and the closing glee).[25]

On subject matter, the role of the traditional artist, apart from the obvious one of entertainment, is to dedicate himself (at whatever risk to his person) to unbridled truth and satirization of social ills, with the hope to alleviate communal suffering. He uses his art to inform as well as to expose certain deviant behaviors in society in an entertaining fashion. Professor Adedeji traces the points of identification in Ogunde's theater with traditional theater, not only to the "organizational and operational practice," but also to the purpose and dynamics of his theater, especially his flair for social criticism. Adedeji cites a classic example of a case when the Alarinjo troupes were banned from performing in certain areas due to their distasteful and unsavory social commentaries:

Sometimes when their sketches were in bad taste, they were stopped in the middle of the act, chased out, and ordered never to return again. A classic example was that of the troupe of Abidogun of Agborako's house, Oyo, in the 1920s. King Ladigbolu I, the Alafin of Oyo, banned the troupe from further performance of the masque of Kudeju because it was a satire on the institution of the famous Are of Alaafin Adelu.[26]

In a similar frame Ogunde was banned on a number of occasions from performance because of his commitment to truth, and the exposure of anti-social behaviors of the powers-that-be, both colonial (as in *Strike and Hunger* and *Bread and Bullet*) and civilian (as in *Yoruba Ronu*). Martin Banham identifies as one of the reasons for the popularity of Ogunde's theater his "willingness to speak openly on other issues of political importance" which not only gained him "a reputation with colonial authorities" but also led to "petty restrictions on, amongst other things, his movement inside and outside Nigeria."[27] Ebun Clark's theater history of Ogunde also contains accounts of restrictions from performance and detentions as in Jos in 1945. Ogunde and his company were banned in the Western Region in 1965 by the Akintola NNDP Government as a result of *Yoruba Ronu*, a play unwittingly commissioned by the cultural arm of the party *Egbe Omo Olofin*. *Yoruba Ronu* is a play whose truth and apocalyptic dimension were vindicated by later events in Nigeria, beginning with the 1966 military take-over.[28] In fact, as late as 1978, Ogunde was still being harassed: *Yoruba Ronu* was again banned on the order of the Information ministry of Brigadier Jemibewon's administration in Oyo state.[29] Yet, Ogunde remained at the forefront of direct involvement in Nigerian politics as he led the orchestra that formed part of Chief Awolowo's campaign team for Presidency.[30] Part of the inheritance of this contemporary theater practitioner for the social import of his work comes from the traditional festival singer who is a social barometer; Professor Ogunba identifies the festival singer as one who develops a keen sense of contemporary events in his locality and also in the larger world [also developing the] attitude of a detective, knowing facts, but keeping them to himself, for a fearless revelation during performance without caring whose ox is gored.[31] Ogunde inherited this biting political edge. Ogunde's aim in this play is to promote social order and humane existence by opposing the forces of tyranny, oppression, and starvation that threaten it.

The source of the theme of *Strike and Hunger* is the General Strike of workers in the post-World War II Nigeria in June 1946. Although the play lacks the vision and the uncanny prophecy of his later play *Yoruba Ronu*(1964), it marks the development of his commitment to society's plight, a sensitivity which he maintained up to the end.[32] The Second World War brought about a significant change in the British economic attitude to Nigeria from one of *laissez faire* to a direct involvement in the economic policies of the colony. The Colonial Government assumed complete control of the colony's economy. The marketing board set up by the Government made prices of products higher than were obtainable in free markets, thereby alienating peasant producers as well as native middlemen and traders. The significant development here was the organization of trade unions with a central co-ordinating body, the Nigerian Trade Union. A more significant reason for the strike was the inflation which progressed with the war, with the cost of living rising between 1939 and 1942 by 50 to 70 per cent. Workers claimed that the cost of living had gone up to 200 per cent by 1945 "with no corresponding relief in wages." Coleman, who recorded this claim emphasized the effectiveness of the action of the 30.000 men who went on a rampage for thirty-seven days for a 70 percent increase in wages. This strike action, which began in Lagos, did extensive damage to the socio-economic life of the colonial administration; the men rendered

> services indispensable to the economic and administrative life of the country; they were railway workers, postal and telegraph employees and technical workers in Government Departments.[33]

Nationalists seized on the strike to promote their Pan-Nigerian Movements. Party and national leaders like Macaulay, Awolowo and Azikiwe played prominent roles in the strike. The strike was successful as it forced the colonial government to review its wages as well as other economic policies. Coleman further stressed the relevance of the strike to the Nationalists' cause, especially as it spread to most parts of the country:

> The Strike served as a dramatic opening of a new nationalist era, [it] marked the beginning of a racial and political consciousness in the north.[34]

Strike and Hunger is a documentation of this event in all its freshness and social relevance.

The opening glee is used here not as a pledge, but as an appeal for mass action. It is also used for plot exposition and a denunciation of the economic policy of King Yejide, the allegorical representative of the colonial rule. The opening glee is an invocation of human and supernatural forces to lend support to the struggle against hardship:

> Araiye ewa kewa parapo kajo jija ebi
> Angeli ebo, Angeli ebo wa waiye
> Angeli ebo wa woran enia
> Tinse alaini ohun ewa wole aiye
> Tin dori kodo lo.
> Come, people of the world, rally round to fight hunger
> Descend O Angels, grant us audience
> Angels, behold the people of the world
> Deprived of the good things of life
> See the world, obverse.[35]

The opening glee above is still part of the indigenous rite at the opening of a festival, a play, or any traditional performed art. The difference is that this homage is not paid to any powerful local force, but to an angel. The glee proceeds to enumerate the threat which Oba Yejide constitutes to human existence in his ruthless imposition of a money-based economy in which the government gives wages that are grossly inadequate for survival. It exposes a system where the government distributes what the people produce. It also proclaims the people's suffering under a foreign ruler (Oba Yejide):

> Gbati ola gun won legun o
> Won gba onje t'Oluwa fun wa lojo aiye o
> Won si ko wa po, won wa nbo wa o
> Bi eni nbo eranko, taiya tomo nfo, sanle o
> Toko taya nku iku ebi
> Gbogbo wa si nramota kato jeun (p. 3).
> And when they were pricked like thorns by wealth
> They snatched from us our God-given daily bread,
> They then feed us in crowds
> Like beasts, wives and children fainting
> Husbands and wives dying of hunger
> And we toil and and sweat before being fed.

The opening glee exposes and comments on the social situation, bringing out the theme and plot of the play. It is also an invitation to action against a demeaning rule:

> Ara mi egbo ara e gba
> E mura ka jija
> E jija lile (p. 4).

My people, behold
Prepare to fight
Fight a vigorous fight.

All the dramatic elements in the play are outlined in the glee, which takes off as a pledge that expresses the Yoruba belief system: a pledge to the Supreme being, and to nature forces like birds and humanity. There is a strong and deep conviction that order and coherence can be restored by a totality of these forces. Like *Ijuba* in traditional art, respect to more powerful forces within a hierarchy of forces that include deities, ancestors, and Nature's elements gives force to this opening glee:

Edumare ye o d'owo re
K'ori wa mase ku iku ebi (p. 4)

.   .   .

Aja to ba f'oju de d'ekun
A ma ke kainkain.
Almighty, it is in your hands
May we not be fated to die of hunger

.   .   .

A dog that underrates a leopard
Will howl in pain.

To pay homage to God to gain his aid in the struggle, the artist utilizes praises encompassing imagery drawn from oral literature. Men are like dogs who despise God/Leopard at the greatest peril to themselves. Yet the God invoked here is obviously the Christian God. But the belief in fate and destiny is a Yoruba concept. Ogunde fuses both traditional and foreign concepts to achieve thematic effect.

The dramatist's social comments, embodied in the opening glee, are built up and emphasized in the main body of the play through the integration of music, dialogue, repetition (of actions, events, or episodes), proverbs, and other elements of oral literature. Specifically, oral poetry functions as a vehicle for social satire and message.

From the start of the opera, by the subtle art of praise-chant, Ogunde reveals that Oba Yeyide has usurped the throne. The praise-poem derives less from admiration than from admonition of the king. It utilizes imagery that can be associated with the king—the river, the ship, and the West. He is addressed as *Oba Ajeji* (strange king), *Oba onile Oju Omi* (king from the ship), *onile erekusu* (from the West). The people build up their verbal salute for the king from their honest knowledge of him, maintaining their traditional respect and acknowledging his aquarial attributes which gain him power:

    Oba erin lo nigbo
    Oba efon lo l'odan
    Yejide iwo lo lokun
    Okun miwo wuruwuru
    Osa mi lu fiwafiwa (p. 5)
    The king of elephants owns the forest,
    The king of buffaloes owns the grove
    Yejide, the ocean belongs to you.
    The ocean tides boil tumultuously
    The sea waves beat wildly.

In acknowledging Yejide's ownership of water—having come from overseas—they are also claiming their own right over the land, a right he now usurps. It is a recognition of order and regularity in nature, an order which Yejide's presence threatens. The roaring of the ocean and the splash and backwash of the waves are not just metaphors for Yejide's vanity, which comes out in his first speech, but pointers to the chaos that will follow if the people are not placated by Yejide. The mounting anger of the oppressed people is symbolized by the rising wave of the ocean and the beating of the tide. Although the above song does not reveal any use of sympathetic magic through incantation, there is a positive affirmation arising from association, a belief in the orderliness and unchanging pattern of nature. Since the king elephant owns the forest, the king buffalo owns the grove, and since the sea-gulls remain on the surface of the sea, come wave, come tide—*legelege o eiye okun* (p. 5)—Yejide will continue to own the sea. It follows in the pattern then that, in spite of the temporary threat, the people will claim back their land. Such an affirmation, built on parallelism between the ordered pattern of Nature's elements (like birds, animals, rivers) and the pattern(s) of human existence is repeated constantly in the play to project the world view that the author wishes to put forward. The above is repeated thrice in the first scene (pp. 5 and 6).

Yejide's own response to the people's greetings departs from customary practice in its boastfulness and contempt rather that gratitude to his subjects. Compare Yejide's response below to Oba Sango's repeated show of appreciation to the *Rara* chants of Iwarefa and the praise songs of the *Oloris* which he expressed through his constant response with the word of acknowledgement of praise—*E seun*:

Oba Yejide: Eyin arugbo, eyin enia
                    Eyin iranse, eyin iwefa

> Eyin eru baba mi
> Mo rire aiye mo rire iwa
> Mo joba laiye mo joba loke
> Eyin enia, egbon
> Egbon egbon riri (ha! ha!) (p. 5)
> You old ones, all you people
> You servants, you messengers
> Slaves of my father
> I'm glorified by nature and by good deeds
> I reign on earth and above
> Tremble, people
> Fear, fear and tremble (ha! ha!)

It is a defilement of a king's traditional duty to his people's obeisance. This is a subtle way of displaying his unfamiliarity with traditional practice, which arises from his foreignness.

The prologue (*orin ako bere*) gives a summary of the theme and the message of the play: the oppression of the masses by Oba Yejide and the call for an open revolt. The body of the play is divided into two acts. The first act, comprising four scenes, treats the events leading to the people's decision to go on strike. It begins with Oba Yejide's decision to control jobs and employ the people on a-penny-a-day-wage, a metaphor for an extremely low wage:

> Oba Yejide: Emi Yejide Oba ogo
> Emi lo ni ise owo
> Ise ori akowe
>
> .   .   .
> Ati ise irin Reluwe
> Enyin ti n wase e mabo
> Ise kobo ojojumo (p. 6)
> I Yejide, the glorious king
> Owner of all handiwork.
> I own messengers' and clerks' jobs
>
> .   .   .
> The railway work is mine
> Come to me, all who seek jobs
> And I will employ you for a-penny-a-day.

The act reveals both the people's docile acceptance of the jobs and the inadequacy of the wages. The second act deals in three scenes with the actual arrangement and execution of the strike, as well as its consequences.

The major scenes show the people's subjection to torture and deprivation in the king's market (*oja elebi*) which make the strike inevitable. The play concludes with harmony and joy as the king increases wages.

Strike and Hunger, like most of Ogunde's plays, is structurally less symbolic and metaphoric than Ladipo's plays. And the language of the play is far less cultic because occasions for the use of incantations, praise poems, and other forms of the complex traditional verbal art forms are few. The reason is not far to seek: Ogunde deals in this play with recent social reality and does so from the ordinary man's point of view. Ladipo dramatizes the complex mythic-ritual history of Sango and Oyo in *Oba Ko So.* The subject of Ladipo's play necessitates the use of ritual metaphor such as incantation, proverbs, and the pithy sayings of old times. The socio-political reality of *Strike and Hunger*—the movement of the peasant masses against oppressive forces—determines the language and form of Ogunde's play. A play for and about the working masses cannot be esoteric if it is to achieve its "tendentious" purpose. Although the play lacks vision and an interpretative dimension, it possesses the "agitative power" one expects from such a committed play as this. It is no wonder that the play attracted such a hostile reaction from the colonial administration in Nigeria.

III
Theater as Farce: The *Yèyé* Tradition of Moses Olaiya's *Tokunbo*

Moses Olaiya's (alias Baba Sala) *Alawada Group* is a theater of entertainment, of farce, which has been much criticized by Nigerian intellectual critics and "serious" writers for its vulgarity and triviality. Ebun Clark described Olaiya's theater as "garish."[36] Tunji Fatilewa described Olaiya to this writer as "clownish" and "socially irrelevant.".[37] Even Olaiya's colleagues in the operatic theatrical mode are no less hostile. Ade Afolayan (alias Ade Love) who started with Olaiya in the sixties told this writer in an interview that he had to part company with Olaiya because he was a "nonserious" theater practitioner.[38] Yet Moses Olaiya was indisputably the most popular, the most commercially viable, professional theater practitioner in Nigeria of his time. Olaiya lacks the profundity of the late Ladipo and the latter's deft handling of mythic-historical material. He equally lacks the political commitment of Ogunde. Yet his ability to treat the excruciatingly funny, the farcical, is unparalleled on the Nigerian stage. His most valuable assets are his ability to provide laughter and popular entertainment.

This study of Olaiya's theater will concentrate on his employment of an aspect of the traditional theatrical heritage—the *yèyé* (fun making, also called *Efe*)—to treat diverse areas of human experience. The study will also identify the attributes of his theater that put him firmly with the popular theater tradition in Nigeria as pioneered by Chief Ogunde and established by Duro Ladipo and Kola Ogunmola. The vernacular theater in Nigeria is purely itinerant and extemporaneous. I therefore examine *Tokunbo*, which I have transcribed and translated from a performance tape of Olaiya's *Tokunbo* (1977).[39]

Although Olaiya's theater belongs with the theatrical genre of farce, his theater shares a lot of attributes with the earlier folk theater of Ogunde and Ladipo. Like the earlier theater practitioners, Olaiya's theater is improvisational and communal. Rather than relying solely on songs and chants for his dialogues, as do his predecessors Ogunde, Ladipo, and Ogunmola, he relies on the incongruous in areas of speech, gestures, and costumery as well as on other physical actions that give vitality to his theater. But, like his predecessors, he has gone back to the traditional theater for the essential elements of form and function of his theater.

The *Yèyé* Tradition

All these dramatists in their own different ways draw heavily on tradition. While the late Duro Ladipo drew his thematic and technical materials from myth, history, legends and rituals, and Ogunde works with the mythical and the secular,[40] Moses Olaiya has taken the traditional form of slapstick entertainment which cuts across ritual festivals and folktales. It is the entertainment form called *Yeye* or *Efe* whose main function is the provision of laughter in the midst of self and public ridicule. In *Yeye*, the traditional artist gets a day off from seriousness and rationality and is empowered by the community to ridicule all forms of rules, individuals high and low, gods, and systems. In the process, he points the way, mostly unobtrusively, to improvement and takes stock of social ills and devious acts. *Yeye* is a kind of low comedy which borders on gentle satire. In the words of Kernodle when he describes farce, it turns "difficulties, restrictions, frustrations and embarrassments of life into laughter."[41] In this way, it provides public entertainment and relaxation for the audience while satirizing what is wrong in society. Adedeji has described the prevalence of the *Yeye* tradition in most traditional performances: ranging from ritual performances such as *Egungun* (masquerades) and *Gelede* (the Mother Earth entertainment cult) to festivals such as *Okebadan*, the celebration of the Ibadan hill-goddess whose festival is a free day of "festivity and license."[42] This tradition of theatrical farce also includes the performances of entertainment groups who convert the cultic and the ritual to the profane in order to earn their living as well as to satirize society. Such groups include the itinerants like the *Etiyeri* (a comic masque who wears a rabbit-like mask) and the *Apidan* theater group (an acrobatic *Egungun* spectacular group).[43] It is this form of traditional popular entertainment upon which Moses Olaiya builds his Alawada theater group upon.

So, in all his plays, Moses Olaiya sees himself as a professional humorous entertainer who comments on the vicissitudes of life. In a contemporary Nigeria where the very nature of life is hard—full of murders, robberies, victimization, and immorality—such a theater that teaches us a way of coping with the absurdities of life, a theater which relaxes us and through humor guarantees our survival and sanity, cannot but be popular. Moses Olaiya employs *Yeye* in his plays—in the manner of the Greek satire—to enable him, publicly, to ridicule all social ills and deviant behaviors in contemporary Nigeria. For instance, his play *Dayamondi (Diamond)* (1978) exposes the cutthroat race after money and encourages honesty and morality. Others, like *Director* (1977), treat the excesses of the power elite in Nigeria (the company directors and the civil servants) who employ people, not on merit, but through bribery and corruption. In all these plays, his theatrical form relies on puns, gesture, incongruities, and mimicry. Through his humourous dialogues, grotesque costuming of the actors, their mimes and pantomimes, the audience is entertained. Yet he makes valid, though light, criticism of society and the social system.

Tokunbo

This play is about an imagined trip by Baba Sala to the United States: the preparation for the journey and the indiscriminate assemblage of various religious institutions to offer prayers for a safe return for Baba Sala (alias Jubike, Lamidi, and later Tokunbo); the visit to his friend Adisa in the heart of America; and his American affectations upon his return to Nigeria. In fact, the title of the play, *Tokunbo* (fresh returnee from overseas), indicates that the play is about the protagonist's physical and psychological experiences before, during, and after the trip to the United States of America. But beyond this general theme, there is a large-scale ridicule of certain social values in contemporary Nigeria: religious hypocrisy and phoniness, to be specific. In this play, Moses Olaiya cites as his example the phony mentality of the Nigerian "been-to." Even from this early stage, it must be remembered that the essential point of Baba Sala's drama is not only the quality of the statement, but the entertainment-orientated power of the scenario.

The play begins then with the preparation for Baba Sala's trip to America. Like all such trips, there is much pomp and pageantry. Well-wishers gather to offer prayers and invoke God to grant the traveler a safe return.

But the main element of this sequence is the dramatist's comment on the unabashed religious syncretism in Nigeria on the one hand, and the hypocritical, holier-than-thou attitude of the various religious leaders on the other. Baba Sala is an adherent of convenience. He is at once a Christian, a Moslem, and an *Egungun* worshipper. Representatives of all these religious institutions have been invited, unknown to the others, to come and offer prayers for their travelling member. With the deft seriousness which makes Baba Sala's farce a convincing one, he brushes aside all the protests of the Christians and the Imams against the invitation of the *Egungun* worshippers who, to them, as to most Nigerian Christians and Moslems, are heathens. As the two religious bodies depart in protest against the arrival of the *Elegun* (the masqueraders), Baba Sala explains his preparedness to accomodate all forms of religions:

| Baba Sala: | S'e e wa ri nkan t'o wa nbe. En, ti irin ajo ti mo fe lo yi l'awon na wa fun. Adua na l'o mbo wa gba. Awon na fe f'adua ran mi lowo ni ona isin ti won na a ni. S'ojo nimi nko b'eni kan s'ota. Gbogbo won ni emi n ba se. (*Tokunbo.*) |
| Baba Sala: | You see, they too are here because of this journey. They too have come to pray. They have also come to aid the trip with prayers, in the manner of their own worship. You see, I'm the rain, I begrudge no one. I ally with all of them. (*Tokunbo*, my translation) |

Baba Sala explains his relationships with all the religions: how he has embraced them through inheritance: "They (the *elegun*) belong to my mother's father's religion. You see, as the *Aladuras* are from my mother's, and the Moslems come from my father's religion" (p. 402). He announces with relish (and to the discomfort of the Christians and the Moslems) his intention to feast on the "slaughter-to-roast" (*apasun*) dog he is about to sacrifice to Ogun. He actually invites his fussy Christian and Moslem priests to join in the feasting on Ogun's meat—dog. This sequence is a humorous manifestation of the indiscriminate religious lives of Nigerians as revealed in Baba Sala's down-to-earth accommodation of the various religions. Wole Soyinka remarked on the lack of any "spiritual conflict" in Africans regarding their ability to operate in many religions (traditional and foreign) at the same time. Writes Soyinka:

> Yoruba society is full of individuals who worship the
> Anglican God on Sundays, sacrifice to Sango every feast
> day, consult Ifa before any new project, and dance with the
> Cherubins and Seraphins every day.... They find it natural;
> no spiritual conflict is created within them and no guilt is
> experienced.[44]

    In his farce, Baba Sala admits openly what the priests do secretly. The complex religious life of the people comes out potently, not just through the speeches, but through the songs, the dance, and the various processions of the Christians, the Imams, and the *Egungun* group.

    The second setting, which is also the second sequence of the play, finds Baba Sala in America, in Adisa's house. This is one of the most laughable scenes in the play, as the language problem provides the main crisis that leads to Baba Sala's sudden departure. Having transported, along with his own ignorance and illiteracy, the noisy atmosphere of Nigeria to America, Baba Sala comes against the hostility of Adisa's girlfriend, Jane. Unable to understand English (and therefore Jane's trivial insult of "don't be silly, don't be naughty"), Baba Sala gives Yoruba meanings to the English sounds of "silly" (as Musili, his mother's name) and naughty (as *doti*, that is, dirty). Thus, in Baba Sala's ignorance, "don't be silly, don't be naughty" means "Your mother Musili is dirty" (see appendix). It is only the timely intervention of Adisa that prevents the show-down that could have ensued from this confusion created by the communication-gap between the Black-American Jenny and the non-literate Baba Sala. Also in this section, we are introduced to the nature of the lives of Nigerians abroad: the hard struggle for existence through hard labor (locally referred to as *Gburu*) as we see in the lives of Mr. and Mrs. Ade; the social pressure that leads Adisa to pretend that he is married to Jenny so as to be guaranteed a work-permit (called "green card" in the play), and the cultural difference between America and Nigeria which the Nigerian abroad must put up with. A very comic example is Baba Sala's disgust when given what was a special treat: a dinner of vegetable salad. The honest anger of Baba Sala at Adisa for not making a pounded-yam or a yam-flour dish is very humorous, yet very critical. Listen to Baba Sala's scornful reference to the vegetable salad prepared in his honor:

Baba Sala:	Emi ni o wa k'ewe tutu mi lai se
	Ewure. Ewure ni mo mo ti nj'ewe
	tutu. E re tomato, e re alubosa (*O da*

95

	awo ru) e gbawo yin o jare. E gbawo yin kuro (*Tokunbo.*)
Baba Sala:	How do you expect me to eat raw leaves when I'm not a goat. Sliced onions and tomatoes (*pushes the plates aside*). Please, remove your plates from my presence (*Tokunbo.*)

Denied a local Nigerian dish, denied the boisterous atmosphere he is used to in Nigeria, and amid general argument and confusion, Baba Sala returns home.

That brings us to the final section of the play: Baba Sala's new self in Nigeria. The humor comes from the difference between the polished, Americanized, title-hunting elite that he craves to be, and the half-baked, phony, poor man he still is. That real position of Baba Sala is revealed by no other than the imbecile, Kariile, when she describes him as a pauper who presses his clothes with a bottle, unable as he is to afford a pressing iron: *A fi igo lo 'so'*. Coming from an imbecile who, as we are told in the play, has only just started to talk properly, the true nature of Baba Sala's status cannot escape us despite the front of a "been-to" that he wishes to show. Kariile further shows Baba Sala's phoniness when she describes him in these words: "*A momi tayin,*", (one who picks his teeth after drinking water—a charlatan). Nothing more confirms this charlatanism than his suddenly superior attitude on his return from his three week visit to America. He embodies the worst part of the "been-to" mentality among Nigerians. Their minds are completely enslaved and they exhibit a nauseating pretentiousness. Soyinka has exposed this obnoxious mentality in his revue sketch *The Child Internationale.*[45] Baba Sala's case is worse than Titi's and her mother's in Soyinka's satirical sketch. He cannot speak English but wishes to act English. So, in a ridiculous mixture of American slang and some Americanized Yoruba, he tries to impress his wife and visitors with his newly "acquired" been-to-ness. Neither his non-literate wife nor the educated Dele can make out what he is trying to say. Dele supplies the right words at the end and the humor comes from the fact of Baba Sala being the fall guy. He calls breakfast "brek" and his wife thinks he means the brake of a motorbike. Plantain is to him "big ba-na-na,", and "dodo" (fried plantain) is "Duudu" because he does not know the English word for it. But the most spectacular social vice which Moses Olaiya ridicules here, and one which supplies the title of the play, is the title-hunting craze that bedevils Nigeria presently. You are either a "Dr.," "Alhaji," or "Chief" or you are not recognized in society. Baba Sala also wants a title for himself:

B. Ojewale: Ein, Ajibike o. Ajibike Jibike!

B. Sala: Look here men. Ee mo b'e se le p'ooko mi?

B. Ojewale: Ha!

B. Sala: Ee mo b'o ti ye ke s'aponle mi niru irin ajo gbogbo ti mo lo. Ti mo de Jos Anjelis, ti mo de York City ati Roy Chocago mo de Paris, London mo gba lo, Roomu la tun gba wa'le. Ee wa mo b'o ti ye ke se pooko mi, a fi ke ma se 'Jibike 'Jibike.

B. Ojewale: Hun aiye re a daa. Bawo ni k'a se ma pe o o?

B. Sala: Se b'o ba je pe Moka (Mecca)ni mo lo, se bi mo ba de, ooko mi na lee tun mo pe mi?

B. Ojewale: Alaaji ni yen na, iyen ti duro. Alaaji ni. B'ode se iyawo re lo, Alaaja ni.

B.Sala: O daa, bi mii ti se lo Haji, iru ilu oyinbo ti mo lo ... to k'e yan lo Moka lee meta. Se ko ye ke ro bee se s'aponle oruko mi ju k'e tun mo laako mo mi.

B. Ojewale: O daa, to mi sona.

B. Sala: O daa bee ba mo bee se mo pe mi, Toks ni k'e moo pe mi.

B. Ojewale: Ko so paa se yi?

B. Sala: Toks. Toks. Tokunbo bee ba gbeeebo.

B. Ojewale: Ahen, aiye re a dara. Tokunbo Ajibike.

B. Ojewale: Well, Ajibike 'Jibike.

B. Sala: Look here men, you don't know how to address me?

B. Ojewale: Ah!

B. Sala: You don't know how to give me regard after all my journeys. I reached Jos Angeles, I got to York City, I reached Roy Chicago ... I got to Paris, I came back through London. I came

97

	back again through Roomu. You still don't know how to call my name except yell 'Jibike 'Jibike?
B. Ojewale:	Well, God bless you, how may we call you?
B. Sala:	If I had gone to Moka and come back, would you still call me by my name?
B. Ojewale:	That one is Alhaji for sure. It is Alhaji. If you went with your wife, she would be Alhaja.
B. Sala:	Alright. I haven't gone to the Hajj. But this overseas that I went ... surpasses Mecca three times and over. Can't you find a way of dressing up my name?
B. Ojewale:	Well, teach me.
B. Sala:	Well, if you don't know what to call me, it is Toks. Call me Toks.
B. Ojewale:	I beg your pardon?
B. Sala:	Toks. Toks. Tokunbo, if you can't hear English.
B. Ojewale:	Better. God bless you, Tokunbo Ajibike. (*Tokunbo*)

Hypocrisy, charlatanism, phoniness, and the title-hunting craze are all prominent social vices which the play calls up for laughter, not for any direct and vigorous attack. Moses Olaiya's plays lack the serious and often virulent indictment of society. The power of *Tokunbo* lies not in the bitterness of its attack, but in its ability to state the absurdities of the social malaise that he exposes. It is a pure farce, which to quote Kernodle once more, is a profound device for "acceptance" of and "adjustment" to the incongruities of life. Farce, he says, "does not discuss whether the world should, and can change. It is concerned with the world as it is."[46] *Tokunbo* ends with hilarious laughter by all the actors at the expense of Baba Sala who makes himself into an object of ridicule in his attempt to be a "been-to." It invites the audience to laugh at its own absurd values. The strength of the play therefore lies in its capacity to entertain its audience, to convert the tragic in society to fun, to *Yeye*. And it is for this ability to entertain and free the spirit that Moses Olaiya is a popular and commercially successful theater practitioner.

Moses Olaiya provided a popular theater of dialogue, music, and dance which attracted Nigerians by the thousands all over the country. With his ability to change easily from the vernacular to the pidgin in the process of performance,[47] he may have located a niche for himself, a place in the Nigerian theater scene, for a very long time to come. The *Yeye* (Efe) theatrical tradition that he adopts is a theatrical mode that will continue to attract popular attention.

The awareness of the potential of this dramatist and the dynamics of his brand of theater mechanics entailing the conscious attempt to give entertainment the primacy of place over matter, over relevance, is disturbing. After all, the Efe/Yeye traditional artist regarded and still regards himself (and his artistic talent) as an instrument of communal will. Olaiya is constantly aborting this tradition in favor of the materialization and commercialization of a communal enterprise—art. The dilemma looms large in our view, when one notes that the choice between an Olaiya with the means thereby of assuming mass-appeal proportions and therefore theater customers, through the art of entertainment and the generation of belly laughs and other much more serious dramatists who pursue the doomed path of hermeticism, is very little indeed. The real choice is the fusion of popular language and theater mechanics with popular message, a vision which deals with the objective lives of the majority of the people in this country, through questioning, dialectics, and participation, employing the mediatory potential of theater.

What emerges from this study of the works of these three leading theater practitioners of the Popular Tradition (Ogunde, Ladipo, and Olaiya) is the closeness of their theater (in terms of theme and structure) to traditional oral performance in Nigeria. And this emerges in spite of their frequent employment of elements or western dramatic models into their works: note their adherence to the use of the proscenium stage in spite of their reliance on an active audience involvement in their performances.[48] Like the traditional artist who regards himself (and his artistic talent) as an instrument of communal will, these dramatists in their various ways put a premium on the communality of their art. It is also pertinent to mention here that, in the eighties and the nineties, on account of technical, physical, and economic difficulties, the one hundred Yoruba Travelling Theaters have receded considerably from the roads. The film and video dramas have taken over in a way that threatens extinction for the Yoruba operatic theater.

---

1   Throughout this study I have used the words *operatic* and *popular* almost interchangeably, to describe the vernacular theater which evolved since 1944 from Christian cantatas but which are based structurally and thematically on traditional performed art.

2   Prominent among these critics are Oyin Ogunba in his essay 'Theater in Africa' in *Presence Africaine*, Vol. 3, no. 58, 2nd quarterly, 1966. See Martin Banham in his book with Clive Wake titled *African Theater Today* (London, 1976), Adedeji in (a)

'Oral Tradition and the Contemporary Theater in Nigeria' in *Research in African Literatures*, vol. 2, no. 2 (Texas, 1971), (b) 'The Alarinjo Theater: A Study of a Yoruba Theatrical Art Form From its Earliest Beginning to the Present Time' (Ph.D. thesis, Ibadan, 1966); also Oyekan Owomoyela's 'Folklore and the Yoruba Theater' in *Research in African Literatures*, same issue as above, and Mrs. Ebun Clark in her M.Phil thesis on *The Hubert Ogunde Theater Company* (Leeds, 1974). Since published as Hubert Ogunde, *The Making of Nigerian Theater*, (Oxford: OUP, 1979)

3   Ogunde's *God and Africa* is also collected in Ebun Clark's *Hubert Ogunde* cited above.

4   J.A. Adedeji's essay 'Alarinjo: Traditional Yoruba Travelling Theater' in *Theater in Africa*, edited by Ogunba and Irele (Ibadan, 1978), p. 50.

5   Adedeji, ibid.

6   Adedeji, 'The Opening Glee in Yoruba Drama' in *Research in African Literatures*, vol. 2, no. 2 (1971), p. 126.

7   Efforts are being made to improve upon this dearth of scripted opera in Nigeria. An example is Ebun Clark's collection of Ogunde plays. Ulli Beier also published a few of Ladipo's plays in *Black Orpheus*.

8   The *Etiyeri* (literally translated as 'ear befits the head') maintains a close link with the Egungun cult, wears mask and most often uses the guttural voice characteristic of the Egungun. Its main function is social commentary and entertainment. A detailed description of *Etiyeri* is Dr. Akinwumi Isola's unpublished paper titled 'Etiyeri: One Type of Social Satire Songs in Yoruba' read in the *Second Annual African Literature Conference* (Ibandan, 11-15 July, 1977). *Gelede* is the only male-performed, female-oriented Egungun in the Yoruba tradition. It is the Egungun of the Great Mother (Iya Nla) who holds sway over, and is the ultimate force of, life and fertility. On any Gelede festival, the Iyalode, the priestess, performs on behalf of the community to appease the witches. Also see Peggy Harper's essay on Gelede in *ODU: Journal of West African Studies*, no. 4 (Ile-Ife, 1970).

9   As is true of the *Alarinjo*, *Etiyeri* and *Gelede* described above.

10 Wole Soyinka, *Myth, Literature and the African World* (Cambridge, 1976).

11 The mythoform theory of Armstrong attempts to establish a universal critical platform for treating all mythical tragedies irrespective of cultural differences.

12 Robert Armstrong, 'Tragedy, Greek and Yoruba: A Cross-Cultural Perspective' in *Forms of Folklore in Africa*, edited by Bernth Lindfors (Texas, 1977), p. 53.

13 Oyin Ogunba, *Theater in Africa*, op. cit. p. 68.

14 Adedeji, 'Oral Tradition and the Contemporary Theater in Nigeria', op. cit.

15 I have used the terms 'religious drama' and 'ritual drama' to refer to such plays as rely heavily on history, myth and whose focus is cultural sympathy with the spirit of the community like *Oba Ko So*.

16 H.D.F. Kitto, *Form and Meaning in Drama* (London, 1967), p. ii.

17 This primordial struggle kept alive by the Obatala festival is treated by (i) Adedeji in *Folklore and Yoruba Drama: Obatala as a Case Study*, edited by R. M. Dobson (Bloomington and London, 1972); (ii) Olorupo Sekoni, *The World in Search of a Viable Leadership: A Study of Soyinka's Scripts* (Ph.D. thesis, Wisconsin, 1977).

18 Wole Soyinka, *Myth, Literature and the African World*, op. cit.

19 Ola Rotimi, 'Traditional Nigerian Drama' in *Introduction to Nigerian Literature* edited by Bruce King (Lagos, 1971).

20 Anthony Graham-White, *The Drama of Black Africa* (London, 1974).

21 Ebun Clark, 'Ogunde Theater: Content and Form' in *Black Orpheus*, edited by J.P. Clark, vol. 3, nos. 2 and 3, December, 1974 and January, 1975, p. 82.

22 Ogunde's topical plays arising from the need of society to use the theater as an instrument to raise social awareness (see Ebun Clark's treatment of Ogunde's committed plays in her thesis, op. cit.) include *Strike and Hunger* (1946), *Towards Liberty* (1947), *Worse than Crime* (1956) and the most popular for its uncanny prophecy and sensitivity of all his plays *Yoruba Ronu* (1964).

23 Bernth Lindfors, 'Ogunde on Ogunde: Two Autobiographical Statements' in *Education Theater Journal*, vol. xxviii (1976), p. 241.

24 Ibid.

25 Ebun Clark, 'Form and Content in Ogunde's Theater' in *Black Orpheus*, op. cit., p. 60.

26 Joel Adedeji, 'Alarinjo: Traditional Yoruba Theater' in *Theater in Africa*, op. cit. p. 37. The history is taken from Samuel Johnson's *History of the Yorubas*, p. 397.

27 Martin Banham, *African Theater Today*, op. cit., p. 10.

28 The military coup in Nigeria in January 1966, which led to the death of civilian leaders like Prime Minister Tafawa Balewa, Ahmadu Bello and Chief S.L. Akintola, vindicates Ogunde's satirical message. The July counter-coup brought Gowon to power and his appointment on release from prison as Vice Chairman of the Federal Executive Council made Awolowo the man with the highest post held by any civilian since the coup.

29 Oyo State is one of the three states carved out of the old western Nigeria by the Murtala Administration in February 1976, when Nigeria was broken into nineteen states.

30 Chief Awolowo, former leader of Action Group party, lead The Unity Party of Nigeria (UPN). Ogunde's active involvement in the party included his composition of the party's Anthem which he played as 'opening glee' for all major campaigns of Awolowo in the 1978 national, election.

31 Oyin Ogunba, *The Ritual Drama of the Ljebu People* (Ph.D. thesis, Ibadan, 1967), p. 110.

32 Ogunde continued to be directly involved in the politics of Nigeria, until his death in 1989.

33 J.S. Coleman, *Nigerian Background to Nationalism* (California, 1963), p. 251.

34 Ibid., p. 259.

35 All page references for *Strike and Hunger* are taken from Ebun Clark's collection of the play in her M.Phil thesis, Leeds, 1974. All translations are mine.

36 Ebun Odutola Clark, Interview with Olu Obafemi, Lagos, January 1980. (Unpublised)

37 Tunji Fatilewa, Interview with Olu Obafemi, Ile-Ife, November 1978. (Unpublished)

38 Ade Afolayan (Ade Love), Interview with Olu Obafemi, Minna, October 1978. (Unpublished)

39 Moses Olaiya, *Tokunbo* (1978), unpublished. All references are to my transcription and translation. See appendix for translations.

40 Hubert Ogunde, the film Aiye - a title which defies a one-word rendering: it is a metaphysical concept which embodies all aspects of man's malevolent nature, either through magic, witchcraft or through plain evil-doing. The film, produced in 1979 with Ola Balogun, is Ogunde's first.

41 George Kernodle, op. cit., p. 248.

42 Professor J.E. Adedeji, 'Form and Function of Satire in Yoruba Drama' in *ODU: Journal of West African Studies*, vol. 4, no. 1 (Ile-Ife, 1967), p. 67.

43 Kacke Gotrick, *Apidan Theater and Modern Drama*, (Goteborg: Po Paterson: 1984) has studied Apidan and impact on modern drama of Yoruba dramatist.

44 Wole Soyinka, 'Neo-Tarzanism: The Poetics of Pseudo-Tradition' in *Transition*, no. 48, April/June, 1975, p. 42.

45 Wole Soyinka in *The Child Internationale*, published with other dramatic sketches as *Before the Blackout*, Orisun Acting Editions (Ibadan, undated).

46 Kernodle, op. cit. p. 248.

47 I have witnessed occasions when Moses Olaiya, in the middle of a performance, switched from Yoruba to Pidgin English. A ready example was during his performance of *Dayamondi (Diamond)* at the University of Ilorin in November 1978. He had sensed the dissatisfaction of his multi-lingual audience with his Yoruba dialogue and changed from Yoruba to pidgin without losing much in terms of providing entertainment.

48 Actually, the playwright-director Ola Rotimi has expressed his impatience with these practitioners of the operatic mode who limit the robustness and vitality of their theater by confining their production within the spatial reference of the proscenium stage. See his interview in *Dem Say* with B. Lindfors (University of Teras at Austin, 1974).

Esu-Elegbara and the Carnivalesque
Femi Abodunrin

One version of the Yoruba creation myth has it that in the beginning there was Orisa. He is depicted as a very old man, who lived at the foot of a cliff, in a very simple hut. He had a slave who secretly hated him. The slave was waiting one evening on top of the cliff, and when he saw the old man coming home he rolled a huge boulder onto the roof of the hut and Orisa was shattered into a thousand pieces all over the world. Now, the story says that Orunmila came, and gathered as many pieces as he could into a calabash, and placed this calabash in a shrine in Ile-Ife, and that was called Orisa-nla or the Big-orisa. But Orunmila could not find all the scattered pieces, so therefore, they are all over the world still and so you find them in rocks, in rivers, and you can also find them in human beings. 1

Some critics have suggested that the slave in the myth is in fact Esu-Elegbara, the Yoruba trickster/god of fate. From this premise, holders of this view affirm that what looks like an evil destruction is in fact a divine plan— to spread the divine essence throughout the world. In contemporary terms, however, according to Hans Witte, "in contrast to the orisa and earthspirits, who attract worshippers on the basis of family tradition, profession, special vocation, Orunmila and Esu are venerated by every traditional Yoruba. The cosmic system would fall apart without the integrating activity of the oracle and the trickster."2

What is certain is that the *Ifa* oracle comprises the sacred texts of the Yoruba people as does the Bible for Christians. But Christian missionaries, prompted by their Yoruba converts on the other hand, had little difficulty in translating Esu, the enigmatic trickster god, as the Biblical equivalent of Lucifer or devil. This translation/interpretation, many have dubbed a libel of Yoruba religion.

My primary concern in this chapter is to examine the trickster god's mediating role in the story of creation, most especially his transgressive tendency and, above all, his willingness to substitute grotesque realism for, among other things, Obatala's plastic refinery.

Literally speaking, any mythic imagination informed by the Yoruba pantheon is endowed with sufficient mythological figures to build its theory on, depending on the ideological inclination of the myth-maker him/herself. The object of our present inquiry is also concerned with why, within this rich repertoire of mythological figures, only three out of the numerous deities represented on the Yoruba pantheon have received significant attention in literary/critical praxis, and these are Ogun, Sango, and Obatala. Because there is no straightforward answer to this dilemma, a convincing critical explanation can only be arrived at if we examine the process of the deification of these mythological figures (as I have done with the figure of Esu in the sections that follow), and identify the ideological implications inherent in their earthly activities. Sango's feudal hegemony can be foregrounded here, and Soyinka's critical observation lends further credence to my reading, when he asserts straightforwardly that Sango is:

> God of lightning and electricity. A tyrant of Oyo, he was forced to commit suicide by factions, through his own over-reaching. His followers there-upon deified him and he assumed the agency of lightning.[3]

With Obatala and Ogun, on the other hand, one should not hasten to make such categorical assertion, not only because they represent "a view of the world" that is complementary to modern liberal-humanist philosophy, but also because, depending on the position of the reader looking through the iconographic details associated with these deities, they are easily digestible as the modern antithesis of the Carnivalesque essence which I will trace presently in the figure of Esu. Indeed, the "friendship" between Obatala and Ogun further depends on a paradox, with the former being god of creation and the latter being god of iron and by extension also of war/creativity. The paradox becomes particularly evident when perceived against the backdrop of Soyinka's figurative articulation: "Obatala (or Oxala) is the god who turns blood into children; Ogun is the god who turns children into blood."[4] Thus the "ambiguous signification" which any reader of these iconographic details, and especially one willing to pass from semiology to ideology must receive, must also generate a chain of questions that could begin from the old question of traditional analysis. The reader will ultimately have to confront questions such as: "What link should be made between disparate events? How can a causal succession be established between them? What continuity or overall significance do they possess? Is it possible to define a totality, or must one be content with constituting connexions?"[5]

Perhaps a logical way to begin to resolve these questions is to externalize concrete historical moments or events that are seemingly disparate in nature and proceed from there to analyze causal succession between them. The issue of continuity and overall significance, on the other hand, depends entirely on whether the reader is seeking to "define a totality" or is contented with "constituting connexions." The futility of any attempt merely to constitute connexions can also be foregrounded at this point, if we take into consideration the fact that this practice is not the true position of the reader who seeks to pass from semiology to ideology. For the third category of reader seeks to apprehend the most radical discontinuities by understanding that they "are the breaks affected by a work of theoretical transformation which establishes a science by detaching it from the ideology of its past and by revealing this past as ideological."[6]

From this abstract theoretical postulation, we may now proceed to externalize the concrete historical events informing the plastic art of Obatala and juxtapose them with the dialectics of power inherent in Ogun's symbolism as god of iron and of war, whose iconographic artefacts include, among other things, metallic ore, and who is often described as the forerunner and ancestor of paleotechnic man. Both deities and their chthonic and transient activities are to a large extent mediated by Esu in his transgressive role and willingness to substitute grotesque realism for Obatala's plastic "refinery" and Ogun's Hellenistic "finesse."

The primordial fault of Obatala is his costly excesses, as he allowed himself to take a little too much of that potent draught, palmwine. His craftsman's finger slipped badly and he molded cripples, albinos, and the blind. His prescription rigidly forbidding palmwine to his followers does not save humanity from the tragedy of this primordial error, as the issue of somatic symbolism has come to define one of the primary areas of ideological struggle. To paraphrase Stallybrass and White, cultures "think themselves" and the opposition between the high and the low truly begins through the combined symbolism of four hierarchies: psychic forms, the human body, geographical space, and the social order.[7] If we single out symbolic connotations associated with the human body and how this informs grotesque realism, we are bound to encounter a system of occluded discourse, in which the low are constituted as the malformed (victims of Obatala's excess?) who are not expected to survive in a world that is informed by the "survival of the fittest" theory and other such philosophical postulations that marginalize them within the social order. Sharing and to a significant extent embodying their plight, Esu carries a deformity in one of his legs and, rather than allow himself to be incapacitated by this somatic disease, he signals the process of symbolic inversion by firmly "anchoring" one of his legs in the chthonic realm, while the other transgresses every domain of earthly transience. Thus:

In Yoruba mythology, Esu always limps, because his legs are of different lengths: one is anchored in the realm of the gods, the other rests in the human world. The closest Western relative of Esu is Hermes, of course; and, just as Hermes' role as interpreter lent his name to `hermeneutics´, the study of the process of interpretation, so too the figure of Esu can stand, for the critic of comparative black literature, as our metaphor for the act of interpretation itself.[8]

With Ogun, on the other hand, we enter into a complex system of "rules" thoroughly informed by the social order, the dialectics of power, and principles of economic well-being. However, it is possible to argue, with Soyinka, that Ogun is not just *an* artistic sensibility, but *the* artistic spirit itself:

The significant creative truth of Ogun is affirmation of the creative intelligence; this is irreconcilable with naive intuition. The symbolic artefact of his victory is metallic ore, at once a technical medium as it is symbolic of deep earth energies, a fusion of elemental energies, a binding force between disparate bodies and properties. Thus, Ogun, tragic actor, primordial voice of creative man is also, *without a contradiction of essences*, the forerunner of paleotechnic man. The principle of creativity when limited to pastoral idyllism, as Negritude has attempted to limit it, *shuts us off from the deeper, fundamental resolutions of experience and cognition.*[9]

To come to terms with this deity whose "symbolic artefact of victory" is "metallic ore," an opposing sensibility to his tragic nature must follow the opposite, humorous path in articulating its thesis or antithesis. The image of "deep earth energies," which the deity also embodies is, one must concede, the very artefact which has transformed men and women from the level of the crude tool makers to a state of technological advancement, which we tacitly proclaim and recognize as civilization.

At the same time, it is also this "energy" which informs past and present "paleotechnic" men's and women's struggle to dominate and rule others like them and control their lives and wealth through acts of war. Indeed, Ogun's metallic ore has supplied the basic raw material through which humanity has transcended the stage of tilling the land with crude implements such as hoes and cutlasses, and supplied men and women with tractors, harvesters, and other farming implements which have made life itself a lot more bearable than it used to be. But it is also out of Ogun's iron that man has fashioned the most lethal weapons, ranging from automatic rifles to nuclear bombs, which are equally capable of wiping out the same civilization built paradoxically on these "deep earth energies." The consequent result which this denouement portends for humanity is equally foregrounded in Ogun's symbolically tragic nature.

In his book, *Iron and Steel in the Industrial Revolution*, Thomas Ashton comes to terms with the fact that even when the art*If*act of "the god of iron" has transformed the mode of existence in industrialized societies, "fundamental resolutions and cognition" also inform us that:

> in the industry with which we are here concerned the *outbreak of hostilities* meant not a diminished but an increased demand for iron in the forms of cannon, gun carriages, shot and firearms, and for steel in the shape of swords and bayonets. Contracts from the Office of Ordnance operated as *food for the Gods* and the industry grew in proportion as the need for munitions of war increased...After each war came trade depression—more intense and prolonged than that expressed by other industries—during which the ironmasters *painfully* adapted their works to the product of peace; and sometimes the process was still incomplete when the outbreak of fresh struggles brought the call for a reconversion of ploughshares into swords.[10]

Ultimately, the object of this enquiry is not complete if we do not state clearly the need for an opposing sensibility to that represented by the tragic spirit and its destructive essence. The opposition concerns the question of hierarchies and those of symbolic inversion between high and low discourses. Foucault's articulation in *The Archaeology of Knowledge* fleshes out these areas of opposition in the following way:

> Beneath the rapidly changing histories of governments, wars and famine, there emerge other apparently unmoving histories: the history of sea routes, the history of corn and of goldmining, the history of drought and of irrigation, the history of crop rotation, the history of the balance achieved by the human species between hunger and abundance.[11]

Because the history of governments and wars, to which we must add the history of statecraft, religion, philosophy, and literature, are the domain of high discourses, their movement has been rapid, compared to the transmuted or cyclic movement of "those apparently unmoving histories"; these concern the experience of the low, whose lives have been profoundly affected by the history of sea routes and perhaps, more importantly, by the "history of the balance achieved by the human species between hunger and abundance." The perspective that any prospective inquirer should adopt, therefore, is as Stallybrass and White further observe, a question of "History seen from *above* and history seen from *below* (which) are irreducibly different and they impose radically different perspectives on the question of hierarchy."[12]

I.

In Obotunde Ijimere's *The Imprisonment of Obatala*, Esu is described on the cast list as the God of Fate. This depiction immediately revises and transcends the contemporary practice of reading or perceiving the deity as a mere trickster.[13]

In *Mythologies*, Roland Barthes provides a useful theoretical framework which this study adopts in reading the position of each category of readers of myths. In Barthes' theory, myths can be deciphered from three basic positions of "reading." Every myth embodies a "duplicity of signifier," "which is at once meaning and form. I can produce three different types of reading by focusing on the one, or the other, or both at the same time."[14]

The first category of readers are those to whom Barthes refers as focusing on "an empty signifier." With these readers, the myth has no ambiguity and the reader is most likely going to find himself before a simple system, where the signification becomes literal again. We can summarize this type of focusing as that of the "producer of myths." The reader at this level starts with a concept and takes upon him/herself the task of seeking a form for the myth. The African/black experience at this level of reading is replete with examples. The following example illustrates the point further.

In translating the Bible from English to Yoruba, the translator, Samuel Ajayi Crowder, West Africa's first black bishop, found himself at various stages at the threshold of mythology, a task made more difficult by the fact that he had to translate myths from one culture into another. Bishop Crowder's task was not a simple one, as he had to find a Yoruba equivalent for every myth from the Christian mythological framework. Thus, in translating into Yoruba the biblical myth of Satan or devil he settled on Esu-Elegbara, the enigmatic Yoruba god of fate. John Pemberton has attempted to set the record straight by reconstructing this age-old distortion:

> As the festival songs suggest that Eshu is one who deceives
> and harms, so too the oriki (praise names) and myths portray

Eshu as the confuser of men, the troublemaker, the one who acts capriciously. So prevalent are these associations that Christian missionaries used `Eshu´ as a translation of the New Testament terms `devil´ and `Satan´. Now, even Eshu worshippers who speak a little English, as well as Yoruba Christians and Muslims, will refer to Eshu as `the devil´. It is an indefensible corruption of the tradition. Nevertheless, Eshu is a troublemaker. His own praise names attest to it.[15]

In performing a Christian duty, Bishop Crowder and numerous Yoruba Christians after him, have consequently produced their own myth, have acted, to use Barthes' words, like "the journalist who starts with a concept and seeks a form for it."[16] However, the threat of complete annihilation which Crowder's translation poses to the original myth of Esu is preserved in Barthes' theory by what he describes as "a false dilemma":

Myth hides nothing and flaunts nothing: it distorts; myth is neither a lie nor a confession: it is an inflexion. Placed before the dilemma which I mentioned a moment ago, myth finds a third way out. Threatened with disappearance if it yields to either of the first two types of focusing, it gets out of this tight spot thanks to a compromise—it *is* this dilemma. Entrusted with `glossing over´ an intentional concept, myth encounters nothing but betrayal in language, for language can only obliterate the concept if it hides it, or unmask it if it formulates it. The elaboration of a second-order semiological system will enable myth to escape this dilemma: driven to having either to unveil or to liquidate the concept, it will *naturalise* it.[17]

The second category of readers of myths focuses on a "full signifier." The reader is able to recognize the meaning and the form of the myth and goes beyond this recognition to unmask the distortion which the form imposes on the meaning, and vice-versa. The reader at this level is able, in Barthian terms to "undo the signification," but rather than see the signification as the embodiment of the association of the meaning and the form, the reader receives the signification as an imposture. "This type of focusing is that of the mythologist: he deciphers the myth, he understands a distortion."[18] A lucid example that is close to my purpose in this section is the role non-white Brazilians living in what Roger Bastide describes as a "a progressive big city," have ascribed to the enigmatic deity. Bastide's articulation of this dynamic process is significant:

The dualism of good and evil thus has the effect of making the educated non-white Brazilians, living in a progressive big city and *steadily rising on the social ladder,* unwilling to have anything to do with the cult of Exu. To practice this cult would only justify the Whites' image of him as an inferior being with a propensity for evil. *Eager to rise spiritually,* he is of course obliged to give African tradition its due and allot a place for the Exus, *but he de-Africanizes them,* and Aryanizes them by means of Judeo-Christian thought. Inventing another false etymology, he derives the name of Exu from Exud, the rebel angel whom God struck down with lightening and hurled from the heights of heaven to the depths of Hell. This makes it easier for him to identify Exu with Lucifer. Yet *this rejection of tradition arouses a kind of guilt.* To identify Exu with Lucifer is to relegate a significant part of Africa to the realm of the diabolical, thus justifying European criticism of the black civilisation. We therefore find a second tendency in Umbanda: *a desperate effort to save this god.*[19]

Bastide's articulation is another historical instance in which the signified has been turned into a red-herring or what Barthes describes as an *alibi* for the signifier's mythic imagination. Again, what is distorted is what is full, the meaning: the myth of Esu is deprived of its history and turned into mere gesture, through which educated non-white Brazilians living in a progressive big city and steadily rising on the social ladder, refuse to have anything to do with the "true" myth of Esu. An integral part of this meticulous process of disavowal is what Bastide has subtly recognized as the de-Africanization of the deity and the imposition of an Aryan soul on him. It is important to note, however, that Bastide's own position is closest to that of the second reader of myth in our theoretical framework: like the mythologist, Bastide merely deciphers the myth by recognizing a distortion that is inherent in his recapitulation. Our concern therefore is not to dwell on this distortion any more, but to focus on the mythical signifier as an irreducible whole, endowed with meaning and form; instead of a distortion, we receive an "ambiguous signification." An integral part of this ambiguity is the question mark that must be placed on the Aryanization of the myth of Esu and how the dualism of good and evil not from an African, but from a Judeo-Christian perspective, can aid a "true" understanding of the history of Esu's myth and its descent into transgression.

Again, if the reader does not see the history of appropriation inherent in the overtly domesticated deity, it is of little importance presenting it in the first instance, "and if he sees it, the myth is nothing more than a political proposition, honestly expressed. In one word, either the intention of the myth is too obscure to be efficacious, or it is too clear to be believed. In either case, where is the ambiguity?"[20]

This important question leads us to the third category of readers of myths in our theoretical framework. The reader at this level usually focuses on the mythical signifier as an irreducible whole, embodied with meaning and form and receives an "ambiguous signification." The reader responds to all the minute components that make up the myth, to its very dynamics and *becomes a reader of myths*. At this level of reading, for example, Esu is no longer an instance or a symbol, and the deity is definitely far from being an alibi for the exploitative yearnings of non-white Brazilians living in "a progressive big city": the deity is the very *presence* of this exploitation. Thus, while the first two types of focusing can be said to be static or analytical respectively:

> they destroy the myth, either by making its intention obvious, or by unmasking it: the former is cynical, the latter demystifying. The third type of focusing is dynamic, it consumes the myth according to the very ends built into its structure: the reader lives the myth as a story at once true and unreal. If one wishes to connect a mythical schema to a general history, to explain how it responds to the interest of a definite society, in short to pass from semiology to ideology it is obviously at the level of the third type of focusing that one must place oneself: it is the reader of myths himself who must reveal their essential function. How does he receive this particular myth today?[21]

The primary aim of this study is two-fold: it consumes the myth of Esu-Elegbara, the enigmatic Yoruba god of fate according to the very ends built into its structure, and within this structural understanding connects the myth to the general history of the dispersal of black people to different parts of the world. Reading the myth of Esu in this way is a critical plunge into transgression and all that it connotes. Transgression is the word that addresses centuries of distortion and partly successful attempts to "control" the myth from liberating the harassed "worshippers" of the enigmatic deity. This control mechanism can be traced to that point in history when the black experience became interfused with Western discourses in literature, philosophy, statecraft, religion, education, and a host of other areas of human experience which have shaped and modeled the black outlook along a certain unambiguous ideological framework pursued by the West.

The reputation of Esu began its critical plunge into transgression from the moment Bishop Ajayi Crowder translated the deity as the biblical equivalent of Satan or devil, and there is no gainsaying in the fact that we are dealing here with a history of appropriation—an appropriation of power. What follows is a critical analysis of this history of appropriation and how it leads to a discussion of high and low discourses. Meanwhile, Peter Stallybrass and Allon White have observed that:

> When we talk of high discourses—literature, philosophy, statecraft, the languages of the Church and the University— and contrast them to the low discourses of a peasantry, the urban poor, sub-cultures, marginals, the lumpen-proletariat, colonized peoples, we already have two `highs´ and two `lows´. History seen from above and history seen from below are irreducibly different and they consequently impose radically different perspectives on the question of hierarchy.[22]

Thus, as Stallybrass and White demonstrate, while relating a general Western history of high and low discourses to the origin of modern thought and expression in *The Politics and Poetics of Transgression*, the myth of Esu is obviously transgressive. The very ends built into its structure reveal it as such.

II.

> In that zone which *our culture* affords for our gesture and speech, (that) transgression prescribes not only the sole manner of discovering the sacred in its unmediated substance, but also a way of recomposing its empty form, its absence, through which it becomes all the more scintillating. A rigorous language, as it arises from sexuality, will not reveal the secret of man's natural being, nor will it express the serenity of anthropological truths, but rather, it will say that he exists without God; the speech given to sexuality is contemporaneous, both in time and in structure, with that which we announced to ourselves that God is dead.[23]

This "rigorous language as it arises from sexuality" only serves the purpose of reinforcing the basic theoretical postulations of Stallybrass and White in relation to the dialectical treatise on high and low discourses. High discourses are sacred, or, at least, upheld to be so from the perspective of their ideological postulators, and share close affinity with literature, philosophy, statecraft, and the languages of the Church and the University: they contrast sharply with the profane or transgressive texts of low discourses, which are the exclusive preserve of a peasantry, the urban poor, subcultures, marginals, the lumpenproletariat, and colonized peoples. The history of this dialectical relationship will lead into a critical appraisal of what Foucault refers to as the "root of this discourse on God which Western cultures have maintained for so long." We will however, come full-circle in our understanding of the historical framework that truly produces the signifying discourse of two "highs" and two "lows" only when we enter into the domain of the semiological order of officialdom through which the upper/middle classes in colonized societies have produced "the Other" in the same manner as their Western counterpart within a monologic linguistic framework. But first, let us examine the movement from the perspective of its ideological precursor: Western culture.

On the plane of simple analysis, God in Western thought is a being with an infinite capacity for controlling the activities of all mortals: being immortal, God occupies a position that is literally unrivalled and often incomprehensible to the earthly beings whose daily life and activities he controls from a vantage point that cannot be attained by even the most powerful among them. This simple definition marks the beginning of a socially and, perhaps more importantly, religiously stratified society. In what can be regarded as one of the most poetic passages in the Bible, the book of the prophet Isaiah captures this hierarchical structure, first as it exists in the kingdom above before spreading to the equally stratified territory inhabited by the earthly subjects of the transcendental signifier:

> In the year that King Uzziah died, I saw also the Lord sitting upon a throne high and lifted up and his train filled the temple. Above it stood the seraphims: each one had six wings, with twain he covered his face, and with twain he covered his feet, and with twain he did fly. And one cried unto another, and said, Holy, holy, holy is the LORD of hosts, *the whole earth is full of his glory.*[24]

Even for a man as holy as the prophet Isaiah, the privilege bestowed on him in beholding the heavenly splendor of the "Most-High" is extraordinary; it epitomizes, more than anything, his own ordinariness *vis-à-vis* the more depraved humanity for and on whose behalf he liaises with the heavenly kingdom. Thus, the apocalyptic vision must be pronounced: "Woe is me! I cried. For I am undone; because I am a man of unclean lips, and I dwell in the midst of a people of unclean lips: for mine eyes have seen the king, the LORD of hosts."[25]

This ontological framework, which Western culture has maintained for so long, is perhaps only rivaled by what Soyinka refers to as the habit of "taking far too literally the annunciation of the Gospel—In the beginning was the word."[26] Both examples shape or inaugurate the belief of Western culture in the twin concepts of the "ideal perfect being" and that which is other than the norm, "the deformed or mutilated self." To come closer to contemporary experience and literary praxis in particular, Pierre Macherey has observed that literature served the useful purpose of carrying "through the ideological task which religion left off":

> The theme already has this value with Defoe, and it could be said that he gives others a formal model: but with Defoe, more than any other, the revelation of order has a critical value; it must have given him pleasure to introduce, at a late moment within this ideal history, *God and the Other.* It remains that the `history´, beyond its anecdotal supports, has didactic significance: it is a complete representation, the visible body on which a theory can be inscribed.[27]

This "visible body of theory" or what Macherey describes further as "the meditation on origins" is the ideological task which literature assumed, which did not seek to liberate people from the dogma of religion, but rather helped in condensing the mythological framework of religion into an arbitrary hierarchy of high and low discourses. It is a meticulous process through which the high defines the low by creating pastiches and parodies of the low as fragmented and marginalized, in short, produces it as "the Other." This defining process is only complete when we examine the general history of the sublimation and repression of discourses relating to the low through which the high order has tried to appropriate and control their spread. Among the numerous terrains which Stallybrass and White have marked as the domain of low discourses (the base language of carnivals and fairs, the language of the peasantry, the urban poor, sub-cultures, marginals, the lumpen-proletariat, and colonized peoples), two are of particular interest to the general concern of this study; the grotesque body of the Carnivalesque essence and the peculiar expe-

114

rience of colonized people in signifying practices.

The first domain, that of carnivals, is perhaps the most sustaining example of how, through language, the middle-class in collaboration with its upper-class mentors has managed to produce, within the same culture, the low as dirty, messy, a symbol of uncouth body movements, ridiculously overindulgent in its eating habits—in short, a whole body of high discourses seeks to represent the low as a grotesque conglomeration of despicable inversion:

> At the same time it began to be marginalized in terms of social classes and geographical location. It is important to note that even as late as the nineteenth century, in some places, carnival remained a ritual involving most classes and sections of a community—the disengaging of the middle-class from it was a slow and uneven matter. Part of the process was the `disowning´ of carnival and its symbolic resources as the culture of the Other. This act of disavowal on the part of the emergent bourgeoisie, with its sentimentalism and its disgust, *made* carnival into the festival of the Other. It encoded all that which the proper bourgeois must strive *not to be* in order to preserve a stable and `correct sense of self´.[28]

> Among the numerous tools which the upper/middle classes have at their disposal in carrying out this act of disavowal, literary praxis is probably the most potent. All the idiosyncratic apprehension of the bourgeoisie is consciously built into a growing body of literary texts and, as Pierre Macherey further observes, Daniel Defoe, for example, "made the island the indispensable setting, the scene for an ideological motif which was only beginning to emerge: the meditation on origins."[29] It is also one of the most profound ironies of the eighteenth century, therefore, that it was while the literature of the period was struggling to rehearse the masses in pluralistic thought and feeling, consciously edging them to believe that more than one viewpoint existed (namely, that of their masters), that "bourgeois society problematized its own relation to the power of the "low," enclosing itself, indeed often defining itself, by the suppression of the "base" language of carnivals."[30] Stallybrass and White have studied this interesting process of the problematization of low discourses and concluded that:

when the bourgeoisie consolidated itself as a respectable and conventional body by withdrawing itself from the popular, it constructed the popular as a grotesque Otherness: but by this act of withdrawal and consolidation it produces *another grotesque*, an identity in difference which was nothing other than its fantasy relation, its negative symbiosis, with that which it rejected in its social practices.[31]

To come to terms with this historical schema, we must understand the signifying process which Stallybrass and White have thematically represented as a symbiotic process producing binary opposition between the official identity of the bourgeoisie and its "political unconscious" which, when placed within a semiological order, "throws into confusion all tight divisions and offers to deconstruct all the tight binary oppositions—proper/improper, norm/deviation, sane/mad, mine/yours, authority/obedience—by which societies such as ours survive."[32] Thus, at the level of official identity, the bourgeoisie enjoys a monologic form of discourse through which it produces mythical symbols of the low as dirty, messy, uncouth, and subservient to appetite. But through the "political unconscious" of the bourgeois class, which only a semiological order can unmask, the production of these abnegating symbols is revealed as a figment of the bourgeois imagination and through it we enter into a simple system by which the low confronts its signifying masters in profound dialogue.

However, it is only when we enter into the mainstream of the peculiar experience of the colonized being that we truly encounter what is earlier demarcated as the discourse of two "highs" and two "lows." The first high is that of the colonialist who, having just discovered a conglomeration of primitive savages in the colonial territory, approaches the subject with the enthusiasm of a reformer. Again, the role of literature in this process cannot be overemphasized. In a recent analytical study of this historical process, Bill Ashcroft, Gareth Griffiths, and Helen Tiffin articulate the unique role of literature in this way:

> It can be argued that the study of English and the growth of Empire proceeded from a single ideological climate and that the development of the one is intrinsically bound up with the development of the other, both at the level of simple utility (as propaganda, for instance) and at the unconscious level, where it leads to the *naturalising of constructed values* (e.g. civilisation, humanity, etc) which, conversely, established

`savagery´, `native´, `primitive´, as their antithesis and as
the object of *a reforming zeal.*[33]

Integral parts of the body of literature which commenced the meticulous
process of reifying these "naturalising and constructed values" are William
Shakespeare's *The Tempest* and its poignant depiction of the primordial
struggle between Caliban and Prospero; Daniel Defoe's *Robinson Crusoe*
and its imposition of a brand new identity and culture on the colonized being;
Jonathan Swift's *Gulliver's Travels* and its portrayal of the cultural and linguistic *tabula rasa* that should pass as the deformed or mutilated self; and, to
come closer to our age, Joseph Conrad's suggestive *Heart of Darkness*. These
are all part and parcel of this "convenient package" of cultural signification
through which the servants of British imperialism commenced the process of
producing the colonial subject. The production of this being of the "lowest"
order has been constructed by Stallybrass and White as complementary to the
same process through which

> the middle-class rejection of the indigenous carnival tradition
> in the late nineteenth century in Europe was a compensatory
> plundering of ethnographic materials—masks, rituals, sym-
> bols—from colonized cultures. In this respect Joseph Conrad
> was doing no more than Frau Emmy in placing `savage rites´
> at the heart of European darkness in the 1890s.[34]

Meanwhile, it is significant to note that it was the first attentive recipients of
the colonialists' myth-making enterprise that were truly "lucky" as they form
what we can demarcate as the second high in our parenthetical location of two
"highs" and two "lows." Defined as low themselves, they can be grouped for
convenience together with the first low order in European cultural discourse,
as they were educated to be nice, clean, well-behaved "little boys and girls":
they also emerged as the "legitimate" producers of the second low, who were
their belated Pan-African counterparts. This category of colonial subjects is
in no way restricted to the Africans in the homeland, but also encompasses
their educated Pan-African counterparts throughout the black diaspora.

III.

> Is literature most usefully seen as a means of access to history (Macherey), or as a way of grasping the present (Lacan and Barthes)? Perhaps the distinction is false? There is no way of grasping the present without a knowledge of history, of the present as part of the process of history. But to understand the text in its historical specificity is not the same as to set it free from its historical moorings, reading it as the work of the present.[35]

Holding the other deities in dialectical struggle, Esu establishes from the beginning the principle of rebellion against every form of convention and opposes all acts of dictatorship by men and deities alike. The enigmatic deity becomes enmeshed in contradictions in the process and his "true" essence becomes further enshrined in profound apprehension. Instilling terror and incomprehension in deities and men, Esu easily attains the contemporary practice of reading him and his relationship with *Ifa* in terms of what John Pemberton describes as "the polarity of order and disorder." In this reading, a major act of incomprehension is evident because the reading is fraught with the age-old distortion and definition of the deity as a mere trickster, "with the capricious element in human experience, or as autonomous energy, libidinal drives."[36] Pemberton has correctly dubbed the reading as a "singular" interpretation of the many facets of the deity, with obvious reductionistic results. The record is set straight by a careful examination of the chant of the *Ifa* priest that places Esu in his proper context as the one who derides the attempts of men to restore order by comparing their actions to one who would try to mend a torn garment with "a spider's web." Thus, an *Ifa* priest will chant:

> The world is broken to pieces:
> The world is split wide open,
> The world is broken without anybody to mend it:
> The world is split open without anybody to sew it.
> Cast *Ifa* for the six elders
> Who were coming down from Ile Ife.
> They were asked to take care of Mole.
> They were told that they would do well
> If they made sacrifice.
> If the sacrifice of Eshu is not made
> It will not be acceptable (in heaven)[37]

This check-and-balancing role and the power over life and death which Esu symbolizes in this regard can only be understood through a careful examination of the role of *Ètutu*[38] or sacrifice in Yoruba belief. To the Yoruba, *ètutu* is the scene of dialectical struggle between life-affirming principles and forces of extermination ranging from poverty, disease, famine, loss, sterility, and isolation to ultimate death. *Etutu* or sacrifice, according to Lienhardt, "is essentially the conversion of a situation of death, or potential death in any of its manifestations, into a situation of life."[39] Esu's involvement in every sacrificial act is not merely central, but as the *Ifa* priest's chant cited above asserts, a sacrifice that excludes Esu can only lead to chaos and disorder. Thus, when a person is asked to make sacrifice with a goat, s/he is also advised "to put the head inside the *ètutu* for Esu."

The *babalawo* or diviner also makes it clear to every supplicant that Esu alone has the special prerogative to transform a situation of potential death into a life-affirming essence. John Pemberton further observes the important role of Esu through a documentation of informed opinions of Esu's unquestionable prominence: Pemberton cites Idowu's acknowledgement of the opinion that although "there is an unquestionable element of evil" in Esu, Idowu recognizes further that this popular assessment of Esu as an essentially evil deity is not shared by the *babalawo*. Pemberton also records Bascom's 1969 brief discussion of Esu as "the divine enforcer" and Abimbola's 1973 reference to the deity as "an impartial police officer, punishing those who have disturbed the order of the universe." From a diasporic perspective, Dos Santos analyses Esu as "the stern controller of sacrifice which is the essential basis of harmony between the various elements which govern life." Idowu notes without comment that "Esu as the approver and bearer of sacrifice to heaven is known to the *babalawo* as Osetura" or the one who brings comfort. Finally, as the one who guards and at the same time transcends the margins of discourse, I quote Ulli Beier's concise observation in full:

> Now your question about order and disorder. Esu has always been called the principle of disorder. Superficially that is true. But remember there is a branch of physics that is called "chaos research". It is based on the assumption that what we perceive as chaos is simply based on a different kind of order. Now take the myth I recited before, about Orisa-nla being crushed by his servant who rolled a rock onto him. Here somebody creates chaos—or apparently so. But when I tell you that the servant was really Esu in disguise (as is said in some versions of this myth) then there is an entirely different significance to it. It becomes a case of divine interven-

tion and what looks like chaos is in reality a new kind of order: instead of a single monolithic god we now have a divine substance spread throughout the world. A new world order, No longer god vis-à-vis the world—but the god and the world being inseparably interwoven. And this is the function of Esu—to create a new order by challenging the old. The Yoruba have always understood that routine is the death of creativity and that complacency is the death of spiritual alertness. Therefore Esu systematically upsets our plans provokes us with the unexpected and keeps us wide awake. Esu reminds us every minute of the day, that we cannot take anything for granted, that we have to live responsibly all the time and that we must work at our relationships with gods and men. If you look at modern life in Europe, how our thinking is dominated and shaped by the media, by advertising, commerce and politics I feel that we badly need Esu in the modern world: our youngsters often turn into zombies. The concentration span becomes shorter and shorter—we badly need the provocation of the trickster god.[40]

Thus, Esu is primordially present in what Soyinka refers to as "a symbolic struggle with chthonic presences," the goal of the conflict being a harmonious resolution for plenitude and the well-being of the community, in all its ramifications. The essence of this conflict and its harmonious resolution, Soyinka also observes, is "a common theme in traditional mask-drama."

Peter Stallybrass' epigraph in an article titled "Drunk with the Cup of Liberty: Robin Hood, the Carnivalesque and the Rhetoric of Violence in Early Modern England" sums up the attitude of the upper class and their apprehension of that class of people among whom "there is such brutality and violence, such debauchery and extravagance, such idleness, irreligion, cursing and swearing, and contempt of all rules and authority. . . ."[41] To this list of uncomplimentary attributes, we must add, Stallybrass's and White's "irregularity of language" without losing sight of the fact that "rhetoric and the regularities of language were no less the structure of the dominant social order."

To reconstruct the concrete history which informs the formation of this attitudinal superstructure, a critical examination of the three domains of folk culture in direct opposition to the "official identity" of the upper class is pertinent. M. M. Bakhtin delineates them in the following order: "ritual spectacles," which includes carnival pageants and the comic shows of the market place; next to this is "comic verbal compositions" and this includes parodies, both oral and written. The third domain concerns what Bakhtin describes as "the various genres of Billingsgate," encompassing aspects of folk culture such as curses, oaths, and popular blazons.[42] Interwoven and closely linked, the basic identity of these domains of folk expression is the humorous aspect of the world which they present, apart from the linguistic code of etiquette which they transgress. Stallybrass also provides a tentative morphology of areas transgressed by Carnivalesque "malformations" in a treatise that includes the substitution of "fast for feast," or sacredness for profanation and the transgression of "spatial barriers," plus the substitution of the noise of the marketplace as the locus of public life, and how this encroaches on the privacy of houses. To these he adds the transgression of bodily barriers, the inversion of hierarchy, the degradation of the sacred, and the transgression of linguistic hierarchy.[43] A subtle articulation of the opposition provided by these aspects of folk expression to the official identity of the upper class is what Bakhtin describes further as the opposition of carnivals to

> the official feast (through which) one might say that carnival celebrated temporary liberation from the prevailing truth and from the established order: it marked the suspension of all hierarchical ranks, privileges, norms and prohibitions. Carnival was the true feast of time, the feast of becoming, change and renewal. It was hostile to all that was immortalised and completed.[44]

Esu's presence in places as diverse as the crossroad, market entrances, market places, king's palaces, shrines within compounds, and divining sessions gives him the ability and power to fulfil all these Carnivalesque manifestations.

To begin with the transgression of spatial boundaries, Esu and his chthonic activities, one must hasten to add, also permeate every aspect of earthly transience, and he does not merely invert social hierarchy, but goes beyond this to prey on the dominant classes. Iconographic details also reveal that the deity deceives gods, kings, and ordinary men as well as demons, witches, and even death. In a true carnival sense, therefore, Esu is primordially "hostile to all that is immortalised and completed," as the following praise attests:

> Eshu, confuser of men
> The owner of twenty slaves
>   is sacrificing

121

So that Eshu may not confuse him
Eshu who confused the head of the Queen
And she started to go naked.
Then Eshu beat her to make her cry.[45]

A major aspect of Esu's symbolism can also be foregrounded at this point, if we take into consideration the *Ifa* priestess D. Lapin's disclosure to Pemberton that "Esu is a representative of ambiguity, the all important foundation of Yoruba philosophy. Esu embodies the fact that no one knows anything with certainty."[46] Very few historians have attempted to refute the fact that the primordial African way of life is built on communal unity and understanding of the individual plight within the cosmic totality. The principle of checks and balances that informed the governance of the old Oyo empire, which made the Oba a mere figurehead who must listen to other hierarchies of power (symbolized by the Oyo-Mesi, the Ogboni cult, and other in-built structures of power) equally made absolute rulership impossible.[47] Esu symbolizes from the beginning the highest attainment of this "African way" through his activities among earthly mortals and in the realm of the supernatural.

Thus, among the other brother and sister deities,[48] Esu also carries out seemingly diabolical acts in ways that are perhaps too light-hearted for the grave implications and results which they achieve. One version of his relationship with Obatala, the god of creation, speaks of his disagreement with Olodumare (the supreme deity) for investing in a single god the herculean task of creation. To prove his point, Esu places a gourd of highly potent palmwine in front of Obatala's hut after a particularly vigorous day in the god's creation role. Thirsty and famished, the unsuspecting deity welcomes the gourd and its content as a gift from the supreme deity himself and drains it to the last drop. Drunk and disorderly, Obatala resumes his task of creation and in the process creates all sorts of deformed people including the cripple, the blind, and the albino. Working with the Brazilian Zora Zeljan's *The Story of Oxala* and Obotunde Ijimere's *The Imprisonment of Obatala*, (versions of the same story) Soyinka arrives at the same conclusion that "The Yoruba asserts straightforwardly that the god (Obatala) was tipsy and his hand slipped, bringing the god firmly within the human attribute of fallibility" and "in Ijimere's version, it is Esu who decides the nature of Obatala's punishment...It is a trial of the spirit."[49]

It is, however, when we arrive at the terrain of the two other roles which Esu fulfils in Bakhtin's schematic morphology, characteristic of grotesque realism, that the deity's Carnivalesque essence becomes inherently manifest and, in an important sense, complete. These roles concern the manifestation of grotesque bodies as provider of an "image-ideal of and for popular community as an heterogeneous and boundless totality" and as "a thoroughly materialist metaphysics whereby the grotesque "bodied forth" the cosmos, the social formation and language itself."[50] Esu fulfils the first function through his powerful presence in "the market place as the locus of public life," and thereby encroaches upon the privacy of houses. The juxtaposition of the aspiration of the upper class against the immediate need of the larger populace to buy and sell, amidst chaos and disorder, is spectacularly captured in the following account of the setting of this conflict.

What is known as Oja-Oba or the king's market is the locus of public activities in every large Yoruba town. Located directly across from the king's palace, activities in the market usually commence at sunset or early evening. This is why the market is also known as *oja ale* (evening market). When in full session, the juxtaposition of the setting of the market and the palace is one of outright chaos amidst buying and selling, making and losing of fortunes on the one hand, against the serene, relatively well-ordered space known as the king's palace, on the other. Uncertainty and intrigue are twin elements associated with the market and all that it connotes in Yoruba belief. In this atmosphere Esu asserts a powerful presence, and the tale is constantly told of a woman who is at the market, selling her wares, while Esu starts a fire in her house. She runs home leaving her goods and before she arrives at the scene of the fire, a thief runs off with her goods from the market. The market also underscores a primary belief of the Yoruba that the world of the living is contiguous with that of the dead, and the two worlds are organically linked with the world of those yet to be born. Thus, it is not uncommon for men and women to return from the market with grandiose tales about ghosts and glimpses of the deceased from other towns. People who die at an early age are believed to be wanderers on the face of the earth and they are constant visitors to market places.

As a reader of myth working along the line of the third category of readers in Barthes' theoretical framework, I receive an ambiguous signification from this tale. To place oneself along the lines of the static or analytical positions of the first two readers is to destroy the myth, by making its intention obvious or merely unmasking it. The true purpose of the third category of reading is to pass from semiology to ideology. Thus, a primary way to begin to read this tale is to externalize those elements of *control* inherent in the juxtaposition of the setting of the organized chaos of the market place alongside the enclosed, relatively well-ordered space that is the king's palace. Having fulfilled the important role of transgressing these spatial barriers (a significant element in Bakhtin's tentative morphology of Carnivalesque essence), the story moves ahead to provide an image-ideal of and for popular community as an heterogeneous and boundless totality. The conglomeration of bodies, encompassing the grotesque boundless totality, at the same time offers the conventional or "sacred," upper class rulership a vantage point from which to view the activities of the popular community. In Yoruba metaphysics, the world view is never complete without the ancestors, the gods, and the unborn. In this sense, the market place as the place that affords the entire community such a coming together, is of overriding importance. Soyinka's observation sums up this relative importance in the following way:

> The past is the ancestors', the present belongs to the living, and the future to the unborn. The deities stand in the same situation to the living as do the ancestors and the unborn. Obeying the same laws, suffering the same agonies or uncertainties, employing the same Masonic intelligence of rituals for the perilous plunge into the fourth area of experience, the immeasurable gulf of transition.[51]

At the scene of this dialectical struggle and controlling every aspect of its intense activity is the enigmatic deity known as Esu. The iconographic details establish him as the overriding controller of the market place, who, in a grotesque, carnivalesque manner, teaches all and sundry the essence of communal existence. Profiteering, wrangling, and greed are rewarded with total loss, as in the case of the woman in the tale, who is in the market (to make profit?), while Esu starts a fire in her house. "It is the day of the thief," as the Yoruba saying goes; Esu will catch up with him in another spectacular fashion. Meanwhile, the woman has been taught a bitter lesson through the total loss of her goods and possibly her house. It is important, as Eva Krapf-Askari observes in her 1969 study of *Yoruba Towns and Cities* that Esu symbolises all that is `impersonal, superficial, transitory and segmental." Thus:

> Eshu quickly makes himself master
> of the market place.
> He buys without paying
> He causes nothing to be bought or sold
> at the market until night falls.[52]

However, the carnivalesque essence inherent in the myth of Esu is only complete when we examine the celebration of Odun-Elegba (the festival of Esu), particularly how the iconographic details associated with the deity and the festival pave the way to a thorough materialist metaphysics, whereby the grotesque "bodies forth" the cosmos, the social formation, and language itself. I have confined my investigation to the feasting and how this culminates in a free flow of abuse, curses, profanities, and improprieties, which are the unofficial elements of speech. By carrying out the research in this manner, it is possible to transcend the current widespread adoption of the idea of carnival as an *analytical* category, which can only be fruitful if further *displaced* into the broader concept of symbolic inversion or transgression. Such speech forms, as Stallybrass and White conclude, being completely

> liberated from norms, hierarchies, and prohibitions of established idioms, become themselves a peculiar argot and create special collectivity, a group of people initiated in familiar intercourse, who are frank and free in expressing themselves verbally. The marketplace crowd was such a collectivity, especially the festive, Carnivalesque crowd at the fair.[53]

Celebrated in prodigious manner, Odun-Elegba truly begins, when

> a black goat is sacrificed in the shrine by the Elebi, the second-ranking Eshu priestess. The blood is poured on a blackened mud image which is the permanent Eshu figure in the shrine. The skull and the lungs of the goat are left with Eshu and the remainder is roasted in preparation for the next day's feast. Others come presenting gifts of kolanut, pounded yam, cocks and goats or pigs. . . . The principal portion of the offering is used in the daily feasting of the celebrants and their guests. Late in the afternoon, on the sixth day of the festival, the Eshu figure is carried to the king's market (Oja-Oba) on the head of the third ranking Eshu priestess, the Arugba (bowl carrier). She is preceded by the higher-ranking priestess, the Elemoso and the Elebi, and followed by bata drummers and other members of the compound.[54]

It is also at the market place that the celebration attracts its equally prodigious following, expanding to encompass everyone present at the market, who can only ignore the chant of the Esu priestess at their peril:

> People of the market, clear the way!
> We are coming through the market gate.
> My Lord is coming to the market.
> My husband, I have arrived.
> Laroye (Eshu), I have arrived.

Baraye, Baraye, Baraye![55]

Pemberton has also observed that at the famous Oje market in Ibadan, no buying or selling can begin until oil has been poured over the Esuoja (market
shrine dedicated to Esu). There is the equally popular Oke-Ibadan festival,
which is a festival of designated abuse, curses, oaths, slang, erotic laughter,
and popular tricks, celebrated around the figure of Esu. Every aspect of the
festival brings to light what Bakhtin describes as *a grammatical jocosa*:
"whereby grammatical order is transgressed to reveal erotic and obscene or
merely materially satisfying counter-meaning. Punning is one of the forms
taken up by the grammatical jocosa."[56] Oke-Ibadan festival transgresses all
spatial barriers to encompass the old and the young, the sacred and the "profane." Also, the prodigious feasting that characterizes the festival is absolute
and to give every member of the society sufficient time to enjoy the spinning
of jokes, all cooking must be done the night before the festival, thus forbidding anyone to cook on Oke-Ibadan day. Groups of young men and women,
going from compound to compound, are licensed to appropriate and consume food being prepared on the day of the festival, simply by sighting
smoke from fire-wood coming from any kitchen. Unfortunately, most of the
punning effects in these erotic jokes are unavoidably lost in translation. I have
recorded and translated some of them as follows:

> *Lojo Oke-Ibadan mo le foko roka*
> *Oke-Badan lanti lanti!*
> (On Oke-Ibadan day, I can mix a pot of
> yam flour with a penis!)

> *Baba da agbada bole, Oko nle*
> *Odagbada bole, Oko nle!*
> (Old man's voluminous robe is spread on the ground,
> but I can see a hardening penis!)

> *Ore meji, jowojowo epon,*
> *Mon bumi, jowojowo epon!*
> *Oni o rojo, ola o re kotu,*
> *Mon bumi, jowojowo epon!*
> (Two friends, flabby-flabby testicles,
> Try to curse me, flabby-flabby testicles!
> Today is not for empty talks, tomorrow, we are not
> going to court - Flabby-flabby testicles!)

Oko Olopa kiki beliti,
Mon bumi, kiki beliti!
(Policeman's penis is imprisoned under a wad of heavy-
heavy belt! Try to curse me, just a wad of belt!)

Oni keke rora goke, Oko nle!
(Bicycle rider take it easy as you climb that hill, I can see
your hardening penis!)

These erotic jokes do not merely work along Bakhtin's notion of "grammatical jocosa," by punning in ways that violate and unveil the structure of pre-
vailing convention and provoke laughter, they also echo Samuel Beckett's
punning pronouncement: "In the beginning was the pun." This sets pun
against official word and at the same time, as puns often do, sets free a chain
of puns. Finally, carnivals, as Bakhtin concludes, "set themselves in punning
relationship with official culture and *enable a plural, unfixed, comic view of
the world.*"[57]

IV.

This theoretical framework, which adopts the act of transgression as concept
and form, ideology and structure, will be employed in "reading" two plays
from the Yoruba/Black tradition. If reading the texts in this way creates a *distance* or *gap*, it is that "gap" which Macherey describes in *A Theory of
Literary Production* as being "large enough to accommodate an authentic dis-
cursiveness," which is the *determining characteristic* between literature and
criticism. For, as Macherey clarifies, what can be said *of* the work can never
be confused with what the work *itself* is saying, because two distinct kinds
of discourse, which differ in both form and content, are being superimposed.

Thus, the *irreducible difference* which this body of criticism is posit-
ing between itself and the body of texts to be examined is that the criticism
is informed by every act of transgression and grotesque realism, as they are
made to represent "cosmic, social, topographical and linguistic elements of
the world." As Macherey concludes, this difference is indeed not one between
two points of view on the same subject, but the exclusion separating two
forms of discourse that have nothing in common. Let us say, provisionally,
that the critic employing a new language brings out a *difference* within the
works by demonstrating that they are *other than* they are.

V.

The Drama of the Hero-Gods: Obotunde Ijimere's *The Imprisonment* and Wale Ogunyemi's *Obaluaye*

> In all the performances of the Travelling Theatre troupes
> ever attended by this writer, a suffusing gregariousness, a
> feeling of being at a public rite, at a communal festivity has
> always been so palpable an emotional and spiritual ambi-
> ence that one could almost feel and touch and taste it...This
> may be one of the deepest psycho-social functions of the
> Travelling Theatre troupes, that they provide for their audi-
> ences a potent vehicle for secular rites of social entropy and
> spiritual solidarity.[58]

Obotunde Ijimere's *The Imprisonment of Obatala* and Wale Ogunyemi's *Obaluaye* represent what I would like to describe as the quintessential bridge between a literary/academic dramatic experience and the so-called Popular Theatre. In David Kerr's recent study of *African Popular Theatre*, a comparison between the popular artist or one "working within the rather rigid conventions of an established genre" and the literary/academic dramatist or one who is able to "experiment with new dramatic forms," is pursued at some length. The comparison, David Kerr concludes, is not to suggest that "a literary playwright...is inevitably superior to a popular professional artist...but that the popular artist sometimes finds difficulty in maintaining the flexibility needed to adjust to a rapidly shifting national political scene."[59]

In their individual and distinctive ways, Ogunyemi and Ijimere are able to maintain this much needed flexibility and as a result able to induce that "suffusing gregariousness, a feeling of being at a public rite, a communal festivity. . . that one could almost touch and taste" which has since sufficed as the distinctive hallmark of the Yoruba Travelling Theatre, so vividly described by Biodun Jeyifo in the epigraph above.

According to Chris Dunton, "of all the major Nigerian authors—certainly among the dramatists—Wale Ogunyemi is perhaps the one whose work cries out to be given more sustained attention than it has attracted up to now."[60] Concerning why Ogunyemi's work has been passed over so cursorily, Dunton also makes the important observation that it is the academic critics and literary historians who have cast aside Ogunyemi's work, and not audiences for whom Ogunyemi's plays represent a constant attraction. Dunton is also probably right in his other observation that much of what Ogunyemi does is controversial, most especially, as Dunton puts it, "for a left-liberal or a non-chauvinist spectator." The sociology of the two categories of potential receivers/critics of Ogunyemi's plays is of particular interest to the general historicity and theoretical thrust of this study. The position of the left-liberal has been foregrounded in the preface to this study as one belonging, in historical terms, to an age when it would require a major act of intellection for the educated African (and his/her counterpart in the Diaspora) to ascribe aesthetic value to our indigenous arts. However, the charge of chauvinism ascribed to Ogunyemi's work is a rather more knotty issue to gloss over. The presentation of patriarchal structures as conflictless, allied to a readily observable univocality (which has accompanied African literature since its inception), has been foregrounded throughout this study as a trait that is reminiscent of an epoch in the development of the literature.[61] Thus without belaboring the issue, it is important to flesh out further the perceived importance of Ogunyemi's work to the general thrust of this study. In his book-length study of Nigerian Literature since 1970, and while declaring Ogunyemi as "one omission I regret especially," Dunton acknowledges that besides the sheer range of his work—which suggests that it merits close study—"there are a number of reasons why Ogunyemi's work provides a reference point for this study."[62] Needless to say, it is not the same reference point that Ogunyemi's work provides for Dunton's study that it does for mine, and indeed it is not in the accompanying pages that "the multi-faceted approach. . . that is not restricted to textual analysis. . . but which takes into account staging conventions, performance history, and—an especially interesting question in relation to Ogunyemi's work—impact on audience" which, Dunton suggests, would be carried out fully. Rather the referential point which Ogunyemi's *Obaluaye*, like Ijimere's *The Imprisonment*, provides for this study exists in what I have described as its staunch defense of a beleaguered philosophical/religious outlook.[63]

Obotunde Ijimere's play is probably even more redolent of this staunch defense of the Yoruba metaphysical presupposition, albeit from a viewpoint far more creatively revised than Ogunyemi's almost propagandist defence of the Yoruba worldview. It is by now a fairly commonplace knowledge that Obotunde Ijimere is indeed a pseudonym for one of the twentieth century's most fervent believers in Yoruba culture and tradition, the versatile Ulli Beier, who first set foot on Nigerian soil on 1 October 1950, precisely one decade before the country's political independence from Great Britain. In an interview with Nigerian playwright Olu Obafemi, Ulli Beier described *The Imprisonment of Obatala* as "based on what I had learned in the very heart of Yorubaland," and explained the choice of the fascinating pseudonym with the following words:

Obafemi: But why the choice of Obotunde Ijimere with all its bizarre connotations?

Beier: Well Ijimere is my favourite monkey. I knew these creatures well. They are dignified and wise. In Yoruba tradition they are sometimes referred to as *Babalawos*. I like the way they look you boldly in the face. The idea of Obotunde is not as strange as you think. There are many such stories linked to Egungun and Oro. But I don't want to drift off into mythology again. The name was a joke: it was bandied around casually between Duro and me and some other friends and suddenly it stuck. It was also a way of signalling immediately that this was a pseudonym.[64]

Finally, it is probably within the parameters of the defense of tradition that important differences also emerge in the writers' creative attitude. According to Isidore Okpewho, where oral tales/myths are concerned, the creative angst of the writers can be delineated into four basic categories. The first tendency is described as "tradition preserved," and a second attitude is labeled "tradition observed." Between the third and the fourth tendencies, however, the ideologically signifying approach is revealed through the use of two potentially radical outlooks; the first is called "tradition refined" and the second, "tradition revised."[65] Thus, while Wale Ogunyemi can be said to have refined the traditional materials at his disposal in *Obaluaye*, it is in Ijimere's *The Imprisonment* that the classic example of the tendency to revise tradition is vividly displayed. In the critical introduction to *Three Nigerian Plays*, comprising Duro Ladipo's *Moremi*, Wale Ogunyemi's *The Scheme*, and Obotunde Ijimere's *Born With the Fire on His Head*, Ulli Beier provides further elucidation to this quintessential difference between the creative attitude that refines and its slightly divergent counterpart which revises tradition:

Like Wale Ogunyemi's *The Scheme*, this play (*Born with a Fire on His Head*) also gives expression to the Yoruba belief that a curse may rebound on the head of him who utters it. The play ends with the *Babalawo*'s prophecy that Aole himself will die the same death he inflicted on the Bale of Apomu. . . . Thus Ijimere's play ventures an interpretation of Yoruba history, according to which the Oyo empire collapsed not so much because of the pressure of the Fulani from outside, but rather because of its internal corruption and degeneration, as symbolised by Alafin Aole.[66]

The same act of creative interpretation/revision can be seen at the heart of Ijimere's *The Imprisonment of Obatala*, which is the object of critical focus in the following section.

Obotunde Ijimere's *The Imprisonment of Obatala*

> The drama of the hero-god is a convenient expression; gods they are unquestionably, but their symbolic roles are identified by man as the role of an intermediary quester, an explorer into territories of `essence ideal´ around whose edge war fearfully skirts. Finally, as a prefiguration of conscious being which is nevertheless a product of the conscious creativity of man, they enhance man's existence within the cyclic consciousness of time. These emerge as the principal features of the drama of the gods; it is within their framework that the traditional society poses its social questions or formulates its moralities. They control the aesthetic consideration of ritual enactment and give to every performance a multi-level experience of the mystical and the mundane.[67]

The heterogeneous nature of Yoruba society dictates the need for unifying myths as well as parallel myths. For a people who value their unity as much as their diversity there is nothing strange about this. Obotunde Ijimere's *The Imprisonment of Obatala* opens with a classic example of the former, a unifying myth.

In this play, the traditional (political) rivalry between the ancient Yoruba cities of Oyo and Ile-Ife is given a unifying dimension when Obatala, King of Ile-Ife and god of creation, and Sango, King of Oyo and god of thunder, are depicted as bosom friends. However, Obatala's supremacy seems apparent, as he is presented throughout the play as the one with the more stable temperament. This depiction would appear to be a tacit acknowledgement of Ile-Ife's and Obatala's ability to lay claim to another parallel myth, and one that describes the ancient city as the cradle of the Yoruba people, and Obatala as god of creation, respectively.

Perhaps more importantly, the multi-level experience of the mystical and the mundane which every performance achieves, as gods, according to Soyinka, control the aesthetic consideration of ritual enactment truly begins at the threshold of these unifying and parallel myths. The quarrel between Heaven and Earth has a philosophical ring to it, and one that is central to the ways the Yoruba view the world. Thus, the hero-gods Obatala and Sango fulfil both the symbolically mystical and mundane roles and further enable man to identify them as intermediary questers and at the same time explorers into territories of "essence ideal." It is at the mundane level, and the level that is perhaps of overwhelming importance to ordinary mortals that the major conflict of the play begins. Ironically enough, it is Obatala who takes the rash decision to visit his bosom friend, Sango, and in the process offends Esu, the enigmatic god of fate. Despite repeated admonition from his thoughtful wife Yemanja that

> Anybody who waits for the buffalo waits for death!
> Anybody who waits for the elephant waits for death!
> Do not provoke the god of fate by this rash trip.
> The kingdom of Oyo is harsh:

Obatala overrules her cautious objection, saying that his "Desire is stronger than Yemanja's wisdom."[68]

At this point, Obatala's dictatorial tendency could be said to be burgeoning into outright complacency. The matter is almost ripe for the integrating activities of the all-knowing *Ifa* oracle and the trickster/god of fate—a check-and-balancing function without which the cosmic system of the Yoruba would fall apart. However, before Esu attains the prerogative to stabilize the spiritual psyche of the hero-god and the situation over which he negligently presides, the all-pervading wisdom of the *Ifa* oracle takes precedent. Obatala consults the custodian of the oracle, the *babalawo*, who, after casting the palm-nuts, chants the ritual verse of the hunter who followed the antelope to the forest of Onikorogbo. The hunter was told to sacrifice in order to avoid death, but he refused. After a spell of fruitless wandering through the forest of Onikorogbo, the hunter was about to return home in frustration, when:

> He met death.
> For a while they hunted together
> At last they found two eggs.
> The hunter wanted to share them—
> But death refused.
> The hunter went home lonely.
> Soon after that famine came.
> The hunter cooked the eggs
> And cooked them for his children.
> Then death arrived and said:

I have come for my share,
There is famine in heaven.
The hunter said: Alas,
I tried to shoot the white patch of the antelope
I tried to extinguish its sparkling eye.
But I hit the iroko tree
I had to eat the eggs with my children.
Then death killed the hunter and his children. (p.9)

Only Obatala's role as an intermediary quester and an explorer into territories of "essence ideal" could have dictated his response to the *babalawo's* divinatory pronouncement:

Obatala: Father of secrets, your nuts portend evil,
     Your prophecy is death.
     But know that my desire is stronger than your knowledge,
     That my eagerness is greater than your wisdom. (p.9)

Recasting his nuts, the *babalawo* comes up with another verse, this time reiterating the prophecy that was meant for the king of Awe, who conquered his foes through patience. Herein lies the "essence ideal" of the god of creation himself, and indeed that of all who are either like him or choose to follow him. For while:

Shango may thrive in war,
Orunmila may thrive through wisdom,
But you (Obatala) will thrive in suffering. (p.11)

The world is a market place where constant struggle and bargaining with the forces of nature are coterminous, so goes the Yoruba saying. The world view is complete only when the intermediary/protagonist quester forsakes both fatalism and complacency, regains his spiritual focus, and only then can he hope to transcend his own self-imposed stasis. Armed with the implicit warning that he would thrive only in suffering, like the king of Awe who conquered his foes through patience, every one of Obatala's encounters with Esu, the god of fate, underscores the latter's role as a representative of ambiguity—the all important foundation of Yoruba philosophy. For Esu, according to the *Ifa* priestess D. Lapin, "embodies the fact that no one knows anything with certainty":

133

Eshu: Wanderer in the forest!
          A single hand cannot lift the load on the head.
          The hand of the child cannot reach the shelf under the
              roof;
          The large hand of the adult cannot enter the narrow neck of
              the calabash.
          The stranger of today could be the friend of tomorrow.
          Wanderer in the forest:
          Help me to lift my load on my head.

Obatala: Stranger by the wayside,
          Your words are sweet,
          But your eyes are evil.
          Yet what you ask of me
          No man can ever refuse:
          For a single hand
          cannot lift the load on one's head.
          {As he helps to lift the pot on Eshu's head, Eshu quickly
          pours the content over Obatala's head and jumps aside}

Eshu: {laughs}: Kindness has never killed anybody,
          But it gives one a lot of troubles.
          {He runs off. Obatala makes to strike Eshu, but quickly
          remembers the prophecy. His arm drops and he stands immo-
          bile. He speaks slowly as if to himself.}

It is scenes like that have earned Esu his reputation as a perpetual trickster.
While testifying to what he calls "the unbroken arc of metaphysical presupposition, and patterns of figuration shared through space and time among
black cultures in West Africa, South America, the Caribbean and the United
States,"[69] African-American critic Henry Louis Gates, Jr. describes the
Signifying Monkey as Black mythology's archetypal Signifier. These trickster figures, to paraphrase Gates, embody aspects of Esu: they are primarily
mediators and as tricksters they are mediators and their mediations are tricks.

However, as *The Imprisonment of Obatala* progresses and the characters grow, Esu emerges as the divine enforcer, symbolizing all that is imper-
sonal, superficial, transitory, and at the same time segmental. Thus, at the
height of his feudal ascendancy, the Sango that Obatala meets in Oyo when
he finally arrives there is not the same Sango that met him at Ife ten years ago
to plead with the Earth. The Sango that Obatala now meets in Oyo thinks lit-

tle of sending a bosom friend to prison at the flimsiest excuse possible. And it is Oya, Sango's, wife who makes the sweeping observation about the decadent state of affairs in Oyo and how a gnawing complacency is reigning supreme in the ancient city with the tacit approval of Sango, the king:

Oya: This city has been filled with slaves
        And this palace with women:
        With yellow skin or long necks,
        With black buttocks or fat thighs
        With breasts like mangoes
        Or palms of soft liver -
        They all succumbed to the owner of the palace.
        Their bodies grow heavy with the king's fruit:
        But alas a curse has fallen on this city:
        Some women die in childbirth; they bleed
        Until their body is drained and dry.
        .....
        I fear that we are paying now
        For the king's injustice.
        No one can maltreat the father of laughter
        With impunity. Creation comes to a standstill
        When he who turns blood into children
        Is lingering in jail. (p.30)

The god of iron, Ogun, who plays a minor role in *The Imprisonment*, reminds the reader that he more than any other deity embodies another ideal (around whose edge war fearfully skirts?). Thus:

Ogun {*jumping up in anger*}: Let us not hear of him.
        We had his peace too long!
        The iron rusted in the smithy
        And the smith grew rings round his waist.
        I had grown tired of the blood of dogs
        Offered as substitute by men
        Who had grown soft and fat like eunuchs.
        The king of laughter had his time
        Now let me quench my thirst! (p.31)

The play ends on a happy note, largely because Sango, apparently harking to the voice of reason, releases Obatala from prison as the timely arrival of the

New-Yam ushers in a festive atmosphere. Obatala's quest is now in an important sense complete. But the epilogue is conceded to Esu, the god of fate, as he watches with an unmistakable note of irritation the heavy slumber of the hero-gods and their subjects:

> Eshu: Now they are happy.
> Obatala rests in the sky like a swarm of bees.
> He watches the world in silence.
> Ogun has retired to the dark forest of Ekiti.
> Idly he watches woodcock and tree creeper.
> He listens to the gossip of weaver birds
> And the prophecies of the owl.
> He understands the wisdom of the hornbill
> And the humour of the cookcal.
> In Oyo the celebrants are sleeping.
> The yam is heavy in their bellies
> The wine is still fermenting in their heads
> Their lust is overpowered by their sleep.
> Their wives are snoring untouched, unhurt
> And undelighted, beside them on the mat. . . . (p.42)

Significantly, for the enigmatic god of fate, the cosmic system he has just helped to reintegrate symbolizes neither victory nor elation!

Wale Ogunyemi's *Obaluaye: A Yoruba Music-Drama*

> For the Yoruba, man is the penultimate measure of all things, absolute justice rests with the gods.[70]

> The-dog-is-looking-at-me
> The-dog-is-selling-honey-at-the-market
> Are the names of the *babalawos* who cast *Ifa* for Ogun
> Who cast *Ifa* for Eshu, who cast *Ifa* for Orisha-oko
> Who cast *Ifa* for Shango, who cast *Ifa* for Orunmila
> Who cast *Ifa* for Shonponna the last born of them![71]

Strict adherence to the world-view of the Yoruba is what rescues Wale Ogunyemi's *Obaluaye* from degenerating into outright propaganda for (it must be said), a beleaguered philosophical/religious outlook. Like every colonized people, the idea of conversion to Islam or Christianity has always spelled doom or, at least, a barely concealed threat of annihilation for the metaphysical presuppositions of the Yoruba. Thus, when no less a person than the Baale or village head gets converted to a rival/imperial religion, in this case Christianity, the entire cosmic system is shaken to its foundation. Like many other aspects of *Obaluaye*, the following is a neo-Yoruba reality around which a contemporary syncretism revolves:

> Olori 1 & 2:   Kabiyesi, give unto the world what it demands,
>   Give Esu his due
>   Give that which belongs to the cult to the Priest
>   So that peace may return.

> All   *Except the Baale*
>   We will observe our tradition
>   We will observe our tradition
>   Christianity doesn't say
>   You understand
>   Christianity doesn't say we shouldn't observe
>   tradition
>   We will observe our tradition.[72]

In Yoruba mythology, Obaluaye or Sonponna is known as "the King who hurts the world."[73] However, the Obaluaye ideal merely underscores another paramount aim of the Yoruba moral system which, according to Sophie Oluwole, is basically a secular one:

> The point is that the gods are made to play a theoretical role in Yoruba Ethics. This does not make their morality a religious system, it does not throw it out of the coffers of philosophy either.[74]

Thus when in the second epigraph above, Obaluaye is described as the last-born of the Orisas, we should not conclude that because he is the last, he is therefore also the least. The myth goes on in which Obaluaye is described as the last-born among the six children of a man called Babaniyangi. The others are Ogun, Esu, Orisa Oko, Sango, and Orunmila. After their father died and while Obaluaye was on errand for his brothers, they shared their father's properties and apparently forgot to leave any for their junior brother. The presence of the oracle Orunmila and the god of fate, Esu, easily integrates the cosmic system seriously threatened as a result of the avarice of the five brothers. And it was Orunmila who told Obaluaye what to do: armed with the advice of his elder brother Orunmila, Obaluaye returned to their father's place in heaven. There he found a bow, an arrow, a stick, and a string which were meant to be his share of their father's properties. Obaluaye then asked Orunmila to consult the oracle for him, so that he may know what to do with his curious inheritance. One of Orunmila's apprentices, called Awolaje, cast the oracle for Obaluaye and told him that he would be more powerful than his brothers if he would make sacrifice. The aftermath of the sacrifice brought Obaluaye into contact with the spirit of their father, who told him that his share of the heritage would not be useless. Returning from heaven and chanting his incantations, Obaluaye shot his arrows to the four corners of the world, and the disease of smallpox spread through the world. After consulting the oracle, the sufferers of the dreaded disease were told by Orunmila to sacrifice to Sonponna: "Then the king and all his people worshipped Sonponna and the disease became powerless. And Sonponna became known as Obaluaye: the king who hurts the world."[75]

Significantly, three of Obaluaye's blood brothers are physically present on the stage in Ogunyemi's play. These are Esu, Ogun, and Sango and indeed the presence of the *babaloosa* also means that *Orunmila/Ifa* oracle is not far away either. Thus the deities with whom absolute justice rests open a drama that presents or at least ought to present man as the penultimate measure of all things. Let the following example suffice to illustrate the point further.

The integrating activities of the *Ifa* oracle and the god of fate, for example (as I have tried to demonstrate in the preceding sections) may be rigid, but are strictly restorative. Adherence to the world-view of the Yoruba means mutual respect for both animate and inanimate objects. For this reason, in Ijimere's play the vulture that carried the sacrifice to Heaven, and one which led to a permanent settlement of the quarrel between Heaven and Earth, is as celebrated and respected as probably the *Babalawo* whose precise divination led to the sacrifice in the first instance. Even though it is for its role as agent-provocateur, albeit a positive one, that the vulture is respected, the depiction is another manifestation of a unifying myth, and one which unites man with his environment, including what we might term the lesser beings within it. The role of the vulture as purveyor is unmistakable, as no less a figure than Obatala, the god of creation, remembers:

How we rejoiced, when the Vulture rose to Heaven
Carrying Earth's sacrifice
And rain poured down once more
After the long drought. (p.4)

In *Obaluaye* however, such a recollection develops into carnivalesque proportions as Orunmila leads both the gods and their adherents through the following chant, complete with the accompaniment of *bata* drums:

Orunmila: (*enters*)
        Do not throw a stone at the snail
        Do not shoot the snail with an arrow
        Do not throw a stone at the snail
        Do not shoot the snail with an arrow
        Whoever shoot the snail with an arrow
        Will fold their hands on their heads and
            lament...

All: *Start to dance to Ogboni music with Orunmila*

Philosophically speaking, therefore, although man may be the penultimate measure of all things, this view of the world still forbids him to kill a fly with a sledgehammer. If he does, as the revellers reiterate above, "he will fold his hands on his head and lament." The analogy suffices, therefore, for the present Baale or village head of Ilode who tacitly or implicitly seems to have forgotten that within this cosmic system everything has been worked out to the minutest detail. As "Ekeji Orisa" or companion of the gods, his position is not just sacrosanct, but he is the earthly representative of the four hundred and one deities among the people. Thus, when his own wives or Oloris lead others to chant "we will observe our tradition" as quoted above, they are merely calling his sagging attention to the view of the world that he seems obviously prepared to abandon. Their song is an accommodating syncretism that welcomes contributions from the alien religion, but not to the detriment or obliteration of their own ways of looking at the world. Thus, like Ijimere's *Imprisonment*, both the multi-level experience of the mystical and the mundane are equally observable in Ogunyemi's play, and the foregoing illustrate the latter. To bring the discussion at this level to some conclusion, it is necessary to spell out what the wilful narcissism of this Baale or village head portends for the world-view of the Yoruba. The vulture in the primordial quarrel between Heaven and Earth might be an agent-provocateur, and one that is celebrated and revered for being just that, but the Baale is an enabler, and in this sense, the one who initiates and endows sacrifices to the gods, just as Obatala and Sango are seen to be doing in *The Imprisonment*, while fulfilling their roles as kings of Ife and Oyo respectively. Contemporaneous with the Baale's roles as an initiator and an enabler is the fact that within the parameters of this world-view,

> Political power could not automatically be translated into wealth—as it happens today. The Oba was a man through whom a great deal of wealth circulated, but he was not meant to accumulate it. He was not even meant to build a house for his children while in office. The Oba had almost unlimited social responsibilities: if a woman had triplets, he became automatically responsible for the upbringing of one of the children; if a woman could not find a husband, perhaps because she was unable to produce children, he would marry her; when a woman gave birth and there was neither husband or father or no other close relative to bury the afterbirth, the Oba had to do it—which meant that he became the father of the child. . . . [76]

At the mystical level, on the other hand, absolute justice—which is the special prerogative of the gods—takes the form of the Baale who, as a result of his refusal to offer appropriate sacrifices to the gods (most especially Obaluaye, the king who hurts the world) contacts the dreaded disease of smallpox. The Baale's role at this level resembles that of Obatala and Sango as kings of Ife and Oyo, respectively, and in this sense becomes like them, a protagonist-quester when he fails to heed the warnings of the *Ifa* priests. The Baale actually dies, and it takes the combined efforts of the two priests in the play, Adifala and Babaloosa, to revive and cure him. Above all, the two priests also combine to offer appropriate sacrifices to Obaluaye with the firm promise that the four hundred and one deities will henceforth be taken seriously and worshipped:

> Babalo'osa: We respect you, Obaluaye.
> We respect you, the small-pox god
> Elenpe Ajobo
> Nana Gbukuu!
> Our respects to you.
> Sonponna owner of uncountable gourdlets,
> Who carries ones charms away to dump in

bush
He destroyed the whole family completely
He attacked the mountain and the mountain
shifted.
The father who goes above
Leaving the whole town to shiver with
fear.
When he goes into the forest
The forest dries up into a desert
Please, Four Hundred Deities
We'll worship you!
We didn't say we won't worship you
What if we do worship you?
..... (p.61)

Finally, because the *Ifa* oracle is firmly in control, we see very little of the integrating activities of Esu, since he made a brief appearance with the other deities at the opening of the play. However, what amounts to the prologue in *Obaluaye* is another concession to Esu, as Ad*Ifa*la leads the townspeople to pay homage to the enigmatic god of fate:

Adifala: Esu Odara is the difficult one,
Esu Odara is the difficult one.
The little father knows no relatives
Citizens of Ilode
Esu Odara is the difficult one.

All: Esu Odara is the difficult one
The little father knows no relatives
Citizens of Ilode
At Odere
Esu Odara is the difficult one! (pp. 81 & 83)

Conclusion

Wole Soyinka: Take Eshu for instance. The stature of Eshu has grown considerably, so that the original myths of Eshu that I knew as a child have grown even more colourful. I believe Eshu became so strong in Brazil because he had to defend himself against the very facile Christian interpretation...

Ulli Beier: ...the "devil."

Wole Soyinka: That's right, and again Wande Abimbola admitted once that these new aspects of Eshu are now found here in Nigeria as well. It is this movement. . . .

Ulli Beier: And of course it shows that the whole thing is alive. . . . [77]

The theoretical starting point of this study concerns what Stallybrass and White describe as "the root of this discourse on God which western cultures have maintained for a long time." To deconstruct the history of this ontological framework, it is important for the critic to become a reader of myth as opposed to a mythologizer or those focusing on an empty signifier, both of whom either make the intention of the myth obvious by merely unmasking it, or destroy it altogether.[78] What the reader must focus upon is the history of the myth, which is very often embedded in its concept and may even be independent of its language. For, through the concept, it is a whole new history that is implanted in the myth, as opposed to the empty nature of the form.

With Esu, the enigmatic Yoruba god of fate, as Soyinka points out in the epigraph above, readers of myths who have focused on the history rather than the contemporaneous forms of the myth have been able to rehabilitate the myth of the god and rescue it from every facile/narrow-minded interpretation.

Even as trickster, the following African-American folktale recorded in Alan Dundes' *Mother Wits from the Laughing Barrel* represents another instance in which the deity bodies forth the cosmos, the social formation, and language itself:

Governor Wallace of Alabama died and went to heaven. After entering the pearly gates, he walked up to the door of a splendid mansion and knocked. A voice inside exclaimed, "Who dat?" Wallace shook his head sadly and said, "Never mind, I'll go the other way."[79]

The dialogue of this tale is the power of the "low" which exploits the "political unconscious" of the "`high" and its erstwhile monopoly of the theoretical framework of "officialdom." The transgressive connotations implicit in this tale can only be grasped when one examines the general history of the dynamics of race relations in the United States. The identity of the Negro voice remains an enigma, a profane discourse of the "low" which has frightening consequences for the "high": "Some think it is God; others think it might be St. Peter. A few Whites assume it is a doorman or other menial."[80] There is little doubt that the tale can be subjected to a myriad of interpretations, but one thing is certainly clear, whether it is God, St. Peter, or a doorman: the enigmatic Negro voice is charged with enough power to send Governor Wallace to hell, a feat which, as Dundes observes, cannot be achieved by centuries of Black power militancy. Ultimately, the interplay of linguistic subterfuge *vis-a-vis* the questions of sanctity and profanity is a matter of history seen from *above* and history seen from *below*—which are irreducibly different and which consequently impose radically different perspectives on the question of hierarchy.

However, as I hope to have shown, it is at the level of the reader of myths that one must place oneself in order to connect a mythical schema to a general history, to explain how it responds to the interest of a definite society—in short, socio-semiotics.

1 As Wole Soyinka observes, at this crucial junction "we are further back in origin, not one engaged in the transitional battle of Ogun, but in the fragmentation of Orisa-nla, the primal deity, from who the entire Yoruba pantheon was born. Myth informs us that a jealous slave rolled a stone down the back of the first and only deity and shattered him in a thousand and one fragments. From this act of revolution was born the Yoruba pantheon." For detail see: Wole Soyinka, *Myth, Literature and the African World*, (Cambridge: Cambridge University Press, 1976), pp.151-2.

2 Hans Witte, *Ifa and Esu: Iconography of Order and Disorder*, (Soest-Holland: Kunsthandel Luttik, 1984).

3 Soyinka, op.cit., p.151.

4 Soyinka, op.cit., p.19.

5 Michel Foucault, *The Archaeology of Knowledge*, tran. by A.M Sheridan (London: Tavistock Publications, 1973), p.5.

6 Michel Foucault, op.cit., p.5.

7 For detail, see: Peter Stallybrass and Allon White, *The Politics and Poetics of Transgression* (London: Methuen Press, 1986).

8 Henry Louis Gates, Jr. "The Blackness of Blackness: A Critique of the Sign and the Signifying Monkey," in *Black Literature and Literary Theory*, (New York & London:

Routledge, 1990), p.287.

9 Soyinka, op.cit., p.150 (my emphasis).

10 Thomas Ashton, *Iron and Steel in the Industrial Revolution* (London: Tavistock, 1924), pp.128-9 (my emphasis) According to Sandra Barnes, today, Ogun's realm "has expanded to include many new elements, from modern technology to highway safety—anything involving metal, danger or transportation"; what Barnes describes as the "*international* Ogun," however, also embodies the "complex ideological systems of which he (Ogun) is also a part." For detail see Sandra Barnes (ed), *Africa's Ogun: Old World and New* (Bloomington & Indiana: Indiana University Press, 1989) pp. X & 2.

11 Foucault, op.cit., p.3.

12 P. Stallybrass & White, op.cit., p.4.

13 See especially, Dierdre L. Badajo, "The Yoruba and Afro-American Trickster: A Contextual Comparison," *Presence Africaine*, 147 (1988); Henry Louis Gates, Jr. "A Myth of Origins: Esu-Elegbara and the Signifying Monkey," *Art Papers* 9, 6 (1985) and *The Signifying Monkey: A Theory of African-American Literary Criticism*, (New York & Oxford: Oxford University Press, 1988) as examples of work that present Esu-Elegbara as a perpetual trickster.

14 Roland Barthes, *Mythologies* (Norwich: Granada Publications Ltd, 1976), p.128.

15 John Pemberton, "Esu-Elegba: The Yoruba Trickster God," *African Arts* 9,1 (Los Angeles) (1975):p.26.

16 Barthes, op.cit., p.128.

17 Barthes, op.cit., p.129.

18 Barthes, op.cit., p.128.

19 Roger Bastide, *The African Religions of Brazil: Toward a Sociology of the Interpretation of Civilizations*, Helen Shebba (trans), (Baltimore & London: The John Hopkins University Press, 1978), p.330 (my emphases).

20 Barthes, op.cit., p.129.

21 Op.cit., pp.128-9

22 Stallybrass & A. White, op.cit., p.4

23 Ibid., pp.30-31

24 *The Holy Bible: Authorised King James Version*, London, New York & Toronto: Oxford University Press) Isaiah Chapter 6, verses 1-3, (my emphasis).

25 Ibid., Is.6, vs.5.

26 Soyinka, op.cit., p.62.

27 Pierre Macherey, *A Theory of Literary Production* (London, Boston & Henley: Routledge & Keagan Paul, 1978), p.241.

28 Stallybrass & White, op.cit., p.178 (original italics).

29 Macherey, op.cit., p.240.

30 Stallybrass & White, op.cit., p.181.

31 Ibid., p.193 (original italics).

32 Terry Eagleton, *Literary Theory: An Introduction* (Oxford: Basil Blackwell, 1983), p. 189

33 Bill Ashcroft, et al., *The Empire Writes Back: Theory and Practice in Postcolonial Literature* (London & New York: Routledge, 1989); p.3 (my emphasis).

34 Stallybrass & White, op.cit., p.172.

35 See Catherine Belsey, *Critical Practice* (London & New York: Methuen Press, 1980).

36 Pemberton, op.cit., p.67.

37 Wande Abimbola, cited in Pemberton, op.cit., p.67.

38 Often translated as ritual, to make *ètutu* is also to propitiate/atone or appease a deity.

According to Wole Ogundele, "the English concept of ritual carries connotations of archaic, pagan (or barbaric) practices, and of benighted beliefs. Mostly used in cultural anthropology, the word is, however, also common in drama, where it roughly means the religious source of secular dramatic action. But within Yoruba parameters, *ètutu* carries none of these outrightly negative or romantic and nostalgic connotations; the essentially religious concept and practice are still alive. Yet, an anthropologist like Margaret Thompson Drewal who has worked extensively with *babalawo* in Ijebu and who evidently has a lot of respect and admiration for the religious and epistemological aspects of Yoruba culture, decides to use the English word instead of the Yoruba one. She agonizes over this choice for a while, but in the end, prefers the English, for the simple reason that the English is better and more universally known, while the Yoruba is not." For detail see Wole Ogundele, "Playing at Modernity: Or the Language Game in Postcolonial Africa", (Being a seminar paper presented at the Institute for African Studies, Obafemi Awolowo University, Ile-Ife, 1996), pp. 9-10.

39 Lienhardt, cited in Pemberton, op.cit., p.67.

40 See Femi Abodunrin, *Iconography of Order and Disorder: Conversation with Ulli Beier* (Bayreuth: Iwalewa-Haus, 1996), pp.49 & 52.

41 Peter Stallybrass, "Drunk with the Cup of Liberty: Robin Hood, the Carnivalesque and the Rhetoric of Violence in Early Modern England," p.45.

42 M. M. Bahktin, *Rabelais and His World,* trans by Helene Iswolsky (Bloomington: Indiana University Press, 1984), p.4.

43 Stallybrass, op.cit., p.46.

44 M.M. Bahktin, op.cit., p.10.

45 Cited in Pemberton, op.cit., p.26. In Obotunde Ijimere's *The Imprisonment of Obatala,* Obatala testifies to Esu's ability to transgress time, to make future become present, and past future, as expressed in the following praise poem:

> Esu confuser of Men!
> When he is angry he hits a stone until it bleeds.
> Having thrown a stone today—he kills a bird of yesterday.

46 Op.cit., p.91.

47 According to Ulli Beier, while "the Orisa all have a very distinct historical personality and their cults are particularly virile in places where this connection is strong, there are some religious institutions though, that cut across Yorubaland and they even play a politically unifying role. The Ogboni society is one of these...All Yoruba people live on the earth, and they must take care not to offend the earth spirit. The Ogbonis therefore have a lot of political influence beyond the wall of their own city." For detail see Femi Abodunrin, op.cit., p.49.

48 Indeed the Yoruba mythological pantheon probably gives more recognition to female deities. Thus in the following *Ifa* verse from *Òkàràn Méjì,* the deity Oya is said to be more dangerous than Sango: The Wife is more dangerous than the husband:

Òkànràn kan níhìín	"When we see one Okanran this way,
òkànràn kan lóhùún	And we see another Okanran that way,
Òkànràn di méjì, a dire;	The signature is that of Okanran Meji, which means good luck.
A díá fun Sàngó, Olúùrójò	*Ifa* divination was performed for Sango, nick-named Oluorojo,
'Bámbí, omo Arígboota-ségun	'Bambi offspring of those who use two hundred stones to defeat their enemies
Nígbà tí nloo gbÓya níyàwó	When he was going to marry Oya as wife.
Ayá rorò joko lo ò,	The wife is more dangerous than the husband

Ayá rorò joko lo   The wife is more dangerous than the husband
Oya ló rorò ju Sàngó   Oya is more dangerous than Sango.
Ayá rorò joko lo   The wife is more dangerous than the husband"
For detail see Wande Abimbola, *Ifa Divination Poetry* (New York & London: Nok Publishers Ltd), pp.98-9.
49 Soyinka, op.cit., pp.18 & 20.
50 Bahktin, op.cit., p.10.
51 Soyinka, op.cit., p.148.
52 Cited in Pemberton, op.cit., p.22. According to Hans Witte, "cowries were formerly used as money. The fact that "Elegba (=Esu) hides behind cowries," as the Yoruba say, indicates that the trickster is present in all money transactions, especially on the market, where strangers come into contact with each other and quarrels may easily arise." Hans Witte, *Ifa and Esu: Iconography of Order and Disorder* (Soest-Holland: Kunsthandel Luttik, 1984), p.108.
53 Stallybrass & White, op.cit., p.28.
54 Pemberton, op.cit., p.22.
55 The Esu figure that is carried into the king's market on the sixth day of the festival is an equestrian figure with a hairtail and armed with a lance or gun—safely interpreted as images of a hunter-warrior. Esu's phallic symbolism is equally prevalent. Hans Witte records the iconographic details of the trickster's carnivalesque/grotesque manifestation in the following way: "The head of Esu is flanked on both sides by a kneeling woman holding her breast, followed by a copulation scene. This sexual emblem, I was told at Erinmo near Efon, can be touched for luck by a woman who wants children or a safe delivery." However, "the phallic symbols in Esu sculpture do not mean that the autonomous nature of the phallus symbolizes the wilful characteristic of the trickster's energy, but rather tones down his male definiteness in order to make it possible for Esu to function as mediator between male and female worlds." See Witte, op.cit., pp. 64 & 110.
56 Bahktin, op.cit., p.10.
57 Ibid.(my emphasis).
58 Biodun Jeyifo, *The Yoruba Travelling Theatre of Nigeria (Lagos: Nigeria Magazine, 1984), p.123.*
59 For detail see David Kerr, *African Popular Theatre* (London: James Currey, 1995), pp.91-2.
60 Chris Dunton, a review of *Chief Wale Ogunyemi at Fifty: Essays in Honour of a Nigerian Actor-Dramatist.* Dapo Adelugba, ed., in *Research in African Literatures* 26, 1 (Spring 1995):160
61 "Maidens, Mistresses and Matrons" are the terms used by Carole Boyce Davies, for example, to describe the majority of the female characters in Soyinka's writing. The same critical apprehension has been expressed by numerous other critics, but as Olu Obafemi reminds us in his 1994 essay, the silencing of the female voice should be regarded as an index "of the prevalent nature of the systematic obfuscation of ideological perceptions of society - a deliberate mystification of the political system in aid of the perpetration of the status quo" which has obscured the emergence of clear ideological positions and trends, and "yet to gain objective appreciation, tolerance of expression, and responsiveness from the dominant socio-political system." For detail see Olu Obafemi, "Towards Feminist Aesthetics in Nigerian Drama: The Plays of Tess Onwueme," *African Literature Today 19* (London: James Currey, 1994), p.84.
62 Chris Dunton, *Make Man Talk True: Nigerian Drama in English since 1970* (London: Hans

Zell, 1992), p.9.

63 For detail see Olu Obafemi, *Forty Years in African Art and Life: reflections on Ulli Beier* (Bayreuth : Iwalewa-Haus, 1993), p.29.

64

65 See Isidore Okpewho, "Myth and Modern Fiction: Armah's *Two Thousand Seasons*," *African Literature Today 13* (London: Heinemann, 1983):2-3

66 Ulli Beier, ed., *Three Nigerian Plays* (London: Longmans, 1967), pp.xvi-xvii.

67 Wole Soyinka, *Myth, Literature and the African World* (Cambridge: Cambridge University Press, 1976).

68 Obotunde Ijimere, *The Imprisonment of Obatala, and Other Plays*, English adaptation by Ulli Beier (London: Heinemann, 1966), p.8. All page references are to this edition.

69 Henry Louis Gates, Jr, "The Blackness of Blackness: A Critique of the Sign and the Signifying Monkey," in *Black Literature and Literary Theory* (New York & London: Routledge, 1990), p.287.

70 Sophie Oluwole, *Witchcraft, Reincarnation and the Godhead* (Lagos: Excel Publishers, 1992).

71 Ulli Beier, *Yoruba Myths* (London & New York: Cambridge University Press, 1980).

72 Wale Ogunyemi, *Obaluaye: A Yoruba Music-Drama* (Ibadan: Institute of African Studies, 1972), p.55. All page references are to this edition of the play.

73 Beier, op.cit., p.45.

74 Oluwole, op.cit., p.71.

75 Beier, op.cit., p.45.

76 For detail see Femi Abodunrin, *Iconography of Order and Disorder: Conversation with Ulli Beier* (Iwalewa-Haus, University of Bayreuth, 1996).

77 *Orisa Liberates the Mind: Wole Soyinka in Conversation with Ulli Beier* (Bayreuth: Iwalewa-Haus: 1992).

78 Femi Osofisan's *Esu and the Vagabond Minstrels* is a classic example of the creative practice that makes the intention of a myth obvious by merely unmasking it. Having portrayed Esu as god of compassion and justice, the moralizing burden imposed on the deity is hardly an aspect of the deity's iconography. Obviously iconoclastic in scope, *Esu and the Vagabond Minstrels* merely unmasks the myth of Esu in a bid to demystify it. Indeed, the entire play can be said to have focused on the contemporaneous forms of the myth rather than its history. Thus the major characters in the play, the five vagabond minstrels having been made to understand their follies, it is hardly surprising that when the unmasking is over that the play closes with the quintessential demystifier: the song "ESU DOES NOT EXIST", paradoxically led by Orunmila. In three stanzas, the song more or less panders to the contemporaneous view of Esu along the lines of what Roger Bastide describes as "the dualism of good and evil" which has the effect of making non-white Brazilians, living in a big city and steadily rising on the social ladder, unwilling to have anything to do with the cult of Esu. According to the song,

    Esu does not exist
    Save in your imagination!

ESU DOES NOT EXIST

And if evil does persist
We must each search our soul. (Original capitals)

The libellous tone of the song could be referred to adherents of Yoruba religion. Meanwhile, at the level of comparative religion, the following example from Peter Fuller's 1985 essay entitled "The Christ of Faith and the Jesus of History" supplies the equivalent of Osofisan's demystification/unmasking, but from a perspective that focuses on not just the contemporaneous form of the myth but also its history:

> A joke has been going the rounds in theological circles for some time now. It goes like this. The Pope was told by the Cardinals that the remains of Jesus had been dug up in Palestine. There was no room for doubt: all the archaeologists, scholars and experts were agreed. Teaching about the resurrection, the lynch-pin of orthodox Christian faith, lay in ruins. The Pope sat with his head in his hand, pondering his position and that of the Church he headed. He decided it would be only decent—whether or not it would be Christian no longer seemed to matter—to let the separated brethren know. So he called up Paul Tillich, the leading Protestant theologian, and told him the sad news. There was a long silence at the end of the phone. Finally, Tillich said: "So you mean to say he existed after all...."

For detail see Femi Osofisan, *Esu and the Vagabond Minstrels* (Ibadan: New Horn Press, 1991), and Peter Fuller, "The Christ of Faith and the Jesus of History," *New Left Review*, 146 (1985).

79 Alan Dundes, ed., *Mother Wits from the Laughing Barrel* (New Jersey: Prentice-Hall, 1973), p.620.

80 Op.cit., p.620.

III.
RELIGION & PHILOSOPHY

Orisha Liberates the Mind
Wole Soyinka in Conversation with Ulli
Beier on Yoruba Religion

U: I wanted to talk to you about Yoruba religion, because you seem to be the only writer who has seriously tried to come to terms with it. Even many of the Yoruba scholars, who do research into language, literature, and history of the Yoruba shy away from the subject—as if they were embarrassed about it. . . .

Now in your own case, given the type of upbringing you had, I have asked myself how you became interested in Yoruba religion. There is an image in Ake that has made a very strong impression on me. You were living in the Christian school compound, that was surrounded by a high wall and when the Egungun masqueraders were passing by outside, you had to ask somebody to lift you onto the ladder, so that you could watch the procession going on out-side. Your upbringing was designed to shield you from the realities of Yoruba life ... and later on your education in the Grammar school, the University in England—they all were designed to take you further away from the core of your culture.

How, then, did you find your way back into it? How did you manage to break the wall that had been built up around you?

W: Curiosity mostly, and the annual visits to Isara—which was a very different situation from Abeokuta! There is no question at all, that there was something, an immediacy that was more attractive, more intriguing about something from which you were obviously being shielded. If you hear all the time "Oh, you mustn't play with those kids because their father is an Egungun man. . . " you become curious: and then you discover that there is nothing really "evil" about it ... that it is not the way they preach about it. Even my great great uncle, the Reverend J. J. Ransome Kuti, whom I never met, composed a song whose refrain was: "Dead men can't talk." One was sur-rounded by such refutations of that other world, of that other part of one's her-itage, so of course you asked questions about it. Yes, and even if I realized quite early on, that there was a man in that Egungun mask, that did not mean that a great act of evil was being committed—any more than saying that Father Christmas was evil.

I had this rather comparative sense and I wrote in Ake that I used to look at the images on the stained glass windows of the church: Henry Townsend, the Rev. Hinderer and then the image that was supposed to be St. Peter. In my very imaginative mind, it didn't seem to me that they were very different from the Egungun.

So one was surrounded by all these different images which easily flowed into one another, I was never frightened of the Egungun. I was fascinated by them. Of course, I talked to some of my colleagues, like Osiki, who donned the masquerade himself, from time to time.

The Igbale was nothing sinister to me: it signified to me a mystery, a place of transformation. You went into Igbale to put on your masquerade. Then when the Egungun came out, it seemed that all they did was blessing the community and beg a little bit for alms here and there. Occasionally there were disciplinary outings: they terrorized everybody and we ran away from them but then, some distance away you stopped and gathered again. . . maybe my dramatic bent saw this right from the beginning as part of the drama of life.

I never went through a phase when I believed that traditional religion or ceremonies were evil. I believed that there were witches—I was convinced of that—but at the same time there were good apparitions. And of course I found the songs and the drumming very exciting.

U: You never really took to Christianity at any stage. . . .

W: Never really—not even as a child. I remember distinctly my first essay prize at secondary school—that was in my first year. My essay was entitled: "Ideals of an Atheist." Yes, I went through all these phases. I just felt I couldn't believe in the Christian god and for me that meant I was an atheist.

U: How old were you then?

W: I was eleven! But I also enjoyed being in the choir—I was a chorister. I went regularly to rehearsals. I enjoyed the festive occasion, the harvest festival, etc. Then we processed through the congregation, rather than sneaking in through the side entrances. At Christmas and New Year I enjoyed putting on the robes of a chorister. On the way to church I went to see my friend Edun, who lived in Ibarapa. And my Sunday was made even more interesting, when we met the Egungun masquerades on the way—which was quite often.

U: Do you remember we went to a conference in Venice, it must have been in 1960 or 1961?

W: Oooooh yes. . . .

U: There was a writer from Northern Nigeria. . . I think it was Ibrahim Tahir. And he made a statement, the gist of which was that Nigeria was, or was about to become, an Islamic country. . . .

W: I have actually forgotten that, but it wouldn't surprise me.

U: I am not quite certain what his real argument was or how it was phrased. But I do remember your rather fierce reply! The gist of which was that both Christianity and Islam were conservative forces that actually retarded Nigeria's ability to cope with the modern world, whereas traditional religions—Yoruba religion at least—was something much more open, and much capable of adaptation.

W: Yes, and for that very reason liberating! I am glad you brought up the issue of Islam, because that was also contributory to my entire attitude to imposed foreign religions.

You know all this nonsense of religious intolerance which is eating into the country now—it didn't exist in my youth! During the Ileya we celebrated with our Muslim friends, because they would send us meat from their ram; the Oba would go to the mosque, even if he was a Christian, and vice versa: during Christmas and Easter, our Muslim friends would come to the house. There was always equality between the religions—acceptance. And that in turn made it impossible for me to see one as superior to the other. And of course, the more I learned about Yoruba religion the more I realized that that was just another interpretation of the world, another encapsulation of man's conceiving of himself and his position in the universe; and that all these religions are just metaphors for the strategy of man coping with the vast unknown.

I became more and more intrigued and it is not surprising that, when I went to study in England I nearly took "Comparative Religion" as one of my subjects; but then I decided that I would enjoy it more, if I just read into it and visited all sorts of places. . . . I remember going to this small Buddhist meeting; I visited the so-called fundamentalist religions, the spiritualist churches. . . I went to one or two seances. I have always been interested in the spirituality of the human individual. So when people like Tahir—and there have been many of them—have made that kind of statement, I have always risen to counter it very, very fiercely. Traditional religion is not only accommodating, it is liberating, and this seems logical, because whenever a new phenomenon impinged on the consciousness of the Yoruba—whether a historical event, a technological or scientific encounter—they do not bring down the barriers -close the doors. They say: Let us look at this phenomenon and see what we have that corresponds to it in our own tradition, that is a kind of analogue to this experience. And sure enough, they go to Ifa and they examine the corpus of proverbs and sayings; and they look even into their, let's say, agricultural practices or the observation of their calendar. Somewhere within that religion they will find some kind of approximate interpretation of that event. They do not consider it a hostile experience. That's why the corpus of Ifa is constantly reinforced and augmented, even from the history of other religions with whom Ifa comes into contact. You have Ifa verses which deal with Islam, you have Ifa verses which deal with Christianity. Yoruba religion attunes itself and accommodates the unknown very readily; unlike Islam, because they know: they did not see this in the Koran—therefore it does not exist. The last prophet was Mohammed, anybody who comes after this is a fake. And Christianity! The Roman Catholics: until today they do not cope with the experience and the reality of abortion! They just shut the wall firmly against it. They fail to address the real problems of it; they refuse to adjust any of their tenets.

U: The Yoruba people have always been willing to look at another mythology and find equivalents in their own tradition. For example: when I first met Aderemi, the late Ooni of Ife—that was at Easter 1951—he told me about the different shrines in his town and he said: "You know, in Yoruba religion we know the story of Mary and Jesus," and he told me the myth of Moremi (Mary) who sacrificed her only son in order to save her town. And he said: "Really, Moremi is Mary." I was impressed, because he could see that there was some basic metaphor that remained valid across a variety of cultures: He knew that the basic truth is the same—only the trappings are different. . . .

W: The Yoruba had no hostility to the piety of other people.

U: Yoruba religion, within itself, is based on this very tolerance. Because in each town you have a variety of cults, all coexisting peacefully: there may Shango, Ogun, Obatala, Oshun, and many more. . . .

W: Even in the same compound!

U: Even within the same family—because you were not supposed to marry into the same Orisha! But there is never any rivalry between different cult groups; they all know they are interdependent. Because they are like specialists: everybody understands specific aspects of the supernatural world. Nobody can know everything. The Egungun knows how to deal with the dead; the Ogun worshippers know how to handle the forces that are symbolized by iron. But for the Ogun worshippers to function, it is also necessary that Shango worshippers and Obatala worshippers and all the other olórìshà perform their part. Only the concentrated effort of all of them will bring peace and harmony to the town. So naturally: when the Christians first appeared, the olórìshà could hardly suspect. . . .

W: . . . .how hostile the new religion would be.

U: I think that tolerance is one of the big qualities of Yoruba culture.

Even the treatment of handicapped or mentally disturbed people—it all shows how much more tolerant Yoruba culture was than Western cultures.

W: Yes. Europeans tend to hide such people, whereas Yoruba religion actually accounts for them.

U: You said before that Yoruba religion "liberates." Can you expand on that?

W: I believe that the truly liberated mind is never aggressive about his or her system of beliefs. Because it is founded on such total self confidence, such acceptance of others, that there is no need to march out and propagate one's cause. That is why Yoruba religion has never waged a religious war, like the Jihad or the Crusades.

U: In fact they never make converts! It is the orisha himself who chooses his devotees. . . .

W: The person who needs to convert others is a creature of total insecurity.

U: There is this beautiful Yoruba proverb: "The effort one makes of forcing another to be like oneself, makes one an unpleasant person!"

W: And even in practical terms, in day-to-day terms, take Shango for instance. Shango becomes the demiurge of electricity, so that this new phenomenon does not become an object of terror; it does not alienate you, because Yoruba religion enables you to assimilate it. The ease with which the Yoruba moves into that world and adapts to phenomena that had not come into the purview of his religion until recently—it means that he does not see the need to protect his family or his town from the benefits of this new technological experience. This is another evidence of this liberating attitude, which becomes ingrained in one. It is not just a bag of tricks that helps you to cope with the world: the mind is already prepared.

The same thing applies to human relationships. Social relationships. The whole experimental nature of what the modern world should be. The way other religions absolutely block your entry into new progressive fronts— Yoruba religion just doesn't do that!

U: It is significant that when a Yoruba says "onígbàgbó,`" (a believer) it means "Christian," because it is nonsensical to say "I believe in Shango" or "I believe in Ogun." One is too secure in one's world-view. I think I have mentioned to you once that remarkable reply of an old olórìshà, to whom his grandchild said: "The teacher said, your Obatala doesn't exist!" He simply answered. "Only that for which we have no name does not exist." He could not be shaken.

W: That is a brilliant way of putting it. And you have been to Brazil and Cuba. In that part of the world you find Europeans—not just Mulattoes—but people of "pure" European descent, who accept the humanism of this religion

155

and who recognize it as their own way of truth. And they cannot conceive of any other way of looking at the world. This a proven ability of this religion, which is well documented.

U: A few days before I came to Nigeria, I received a letter from a Portuguese student at the University of Munich. She came across a small community of olórìshàs in Lisbon and again she found this a more realistic and intense way of looking at the world.

W: I know a number of people like that. On the other hand, what you said earlier on about Yoruba scholars and their reluctance to come to terms with Yoruba religion. . . it is a very curious phenomenon. . . .

U: So you agree with my estimation?

W: Oh yes, I agree with it absolutely. And the worst part of it is that those fellows who speak about "false consciousness"—and I don't just mean the dying breed of Marxists—they are all totally preconditioned. Even when they are trying to be objective about African religion in general—or about their own traditional belief system—they are totally incapable of relating to it. They say: "This is a contemporary world. What use is our traditional religion today?" and I feel tempted to say to them: What use is a system of beliefs like Islam and Christianity in the contemporary world? And they cannot see that they have totally failed to make that leap: to take Yoruba religion on the same level as any system of belief in the world, that they are committing a serious scholarship lapse. In other words, they are totally brainwashed by what I call these "elaborate structures of superstition"—Islam and Christianity particularly. They have accepted these as absolute facts of life which cannot be questioned.

They lack the comparative sense of being able to see Yoruba religion as just another system - whether you want to call it superstition, belief, worldview, cosmogony, or whatever—you have to do it on the same level with any other system. Once you do that, many questions which have been asked become totally redundant, because they have not been asked about other religions. But when our scholars come up against their own religion, their faculty of comparison completely disappears.

U: There is a whole body of prejudices—which have their roots in the ignorant or malicious misinterpretations of missionaries—and which still persist in the minds of many Nigerians.

A typical one is the accusation that the Egungun try to "decieve" women and children, by pretending that they are spirits. Whereas of course every child knows that there is a man in the mask. . . .

W: Absolutely! I did.

U: Everybody knows that the mask is carried by a dancer who is specially trained for that task—but at the height of the dance he becomes the ancestor. That is a totally different matter. These "wicked" men who allegedly try to intimidate women—can't people see that during the Egungun festival they are in fact blessing women and that those who pray for children dance behind them?

W: And again, if you take the communion: here is a thing that happens every Sunday, sometimes twice a week. In which the officiating priest actually gives you a wafer and says "This is the flesh of Christ" and he gives you a drop of wine and says "This is the blood of Christ". . . .

U: Another defamation of Yoruba religion is the notion that it is a form of exploitation of the people. But surely it is much less so than Christianity! Take a babalawo, for instance: When you consult a babalawo, you put down threepence—a token fee—there is no money involved in divination. Have you ever seen a rich babalawo?

W: (laughs)

U: A traditional babalawo was a poor man. He was not even interested in being rich. In fact the whole society did not even know wealth in our modern sense. What kind of possessions could you own, that others didn't have? Another Agbada? Everybody had enough yams to eat. Everybody lived in a spacious compound that would accommodate him, his wives and his children. Everybody had enough clothes to wear... everybody had access to land. What else could you want? There was nothing to buy.

The grand old olórìshà priests I knew in the fifties: the Ajagemo of Ede, the Akodu of Ilobu ... they were poor people, in spite of their influence. There was no such thing as a fat priest. Whereas now: some of these new Churches really do exploit their congregation. Only a week ago one of these self-styled "prophets" went to see a friend of mine and told her: "I had a vision. The child you are going to give birth to will be born dead, and you too will die in childbirth. The only way you can survive is to fast for three days without water and to give money to the Church!" Now here is not only exploitation but also blackmail!

W: It is happening all the time. All the time. This whole spate of prophesying, this competitive mortification of people is nothing but an attempt to bring powerful and wealthy people under the control of the priest. Even ordinary individuals are not exempted. They have succeeded in some cases. Oh yes. They rush to them and say: You must do this and that. And sometimes when people take no notice of them, their relatives will! There was a relation of mine, he got so frightened when one of these prophets predicted a likely death for me, that he ran to him and asked him what to do. And I said to him: I will curse you, if you go again to that church. I will follow you there and break up that ceremony. So they do succeed on so many levels and it has become competitive. . . .

U: Now let us talk about the way in which some of these traditional Yoruba concepts have been used in your plays. If I am not mistaken, it was in A Dance in the Forest that you first used some kind of Yoruba symbolism in a play.

W: Yes, of course by that time I had written the draft for The Lion and the Jewel, but that was a very different thing. It was on a different level.

U: The striking thing about A Dance in the Forest is the character of Ogun. This image of Ogun has accompanied you through your later writing; but it has been said that the Ogun of your play is a rather personal, "unorthodox" orisha—that you have, in fact, created a new kind of Ogun.

W: Hmmm ... that is true.

U: But of course, even in purely traditional Yoruba terms, that is quite a legitimate thing to do. Ogun has never been a rigid defined being; the orisha can only live through people—by "mounting somebody's head"—you could go so far, to say that when the Orisha fails to manifest himself in this way through his priests and worshippers, he ceases to exist. If the priest who personifies Ogun is an unusually powerful olórìshà he can modify the image of Ogun. So that even in Yoruba tradition Ogun consists of a variety of interrelated personalities.

Any traditional priest would accord you the right to live Ogun your own way, in fact they would think it the normal thing to do. You recreate Ogun—or perhaps one could say you are sensitive to other aspects of his being. Because Ogun is a very complex being.

W: Yes, indeed.

U: It is again the typical Yoruba openness and tolerance that we are talking about. It applies not only to the relationship between the different orisha cults, it also applies to the variants of interpretations within one and the same cult group.

W: And in the diaspora of course, the same thing. The concepts of Orishanla or Oshun are very different in Brazil or Cuba; and in turn the manifestations of the orisha over there have affected the interpretations of some of the scholars and they in turn have transmitted some of these ideas to our most traditional priests. So that when you speak to a Babalawo you may notice a new perception, a slightly altered perception.

U: Actually Pierre Verger was instrumental in establishing contacts between Brazilian olórìshà and their families in Dahomey and Nigeria. Messages were sent back and forth, which were ultimately followed by exchange of visits. Today there is quite a bit of movement between the two countries. Look at Sangodare, for example: the young Shango priest who grew up in Susanne Wenger's house. He was invited to Brazil four times by groups of olórìshà.

W: Take Eshu for instance. The stature of Eshu has grown considerably, so that the original myths of Eshu that I knew as a child have grown even
more colorful. I believe Eshu became so strong in Brazil because he had to
defend himself against this very facile Christian interpretation ...

U: ... the "devil."

W: That's right, and again Wande Abimbola admitted once that these
new aspects of Eshu are now found here in Nigeria as well. It is this movement. . . .

U.   And of course it shows that the whole thing is alive. But you know
what Melville Herskovitz thought about Verger's travels between Brazil and
Nigeria? "Terrible man," he said to me, "he is destroying laboratory conditions."

W: Oh perfect! That's perfect. That's beautiful: it really sums up the
whole lame battle scholarship faced with a living phenomenon.

U: Now the Ogun you created in A Dance in the Forest stresses particularly the creative aspect. He is not merely the warrior, he is also the creator!

W: This was for me very obvious, because the instrument of sculpture
belongs to Ogun; many sculptors are his followers and so is the blacksmith,
again a very creative person, not just an artisan. And then of course there is
the Ijala --he is therefore by implication the father of poetry. All this made
me delve more into the complexity of Ogun and, given my own creative bent,
I explored that a lot more. And also given my own acknowledged combative
strain, I found a fine partner in Ogun. It was a kind of liberation for me, having grown up in a narrow form of Christianity.

U: Which is very simplistic.

W: Very simplistic, everything has to be black or white: you are either
a good child or a bad child. When I grew up and was given a little bit to self-
analysis and introspection, I wondered why I should be inclined towards the
creative—I really feel alive when I am creating—while at the same time I
would readily drop my pen or typewriter without hesitation and pick up whatever combative instrument necessary. . . . Yoruba religion made me see that
there was no contradiction—it was the most normal thing in the world to
have within the same person these two or more aspects.

U: Each orisha contains and bridges contradictions, and human beings
are the same. To pretend otherwise is hypocrisy. People don't realize how
unrealistic Christianity is. Yoruba religion portrays the world as it is and
makes you live with it, the way it is. It teaches you how to turn a dangerous
situation, how to diffuse tension, how to turn a negative situation into something positive even. But in A Dance in the Forest you created another character called Esuoro. I find it hard to relate this figure to any Yoruba
tradition—I am tempted to say you simply invented him.

W: Oh, that was purely dramatic. That is something I have not taken beyond the pages of the book. It's purely dramatic. I created him in the same way, I suppose, in which Puck was created by Shakespeare, taking parts from various mythological beings. As you know: Oro is one of the most intangible beings ... so I fleshed him out, some-how.

U: By far the most important statement you have made about Yoruba culture is your play Death and the King's Horseman. I don't know whether you remember this, but it was Pierre Verger who found out about this famous incident in Oyo. He was even able to verify it, by writing to the District Officer, who was then living in Canada.

W: I do remember that you gave me a kind of summary of the story.

U: I thought that the material was crying out for a play. But for several years, you didn't do anything with it.

W: Well, I wasn't ready for it.

U: I then gave the material to Duro Ladipo who produced Oba Waja in 1964. Then, maybe a decade later you wrote The Horseman. What was it then that prompted you to go back to this material finally? What new insight had occurred? What new preoccupation with Yoruba religion, maybe?

W: That's a question that's always very difficult to answer. Because it has to do with the entire active creative process: gestation, something that takes place on different levels of consciousness or sub-consciousness. But don't forget, I wrote this play in Cambridge, when I was there for a year as a fellow in Churchill College. And it could have been the resentment of the presumption! Because you know in a Cambridge College named after a personality like Churchill, you have encapsulated the entire history of the arrogance of your colonizers; the supercilious attitude towards other cultures, the narrowness, the mind closure—it could be all of that. It was not a year which I enjoyed particularly. There were a few stimulating intellectual contacts, which made it worthwhile; but I think there was the basic underlying question "What the hell am I doing here? What the hell are we doing here?" I felt like a representative; a captured, creative individual having to deal with another culture on it's own terms, in it's own locale. And passing the bust of Churchill on the top of the stairs almost every day—with all that Churchill meant. The big colonial man himself! It could have been all of this that brought back the memory of this tragic representation of the way their culture would always impinge on ours. I suspect that is the way it must have been. I must have been tempted to challenge this: How dare this smugness be! How dare it be exported!

U: They came without the least attempt to come to terms with the culture they ruled.

W: Hardly ever!

U: This was particularly so in Southern Nigeria. They referred to Yorubas and Igbos as riff-raff, whereas Northerners, of course, were gentlemen.

W: Of course, the North appealed to their sense of feudalism.

U: You have given a very plausible explanation for the immediate stimulus that prompted you to write this play. But of course the far more difficult question is: what actually happens in the poet's mind? What are the secrets and maybe subconscious processes that produce the particular images and the particular kind of magic of a play like Death and the King's Horseman? This is almost unanswerable, and many writers would simply refuse to be drawn into any discussion about it. But you have in fact attempted to find a metaphor for the creative process which you described at length in "The Fourth Stage." I am fascinated by that essay because it seems to me that you are giving a very Yoruba explanation and one that seems to have some parallels in Yoruba religious thought. You speak about the artist going on a kind of journey; a trip into another dimension from where he returns with a kind of boon . . . and inspiration . . . but maybe you better summarize it yourself.

W: I think what I was referring to was the mystery of creativity itself. Which is almost like a dare, a challenge of nature's secrets. One goes out almost in the same way in which Ogun cleared the jungle—because he had forged the metallic instrument. He is very much the explorer. The artist is in many ways similar; each time, he discovers a proto-world in gestation; it's almost like discovering another world in the galaxy. The artist's view of reality creates an entirely new world. Into that world he leads a raid; he rifles its resources and returns to normal existence. The tragic dimension of that is one of disintegration of the self in a world which is being reborn always, and from which the artist can only recover his being by an exercise of sheer will power. He disintegrates in the passage into that world. He loses himself and only the power of the will can bring him back. And when he returns from that experience, he is imbued with new wisdoms, new perspectives, a new way of looking at phenomena. I was using Ogun very much as an analogue: what happens when one steps out into the unknown? There is a myth about all the gods setting out, wanting to explore and rediscover the world of mortals. But then the primordial forest had grown so thick, no one could penetrate it. Then Ogun forged the metallic tool and cut a way through the jungle. But the material for that implement was extracted from the primordial barrier.

This I took as a kind of model of the artist's role, the artist as a visionary explorer, a creature dissatisfied with the immediate reality—so he has to cut through the obscuring growth, to enter a totally new terrain of being; a new terrain of sensing, a new terrain of relationships. And Ogun represented that kind of artist to me.

U: I can find parallels to Yoruba concepts here on several levels. The artist as the "creature of dissatisfaction with the immediate reality" is really very reminiscent of the orisha, who starts life as a human being—a king or a warrior—but because of his dissatisfaction with the immediate reality "leads a raid into that other world", losing himself on the way: Shango hanging himself at Koso, Ogun descending into the ground at Ire, Otin turning into a river at Otan Aiyegbaju—all these are examples of the creative human being breaking through the limitations of ordinary human existence.

Of course, the orisha does not return—he undergoes a metamorphosis and becomes a divine being. But he is there to remind us of the existence of that other world, to remind us that we can dare to penetrate, however briefly, that other sphere of existence.

Similarly the olorisha going into trance crosses the border, "rifles the resources" of the divine world and returns with a new understanding. His personality undergoes significant changes through such repeated experiences. The maturity of the old orisha priests, their wisdom and tolerance, their insight into the human mind are the result of these raids into the divine sphere. Am I right in thinking, that this is something very similar—almost identical to the experience you are describing in the "Fourth Stage"?

W: Yes, definitely!

U: I think you can describe the act of the priest who goes into trance also as a creative act; because he has to personify the orisha, recreate him through his performance, through song and dance. So in that sense there may be some real hope left: for a while we must helplessly watch the culture crumble in front of our eyes, there are still some individuals, like yourself, left who can capture something of the spirit of this culture through the very individual process you have described and who can keep the orisha alive in some new form of existence.

W: There is a lot of hope left. I'll give you an example: when I gave a lecture in Ibadan recently titled The Credo of Being and Nothingness, when I explained certain aspects of Yoruba beliefs, the role of the orisha, the reaction, the forcefulness of response which I could see on the faces of the young people was really very encouraging. It was more than just an expression of their misgivings towards the way in which they were brought up, more than just a feeling of deprivation. These young people are really looking for new directions in their lives. I believe there is real hope.

Sangodare Gbadegesin Ajala
Sangodare and Susanne Wenger

The spread of Christianity and Islam and above all, the cancerous growth of Western materialism have destroyed the Yoruba way of life to a very large extent, just as thousands of other cultures world-wide have fallen victim to European economic interests during the last forty years. But Sangodare Gbadegesin Ajala remains one of the last remaining representatives of traditional Yoruba culture, and is one of Nigeria's finest artists.

When Sangodare was born in 1948, Yoruba religion was still very much alive. In his native Oshogbo the ancestral masquerades were still dancing in the market place (albeit in front of the mosque) and in an annual procession fifty or sixty magnificent carved images were taken out of their shrines and carried in procession through the town. The festivals of the ancient gods, particularly those of the river goddess Osun and the thunder god Sango were celebrated with great splendor.

Sangodare's father was a famous Sango priest and dancer, who was a very old man when his first child (Sangodare) was born. He was born in the 1870s and would therefore have experienced Yoruba culture at the height of its power. When he decided, in 1959, to have his eleven-year-old son initiated to become the incarnation of Sango, he must have been fully aware of the huge burden he was placing on the child's fragile shoulders. He must have known that Sangodare would need enormous strength to be the living incarnation of a god in an increasingly hostile world.

Yoruba religion never relied on a book that professed to be an unerring and unchanging truth. Yoruba gods do not manifest themselves through a sacred text, but through a living person, who becomes his incarnation—not unlike a Tibetan lama.

To let the god "ride one's head" requires unusual concentration and strength on the part of the chosen one; it also requires considerable concentration and ritual knowledge on the part of the community of priests who prepare the initiate for his task.

As the community of worshippers is shrinking, and as they have become more and more aware that the future of their way of living is being seriously threatened, their task becomes harder, the effort they must put into an initiation becomes greater each time.

When Sangodare was initiated in 1959/60, important priests traveled from far and wide to Oshogbo to assist in the task.

For one so young to be given such great responsibility in life is unusual. In Sangodare's case his responsibility became even greater, because he had to carry it out in a fast-changing world. He is the first Sango priest who must make a living from another profession. He lives in a community that, as a whole, has little time or respect for his god. Most of his friends and acquaintances are Moslems or Christians, at least nominally so. He is the first Sango priest who has become literate in Yoruba, the first to speak English, the first to have traveled overseas. Rather than withdraw and retreat from the world that has become hostile to the Yoruba gods, he carries his burden proudly and with dignity. He practices his rituals with integrity and has earned the respect not only of his fellow worshippers but of the community at large. His reputation has spread to Cuba, Brazil, and the United States, where descendants of slaves practice adulterated forms of Yoruba religion. He has made several trips to Brazil to help people to find their way back to the true core of the religion.

To bridge two such normally incompatible worlds is a great personal achievement and is proof of Sangodare's integrity and strength. He was helped by two unusual circumstances, however: First, after his father's death, he was taken to Susanne Wenger, to be brought up with several other children she had adopted. Susanne Wenger is an Austrian artist who had herself succeeded in bridging these incompatible worlds, but moving in the other direction: coming from a Western intellectual background she accomplished the giant task of becoming initiated into the Yoruba cult of Obatala (the creator god) without ultimately abandoning her own background. Susanne Wenger has evolved the concept that creation of new Yoruba religious art generates a kind of energy, that can replace the role that elaborate religious rituals once fulfilled.

Sangodare's artistic career is the second powerful influence on his life. Becoming an artist has provided him with a means of communicating with people world-wide. Being an artist, whose work is concerned almost exclusively with his religious experience, Sangodare is able to lead a "modern," virtually international life, without abandoning his roots. In other words, art is for him the bridge between traditional Yoruba wisdom and the changed world of which he has become a part.

As more and more Westerners have come to doubt the values of their own culture, as more and more young people are watching with horror the destruction of the earth that has been wrought by their fathers in a single generation—a like Sangodare may well become a key figure in the spiritual salvage operation which a new generation may embark upon.

Batik in Yoruba Land

Batik is not an ancient craft in West Africa. Various tie-dye techniques and indigo dying have been practiced for centuries, but the use of batik is of recent date.

The Yoruba people refer to any kind of indigo pattern-dyeing as "Adire." The art of Adire was practiced solely by Yoruba women and its sole function was to create items of female clothing—wrappers and head-ties. In the 1950s a Yoruba market was a startling sight: Every woman was dressed in Adire, but the variety of tones produced from a single dye stuff was truly amazing; Indigo, according to the dyeing technique, is capable of producing both cool and warm shades and it ranges from very light greenish blue, to a very deep purplish black.

It is not certain when the Batik variety of Adire was first introduced, but we know for certain that "Adire Eleko" were produced in the 1920s. Unlike the more widely known Indonesian batik, "Adire Eleko" does not use wax as a dye resist, but starch made from Cassava flour.

Susanne Wenger learned this technique in Nigeria and exhibited large pictorial batiks in Paris in 1956. Subsequently she experimented with wax, which allowed her the use of multiple colors.

It is from her that a number of young Yoruba acquired the wax batik technique in the early sixties. Adigun Olosun, Atanda, Isaac Ojo, and Sangodare are well known artists in Nigeria today, but Sangodare is undoubtedly the most inventive and the most successful.

Sangodare On Himself

The autobiographical sketch by Sangodare and Susanne Wenger's recollections of Sangodare's childhood published in the following pages are based on interviews recorded by Ulli Beier in 1985 and 1987 respectively.

I was born in 1948 in Oshogbo. My father was Ajala Atanda, a famous Sango priest. He was the Jagun Sango and a great dancer. During the Ataoja's Sango festival he would perform magic in the palace. By the time you came to Oshogbo, he was very old.

When he was seventy-eight years old, he still had no children. Then during one big festival a priest was dancing and Sango entered his body and he called my father and said: "Ajala, next year you will marry a new wife and she will give birth to a son, whose name will be Sangodare." My father was laughing: "How can you talk like that. I am old enough not to have children any more!"

But the following year he went to a friend's town in Kwara State. The town was called Esao. In the evening he was sitting with his friends, drinking palm wine. They were discussing religion and looking about. Then my father saw my mother walking along the street; and he called after her: "Come, this lady! I love you. I will take you to Oshogbo: I want to marry you." My father was just joking like that.

In the night my mother dreamt about my father. And she thought: "Ah, what can I think?" Then in the morning she told her mother: "I saw an old man. He said he wants to marry me and take me to Oshogbo." My grandmother said: "No problem. You can go there. I like it."

So on the third day, my father met my mother again and they discussed it. Then he married my mother, and when the next Sango festival came, he presented her to the people, and they prayed for her and made a little sacrifice. The following year she was already pregnant. Then, when I was born, they called me Sangodare.

But for five years I never got up! I was crawling about on all fours! For five years I didn't walk. They used medicine, they do this and that—but I was not cured. Then they made sacrifice to Sango, and the Orisa said: "He is my son. Don't give him any medicine, just give him water." Then they took me to the Osun shrine near the river, and they brought me water every morning. Then the next week I started to walk!

In 1955 there was an epidemic in Nigeria: smallpox! Many people got sick, many people died. I too got really sick and my whole body got covered with marks. Then they took us to the farm, about twenty-five children. They made fire in a bamboo tray, because that is one of the medicines. About ten of us survived, and the marks have all disappeared from my body.

In 1960, I think it was in January, my father prepared the Sango initiation for me, and important priests came from all over Yoruba country. Bandele of Otan was there, and the Magba Sango of Ilobu and so many others. Then I had to spend some days in the shrine and after 46 days they brought me out to present me to the people. They took me all round the town, dancing and singing with Bata drummers. We had to stop at the house of all the important Olorisa, and when we came through Ibokun road we stopped to greet "Mama." Then Mama came out and saw me for the first time.

But there, on Mama's verandah, was a woman who was called Bioyin, who had a petty trade and she was selling milk and beans and tobacco; she did a little trading there. Then I saw a small pair of scissors in her tray and I said: "I want to buy this thing, I want to buy this thing." Then there was trouble; they said: "You can't do that!" In the end, Mama bought me the scissors.

Later Baba Olosun brought me to her house to make Ose and I was dancing. By that time you were here.

Then Mama took me to live with her; and I stayed here for many years, but when I had to attend a festival I would go and come back after the ceremonies.

A year after my initiation, my father died. Before he died he told Layi Olosun : "This is my son. You must teach him about our religion. You must teach him how to divine with cowries. " Then Layi brought me here, because he is a close friend of Mama's. Always Mama gave me food and I would be eating. She gave me threepence. Then we came home and I said to Layi: "Baba, I love this woman. Can you arrange for me to live with her?" Layi would say: "You small boy! What are you talking about." So I didn't say anything, because you must respect your elders. Then one day Mama said: "Do you want to stay with me?" I said: "Yes Mama." Then we told Baba Olosun.

So I moved into her house and I have been living here for 24 years. I started to make batik in 1969 with my own idea. But before then I attended the workshop at Mbari with Georgina and Susanne. I was there! But I was very young and I was only playing! I remember we had an exhibition at the end of the workshop and people were dancing. But I didn't know what was good in it then. I was just doing it for fun.

Now in 1969 Susanne had a very old friend, an Osun priest called Baba Lakokan. He had a bad leg; and he was too old to wash his clothes. So Mama was always washing his clothes and I too was doing it. One day I got tired and I said: "Mama, I am not doing it again, he is not my father!" But she said: "You must do it, he is an old man."

Then the third day, I said again: "I am not doing it." Then Mama beat me very well and she said: "Sango, you must go to Ile lyadudu and spend fourteen days. Then after fourteen days I will decide, whether you can come back or not."

Then I returned to Ile Iyadudu in 1970. Then some people there were abusing me always and calling me "Omo Oyinbo." Then I decided not to return to Susanne's house.

Then Susanne decided after fourteen days that the quarrel was over and she called me and said: "Sango, it is enough, come back." But I said: "Mama I won't come back anymore. I want to stay at Ile Iyadudu and learn a trade." And I didn't care that I had no good food—nothing! Then I decided I wanted to learn to read and write, but I could not go to school, because I plaited my hair ; and the teachers refused to let me attend school unless I cut my hair. In those days, if you wanted to got to school, you must be a Moslem or a Christian.

Then I began to teach myself. And anytime I didn't understand something, I would call a small school boy: "Hey boy! What is this?" Sometimes I would get them to read for me; then I memorized it and then I read it and read it and read it again, until I master the reading and the spelling!

Baba Olosun gave me some memory medicine—we have it!—and within just six month I learned everything. And I was really happy now, reading novels and some little books.

And Baba Olosun, whenever one of his friends taught him a new medicine, he would call me and ask me to write it down.

I tried to teach myself English too, but it was very difficult for me, because I had no teacher.

Now during the Nigerian civil war, the people liked the "Kampala," and they were making it everywhere. I saw it in the street. And one day I saw a woman working on it and I said: "Mama, how are you doing it?" And she said: "Ah, it is very hard!" I said: "I want to be your apprentice." Then I watched her and I helped her to make it and she gave me 5 shillings a day, and I took the money to Baba Olosun. Then one day I said to her: "Mama, maybe you have a yard of cloth; I want to make a design for you." Then I went home and melted some candle wax and made a design and dipped it in different colors. When the woman saw it, she said: "Sango, you are master at this thing," and she increased my money to 10 shillings a day.

There was a boy who was a cook in Mama's house, and he said to me: "Why don't you just make batik, I will sell it for you." So I borrowed 30 shillings from him and I bought cloths and I made a batik in five colors. He went to Lagos with my batiks and he came back and said: "The people love it." And he gave me £45. I was very happy. I bought more material and started to make batiks in seven colors. But when I gave them to the boy to sell, he never came back with any money, and so I got fed up.

Then I tried to become a bricklayer, because the woman who was making the Kampala cloth had gone to Ghana and I had no more means of income.

In 1973 I met Mama in the bank, and she said to me: "Sango, are you still in Oshogbo?" And I said: "Yes, I am still in Oshogbo." Then she said: "Don't be annoyed anymore. It was the work of Esu. I was teaching you about life, -that's why I beat you. Come back." I said: "Mama, I don't want to come back, because I need to learn; I am now making batiks myself." Then she said: "Very good, if you want to make batik, I will help you."

So that was how I returned to this house again and now I started to make real batik. I began to have new ideas. In 1975 Mama arranged for one of my works to be included in an exhibition in London. So I made a batik with ten colors for it. From then on, my batiks were shown in different countries overseas, but I never went there.

In 1978 I had my first exhibition at Ibadan, in the Institute of African Studies. It was very successful, people liked my work, and I got money there.

Then I got another exhibition in Ibadan and this time I made batiks with 21 colors. Then I had a one man show at the Goethe Institute in Lagos and I used 23 colors!

I had a lot of exhibitions in Lome, organised by an Austrian businessman, and Mr. Perlinger, who showed my works in Wọrgl, in Austria.

The first time I went abroad was to Brazil: I was invited to the Orisa World Conference in Bahia. They were talking about Yoruba religion and how it is practiced in Nigeria and in Brazil and in Cuba. There I met some people from Sao Paulo and they invited me to return to Brazil the following year in order to make some initiations for them. Altogether now, I have been to Brazil four times.

I have been to many of their "Candombles." They love Orisa very much and there are many white people worshipping Sango! But I have some difficulties with them; because the way they are doing it, they mix it together with other religions from Angola and other parts of Africa.

So one has to compromise, if one wants to make initiations there. They have written to me, asking me to come again. But I wrote back to say: It is not now. First I want to prepare for this exhibition in Vienna, so that I can earn some money. Because when I go to Brazil, I am not taking any money at all from them; I am doing it for my Orisa. Before I went to Brazil for the first time, I asked my Orisa, whether I should go on that trip and he said: "You can go, but don't ask for any money there!"

So that's why I am not going there yet. Once I have had my exhibition, I will spend part of the money to make the Orisa come up in Brazil. They all want to worship Orisa there, the Africans, the Whites, and the Indians. But I don't like the way they are doing it, it is not good. You can find Orisa priests in Brazil who make bad medicine, even to kill a person. That is tabu! An Orisa priest can only make medicine to cure. So I will teach them the right way.

This year I went to Vienna for the first time. Wolfgang Denk had arranged a big exhibition for Susanne and Susanne asked him to send a second ticket, because she did not want to travel alone. At first he wrote to say it was not possible to get another ticket. Then I said: "O.K. I like it. You go there, do a good thing over there and carry our news." But later on the Austrian ambassador came and said he had a ticket for me too: so I was very happy.

Then Mama made her big exhibition and many people came from all over Austria and even many Nigerians came and we had a very good time talking to so many people; and every day we got to another house to make party and have dinner. I carried a couple of batiks with me and people liked them but Wolfgang Denk told me: "Don't sell them. Work more and make a big exhibition." So that's why I am now trying to finish this big work.

In Vienna I saw snow for the first time. It was very cold, but I like it! A great snow: All the trees were white and all the mountains white and some of the small rivers were covered in ice. Too much snow—but I really like it!

Susanne Wenger on Sangodare

I am not good at remembering dates, but I know that Sangodare came to me directly after his initiation. His father was a very famous baba elegun, a very powerful priest, but already ancient. Then Sango suddenly told him that he must marry a new wife and that he would have sons. And it was rather like the story of Abraham and Sarah, because the elegun and his friends laughed, thinking that Sango was merely joking.

But Sango insisted and the Elegun married Sangodare's mother, who was still a very young woman. The oldest of the three children that were born to him was Sangodare.

When the old man felt that he might die any moment, he had his son initiated. Sangodare was still a small boy when they made him the incarnation of Sango, in succession to his father. It was a most dramatic situation. Before the initiation the father kept stroking the boy tenderly, saying, "You are still such a small boy" and the child did not understand what the father was saying to him. But the father knew that the child had to go through this very difficult initiation and he probably foresaw that it would be an unusually strong ritual.

For a while the child had to live a very unusual life in a shrine, after that he was presented to the town. At that time there were still many strong Sango priests in Oshogbo, and many came from far away: the beautiful Iya Sango from Ifon and her friend from Oyo, and priests from Ede, Ilobu, Otan and Ila-Orangun, they all came to take part in this procession.

Everybody was very excited when this child wore plaited hair for the first time, and they were shouting the Oriki of Sango and they laughed and danced and beat the Bata drums with immense energy. Of course, they also came to my house, it was very moving—this little boy who had just gone through such a difficult initiation; I treated him like a real Olorisa and gave him three shillings with my left hand.

Then suddenly I heard the new Baba Sango cry bitterly outside. There was this woman, who was married to Asiru's father ; we called her Bioyin, because she was selling snuff and she always called out "Like honey, like honey. . . ." She was a petty trader, who had a little stand outside our house. In any case, the little Baba Sango had seen a small pair of scissors on her tray; and since he'd always wanted to have scissors but never had been given any, he bought them with the three shillings he had received from me. But the priests said, no, all the money has to go into the same pot and they took the scissors away from him. Well, then I said: "Let the money go into the common fund, and I will buy him the scissors." That impressed him a lot; and also the fact that I treated him with great respect, because at that moment he was the incarnation of Sango. Of course the others treated him with respect too, but then they had to burst out laughing again, because their Sango was so tiny!

Before the procession moved on, Sangodare said, "I am coming tomorrow. Tomorrow I am coming to see you." And I said, "Good." The following day he came, and we greeted him very politely. We had bought o`kà which is one of Sango's favorite foods, and we arranged it all very nicely. The children knelt down to him, as you do for an important person. Then he ate, and when he had finished eating, he said: "I am going to bring my loads. . . ." And then he moved into my house.

He was an incredibly wild child. He was famous for climbing on the roofs and then running through the town across the corrugated iron sheets. That's how he made his short cuts. I remember one day entering a taxi and he asked, "Where are you going?" and I said, "To the post office." And when I got to the post office, he was already there to greet me. Life was always very dramatic with him!

Soon he began to paint; first he made these very rough pictures with emulsion paint on hardboard. I liked them very much; I think I may still have one or two of them. But he destroyed them whenever he could! He tried to provoke me with that, too, because I had expressly forbidden him to do so. He liked to use his paintings as a dust pan! Once I said to him, "It is as if you use yourself as a rubbish pan," which prompted him to it again immediately. I was really annoyed and I gave him a swipe at his head with an exercise book that I happened to hold in my hand. Of course, I didn't really hurt him, but he was outraged and he ran off and away. I remember it precisely: he was wearing a blue velvet gown that I had bought him for his annual Sango festival. With this conspicuous gown he was seen everywhere, but nobody could catch him. For days on end he slept in those shiny tin huts, that had been put up for the coming elections. When no one was at home, he jumped in through the kitchen window and got himself something to eat. Neither the hunters nor the police could catch him; he was much too fast and too clever for them.

Finally Layi Olosun tied on his famous ondè and soon afterwards he came leading Sangodare by the hand. Layi Olosun always appeared, unexpected, whenever I needed him. Like the time when a madman tried to kill me and suddenly he appeared from nowhere and quietly took the raging man by the hand and led him away.

Sangodare stayed another two years with Layi; then I couldn't stand it anymore and said: "We belong together." And I gave him the two rooms which have remained his studio until today. And I said to him: "You are far too strong a person, to simply live in the house with all the children. Take these rooms, live there as you like, and we see each other when we feel like it."

Then he came back and started seriously to work on batiks. He had often enough watched me do it before; it was a perfectly organic situation. He understood me far too well and he was far too intelligent even to be tempted to copy me. The only thing he adopted from me, maybe, was this way of letting your imagination really go wild. That was good, because he could live out this power, this ritual power that he has. He is the perfect example of what I call "art as ritual."

At the same time he also started to learn "mekaniki." As a small child he always carried around dangerous iron objects; he was always holding some sharp piece of metal in his hand; and given his temperament that made me pretty nervous. Then I said: "Since I can't send you to school, you have to learn some trade, and if Ogun is so strong in your life that you always walk around with iron—woulddn't it be a good idea if you became a mekaniki? Because there is no future anymore in becoming a blacksmith."

It seemed the right thing to do, because Sangodare was very clever with his hands, and he still is; he can even repair watches! Unfortunately, the mechanic we apprenticed him to didn't teach him much; because he also ran a business renting out bicycles, and whenever one of his clients stayed away too long, he sent out Sangodare to retrieve the bicycle. We soon realized that he would not learn a trade in that place. He also made an attempt to become a carpenter, but that didn't work out either.

I could not send him to school, because as an adósù he had to have plaited hair, and of course he also wore an òjé on his wrist. In those days the teachers shaved the hair of children and they tore all religious symbols from their bodies. I could not expose him to such a traumatic experience. I once took him to University College Hospital in Ibadan, and before they even removed his bandage, they tried to cut his hair. We could only stop it, because we had some personal friends among the doctors. Schools and hospitals saw themselves as pioneers of "progress" in those days, and they did everything they could to eliminate the "backward" Yoruba religion.

Even though he never went to school, Sangodare taught himself to read and write Yoruba and in the meantime he even learned excellent English. I remember him lying on his belly in that room up there, with a book in front of him, and he wouldn't answer anybody who talked to him. For a few weeks he concentrated totally onto his task. An Adosu, like him, can muster great power of concentration.

The young people also teach each other, and this works so well, because there are some really fine young people who have grouped themselves around Sangodare. There are no class differences amongst his friends: some are peasants and others are university students, but he is always recognized as the strongest. Often they discuss things until late at night, and they always find some worthwhile topics.

Sangodare now lives almost exclusively from his batik. He has developed his own technique. He does not use wax as hot as I do, because he does not want to have as much craquelé. He sometimes paints the colors on with a brush, whereas I use almost exclusively dying techniques.

His themes are derived almost exclusively from the Orisa myths, which play such a central part in his life; and he creates these batiks with a wildness and an explosive power, which are typical for the Orisa whose incarnation he is.

Death and King's Horseman
A Conversation between Wole Soyinka and
Ulli Beier

INTRODUCTION

Wole Soyinka's play Death and the King's Horseman is based on an historical incident that took place in the Yoruba city of Oyo in 1946. According to an ancient custom the Elésin Oba, the commander of the King's cavalry, was to follow the deceased Alafin (King) into the other world, so that he could lead him across the final threshold into the world of the ancestors.

As soon as an Elésin Oba has this important title conferred on him, he commissions the splendid gown in which he is going to die, when the appointed time comes.

Throughout his lifetime he enjoys great power and privileges. When the day comes on which he has to follow his master, he dresses in the gown of death, dances through the town with drummers and praise-singers and is given the highest honors by the entire population. As the sun begins to set he returns home, sits down amongst his relatives and friends, looks into the sinking sun, leans back and dies—by an act of will. His death is the climax and fulfillment of his entire life.

When the ritual was to be celebrated in 1946, the British District Officer went out and arrested the Elésin Oba and threw him into jail because, according to British law, attempted suicide is a criminal offence. The Elésin Oba's son, who was at that time a trader in the Gold Coast (now Ghana) rushed home in order to bury his father. On seeing him alive he was so horrified by this abomination, that he committed suicide on the spot. The Elésin Oba in desperation over his failure to accomplish his sacred task also committed suicide—but now it was too late to accomplish his ritual mission.

These are the historical events, as they were originally researched and related to Pierre Verger in the early sixties. The conversation between Wole Soyinka and Ulli Beier touches on some of the cultural, religious and ethical issues raised in the play.

U: In your introduction to Death and King's Horseman you issue some very fierce warnings to would-be producers. You tell them in no uncertain terms that you do not wish the District Officer to become the key figure by making him "the victim of a cruel dilemma." Above all you object to that facile cliché of the "conflict of cultures."

As for the role of the District Officer, it seems to me that Pilkington is too banal a character to be even capable of becoming the "victim of a cruel dilemma." He is far too convinced that he is right.

The other point you raise is more complex. Because on the surface, at least, there is a conflict of cultures here. Do you see this play as an internal conflict of Yoruba culture, that is merely sparked off by an external event?

W: First of all, there is a background to this particular note: it was written after an extraordinary blurb on my novel Season of Anomy. I did not think that it would be possible for any human intellect to read A Season of Anomy and say this novel was about the conflict of the old and the new African culture. As you know we have been through this a lot. Many poets in a certain period have indulged in that shallow cliché. They could not see any other issue at all and some of it was really awful literature.

U: Dennis Osadebey : "My simple fathers in childlike faith believed all things" and so on ....

W: Mabel Imoukhuede!

U: But she basically only wrote one poem in that mood.

W: But the others carried on for so long. We have been discussing that phenomenon and its short-lived influence a lot. We thought we had dealt with it. Then years later this novel was published in America and I could not believe what was written so authoritatively and implanted on my book. Not just a review—which I could ignore.

But my book was actually made to carry the burden of this reductionist summation. So that's why the introduction to Death and the King's Horseman was so strong—I wanted to caution everybody!

But having said that and explained the source of it—I also consider it true and it has historical justification. For example: one of the major wars of the nineteenth century was triggered off by a very similar event; in this case it was the Àrè`mo`, the eldest son of the Aláàfin, who refused to commit suicide, and he was even supported in this by his father, whom he was to succeed to the throne.

U: Yes, it was Aláàfin Atiba, who in 1858 abolished the age-old custom that the Àrè`mo`, his eldest son, had to die with him. For many centuries the Àrè`mo` was considered as the King's co-regent, but he had to pay for this sharing of power and privilege by dying with the king, just as the Elés`in Oba died. Atiba loved his eldest son because he had been a very loyal son who had shared many dangers with him, even before he became the king. So he got the support of the powerful war chiefs of Ibadan to help him change the custom.

W: But Kurumi the ruler of Ijaye declared this to be an abomination! He never accepted this change, and when Atiba died and Adelu was actually installed he went to war over it. But what is significant about this is the fact that this King was not a Christian. There is no record of European or missionary influence on his decision. In other words: this was a revolt against certain acceptances within the traditional set up. So if you want to look for the root of certain tragic experiences in Yoruba history, you don't have to go outside. The story of the E`lé`s`in O`ba, which you told me years ago, takes on a global dimension and this enables me to interrogate the morality and the history of those who point the finger on the Yoruba as being barbaric and having primitive customs; it gives me that combative dimension to examine the whole meaning of existence and how different people interpret it. It enables me to look at the conflict of honor and obligation. You are quite right in saying that at the beginning I do make the District Officer rather a cardboard figure, but towards the end I do hope that I succeeded in giving him some moment of dignity. He is now confronted by a situation, which he has never in his life anticipated and he responds to it with a little more sensibility. I even make him best the E`lé`s`in O`ba in an argument utilizing a proverb of his own people against him—to silence him!

U: "The elder grimly approaches heaven and you ask him to bear your greetings yonder; But do you really think he makes the journey willingly?" But you are very right in saying that a culture constantly transforms itself and a situation arises when an age old custom becomes difficult to carry out and eventually becomes unacceptable. I remember that in the mid-fifties, the Ogun worshippers in Oshogbo found it hard to carry out the sacrifice of a dog and they employed somebody from outside the cult to do it for a fee. Another, rather more severe example, is the conflict between politicians and traditional rulers in the mid-fifties. Kurumi of Ijaye, as we know, was unable to dislodge Oba Adelu and the people of Oyo accepted the new ruling that the Arè`mo should not die. They insisted, however, that in future the Arè`mo` should be sent into exile after his father's death and that he should be disqualified from succeeding his father. Now you remember that in the 1950s the Action Group government ordered an enquiry into the affairs of the Aláàfin of Oyo. The British commissioner could not find much evidence of the alleged corruption and exonerated him. But the politicians did not accept the verdict and they sent the King into exile in Ilesha. Then they went ahead and brought the Arè`mo` back from exile to be installed as the next Aláàfin.

In other words they installed the one person who was not supposed to become King! I sometimes wonder whether this was done from ignorance of the customs or whether it was a deliberate, calculated attempt to destroy the institution of kingship.

W: I think this was a deeply calculated move to break a certain mould, a certain tradition, through an act that amounted to an "abomination" in the eyes of many. They were a very anti-feudalist party. They operated not merely through such negative, aggressive means, but operated also by catapulting some powerful monarchs, like the O`ò`ni of Ife into the political arena where they now came under control and became themselves enticed and absorbed in the new dispensation. They were very wily—they knew what they were doing. And even from the very beginning—before they officially embraced socialism—they were at heart pretty republican.

U: Now, the play has several controversial issues and one of them is found right in the first scene: I am referring to the demand of E`lé`s`in to have a new bride, before he follows the Aláàfin into the other world. I don't know whether this goes back to some tradition or whether it is merely a dramatic device that you invented. One thing I know is that the E`lés`in O`ba enjoyed certain privileges during his life time and one of them was that he could claim any woman—like the O`ba himself

W: Oh yes: the traditional gbé`sè`le—"I place my foot on her," a privilege that applied not only to the reigning monarch, but also to the Arè`mo` and the E`lé`s`in O`ba. The head of the King's cavalry could go to the market at any time and demand any goods or any woman. And you would be surprised how many Oba are still trying it today. I know one instance in recent years—I talking about five years ago. This ruler went to visit his daughter on the university campus in Ibadan, she came to see him with a friend, a girl who was already married. The Oba sent two of his chiefs with staffs of authority to her the following day, summoning her to his palace, and he told her in plain terms that he had decided to marry her. When she explained to him that she was already married, he said: "Oh that's alright: I'll send for your husband and let him know what is my decision." The girl refused, but he harassed her so much that in the end she had to send a delegation of elders to him asking him to desist.

U: Yes, but surely whatever the traditional privilege of the E`lé`s`in was, there is a clear indication in the play that at that moment this was not appropriate. Because at that moment his thoughts should have been somewhere else.

W: Oh, of course!

U: His indulgence in fact weakened his resolve.

W: He himself actually admits that at a later point.

U: He blames his new wife for the "mystery of the sapping of his will."

W: But my position on this is somewhat dual. First there is a kind of image in my mind. There are the Abàmì O`mo`, the supra normal children who from childhood on are considered Alàgbà—grown-ups. They have unusual privileges. They sit down with adults and participate in the conversation. Tunji Oyelana has such a child. She utters the most unbelievably perceptive statements about things. There are children like that, and of course, Yoruba society has a place for them. Naturally I have always wondered about such children and in a drama like this, when human weakness comes into conflict with a sense of duty and with one's perception of being virtually one step away from the land of the ancestors, there is a hovering sense of symmetry.

U: Between the child that has just come from the other world and the old man who is about to go there?

W: Yes. All this is just part of the metaphysical aesthetics operating in my mind. I try to use this ambivalently—also as an expression of the man's weakness. In other words: how do I make it happen? Of course, I could have just made the woman donate the daughter to the E`lé`s`in, and not make him feel guilty about snatching her from someone else, but then I would lose the element of humanity in the man. He becomes self indulgent—with the connivance of the entire city—he tries to prolong his sensuality, which is his definition of his being at that moment. I put myself in the man's position—not just as a human being, but also as a product of that particular environment, both the physical environment and the spiritual one. And at the back of my mind there is the constant awareness of this Abàmì O`mo`—the extraordinary child. At that moment I could not resist the proposition that the loss of this person from the community would be compensated for by the planting of a seed; not just in the sense that one man dies and a child is born, but in the sense that this child will also be something special, something extraordinary. A suggestion. . . .

U: . . . that the child would become an Abàmì O`mo`. . . . Of course E`lé`s`in himself is a very unusual person.

W: And he believes also that he is creating something very unusual.

U: The child could even be the same person reborn. After all, the E`lé`s`in says to Iyaloja : "let my going be like the death of the plantain," meaning that he will renew his existence constantly like the plantain does.

W: It could be the same, but in any case it would be a very unusual person. So, yes, there is this man's weakness and he indulges himself, but at the same time, when Iyaloja says: "What I hear is no longer the voice of the living. . . ."

U: She has to honor that.

W: This is something different, this is not just a self-indulgent old man. He has prepared himself for this in the proper way and he is ready to do it. I wanted to leave it as ambiguous as possible: all the various suggestions.

U: The point is that Yoruba culture can produce the kind of mind that is capable of performing such a feat. . . .

W: . . . to sustain it, to totally believe in it and find it viable, and even to hold it up against another culture. In fact one thing that convinces me of the validity of such a world-view is the fact that it can stand up to the alien, with its arrogance, its claim of superiority which is not based on any evidence. In some sense the District Officer and his interference reinforces the values of that society. This has been true for centuries. There are converts, no doubt. But on the whole—look at Yoruba society even today. Even in Lagos that society still holds on to certain elements of tradition.

U: Let us return to the District Officer. It is true that towards the end, you have made him more sensitive, more responsive. But he never grasps the simple fact that the value of life is not its length. To him the prolongation of life is what life is all about. Even a meaningless life must be prolonged at all costs. It has not occurred to him that life has a natural span in which it must fulfill itself. . . .

W: Yes, but the problem is that in Europe the dissidents from this point of view, the so called euthanasia volunteers—they are also problematic, like that doctor in the United States who virtually sets up suicide gadgets to enable people to kill themselves. I followed that very carefully. There are doctors who are being faced with the evidence of the uselessness of existence at a certain point, whether it is age or terminal disease or coma, I respect their point of view very much. But unfortunately they cannot conceive of how to integrate their philosophy into society. The result is this American doctor who hawks around his suicide machine. That in itself is for me part of the decadence of society. If you read his pronouncements—he's a man on an ego trip, a man on a power trip! He's a man who enjoys wielding power over life and death. He's invented his little machine, he's appearing before the cameras and he says: take me to court! He does not know that this requires a communal answer. That it requires a communal mental reformation. This seems to confirm the belief in Yoruba society: that life has an end if there is no more purpose left in it.

U: And again: death is painful when the person was too young to have fulfilled his purpose. Death can be joyful, if the person has fulfilled his life. And who can have a more complete life than the E`lé`s`in O`ba, whose death is not an accident but the climax of his life? I cannot imagine such a total fulfillment in any other society.

W: Right, I cannot think of any. . . .

U: And then there is this other misunderstanding that is embedded in the European position. There is the notion that the E`lé`s`in O`ba is enslaved to some bloodthirsty potentate who forces him to commit suicide. But on the other hand, the District Officer with his superior morality, arrests E`lé`s`in because he is committing a crime—not against himself—but against the Queen of England!

W: That is correct. He is depriving her of one of her subjects!

U: How absurd can you become? Is it not a worse enslavement if the Queen can say, "You can't kill yourself, because your life belongs to me"?

W: That's why I made Sergeant Amusa—who is the comic figure in this play—insist that it is a crime: "You are committing death, its against the law!" But whose law?

U: But that was the position: you actually got jailed in Britain for attempting suicide.

W: Yes, until recently. It was not treated as a form of disturbance or illness. Nobody was looking for the cause: it was simply treated as a crime. The first time I read about it was when I was a student in England. Somebody tried to commit suicide and was jailed. It blew my mind! Now in Nigeria there was a similar case. The judge was obliged to sentence him to three months, but if you read the judgement you could see that there was a very different attitude. No moral indignation. The judge was trying to help. He told the man: life is not as bad as all that. You have a family, you have friends. Try and make a new start. Maybe, he said, these three months will be a time of reflection for you. It was a humane attitude.

U: Europeans have another difficulty with this play: they cannot believe that the man actually dies by an act of will. They are convinced that he must take poison. I have no difficulty with this at all. Having lived in Nigeria for so long, I know that people are trained to develop certain faculties of the mind which our society has always suppressed.

W: I have experienced many similar incidents with persons quite close to me. I know that wives decide to die after their husbands and mothers after their children. There was a time when my sister was very ill and it looked as if she might never recover. She had been operated on and for days she was suspended between life and death. My mother used to sit by her bedside, watching her. And when I visited my sister in hospital, I could tell that the woman had made up her mind: If my sister was not going to survive that illness, she would go before long. She would certainly not remain alive to see one of her children dying. I could tell, it was very obvious: the way she sat there, sighing from time to time and the way she looked at me when I came in. She seemed to be saying: fate has played a dirty trick on me. Not long after my sister had recovered, my mother and her circle of friends held a feast. My late friend Femi Johnson was there and he observed the things between the two of us. She had cooked some special vegetables, some Efo Sokoyokoto. She was serving around this vegetable, and it was like a communion. When she came to me I refused to take any of it. And she said: "Alright—that is your business." She was implying: "I know you know why I am doing this; if you don't want any of it—that is your business." I just turned away. I knew that woman has made up her mind and I wasn't going to partake in it.

Not long after that, I was travelling to Ghana. I was teaching in Ife at the time. It was an early flight and I was standing in a queue a long time before the counter opened. When I approached the counter, I suddenly picked up my bag and said, "I am not travelling." I told the driver, "We are returning to Ife." I went back to my house and I sat there for a long time. I wasn't sure why. I hadn't spelled it out. I just knew I wasn't going to travel. I sent the driver to pick up my mail and shortly after that Yemi Ogunbiyi came to the house. He started talking to me in a consoling voice and I said to him: "What are you talking about?" Then he said: "Oh—I thought you had heard!" That was the moment when I understood that my mother had died! But that is not the end of the story. I had spent the previous night in Ibadan with the Aboyades. So when the message came, I had already left Ife. People were looking for me everywhere. They went to all my friends in Lagos. By the time they came to the Aboyade's house I had gone; but Mrs. Aboyade kept saying to her husband: "Wole has not traveled." He said: "Don't talk nonsense. He left before 6 o'clock this morning." But she insisted: "No, he hasn't traveled."

So you see it is not uncommon for Yoruba people to decide on the time of their death. Sometimes they call their family together. They distribute their property among them and then they go. Or they do it more secretively, like my mother.

U: It reminds me of another recent incident. You know that Asiru Olatunde, the Oshogbo artist, died recently? He had been ill for sometime, and his daughter Sinawu got very worried. Every weekend she came up from Lagos to visit him. One day he said to her: "You don't have to come here every week to check up whether I am still alive. I am going to die next Saturday at five o'clock." And he went exactly at that hour.

W: Yes, yes. I know very precise announcements like that.

U: Then there are the very old olórìshà who have acquired tremendous spiritual power during their lives. They are so old that their body has nearly wasted away but their mind is very active and very strong, and they rule the household with great power—lying on their mat. When they decide it is time to go, they send their eldest son to the farm or the bush and say, "Dig under such and such a tree. And when you find this medicine that I have buried there, destroy it." The moment the medicine is destroyed, the old priest releases his hold on life.

W: There are these various moments for cutting through the thread of life. In Death and the King's Horseman it is the dance of death, through which the transition is accomplished. But it is not only old people who can accomplish this. There are even children. . . .

U: Àbíkú!

W: Yes, the àbíkú not only threaten to die, they sometimes announce the precise time of their death. They threaten and suddenly go. But the abàmí do it more gently. They may say to their mother: "I hope you won't mind. I hope you won't worry too much. I will be going at such and such a time. . . ."

U: Of course, the real tragedy in this play is not death, but the man's failure to accomplish death. Elé`s`in has to face the horrendous fact that he could not accomplish it and that in the history of the Yoruba he was the first person to fail. The sense of continuity is very strong in the culture and even in less potent situations—say during an annual sacrifice for Ogun—the people pray, "We have met here today and we have done it again, as our forefathers have done it; and we pray that we shall meet again next year to perform this sacrifice." For somebody to suddenly realize that he cannot do what he was chosen to do, that he cannot accomplish what he had prepared for all his life. . . .

W: ... it is the end of his life.

U: More than that, even: it is the end of the community itself, up to a point. I have witnessed situations that were not dissimilar to this. Many of the feats olórìshà accomplish during ritual performance can only be achieved if the entire community are concentrating on this one action. And if that kind of communal concentration is not there any more, then the individual performer can not carry it any more. I am thinking of the bàbá e`lé`gùn S`àngó for example, during the annual Shango festival.

I have recently seen a Shango ceremony in Ilobu. Ten years ago these festivals in Ilobu were mind-blowing events. But now nothing happened. The small crowd that had gathered was part curious, part hostile. They did not participate in the event. The handful of priests could no longer evoke the power of the god. Shango did not manifest himself. The ceremony was a sham.

I remember even in the fifties, when such feasts were still very powerful, how disturbing the presence of a single alien person was. I never took Europeans or upper-class Nigerians into such ceremonies. But when one of them found his way there by chance, I felt extremely disturbed by the alien presence. How much more disturbing must they have been to the person who had to carry the burden of the performance.

W: Yes, I made this point in one of my essays in Myth, Literature & the African World. What I tried to do is to define the thin line between the possessed actor and the possessed representative of a god. That very grey area, when the ritual role that has already been predetermined is carried out almost with the precision of a rehearsed piece, but indicating that the possibility only exists when the potency of the crowd -that is the communicant chorus has reached a certain height, a certain level, a certain pitch. Then it becomes the reinforcement of the individual. They transmit their own communicant force onto the head of that individual, and at that moment there is no question at all that the individual becomes the voice of the entire people. It's like the transfer of all the individual potencies to the protagonists and the protagonists move into the arena of the gods. But for him, to attain that level when he becomes the embodiment of the deity—where he crosses the threshold into the world of the deity—it requires the complete and total potency of that communicant crowd.

That is for me the real meaning of the chorus in ritual Yoruba theater. It's not just people repeating refrains and sympathizing and empathizing with the individual going through his travails. No, the chorus is in fact the force which enables an actor to become the embodiment of the role.

U: The proximity between religious ritual and some kinds of theatrical performance that you are talking about, became very evident in the late Duro Ladipo. Over the years his performances of Oba Koso became more and more like ritual and he became more and more a personification of Shango.

W: That's right. And Duro, having separated the audience from the stage, compensated

for it by the charge which, through rehearsal, he had given his actors, who were   equally possessed. They were oblivious of the audience. Something was taking place on that stage which could use the audience, but which did not depend upon it. It was Duro himself, his wife Abiodun, Tijani Mayakiri, and Ademola Onibonokuta who between them carried this charge. I believe you were not in Nigeria when Duro died, but did you hear what happened...

U: Yes, thunder!

W: Unseasonable! And of unprecedented dimension. It was incredible. Such incidents really make you wonder. . . .

U: But let me come back to E`lé`s`in. Was he being carried by his chorus? Or was the crowd wavering?

W: Oh no! The support was there. It had not reached its climax, before the intrusion   came. But there is no doubt that, left alone, he would have accomplished his task. He was ready, he was prepared. And again: he could have made it in spite of this intrusion if, however, his weakness had not been present.

U: The terrible thing is that, once such an ancient ritual cycle is broken, it can never be revived again. This is really frightening. Because for centuries a powerful ritual has been carried out that binds the community together, and that strengthens its ties with the ancestors. Then something interferes which, in itself, is rather trivial, and the person causing it is himself rather banal; and yet this trivial incident has this enormous negative power.

W: Yes, it is often the trivial incident that has the most profound and far-reaching consequences! And that's why for me the play is not just a thing in itself; it's a parable. A parable for many things that have happened to Yoruba society. A parable of history.

U: There is a photograph in Ajisafe's History of Abeokuta that shows the Aláké Gbadebo with Governor MacGregor. The Aláké is a giant of a man, not physically, but spiritually. A really powerful man. And next to him is the British Governor, pale, spindly, in a kilt, looking a trifle silly, perhaps. And yet this man, through his negative thinking, can destroy the whole powerful and meaningful world that his opponent stands for!

W: Of course we must never forget that the colonialists were able to utilize the dissidents in other societies, who have their own motivations, their own ambitions. You don't just do it frontally, with guns. You can rely on the meanest, on the weakest individual to exploit the situation. But basically every society carries within it the possibility of change, positive or negative. And that's why every society must constantly reexamine itself, its values, its customs, its procedures, so as to reduce as much as possible these drastic changes, these insertions of alien solutions to their problems.

U: West African societies were in a relatively strong position to handle such processes, because of their very size, their highly organized political structures, and their flexibility. In the tiny communities of Papua New Guinea, these confrontations were much more dramatic. A typical case is the village of Hopaiku in the Papuan Gulf. In 1930 the missionaries had made very little impact. There were only about 30 converts in a population of several hundreds. But one night, the Christians went and burnt down the sacred Eravo, the ceremonial house in which all powerful objects were kept. The next morning the elders sat down together and discussed the crisis; and they came to the conclusion that there was little point in re-erecting the Eravo. The place had been desecrated; the community was divided; the taboos had been broken. "Our ancestors," they said, "have protected us all the time until now, but they are powerless against these newcomers." Very few cultures have taken such a conscious decision. . . .

W: It's like cultural suicide.

U: But basically it's a process everybody goes through.

W: Yes, but on different levels of gradation. People may come back and pick up pieces, may realize that there are some things that they really need after all—and then these pieces grow again, but perhaps in a stunted form like an amputated tail of a lizard. But the Yoruba and the Orisha seem to have been singularly well adapted for this kind of situation—partial suicide and then again resurgence with greater profundity in certain unassailable aspects of their culture.

U: The flexibility of Yoruba culture has been quite exceptional. If you look at the Yoruba Orisha, you will find that the Yoruba have absorbed cultural elements from all directions: Shango has strong connections with Tapa in the north; Sonpona comes from Atakpame in Togoland! Many elements have been woven into a complex tapestry with different threads overlaying each other. Look at the thunder god alone: there is Shango the royal figure from Oyo—but in some villages in the Republic of Benin Shango is a woman and the wife of the thunder god Jakuta! Then there is Oramfe, the Ife thundergod, who probably preceded them all. It is this very capacity to absorb different cultural elements that has given Yoruba society its rich texture.

W: Another good example is the Igunnuko, many Yoruba don't even know any more that they have adapted this masquerade from the Nupe.

U: We have been talking at length about the difficulties Europeans had with this play. What about America? I know that the critics could not make much sense of it, but what about your Black American cast?

W: Have I never told you this? In Chicago, the phenomenon of possession became so prominent that some of the actresses and some of the actors had to be permanently exempted from the death scene—because they just fell into trance! The girl who played Mrs. Pilkington, for example, she had to keep a distance from that scene back stage, otherwise she was seized by the most weird sensations. She just felt her head swelling: she found herself being transported in a very different world. She used to go very far away, so she could not hear the music on the stage. But as for actual physical possession—that was not funny at all. Even in New York—the girls were all born and bred in that big city, and yet I had to choreograph them out of it. When the death dance began, I just had to move them out of hearing. One girl in particular: she really scared us one day because we could not bring her round again till the end of the play.

We were losing our chorus! So I had to think up some device to counteract this: I gave them kola nut and orogbo to put under their tongue and I told them that the moment the emotion started they should bite and chew it slowly, so that the bitter taste in their mouth should to an extent counteract the intense sensibility of the moment. It worked for some of them. And one final thing: One night, I was told a white woman in the audience became possessed and she had to be carried out.

U: What does it signify? No doubt you must have used very evocative music.

W: I had Tunji Oyelana with me and Yomi Ogunleye and we worked very hard to get the right tonality and rhythm to get a numinous effect.

U: At the same time I feel that they were ready: there was something lacking in their lives. They must have been highly receptive to start with.

W: Definitely, because a possession cannot be forced on anybody. You have to open yourself to this possibility.

U: I have come across only one case when a person went into a violent state of trance—against her will, as it were. This was at Ibadan in the mid-fifties. There was a British architect who was an ardent and, I must say, ruthless collector of antiquities. On one occasion he entered a compound in Ibadan, where he heard some drumming. There was a ceremony going on, which appeared to be of a more intimate nature. Most Yoruba festivals are very public, but apparently this one was not, and he was asked to leave. However, he wouldn't budge. Perhaps he was hoping to locate some carvings which he might purchase later. The celebrants became visibly annoyed, but that did not appear to worry him. Suddenly his wife became very disturbed. "Please take me home," she said. "Something strange is happening to me. My head feels like its growing big, and it seems to have separated from my body." The husband got alarmed and took her home immediately, but in the car she began to talk -incomprehensibly and incessantly.

W: Speaking in tongues!

U: Yes, and she continued for three days and three nights until the priest, who must have imposed this state on her, released her.

W: It is very taboo to use your spiritual powers in this way, but the priest, whoever he was, acted under extreme provocation.

U: One final thing. This European notion of "suicide" is very far removed from the ritual that takes place in Death and the King's Horseman. If you look at the mythology about the Orisha, there is always some form of so-called "suicide" involved. Shango actually hangs himself. Ò`tin throws herself on the ground and becomes a river. Olúorogbo ascends to heaven on a chain, and Ogun descends into the bowels of the earth. In each case there is a metamorphosis from one form of existence to another. It always arises from a sense of tragedy: from a feeling that without this transition you cannot become what you are meant to become.

W: You have come to the end of your mission in this particular existence. How you come about that knowledge varies. But as you pointed out, it is usually in the tragic mode.

       And it is true that tragedy in Yoruba mythology and culture is not perceived as the termination of existence. Yoruba tragedy exists in a world that believes very much in the interflux and almost equal partnership or collaboration between the living and the world of the ancestors.

It believes that one world cannot exist without the other. If you have a world which accepts this totally, the word "suicide" is meaningless. The tragic experience then leads to a new sense of awareness.

The Yoruba mythology of the Àbíkú, the Abàmì O`mo`, the Òrìshà of anthropomorphic origin, all speak of a particular perception of life which contradicts the very simplistic European translation of "tragedy" as something terminal and of no benefit to the communicant chorus. In Yoruba tragedy the chorus imbues the protagonist with the very energy that leads to his transformation and his eventual return to the living. This is really the essence of the Yoruba perception of living. That is why the Egúngún come out in our midst as a reminder of the world of our ancestors: People realize that there is a man underneath the mask, but it is a symbolic representation. It may require less energy, a lesser act of the will than, say, the priest who becomes the embodiment of Shango. But at the same time, you know, after going through the ritual in the sacred grove, some Egúngún have to be restrained, when they come out in the mask. So its a whole world of perception. Suicide in European terms is a negative act. It is of no interest except for the individual concerned, and it's terminal.

What we are talking about in Death and the King's Horseman is an experience of an entirely different kind: a widening of the horizon, a progression from one sphere of existence to another.

IV.
ART

Youruba Aesthetics
A Conversation Between Rowland Abiodun and Ulli Beier

U: This spectacular exhibition of Yoruba Art, in the Museum Rietberg here, has sparked off a whole new discussion on Yoruba aesthetics. But so far the discussion has centered entirely on art, and nothing has been said at all about the concept of beauty in the everyday life. For example, would Yorubas talk of a " beautiful" flower?

R: I don't think so.

U: Compare that to the cultures in Papua New Guinea, where people constantly decorate their hair with flowers, where they hang garlands round their neck, where they use flowers as color! They even plant flowers along the highway to beautify the road!
On the other hand, for Yorubas a plant must either be edible or it has to have some medicinal use; otherwise they don't care about them. I have not seen Yorubas planting flowers for decoration. The only tree they might plant in a town is the *peregun* (Dracaena Fragans) because it has certain magical qualities and its presence is needed in many shrines.

R: That's right.

U: So there is a completely different aesthetic feeling here.

R: Well, aesthetics in everyday life among the Yoruba has to start again from *ìwà*. The concept of *ìwàlewà* goes beyond artistic things. It goes to the very core of a person' s identity, of his *being,* his character, his behavior.

U: Maybe we can apply that to plants. Do you remember that outside the gate to the Osun grove there were three mighty trees? These trees were interlinked in their crowns. They made a very powerful group: they were very sacred and you really felt you were in the presence of *orìsà*. The European visitors invariably said: "What beautiful trees." But Susanne Wenger used to say: perhaps we simply call such trees "beautiful" in our culture, because we are incapable of understanding or defining the spiritual being of such a tree.

One night one of those trees suddenly fell to the ground and to the Osun worshippers that was a great disaster. They then commissioned a carving to be placed in the Osun shrine at the king's market—as a replacement for the tree. Perhaps the spirit of that tree had to be transferred to that ère.

R: It has to do with the concept of *completeness.* The Yoruba say: If two people go on a journey and only one of them returns, the one who returns lonely will feel ill at ease. It's just like *Ibejì:* two of them come into the world. If one twin dies, you have to make an image to complete the pair. Otherwise the life of the survivor will be in jeopardy....

U: Because if the completeness is not restored in this world, it will have to be restored in the other world.

R: Exactly! Only completeness can give you assurance. The falling tree has left a gap; you are in a state of suspense. You are ill at ease. Because that tree was seen as a spirit tree. A tree has power. Where can that power go? You have to give it ahome. Think of the Ogboni images, too: in the *èdan ògbóni* there is always a pair, male and female, linked by a chain. The Yorubas have never had the concept, that man was created separately from woman... they are always thought of as having been created together.

U: Unlike the Bible, where the woman was merely a divine afterthought— a divine mi*stake,* to be precise; because after all it was woman who destroyed the original divine concept of the world.

R: Whereas in a Yoruba shrine you find mostly *a pair* of images: a man and a woman always go together.

U: Let me ask you about another aspect of beauty: the beauty of women! Because, surely, men must see certain aspects of beauty in a woman, that have nothing to do with character, that are purely physical, that have to do with forms and shapes and   colors. I know one such criterion of beauty, which is often represented on carvings, especially on Ifè bronzes: they are fine parallel lines round the neck. They are referred   as   "natural   necklaces." Another is a gap in the upper front teeth: that is also often represented in wood carvings. Now, what other criteria are there?

R: In the *Ifá* divination verses we have a brief comment on this:

> *Whiteness enhances the beauty of teeth*
> *as rings enhance the beauty of the neck*
> *and as heavy breasts enhance the beauty of a woman*

U: The carvers do indeed represent a woman's breast always full and pendulous...they are the breasts of a woman who is feeding a baby.

R: Of course, "heavy" here means "heavy with milk."

U: The beauty lies in the fact that the woman has fulfilled her function as a mother...which is very different from the European concept, where even grandmothers attempt to look like girls and where some women feel that feeding a child "spoils'their breast.

The different concepts of beauty here have to do with different attitudes to age: in Europe, "youth" is a highly overrated ideal, not only women but also men take a great effort to "stay young." they actually fight the natural aging process. Whereas the Yoruba respect the wisdom of age, and appreciate the calm and equanimity it can bring. . . .

R: Old age is seen as the climax of life! But there is another criterion of beauty which has to do with grace. You know the popular saying:

> *A person who carries a basket of eggs on his head*
> *must walk with measured steps.*

U: But actually the implication is that a person should always walk as if he was carrying a basket of eggs on his head! He should *always* walk with grace, with a certain poise...it all amounts to *ifarabalè*, doesn't it?

R: Absolutely! So when you are looking at a woman, you are looking at these qualities.

U: The gait has to portray a kind of calm.

R: Yes, and when the woman is dancing, her head has to remain very calm. It is sometimes hard to understand how it is possible to control the head, when the body moves so energetically.

U: That is *tutù*.

R: Yes, indeed.

U: One thing that is striking about Yoruba carving—something that strikes you if you come to it from another culture—is the profile of the head. The way the head sits on the neck: there tends to be a line that starts at the back of the head and runs right down to the chin. The head is poised, perfectly balanced on a rather long neck. Often the chin is relatively high—as if the figure were indeed carrying a head load.

R: This is not surprising, because as small children we learn to balance things on our heads, and the creation of perfect balance is also one of the concerns of the carver.

U: There is another interesting aspect to the Yoruba attitude to female beauty: whereas in Europe people have certain preferences of color—say they prefer blondes—in Yoruba *oríkì*, women are being praised for whatever characteristics they may have. In the *oríkì* of the Ogooga of Ikere it says:

> *He is the husband of the black woman*
> *and the husband of the yellow woman.*
> *He is the husband o the fat woman*
> *who sells tobacco in the market*

In other words: the woman is beautiful, because she is what she is.

R: You've got it! You have put your finger on the most vital principle of the Yoruba, which has to do with *conceding to each person his own individual character,* even if it may not be pleasing to you.

We admire Sango, even if he is quick tempered. We admire Obatala, even though he got drunk and created albinos. We admire Ogun, even if he "bathes in blood." We admire Esu, even though he can belong to two opposing sides without feeling ashamed.

So we can admire a woman because she is fat or because she is thin: thus Osun is described as a corpulent woman, too fat to be embraced by the waist! So it is *the acknowledgement of the thing for what it is.*

U: There is a hunter's poem in praise of a thin woman:

> *She falls against a plate*
> *the plate does not break*
> *she falls against a mortar*
> *the mortar splits right down the middle*

It is a joke, of course, but I still feel that it tries to convey the idea, that even though the woman is slight of build, she is not insubstantial.

And here we come to another point where Yoruba ideas on beauty differ very much from those of Europeans: once a man or a woman has reached a certain status in society they are expected to look substantial.

R: You are right! There is an *oríkì* in which the *Olówò* is called "The father of mountains." so his size, his bulk indicates stability.

U: Even the dress of the *Olówò*, the way it is decked out in layers of cloth, until he looks like he is wearing a crinoline.

R: Exactly! It has to do with fecundity! The *Olówò* is also called "The prolific banana tree that bears many fruit."

U: The bigness means also: he is so strong, you cannot shift him

R: Immovable! He is able to withstand all kinds of problems. It is a metaphor for strength, for endurance—nothing can move you. That is actually what you call *baba:* 'somebody you meet in the hut, well seated."

U: Somebody who has equanimity.

R: A person who has reached the position of *Baba*—an elder—"must not fly around like a butterfly." It has to do with *sùúrù*. Once you ascend that position, you need a new kind of aesthetic consciousness, to be able to hold that position. It does not matter who you were before, as soon as you move into the position of a chief, priest, king, you need this stability, you must radiate that presence. Look at the image of the elephant:

> *Ajanaku*
> *where he treads once*
> *the grass will not stand up again*

or:

> *when an elephant passes*
> *nobody will say*
> *what was this thing*
> *that just passed?*

When you see an elephant, *Please declare* that you have seen an elephant.
U: His presence is undeniable. But what it *also* means is that people change their physique when they change status, which means that beauty is dictated by an attitude of mind. A person looks what he wants to look like.

I can give you another example of it. In 1951 the British Council had arrangeda function in honor of their sewing class; and there were all these substantial and dignified Yoruba ladies walking about in rather plain European dresses which they had sewn themselves. They looked impossible, they just didn't seem to fit into these straight, shift-like artificial silk frocks. And I thought then, that Yoruba women should never give up their own traditional clothes, which had been developed for their own type of beauty. But then, only a few years later, you could see young Yoruba air hostesses, who looked like PANAM or Lufthansa adverts. So here again women developed the kind of figure they wanted to have; a case of mind controlling the body.

Then to give you a much stronger example: *olórìsà* are certainly beginning to look like the image they have in their minds of their *orìsà*. A Sango worshipper doesn't look like an Obatala worshipper.
R: No, no!
U: In the fifties, when the *òrìsà* was still very strong, you could identify an *olórìsà* by simply looking at his face. His physiognomy changed as he got more deeply involved with his God. Even today: a face like that of

Sàngódáre Gbádégesin Ajàlá (the batik artist) could not belong to anybody but a Sango priest.

So beauty—the specific *type* of beauty a person may have—is decided from the inside. It is truly an illustration of *iwàlewà*—character is beauty.

R: The character and the beauty, the power and the concentration of a face can only build up over the years.

You know this cloth you are wearing is almost like *etù*. You know that *etù* is called the cloth of an elder. And they will tell you why: because it can absorb dirt! The things that a young man cannot take, the insults he cannot endure, an elderly person can take it and rub it off.

U: It's like the saying:

> *A young man can have as many embroidered gowns*
> *as an elder*
> *but he can't have the rags of an elder.*

R: It's like loolding at an *Egúngún* costume. Never mind the bright beautiful velvet on the top! It's the layers of ancient, faded, and ragged cloth he's wearing underneath, that counts.

U: The accumulated power, built up over generations!

R: That's right. It's the history of the mask. If you start a new mask today it cannot have the power. Such spiritual power has to be built up. So we could say again: the beauty of the *Egúngún* is not his colorful costume, his dazzling exterior. The real beauty of the mask lies in it's spiritual power. And again: different masks have different personalities, different characters, and we admire them for what they are. We worship the specific power they represent.

U: If we return briefly to our starting point: the beauty of women. We can say then that a woman is beautiful because she is yellow, another is beautiful because she is black, one is beautiful because she is fat, another because she is slender.

R: That's right. It's only the woman who has no character who could be deemed to be ugly.

U: In fact, I remember that some forty years ago, when people's lives were still directed by their *òrìsà*, there was hardly a woman who passed our house in Ibokun Road who didn't have a personality, an attraction, some radiation ... whereas if you walk through the streets of Lagos nowadays you may pass a lot of people without being aware of a face. That is because people are harassed, they have neither patience nor *ìfarabalè*. If they have character, they are hiding it.

R: Only that which has lost its identity can be called ugly.

U: This explains, then, why *òrìsà* worship creates beauty, because it strengthens the identity! There is an *oríkì* that says:

Sango imparts his beauty to the women with whom he sleeps.

It's a metaphor, I think, for the spiritual power the worshipper *(ìyàwò orìsà)* receives from the god. In this connection it is interesting also that the *oríkì* of the *òrìsà* hardly ever mention their physical characteristics. They concentrate on the spiritual being, the power, the personality of the gods. Very occasionally they talk about things like "dainty feet painted with cam-wood" or "white cowrie shells gleaming on black buttocks." the only thing these *oríkì* refer to constantly are the eyes: they speak of gleaming, shining, sparkling eyes.
Osun's eyes "sparkle in the dark like the sun on the river." Obatala's eye "is laughing." Oduduwa "shines like 200 stars." the light that shines on Ogun's face blinds our eyes. "Osumare watches the world with the black eye" and he is "sparkling like the sun." Erinlè "sparkles like fire, when the lights are extinguished." Ososi is a small man with sparkling spirit whose eyes "fill one with fear. . . ." so it has all to do with luminosity, with radiance, with a shining spirit.
R: Shining has to do with completeness: *dídán*. Something that is completed and ready for use is often described as 'shining" in Yoruba.
U: Perhaps we could also say "fulfillment." the fulfillment of a personality or the fulfillment of an artistic work. The Yoruba artist aims at a shining surface. He gives the carving such a smooth surface, that it reflects the light. Some carvers even nail white metal across the eye of the *ère* to give it that luminous look that the *oriki* describe.
But the real completeness of the carving comes with time ... the handling by generations of worshippers that produce the patina.
R: That's right. To the Yoruba the work of the carver is only the first stage in the completion of a carving. Maybe the most important stage, but only a stage.
U: There is one other thing that worries me. We all agree that the Yoruba artist follows some very clearly defined aesthetic principles. To what extent he actually verbalizes these principles is really irrelevant. After all, some European artists never talk about their work. Picasso never bothered to analyze his paintings. But the question that arises is: to what extent do the users of the images understand the aesthetics of the art and to what extent do they care about them?
Years ago I felt shocked when I saw a toby jug in an Osun shrine, which some facetious British District Officer had "donated" to the priests.

Today, in the light of what you have told me, I can understand their attitude more easily: no Osun worshipper could ever imagine another human being to be as cynical as this colonial official. So they must have assumed it represented *his òrìsà*, and however weird it must have looked to them, they respected it's idiosyncrasy. They conceded it its own individual character.

But how do they handle their own carvings? Many of them, during a ritual, are being painted with red and white stripes or with dots. They are being painted in the way in which initiates were once painted during certain rituals. This does give the images a kind of mystical presence, but the forms the artist had created have been obscured. You can no longer see the delicate incisions on the surface, which have been caked up with paint. Lines and dots rudely cut across his shapes and obscure his proportions. During the annual *ère* festival in Osogbo, all the images from all the shrines are carried in procession through the town and then exhibited in front of the palace for the day. But they are heavily painted, so that the general public will never know about the artistic intentions of the wood carver, this being the only opportunity they have of seeing the images. In the Osun shrine at the King's market of Osogbo, the carvings are permanently in this painted state.

R: I have no answer to that. First: I talked to Lamidi Fakeye. I said to him: "Tell me in one sentence, what was the greatest thing you ever learned as a carver?" After thinking a long time he answered: "It is *ifarabalè* that we go to learn."

It is true that the carver takes time to carve certain details. He gives his work a certain surface. And then it is obscured. But there are categories of carvings. Some are not complete without paint—like *Gèlèdé*. So for their completeness they need color. Which means that the carver's work is only the first stage—though a very important one—towards the achievement of completeness.

And just like an *Egúngún* mask, the carved image will not be considered complete, unless it has undergone certain ceremonies. It has to be "empowered" or it will not mean much.

There is an accumulative process: the carver, the painter, the ritual and ultimately the user, all add to it's potency. The character of a work may even change as it is passed on from one user to another over the generations.

U: But does this not simply mean, that in spite of all these Yoruba aesthetic criteria, that have been identified in recent years, there is something which is far more important in the eyes of the Yoruba and which *overrides* all the aesthetic considerations?

R: That is true. But is this not what we are talking about? The identity of a work of art, its *ìwà* has precedence over everything. Because if this is not fulfilled, then the artist has failed.

U: Alright. Let us put a theoretical case. A highly unlikely one, but nevertheless, suppose a great artist like Olowe of Ise produces a superb Epa mask, something that we would call a masterpiece. Now supposing that during the ritual to empower the carving, something has gone wrong: *Ifá* rejects the carving, or the intended owner has suddenly become a Muslim or whatever, supposing the ritual does not take place. Then what *is* this incomplete carving? What happens to it? It could only be thrown away, because the society has no use for a carving whose value rests *only* on it's aesthetic beauty.

R: Yes, it's possible.

U: This reminds me of the famous case of the carver Bamigbóyè: one of the greatest artists in Ekiti. As a mature man he was persuaded by a well-meaning British education officer to teach carving in a high school. So he suddenly began to make carvings, of which he knew in advance they would never be empowered by any ritual and would never be put to any religious use. Such carvings were useless, meaningless objects to him, and all one could do with them was to sell to Europeans. And as soon as this situation arose, Bamgboye *lost his sense of aesthetics.* His forms became feeble, some objects were toy-like imitations of his own former works!

R: Well of course, they had no identity, they had no *ìwà*.

U: We could actually use an example from Yoruba mythology. It says that Obatala formed human beings out of clay, but that Olodumare had to breathe life into them. So Obatala is the artist, he creates the shape, but without the ritual action of Olodumare, these beings can never come to life. They remain useless lumps of clay.

Therefore it seems to me that, in all the recent discussion on Yoruba aesthetics, it has been ignored that all aesthetics has a different *place value* in Yoruba society from ours.

We tend to place the value of aesthetics so high, that we disregard the meaning, contents, and *ìwà* of a work of art completely. And this is what has happened in this particular exhibition here in Zurich: Yoruba values have been turned upside down. The *Èsù* figures right at the entrance to this exhibition are like a symbol of this: in a Yoruba shrine these little *Èsù* figures hang head down and they are partly hidden in a cluster of cowrie strings. Here the figures have been displayed in (what is to the organizers) the "right way" up. We can now admire the skill of the carver, but the *ère* has lost it's meaning. The whole idea of it is that *Èsù*, who constantly upsets the equilibrium and turns the world upside down, is here again demonstrating his contrariness.

R: That is why I felt it important that Muraina came into the exhibition with us. Because to me these carvings are not complete without the *dùndún*, the songs and the dance. They authenticate the carvings. They give it sanction. We have to look at them in the right context of performance—of ritual performance.

199

U: You know what Muraina said to us after seeing the exhibition? He said: "If one went through this exhibition lonely, with no other person around, one could become frightened." I said what gives you this feeling? He answered: "It may have to do with the fact that the exhibition is underground, but it is not only that. I almost felt as if the objects themselves ought to be frightened of being there! As you walk down those steps, the first thing you see is that Èsù in a small glass case: it looks captured!"

R: Muraina responded to the isolation of the objects.

U: He responded to what was to him the artificiality of the context. In fact he said: "It is like some scientist's laboratory: as if the carvings had been taken there for experiments." R: It is reduced to an academic exercise, the objects have been treated so much like artefacts. A distance has been created between us and the art works. But then there is always the "usefulness of the useless": it teaches you one thing, but then you lose many other things in the process.

U: One could argue, of course, that any art work can be evaluated as pure form, that the form as such makes a certain impact on us, whether we understand how it arose or not.

R: Exactly. It has become art history, with dates and periods and styles. . . as wonderful as that is! We are now at a crossroad, at a point where we are stripping Yoruba art of contents. Where we are "leaving it naked" as Georgina says. And that is dangerous! Because orò does not go out unclothed. He must never be seen naked! If you ran into orò naked it would be a catastrophe! And this exhibition is not clothed. It is naked and that is why it can frighten one. *I have to change my way of thinking, before I can be comfortable with it.* I have to wear my Western thinking cap.

U: There is now a certain danger, too, that people will use your own work on aesthetics to say: Well, after all it was wrong to say that African art has been merely functional. It now has been proved that there have been very clear aesthetic principles which the carver followed. And this justifies an exhibition in which the art work is treated as pure form. It justifies turning Èsù the "right" way up. So in some sense they are misinterpreting you.

R: I think you are right, but then, you see, things have gone too far in the other direction. Anthropologists and art historians have long been saying that African artists had no conscious idea of aesthetics at all and that they could not be regarded as individual artists, because they were merely *copying* a master. So it has been a very necessary development to point out that African art is not anonymous, that there are individual masters who can be identified. So this was a necessary development.

But I agree: it is equally wrong to isolate the objects from their cultural context. Because, if you do that, you mainly serve the interests of the collectors.

There are many people who want the objects—but they are not interested in the people.

U: That is very true, and we saw a striking example of that during the last few days. We had Muraina Oyelami here, a great Yoruba musician and artist. Nobody was curious to know how he felt about the exhibition. He was simply ignored.

R: Some visitors used the exhibition like a market place: one of them actually said to me: "This carving here, do you know the owner? I might want to buy it."

Sometimes I feel that we academics become the undertakers of cultures. To some academics these works are mere examples, which they can use as illustrations in some of their seminars on this or that. But to be fair: we cannot expect others to have a personal stake in the culture, like you and me.

U: If the principle of Yoruba aesthetics is *ìwàlewà*, as you have explained so convincingly in much of your writing, then we must say that the concept of this exhibition goes right against that principle. And yet I must confess, that this (to us) "unnatural" and perhaps even uncanny isolation of the art works does make a powerful impact. It is startling in it's own way.

R: Yes, there is something we must be grateful for. Because even the most skeptical, the most conservative people will be humbled, when they go through this exhibition. They cannot help admiring the sheer technical perfection of these art works, the grandness of concepts, the antiquity and consistency of the culture.

U: I think people will necessarily be impressed by the dignity and the integrity of the culture. And maybe, hopefully, the sensitive visitor will become aware of some other force, some other way of life, some other vision of the world, that produced these magnificent works.

To Organize is to Destroy: The Oshogbo Art School
Georgina Beier

In 1985 an art teacher from a French University took a group of twenty students on a trip to Nigeria, to visit the "Oshogbo Art School." It seemed an interesting and adventurous project: they were going to look at the syllabus, the teaching methods, and the overall philosophy of the famous African art school that produced such internationally famous painters as Twins Seven-Seven, Bisi Fabunmi, Muraina Oyelami, and Rufus Ogundele. But when they arrived in Oshogbo they had a shock—there was no building called the "Oshogbo Art School"; there were no classes and no teachers. Gradually, of course, they got to meet the artists, who had followed their own lives and careers and were now living scattered in Oshogbo, Ife, Iragbiji, and Okemesi.

When the students asked the artists: "How did it all happen? What made you become artists? Who taught you? What was it like—in short, what exactly went on in Oshogbo in the 1960s"?—they were given lots of anecdotes and entertaining stories, but they finally returned to France, not being any the wiser; for none of the artists had been able to capture in words the spirit of euphoria that moved them, and the "secret of their success" was as inexplicable to them as it was to anybody else.

I have often been asked those same questions and sometimes I have tried to write about it. But my attempts to explain what happened at the workshops and to define my role in them have always been unsatisfactory, because I am not a writer, and it seems to me that there are limits to the ability of language to capture an experience.

It is rather like a portrait photograph. Undoubtedly the camera will capture a likeness of the person, but it fixes a fragment in time, it reproduces a tiny, fleeting aspect of the subject, rather than the whole personality. If we had the kind of "school" the French students were looking for—a school with a building and entrance examinations, with registration fees and timetables and salaried teachers—then, of course, there would be no problem at all in describing it. But to organize creativity is a contradiction in terms; that is, after all, the meaning of Chuang Tsu's famous saying, which I have chosen as the motto of this article. When I came to live in Oshogbo in April 1963, I did not come with the intention of running an art workshop! Some dramatic events had already begun to transform the image of the town: the Mbari Mbayo Club had been opened the year before and Duro Ladipo had already given his first (somewhat raw) performances of *Oba Koso*, the play that was to bring him world acclaim. A five day art workshop conducted by Denis Williams and Jacob Lawrence in 1962 had produced a talented young artist, Jacob Afolabi, who was, however, rather at a loss about what to do with his talent.

Asiru Olatunde was already working on his aluminum panels. In August 1963 Denis Williams returned for a second workshop. I did not participate in this, but I invited Therese Cronjé, a fifteen-year-old South African girl, whom I had taught in Zaria, to take part. She was the daughter of Sue Cronjé, a political journalist who had to escape from South Africa because of her outspoken, critical views. Therese contributed to the workshop a number of paintings of great lyrical beauty, of which only one seems to have survived. I was interested to see that the Nigerian students were in no way influenced by Therese's work, even though she was more experienced that they and she went about her work with considerable certainty.

It was during this workshop that Rufus Ogundele realized that he wanted to become an artist. The original plan had been that Denis Williams should return every weekend to Oshogbo to work with Jacob and Rufus; but he soon found that his heavy commitments as a university teacher and researcher at the University of Ibadan made it impossible. So the task of assisting these two young artists devolved onto me. They were then working with emulsion paint on large sheets of hard board and had evolved a curious technique. They drew the outlines with a fat brush dipped into black paint; then they filled in the spaces around the lines with areas of flat, pale color. This created a marvelously lively line, like a jagged dance rhythm. What disturbed me, though, was that they worked in much the same style, in spite of their very different personalities and age. Rufus was only fifteen at the time. The problem was to make them aware of what they had achieved, without producing the self-consciousness that could kill their freshness. The paintings themselves—which were basically conceived in black and white—suggested that linocut might be a sympathetic medium; because linocut can be a bold medium, and in cutting a line one becomes more clearly aware of its quality than drawing it with a pencil. It was through this medium that Rufus and Afolabi matured in different directions: Rufus´ work became more and more angular and energetic, while Afolabi's shapes acquired an undulating flow. In 1964 I was asked to conduct the third Mbari Mbayo art workshop and this became a truly exhilarating experience.

Muraina Oyelami has best expressed our feelings at the time: "When you find yourself in a strange town, you have only your character to rely on." Like the "students" I entered new territory. I learned a lot. I realized that I had an instinct for discovering the visual element that is unique to a person. Running a workshop is not simply a matter of providing materials and "encouragement" and letting anything happen. It is like hunting for the original element, trapping it and making it safe, before it gets confused with so many other, alien elements. An artist could find himself in the position of a chemist who is unable to analyze a potion because the original components of it have changed their nature.

I am saying this with hindsight: at the time we weren't thinking about it, we were just doing it. When one thinks too hard about these things, one becomes blind. The Yoruba people say: "The one who thinks of nothing but the irritation of the itch, will scratch himself to the bone." I was not working with preconceived ideas, I had no theories—I still haven't. The participants themselves had no fixed ideas about why they were there or where it would take them. The workshop quickly developed its own momentum. Ideas grew in different directions at breakneck speed. When the five euphoric days were over, several very distinct artistic personalities had emerged: Twins Seven-Seven, Bisi Fabunmi, and Muraina Oyelami, and we had all grown so close together during this common experience that it seemed natural for us to continue working together. I set up studios in our house and in the museum of the Ataoja's palace and until we left Nigeria for New Guinea in December 1966 we saw each other every day and discussed our work. Others, equally gifted, were too heavily committed to the theater; Tijani Mayakiri and Ademola Onibonokuta were the lead actors of Duro Ladipo's company, and they could not devote themselves to painting, until the left the company a few years later. It must be stated here, that the existence of the theater company, to which they all belonged, had made my work a great deal easier: because already these young people had developed a lifestyle of their own; they were open-minded and anxious to discover their potentials; in fact, the evolution of Duro Ladipo's plays proceeded in a manner that was akin to the evolution of our art workshop. Duro's masterpiece *Oba Koso* was not planned or achieved in a single production: it took several years to arrive at its ultimate greatness. When we look at photographs of the first performance of *Oba Koso* today, they look quite flat: the actors stand a little awkwardly against a completely plain backdrop. On some of the pictures there are flashes of great dancing, but there is no indication that Duro will ultimately come so close to being the true personification of *Shango*. All the same, the photographs do not tell the full story. Because, even then, Ulli sensed the enormous strength of the man and he gave him that most precious of gifts—time. It allowed Duro to put together the investment of energy and imagination from a number of people, and to create that explosive, intense opera that had the power of making many Yoruba people re-examine their attitude to Yoruba religion and history. His wife Ashake, the actors Mayakiri and Onibonokuta, and Ulli himself all contributed elements to the play's growth and the artists made it visually spectacular, without using theatrical gimmicks.

The greatest thing Ulli did for Duro was that he brought no preconceived ideas into the relationship. Being older, more experienced, the representative of the university, and potentially a figure of authority, he could have killed the play by imposing his own ideas. Instead, he was always willing to allow himself to be surprised. He had already learned the wisdom of the Yoruba proverb: "The effort of forcing another man to be like oneself makes one an unpleasant person." If a professional theater director had been employed in those early days to organize the company, slick up the production, finalize the script, plot entries and exits, determine the exact length of each speech, etc., he might have produced a smoother performance in terms of conventional theater, but he would have suppressed all possibilities of improvisation and stifled the play's organic growth. In the same way, I would have stifled the development of the artists if I had plotted out a three-year course. Even a time-table would have been destructive. Our driving force was creative motivation—and that does not fit into office hours.

Twins Seven-Seven says: "Perhaps the most important thing I learned from Georgina was energy..." and I thought I had learned that from Yorubas! We all motivated each other's energies! We worked furiously in those heady days; we slept little and we lived for the daily surprises that we discovered in each other's work. For such an euphoric situation to develop, the time, the place, and the human chemistry have to be right.

The Hunter, The Antelope, and The Trap
An interview with Georgina Beier

Q.   I think it is true to say that the London suburb of Sutton was culturally one of the bleakest environments in which a child could grow up! I believe there weren't any pictures in your home. . . .

G.   Well, there was the "Lady of Shalotte" in a relative's house: a sepia-tinted reproduction of a Pre-Raphaelite painting. We weren't supposed to look at her, because she had no clothes on. . . .

Q.   You mean the one floating down the river?

G.   Yes. The room was usually closed. It was the "parlour" that was used only on Christmas day or important family feasts like weddings. I had to sneak in to look at it.

Q.   So that was the only work of art you encountered in your childhood?

G.   There were granddad's palm trees. They were watercolors. My father's father—he painted the Sahara.

Q.   Had he been to the Sahara?

G.   No! But he painted date palms in the sand. They are still in my parents' house. I used to look at them a lot as a child. But that was all the art I was exposed to. So "culture" was the *Daily Mirror*.

Q.   Did you read it?

G.   Yes. There were no books in the house, except a children's encyclopedia that my painting grandfather had bought. I read everything in it, from deep sea divers to electricity systems. My parents sent me to the adult section of the local library, to ask the librarian for a "murder" or a "love story." The thing that interested me about the *Daily Mirror* were the mail order adverts, which enticed people to send in a few shillings for a "smashing dress." These little adverts were accompanied by illustrations—they were awful drawings!—but I copied them, dreaming of becoming a fashion designer!

Q.   Were these your first drawings?

G.   No... I used to copy last year's Christmas cards and then send them back, hand-painted, to the same person the following year. You got silver dust and sprinkled it on with a bit of glue, to get the glitter. It took three months—there were so many cards. It was also a matter of money, of course, but it was fun.

The first "serious" painting I made was a ship at sunset and ... ah ... a ballerina. That was in the Saturday morning art classes. I had just started Secondary School, so I must have been twelve.

Q.   What made you want to go there?

G.   I loved drawing, and I thought I'd get an education. But it was so boring ... terrible. . . .

Q.   What happened in those classes?

G.   You were just given a sheet of paper and you drew ... but you didn't really know what to do. But every year a lot of energy was put into doing a painting for a competition that was run by a newspaper. A lot of kids tried to win a prize. That's when I did the ballerina. I can still remember it—it was quite disgusting. I put her on a glass floor in a pink tutu—but trying to get a reflection in poster paints was hopeless.

Then one day somebody came into the class and asked: Does anyone want to do life drawing? I didn't know what life drawing was, so I put my hand up, because I was bored.

I think they had to have a minimum number of students to keep the class going, so they picked up anybody. They were desperate. So I was taken upstairs and there was a black lady standing there, stark naked, and my Geography teacher was drawing her. And my God, he blushed! She was the first naked person I'd ever seen.

I made copies of my drawing and sold them to the boys at school: three pence black-and-white and six pence colored. I don't think I sold that many, but they all looked.

And there were other drawings. I drew Elizabethan costumes on dozens of A4 sheets. I loved history: all those ruffles and velvets! I must have done fifty or sixty of them one weekend and the teacher put them all round the class, like a frieze.

Then I drew wattle-and-daub houses of the early swamp dwellers in Britain. I loved that architecture and dreamt about living in such a dwelling, and having a little boat to travel from one hut to the other. You can imagine that growing up in Sutton, you really have to imagine you are living somewhere else. So at times you are living with ruffles and lace and beheadings and another time you lived in a mud hut in a swamp.

Q.   Well, one can look at it on this obvious level: what kind of art were you exposed to as a child; what were the first drawings you made and so on. But there is another level of experience, which is more basic, perhaps more essential. We might also ask: when did you first become aware of color; of shape ... this kind of awareness need not have anything to do with art lessons.
. . .

G.   Well, the shrapnel collection during the war! We children thought that these were splinters from exploded aircraft—it's molten metal that falls out of the sky and sets; like toffee, when you drop it into ice cold water, to test whether it is hard enough.

The shrapnel pieces are rough; they are grey and shiny, like the antimony they sell on Nigerian markets. Quite beautiful.

Some of them had long spiky threads, extending in all directions. We kids made shrapnel collections and we evolved our own criteria by which to evaluate them. You could swap the most beautiful pieces for marbles—and marbles were scarce during the war.

The ones with the long thin threads were considered the masterpieces. The best way to get the good ones was to stay out during the air raid ... so that's what I used to do. The pieces were still hot! And then there were the flares! Green for OK and red for danger: messages to our pilots flying past my bedroom window. That was beautiful—like fireworks, which I had never seen ... and then after the war, everything went dead. During the war we lived with daily tension and we got used to it. The adults would say: "Poor kids," but we didn't know anything else.

Q.   When did you first become aware of color—what made you conscious of colors?

G.   My first strong responses to color were negative responses. My mother knitted a green pullover for me—and I hated that color. It was so crude! It took me years before I could use viridian green in a painting ... on the other hand, ladybirds! That was real color; I followed them around for hours. They are really bold: scarlet with black spots. And then the Red Admiral—that beautiful butterfly, its again red with black spots! It was a strong color—marvelous that red flitting about. Later, when London was polluted by smog, people thought it had disappeared—but it had merely changed its magnificent wings for a dull grey, to match the smog. I suppose we were brought up with color prejudices, too, which took time to break down. When Diana Dors appeared in our suburb with a pink chevrolet, I thought it was shocking! Cars should be grey or black—but a pink open car ... I thought that was really vulgar; and it was a shocking pink! I was may be ten. . . .

Q.   I suppose the bleakness of your environment must have been depressing. Did you ever feel deprived as a child?

G.   No, not really, because when you have imagination, you can experience all kinds of wonders in fairly ordinary things. One of the most absorbing experiences for me as a child was to watch bowling.

Q.   Bowling? I always thought it was a most boring exercise. What did you see in it?

G.   One thing is that it is very quiet. I used to stand there with my nose through the expanded metal wire. Other kids didn't go there. So I was completely alone. There was peace, marvelous peace, just watching an expanse of green grass, that was so smooth. I didn't watch the players—but it was good that they were white on green. The magic was the ball—moving so smoothly and relatively slowly. And some had a white spot on them—it was soothing, like a massage. It made you feel totally smooth and calm. I was very little.

Q.   You make me visualize it myself now: the white spot on the ball draws a kind of looping line. . . .

G.   A firm line—like engraving!

Q.   So this experience somehow took you out of the hustle and banality of daily life.

G.   Yes, you can find the whole of life in the most deprived circumstances. It is very small details, that can make you aware of the world. I first became aware that books are wonderful things, because of the way one of my teachers held a book—as if it was sacred. It was a book of poetry; and even if I did not understand it, I love the way she was turning the pages. I had never met anybody who loved books like that.

I had been told that I ought to like literature, but how could I, when virtually all I had access to was Enid Blyton?

Of course, there was the Children's Encyclopedia; and it contained a page with passport-size photographs, of the races of the world. There was a Slav next to a German and I remember thinking: why worry about the insignificant differences between those two, when there is the Congolese Lady with the elongated neck that is covered in brass rings. I thought she was the most beautiful creature I'd ever seen. That was the most wonderful picture of my childhood: I would look at it again and again.

I think that as a child you collect your life, bit by bit. Because every child has access to similar images but they all pick different things. Its really what the Yorubas call "choosing one's head," isn't it? I mean the notion, that before we are born, we are taken into a garden, where we have the opportunity of choosing our own "head," our destiny. The Yoruba are quite right: you do it by selection, and you can find your own destiny, provided you are not deceitful. . . .

Q.   Of course, if you were to say: "I ought to like this," then you don't choose your life, you allow others to direct (dictate) it.

G.   It makes me feel utterly uncomfortable, when I am trying to like something because I ought to: that's why I felt so uncomfortable at art school; utterly miserable.

Q.   You could elaborate on this Yoruba image, because they tell us that when you come into this world with a "bad" head, you can still manipulate your fate in various ways. It is within the capacity of a human being to improve his destiny. One could say that fate didn't exactly play into your hands, but you picked the little gems that were there.

jis around. Always. However miserable

G.   There are always some jewels around. Always. However miserable you are. continuing process, really; it's not just

Q.   So "choosing your head" is a continuing process, really; it's not just a single dramatic act in the heavenly garden ... it's all those little choices that you keep making. . . .

G.   But the Yoruba have this too: if you are an Obatala kind of person, rather introvert, and you find yourself in the Shango cult, things are not going to work out for you, because you made the wrong choice. But then they are lucky, because they can go to the oracle priest to have themselves sorted out. . . .

Q.   On the whole, you seem to have been pretty astute in your choices in life, but what made you want to go to art school? Was that not maybe, one of the few wrong choices in your life?

G.   No. It happened by accident. It never occurred to me that I could go to art school. But then I did a self-portrait which won the competition that was held annually by Bentals Stores. I tried to be like Rembrandt then; I must have come across him in the Encyclopedia. The competition was judged by the Principal of an art school, and my headmistress arranged an interview with him. She said: "Do you want to go to art school?" It came as a complete surprise. I was learning shorthand and typing at the time. I quite liked shorthand—I mean the squiggles of it. But once I'd mastered it, it become so boring! I don't quite have the organized mind to go with it. "Something to fall back on," my mum had said; so I did: on my bum! My first job lasted a day! The second one, half a day. So that was my career at the office.

Q.   Well, what happened at the art school?

G.   I only stayed nine months—I ran out of money; maybe just as well.

Q.   Did you learn anything? Was it useful to you?

G   Mmmmmmmm. . . .

Q.   Did it help you in any way?

G.   No.

Q.   You actually developed a hang-up about painting. I remember that in the sixties you did everything with complete ease: sculpture, graphic art, theater design, murals ... but when you worked on a canvas, you always labored over it. What made you self-conscious? What was the fashion at art school at the time?

G.   Utrillo was popular with the students ... a lot of black and white and Bratby's kitchen sink. He" d actually gone to that art school and got thrown out, for having no talent. The Principal painted like Spencer; Mr. Bulmer did Bonnard; the sculptor did Marino Marini. It was all old hat; nothing exciting. There were different things that were interesting: the man who ran the general introductory class, he worked in theater—professionally. He gave an introduction to architecture, and that I liked, because it made you look at buildings; you became much more aware of your surroundings. Or he brought a trunk full of old costumes from the theater and helped us produce a musical. That was fun; it was like life—not still life or life class.

Q.   Did you have to go to life class?

G.   Oh yes, but you see, I thought I was wrong. I couldn't understand why I didn't enjoy it. But I just didn't like this kind of drawing at all. I liked the models though: a big fat woman—Pat Hall! She was huge with tiny, tiny feet; you wondered how she could possibly balance on them. And there was another woman: Marjorie. Her face was old, but her body was so youthful; and she lived in a little bedsitter near the British Museum with about 200 budgerigars in it. A real eccentric ... I liked those people. And then there was Mr. Newton, one of the teachers, who looked like Stalin. He was a communist. I'd never heard of communism, till then. He was invited to a function at the Soviet Embassy, when Stalin died, but he got thrown out, because they thought he was a cheap impersonator! It was a good time in a way, but not for art, for other things. I learned about books—I'd never heard of Dostoyevski or Zola before. I discovered Jazz. But it was just as well, that I ran out of money.

Q.   How did it affect your painting—I mean the fact that you were laboring over them.

G.   I don't think it's fair to blame everything on the teachers; because another thing is, it takes time to grow up. It's different for a Nigerian. The Oshogbo artists in the sixties, they had something real. They had literature in their heads. Poetry! Just think of the imagery of Yoruba poetry. What a marvellous thing to come from. But I grew up with nothing. So you have to fill that gap ... I don't think you can blame the art school for having an empty head ... but they don't jolt your head either ... they don't shock you ... they just go on doing the same thing. I hadn't been introduced to Gaudi at art school! It was all Michelangelo and Henry Moore, etc., etc.

Q.   And you weren't supposed to be critical of sacred cows like Michelangelo.

G.   No, but I was ... it seemed to me repulsive—he had too many muscles in the wrong places everywhere. I thought his line was too fuzzy, and I found that unpleasant. I liked a clean line ... but there was dead silence when I said it, because you weren't supposed to make such a statement.

But I must say, I would find it difficult myself to teach in such an environment. What do you do with all these kids when some have more talent and others less, but none has any grasp of his own individuality, none of them has anything to say? It's a self-conscious sort of teaching.

Q.   You say the art school didn't jolt your mind. Then what did, in the end?

G.   Well, Nigeria!

Q.   In what way; what exactly happened?

G.   I think one just becomes a piece of flotsam in the river and you let the water carry you along. Because I didn't go with any preconceived ideas—none. I didn't go to study anything either. . . .

Q.   You didn't have a purpose. . . ?

G.   I wanted to live—to digest—this huge, strange country.

You are not really aware of what's happening. It's simply excitement. So many cultures! And the landscape. Not its beauty—its harshness. The Jos Plateau with its rocks, and the way it falls suddenly, into jungle. Ways of life!

Not one way of life—many ways of life. You had no idea how it worked and how these societies organized themselves. Sheer wonder!

There is nothing—absolutely nothing—that reminds you of Europe. This is not disturbing, only exciting. A relief actually. You can't form opinions, because you don't know anything. You have new experiences all the time; you have to learn, adapt, readjust continuously. So it's really like starting again.

Q.   You have often referred to Nigeria as your real home. What gives Nigeria that unique position in your life, when you've lived in so many other exciting places like New Guinea and Australia and India?

G.   People say that when they feel sick, really sick, they have a sudden longing for some dish their mother cooked when they were young. Well, when I'm feeling really ill, I think of palm oil soup.

Q.   OK, I guess I asked a stupid question.

G.   Well you can't really analyze these things. Otherwise you become like the poet who is asked to explain why he loves a certain woman and he says: her eyebrows are like half moons, her cheeks like peaches—it doesn't mean a thing. . . .

Q.   Maybe you should say something, briefly, on the Oshogbo artists, on your workshops. After all, the artists who emerged from your studio in Oshogbo have received considerable international recognition; and you have maintained a close relationship with them for twenty-five years!

G.   Well, there's not much one can say—except, I'm not a teacher.

Q.   You may not be a "teacher" in the conventional sense, but somehow a lot of young people, both in Nigeria and Papua New Guinea discovered their vocation as an artist, when they came into your orbit. . . .

G.   I hate the word teacher, because it implies authority. We think of a teacher as somebody who tells others what to do. But I believe in the Yoruba saying: "The effort of forcing another man to be like oneself, makes one an unpleasant person."

Q.   But your own approach, how did you develop it and what does it consist of. . . .

G.   I didn't learn it—I only discovered it

The first thing is not to be complacent. You cannot think that you know. You cannot know what new idea is coming into the mind of a man like Twins Seven-Seven, nor should you attempt to. You can't have order, you can't plan. You've got to be alert, ready to respond to any new development. It's the recognition! They throw out an idea casually, maybe it's rough and untamed, but you can see where it can go. But more important than sparks of brilliance is character. I have seen lots of people—kids, old people—produce marvelous pictures. But you've also got to have motivation, strength of character, single-mindedness. Talent without energy. . . .

Q.   It fizzles out.

G.   The important thing is for the artist to find his own individual road. The Melpa people in the Western Highlands of New Guinea have this marvelous term "Noman." It signifies the need for a person to express what he really is even if his artistic ideas contravene convention. If a person feels strongly about something, he must follow his "Noman," otherwise he will destroy his character. And that really requires a special kind of discipline.

But how do you get that person to recognize this quality in himself; that is the real problem. And what that means is to believe in somebody, to have faith. There was never any question in my mind that that group of young people in Oshogbo had enormous potential ... at the same time you have to approach each "student" differently, have a different relationship. . . .

Q.   ... you must be able to respond to each new move the artist makes, each new direction he takes. . . .

... and that means forgetting yourself totally; you have to concentrate your entire mind on recognizing what makes these artists different.

Q.   There is also the need to exercise considerable restraint. I know this from teaching creative writing; its easy to see how a piece of writing can be improved; its tempting to polish it up ... but you need the patience to let him find his own solution, otherwise you destroy all the potential that's there.

G   If you have the admiration for their talent, then its simple. And it doesn't begin and end in the studio. Our lives were totally involved, to the point of solving their marriage problems, of bailing them out of jail. And one had to be available 24 hours a day.

Q.   If you are an artist yourself, does it not interfere with your own work, if you have to efface yourself to that extent?

G.   No: a woman is so sensitive to the presence of a new-born baby, that she would never roll over it in her sleep; but it doesn't mean she is effacing herself as a person. And another thing is: the insights come as a sudden flash, and when that happens you tend to make the right statement. And of course, a student must feel at ease to criticize you. . . .

Q.   Did they ever criticize your own work?

G.   The incident that comes to mind is of Sam walking into my house one day; he turned my painting upside down and said: "That's better, Ma," and walked out again.

Q.   Another thing that would have helped your Oshogbo workshop is that the whole aura that surrounds art in Europe did not exist.

G.   Well, in Europe I must isolate myself from my environment to work; in Nigeria I could have young Waibi sitting on my desk, sharpening my pencils, and I could go on drawing.

Q.   Yorubas can have this calm. . . .

G.   Yes. On the street there is all this shouting and bustling and yet, when people come to visit you, they just sit down quietly and their presence doesn't disturb you at all. They carry their privacy with them. Since they haven't got any physical privacy, they create it in their mind.

Q.   That is a wonderful thing. You can live very close together, without disturbing each other.

G.   And that affected the whole "teaching" situation.

Q.   Another thing that would have helped the situation enormously was the fact that there was no "art scene" in the European sense at all. No marketing. . . .

G.   There was just this exciting activity! We never thought about selling or how to survive. There was no motivation, except to create!

Q.   Bisi Fabunmi says, in the catalogue to his recent exhibition: "We had no idea that such pictures could be sold. But in the morning, when you woke up, you simply felt like going to the studio ... and when a picture worked, it made you happy." So these artists worked in a context utterly different from the contemporary European scene: no galleries, no art establishment, no "-isms," no cultural pressures. Does that make them somewhat akin to what Jean Dubuffet called "Art Brut" or "Outsider Art"?

G.   No, no, no. Its different. Besides, I hate definitions; they are a trap, like a portcullis that's slammed down and locks you into the castle. People are always trying to define, label, and cast the artist into a mould, whereas we are leaping ahead into new discovery.

Q.   Let's come back to your own paintings: You have recently said of your large Sydney paintings—the work you did in the late seventies—that they were too preoccupied with textures and paint quality. Are you trying to say that these beautiful qualities were really a kind of diversion?

G.   I think what happens is that one has too much respect. Rembrandt's "Man with the Golden Helmet"—that is glorious paint. But once you have actually understood paint. . . .

Q.   Once you have acquired the facility with paint. . . .

G.   Then you are free to throw it away.

Q.   But it has taken you many years to feel that you can now. . . .

G.   ... just paint!

Q.   You've had this strong concern with paint quality since the Oshogbo days, since 1964 till. . . .

G.   ... till I came to Bayreuth, virtually, in 1981. It happened here. Strange, that freedom.

Q.   You once said that your problem was to get the drawing strong enough.

G.   Well, really, you have no path. The direction is fuzzy. The road is not clear. So you use paint to try and find an image, to read images into it. But the problem comes when you have marvelous, beautiful paint, but there is no image in it. Then you don't want to destroy it, because it's so beautiful.

Q.   ... then beauty is a trap.

G.   Yes, but that's gone now. But of course, you still go on searching and finding. . . .

Q.   Why do you think it happened here in Bayreuth?

G.   Well, God knows, but it may have to do with scale. In Sydney I worked on large canvasses: six by three feet. . . .

Q.   I remember you had this anxiety, that when you start on such a large canvas, you need six clear weeks without interruption; because when the flow is interrupted, you might lose the mood.

G.   The other thing is permanency: when you make one of these little paintings and you've fucked it up, you can throw it away. But these big paintings—there's a terrible feeling it ought to be perfect, and permanent, and you keep on laboring over it.

Q.   ... and it hangs there like a reproach.

G.   Exactly.

Q.   Actually, my father said, that's why he stopped painting. When you play music, he said, you enjoy doing it—and then it's gone and you can start again. But when you make a picture, you get a hangover afterwards. He enjoyed the act of painting, while he was sitting in the landscape, but then afterwards, when he looked at the finished painting he saw what was wrong with it. . . .

G   That's right. And the moment where you begin to feel you can throw it away, you've lost your hang-up. And that's where you must blame the art schools really. They teach you to be precious. . . .

Q.   What made you suddenly reduce the scale of your paintings?

G.   I travelled so much and I got tired of carting them around. So I reduced my canvas from 6 x 3 feet to 6 x 6 inches. It means that I can concentrate on this little thing and I can finish it in one mood in the middle of the night. It's the short story, as opposed to the mammoth novel. But then these little paintings looked so much better in a group, and so I started to put them, like chapters, into one frame. And still I have the freedom to know that if any panel is no good, I can just throw it out. But it's never happened, because the anxiety is gone.

Q.   When you start one of your now famous conglomerate paintings of twenty-five separate panels ... what happens? Do you plan it all in detail, or do you just let it roll? Just how do you start painting?

G.   The little ones, in 1981, I drew straight onto the board. But there was always an idea, so it's like sketching in your head. But it's always a matter of concentration. Even these big new drawings, which are 2 x 1 meters and which must be done pretty quickly—you have to get into the mood, where, if ants were biting you all over, you wouldn't feel it. Unless you are truly concentrated, nothing will go right.

When I start one of these complex paintings, I have the twenty-five boards all laid out in front of me. When I draw the first line—even if it's only two inches long—I can sense if it's wrong, that this line will lead to failure. This is the sensation you live off: you know when it's right. You just feel it. If the first mark is right, everything will follow through. So I end up with a drawing that covers all the twenty-five boards. Then I paint it all blue—Prussian blue. Because I hate to paint on a white ground.

Q.   But, of course, your drawing shines through the blue ground.

G.   Yes, that's the core.

Q.   Then the real problem, and I know this from writing, is how to start. Then how do you do this: do you have a method?

G.   No, there is no method, because each painting poses a different problem. There has to be a daily discipline. If one waits for inspiration, one waits forever.

Once you have achieved concentration, you know what to do. So I look at the line on the blue panel, and I know that the snake must be pink. There is no reason or logic in this. Once the python is pink, I know, that the lady should, not could, be yellow—and so it grows. It's quite surprising to me, to see things happen. The process reminds me of a Yoruba proverb: "Everybody is born into this world to become something, only we don't know what." So each painting is born into this world to become something, but I don't know what.

Q.   One of the surprises that happened in these new paintings are these creatures, these snakes that begin to slither into them. . . .

G   There is one thing, it's a good device.

Q.   Linking something?

G.   It's a line. A snake is a line ... a beautiful line.

But also: they are everywhere. People say: "Maybe you have an obsession." That's because they don't grow up with snakes. But I lived with them for years. In that house near Zaria (Northern Nigeria) they were everywhere—hundreds of the damn things: behind the fridge, under the bed, in the bush ... that's how it was. Europeans wouldn't think it odd, if I put a pussycat into my pictures. And snakes are very lovely really. I am not particularly fond of them, I wouldn't want to keep one.

Q.   But I do think they are beautiful. You never painted a monkey, in spite of the fact that you kept so many.

G   Noooo, they are too wonderful. Maybe their character is somewhere in my pictures, but not him in body.

Q.   Perhaps we ought to talk about the reception of the work by the public. It is really amazing how popular these recent paintings of yours are. You could have sold each one of them several times over. . . .

G.   Yes, it's ironical ... just when I have decided I don't want to sell my paintings anymore.
But it's true, they respond very warmly ... a lot of people.

Q.   It's only those who think they know about art, who come up with the occasional stupid comment like: "It's very interesting, the way you have used that African imagery. . . ."

G.   They are blind! I am infected with the life, not the imagery. It's much more an indirect thing.

Q.   Much more subtle. I think Olu Oguibe's comment throws some light on this issue.

G.   He is a very bright fellow, really, and a very promising young artist himself. At Nsukka, I gave him reproductions of my paintings to look at. . .
.

Q.   ... and I remember his first comment. He said to me: "This is a celebration!"

G.   But then he went to a lecture of yours on Aboriginal art and afterwards he came home and said: "Now I understand, why the paintings are so different. They are like Aboriginal paintings; you are using all those dots. . .
." Now he wouldn't say it's like African art, because he knows too much about it. Fortunately, I had those reproductions with me at the time and I showed them to him and I said: "Show me where the dots are" and he said: "Oh no, there aren't any." That's a good example of how people read things onto paintings.

Q.   It stems from a habit of constantly trying to interpret a picture in terms of other pictures ... of searching for labels. . . .

G.   Actually, Herr Schmidt, from the Bank, he was marvelous when he commented on Bisi Fabunmi's paintings. He said: "There's no word for it, they don't fit. This is a thing of its own." This kind of spontaneous reaction is rare. . . .

Q.   To end with, we should talk about this particular exhibition: You have some very contrasting elements in it.
The real core of the exhibition is formed by these new paintings. But before you get to them, you pass through a room of these very pure line drawings. Perhaps you can say that this is the raw material from which the paintings are made.

G.   Yes, it's always changing through, and I can use the same drawing in different situations. For example, if you have a drawing of a little head and you can use it in a painting. Then you forget that you've been using it, and it reoccurs on an appliqué. He's always different, but like the same person, showing different sides of his character. But you also create new characters all the time. . . .

Q.   People will find it easy to relate these drawings to the paintings; but what about the first room, where you have these very large, spontaneous drawings, nearly three meters high. . . ?

G.   It's just a matter of scale. If you were to reduce these drawings to, say, half a meter, you would clearly see it's the same type of drawing. But it's also like theater, that room. I only wish, I had some dancers! The idea is, to jolt people out of that deadly "Art Gallery" mood.

These big drawings are rough things; but it's good to work quickly sometimes. I spend a month on a painting. . . it's difficult to make these twenty-five panels all work together. There are so many complicated color relationships; and it has to have rhythm, harmony. . . .

Q.   If I try to sum up the different things you have said about painting, it seems to me to be a continuous process of solving problems.

G.   When a problem is solved in painting, I feel transparent, physically transparent. The code is cracked, the trap is released. Imagine the antelope, caught in the hunter's trap. Imagine him being released and lightly bouncing off into the bush. In my own case, I am the trap, the hunter and the antelope.

CHARACTER IS BEAUTY

V.
YORUBA SOCIETY

Womanhood in Yoruba Traditional Thought
Sophie B. Oluwole

INTRODUCTION

Very few writers today have the temerity to deny the existence of a nearly universal discrimination against women in all ages. This assertion is based on the raw facts of human experience documented in several studies of different human cultures the world over (Grimshaw 1986:36).

Discrimination against women in present-day Nigeria is not a new phenomenon. Some 100 years ago, precisely at the inception of colonial rule, pregnancy and/or marriage marked the end of an educated woman's career. Each of the two also earned her instant dismissal from the university. This is still true of students in secondary schools in most countries of the world. Today, the educated woman in Nigeria has made some progress. She can now marry and retain her job or continue her university study. But until very recently there was no maternity leave with pay. These are now a woman's right even though a single parent, who needs more money to care for herself and the baby, still receives half-salary during her leave. A female lecturer in most Nigerian universities today receives no house allowance once her husband is provided residential accommodation. Yet every lecturer's contract includes the provision of this accommodation or some allowance in lieu of it.

The present concern of most female activists is to show the inadequacy of conventional reasons as justification for these discriminating treatments of women. The final goal is to fight for justice and achieve it. The primary aim of this paper goes beyond this. My interest is to investigate the role some cultural philosophies have played not just in justifying the unjust treatment of women but in providing the metaphysical and epistemological bases for negative and positive conceptions of womanhood.

My illustrations will be drawn from both Western philosophy and

African traditional philosophy. In other words, my mission is to critically examine how philosophy as a discipline has tactically contributed to the oppression of women, when philosophy is defined as consisting of principles underlying reasons for the different arrangements of men (and women) in society. (Kwasi Wiredu 1980).

The Metephysical and Epistemological Origin of the Oppression of Women in the West

At the level of poetic and philosophical imagination, man regards every object of experience as having an indubitable surrealist existence. When Thales sought to establish the fundamental stuff from which everything came into palpable reality, he did not deny this surrealist view. What he did was to introduce a dualism which entails an implicit classificatory element. To talk of something as fundamental is to imply that others are subsidiary or may be inferior. Metaphysics as practiced in the West, therefore, started as an otherwise objective study of nature but with an inherent disguised form of evaluation. This point came out clearly in the works of Plato and his successors and the trend has not changed much even today. Metaphysics as the search for absolute certainty entertains an epistemology which regards truth as superior to opinion (not falsity), and prizes knowledge higher than belief (not ignorance).

The scientist today operates on the epistemological view that knowledge comes to man through the five senses. With or without the aid of scientific equipment he sees the sun, feels its warmth, and recognizes it as the basic source of energy to all living creatures. The physical-biological effect of the sun leads man to the conclusion that the sun is a giver of life. But the same scientist, through the same media, knows that the light from the moon is a reflection of that of the sun, even though the moonlight is of less value to living things than that of the sun. Here again an objective observation of the sun and moon reveals a sort of interest in their comparative importance. At the level of Western symbolism, therefore, the sun represents royalty while the moon stands for subservient existence.

Many good reasons can be given for the initial discrimination between primary and subsidiary levels of existence, between the harsh solar energy and the colder one of the lunar sphere. The categorization of objects, experiences, etc. into different types can therefore be justified on purely rational grounds. The distinction between truth and opinion, between primary and subsidiary existence, between man and woman amounts to carrying out purely objective descriptions of nature and the elements of human experience.

But the problem becomes different when we come to regard these classifications as evidence of some basic evaluative qualities or lack of them.

Hellenic civilization recognizes the dualism both in nature and in human experience. But philosophy, in its system of building abstract theories based on this dualism, involves itself in human judgements which misidentify natural differences as elements of positive and negative values. In short, natural characteristics are not just regarded as signs of value differences but as canons in terms of which virtues and vices can be adequately determined.

When philosophy eventually broke into distinct disciplines, the same type of value assessment was extended to different types of human rational endeavors. While some rules and principles are regarded as universally valid, others are seen as of restricted relevance. The rigor and completeness of proof, the logical and empirical demonstration of claims have precedence over sympathy, sensitivity, and homage to human interests. As modes of classification, these two sets of canons appear as inevitable, purposeful, and objective. This so-called scientific attitude thus separates the objective from the subjective, the primary from the subsidiary, the weak from the strong-and this on the claim of differences of veritable qualities. Science, we are told, concerns itself with the objective world while the humanities deal with the subjective problems of human thought and existence.

So far, the fundamental practice of discrimination between the objective and the subjective is supposedly value-neutral. But then, the way in which most Western thinkers from various ages used concepts like primary and subsidiary, objective and subjective, strong and weak, principles and sensitive should leave no one in doubt that some logical (or is it traditional?) relationships were seen as existing between these two sets. To many writers, the first set of ideas, qualities, etc. suggest positive values and the second set connote antithetical ones. To say of a person that he/she is strong, objective, and principled amounts to some sort of praise. To revert to the second set is to imply some condemnatory assessment of a person's behavior, character, attitude, and so forth.

The movement from pure metaphysical and/or epistemological understanding of nature to the categorization of natural objects and qualities into strict patterns of identity inadvertently led the West from mere description or analysis of facts to interpretations of such facts in biased terms. This is why I agree with Robin Barrow (Barrow 1982:7) that discrimination comes naturally into the world of human experience; what does not are human prejudices and biases. In other words, man discriminates every day and justifiably so. To call X a man and Y a woman is to be involved in a purely classificatory discrimination. But to treat Y differently in ALL THINGS just because Y does not belong to the class of X is to be involved in an unjustifiable absolutism. For while there may be some occasions and good reasons for treating X differently from Y, there cannot be such good reasons for treating them as two parallel lines which never meet.

What intrigues me at the level of philosophical thinking in the West is not how individual philosophers have undervalued women or what irrational justifications such thinkers gave for their attitude. Instead, my primary concern is with the Western philosophic conception of womanhood. And these two—the unfair treatment of women and the philosophic attitude to womanhood—can, to my mind, be adequately separated. This is without prejudice to the fact that one may be seen as a justification for the other. It is one thing to treat women unjustly because they are women; it is another to have a negative conception of womanhood.

There is abundant evidence in Western literature to prove a negative philosophic attitude to womanhood. What this means is not that being a female is unnatural or biologically unrealistic. Rather, womanhood stands for a scale of paradoxical qualities and values such as intellectual and physical weakness, the last to be created, the ephemeral and fickle-minded. This understanding is consonant with Thales' notion of primary and subsidiary existence, without implying, however, that Thales or his associates ever subscribed to the values imposed on his categories.

Judeo-Christian thought is sometimes seen as distinct from Hellenism. But at this level both share similar conceptions of women. Man is the primary stuff from which a woman was originally made. The woman caused the downfall of Man and by implication that of his descendants. Sinful Eve put an everlasting blemish on Saint Adam. This notion of "perfect" goodness and "absolute" badness was extended to Nazareth centuries later when a biblical character ejaculated: "Can anything good come out of Nazareth?" The reference of course was to Joseph and Mary's child JÈsùs Christ. This disparagement of JÈsùs Christ as it is now being inferred, stemmed not only from his provinciality and rusticity but also from the fact that Mary was pregnant before entering Joseph's house (Diop 1959: VIII). It is against this biased Western attitude towards womanhood as a sub-species that I wish to compare and contrast African philosophic conception not of woman but of womanhood.

Womanhood and Feminism in African Traditional Thought

Apart from the disputed claim that African thought in general exhibits an intellectual paradigm in which intuition, sensitivity, and homage to human interest play prominent roles (Cheikh Anta Diop, Aimé Césaire, Leopold Sedar Senghor), there are numerous instances in African folklore which bear testimony to a less prejudiced attitude towards women and womanhood. As it is said of people in other cultures of the world, the Yoruba, for example, recognize the distinctions between men and women. In tradition, women are expected to perform a number of roles different from the ones men are supposed to perform. Particular assignments have been seen either as unfair and/or based on false claims about the nature of the woman. But how exactly do the Yoruba people view womanhood? What does womanhood portray in Yoruba thought and philosophy?

Going from the level of metaphysics and epistemology, the Yoruba sage does not subscribe to any form of absolutism. He recognizes the dualism in nature but does not attempt to reduce everything to one category or regard a natural feature as absolutely positive or negative. The world, he knows, is full of characters and events which can be either good or evil, though not in any absolute sense. Instead of trying to deny the existence of Evil as many Western thinkers have done, the Yoruba sage neither regards God as the Creator of the world nor as a Perfect Being. The Yoruba God asks some questions and acknowledges the place of new knowledge; *Ajala*, the maker of destiny and therefore the agent indirectly responsible for Evil, was not God-not even a perfect man but "an incorrigible debtor ... an irresponsible man" (Abimbola 1976:116). Thus the Yoruba thinker recognizes Evil as real but he does not regard it as having independent existence or disreality as proof of God's incompetence or His limited goodness.

To the Yoruba it is true that knowledge or even truth, unlike its Platonic conception, cannot be absolute or everlasting. This is why he comes to the conclusion that *"Ogbón odún ní, wèrè è è mí"* (Wisdom this year is folly next year). Every truth gained through whichever means remains tentative at the level of opinion as Kwasi Wiredu, for instance, argues (Wiredu 1980). Consequently, there is respect for the views, opinions, and knowledge of others. Another Yoruba proverb states *"Ogbón ológbón ni kì í á pe Àgbà ní wèrè"* (The sage benefits from the wisdom of others, hence it is anathema to call him a dunce) and contrary to a popular view, wisdom is never restricted to the adult or a portion of humantiy: *"Omodé gbón, àgbà gbón a fí dá Ilé Ifè"* (Children are wise, elders too are wise, this is the fundamental principle of Yoruba culture).

The Yoruba may separate adults from children, but the action is not an excuse for the former's permanent discrimination against the latter:

Owoó omodé ò tó pepe
T'àgbàlagbà ò wo akèrègbè
Isé èwe bá be àgbà kí ó máse kò
Gbogbo wa ni a 1'óhun se fún ra.
The hands of the child do not reach
up to the mantelpiece.
Those of an adult cannot enter into a gourd.
Whenever the child appeals to an adult
for help the request may not be denied.
We exist to collaborate with one another.

The Yoruba attitude, therefore, is to recognize differences in man and nature without converting them into stereotypes. This general attitude is extended to moral distinctions. Rather than conclude that nothing good came out of Nazareth, the Yoruba sage admits that "*Inú ikòkò dúdú ni èko funfun ti jáde*" (Out of the black pot the housewife produces white maize pap). The idea is that whiteness and blackness as colors are interpreted; they do not symbolize permanent evil and good qualities respectively. We can infer also that an object or a human being that is not good today must be so tomorrow. Finally we have the philosophic principle that "*T'ibi t'ire 1 ójó n rìn*" (Goodness and Evil constitute an inseparable pair).

Womanhood in Yoruba thought symbolizes a—and not the—position of honor. In politics, specific roles are constitutionally reserved for women. And also in religion, woman sometimes ranks higher than man (Johnson 1921:63; Mba 1982:327). In socioeconomic arrangements, women are at the forefront and their contributions have always been recognized. For instance, men do not engage in the sale of farm products on market days. Most crops are grown by women (Ezeigbo 1990:153-154), except that nowadays most of them have become office workers and traders in urban centers. However, the essential role of women as "*Iyá*" (mother) has survived and continues to be defended: "*Orìsà bí iyá kò sí, iyá là bá má a bo*" (Mother is the only deity worthy of worship. This proverb clearly endorses the woman's inalienable position, like that of priest or sage, in every age and society. For the Yoruba people "*Iyá ni wura, baba ni dígí*" (Mother is gold, while father is glass).

There are two points that I wish to stress about Yoruba traditional thought. Firstly, the Yoruba view of life does not consist of classifying objects or human experiences into permanent classes meant to symbolize specific values. For example, the woman is at once mother, daughter, wife, merchant, and priestess. Secondly, it follows from the above that the woman is not regarded as an embodiment of evil. For example, Shakespeare, the arch-poet of the West, said: "Fraility thy name is woman!" Hamlet was addressing his mother. This would have been an abomination to a Yorubaman. For the Africans, the woman can be a philosopher-queen and enjoy the confidence and support of the entire menfolk (Mba 1982; Diop 1959:Xl).

Feminism and Human Values

A comparison of Western and African (Yoruba) conceptions of womanhood reveals that a clear distinction is made between natural discriminations which mean no more and no less than the recognition and classification of objects into natural types. But a number of feminists have argued in a manner which seems to deny the necessity for this otherwise purely rational exercise. Such a radical position appears to me to have little or no intellectual credibility. It is an error, as Barrow rightly argues, to believe that all forms of discrimination inevitably involve indirect acts of evaluation (Barrow 1982:Chapter 1). While this error is understandable in relation to the history of Western thought, it is not necessarily so in all other contexts. After all, there have been societies where womanhood is seen as dignified. Manhood can still be appreciated in its complementary role, even if male chauvinism is anathema to the civilized and fashionable world today.

I am aware of the charge of injustice against women in many African traditional societies, including that of the Yoruba. Such charges are based on the fact that although women are represented in councils and secret societies, for example, the number of women representatives falls short of equal treatment in view of their overall population (Mba 1982:Chapter 1). But the question of equality is a philosophically problematic one. Of course we are reminded that justice cannot consist of equal representation alone, just as all men or women are not treated the same way. In Yoruba society, a single female representative who performs the role of a regent, *Ìyálóde* (Women leader) and *Erelú* (Women leader in Ògbóni or Òsùgbó fraternities) wields more power than the other members. But one condition she must meet is that she has passed the age of menopause. This is to me not necessarily negative discrimination. No society, it is accepted, operates without its code of conduct in public affairs. A woman does not become a man and, by implication, a superior being when she destroys her femininity; she only performs better in some spheres once she is able to overcome weakness in her life and circumstances. For democracy to work in modern life, for example, only a man aged 25 years in Nigeria or another man aged 40 in America can aspire to certain positions in public affairs.

If the woman was not a child-bearer, she would not have remained at home and become a spinner, a weaver, pot maker, etc. She would not have had all the time, knowledge, and experience to manage the economy both at the domestic level and also in other areas of her involvement in society. The African woman in the past was many things rolled into one individual. From historical records, it is known that she could be a war leader like Queen Amina or Queen Nzingha, or a business magnate such as Madam Tinubu of Lagos (Diop 1959:IX).

The unequal treatment of men and women does not therefore necessarily amount to an act of unfairness, at least in Aristotle's definition of what is justice. What is wrong and unacceptable is to base human values on group/class properties like race, gender, or religion. The fact that a woman, for instance, possesses less of brute force than a man does not scientifically or rationally justify the view that women constitute a class permanently weaker or inferior to men folk (Mba 1982:290). Variations in the numbers of men and women in palaces, councils, etc. in a Yoruba social and political set-up do not support any claim of a general devaluation of women. The powers of *Ìyá-Oba* and *Ìyálóde* show that a single woman representative on the council can upset the decision of the entire council. And the reason for this is simple; the single woman represents womanhood and as such she enjoys an influence commensurate with the elevated position. A short Yoruba poem from oral tradition adequately demonstrates this:

Dá'gi ké,
Dá'gi ké,
Aáké ò le è dágiké,
Dá'gi là,
Dá'gi là,
Elìlà kan ò le è dá'gilà,
Bí ò s'Erelú
Osùgbó ò le è d'áwo se.

Cutting alone,
Cutting alone,
The axe cannot cut alone,
Splitting alone,
Splitting alone,
The wedge cannot split alone;
Without the Erelu (i.e., the female representative)
The Osùgbó secret society cannot operate.
(S Obande 1973:6).

230

This point, then, is that human evaluation will run into difficulty if and when it is based on merely accidental qualities. The United Nations and the constitutions of most countries have a definite stand in this matter. What all the defenders of human rights uphold is that human value and dignity shall not be violated in any assessment based on recognizable differences. Nevertheless the present situation calls for self-rediscovery, for it is doubtful whether any culture in the world has attained this neutrality in judgement and consequently succeeded in formulating absolute principles underlying the different arrangements of humans in society.

The argument I have tried to pursue here is meant to demonstrate that Yoruba traditional thought is less prone to the violation of womanhood. The difference I have noticed between Western and African attitudes to womanhood is that whereas the system of morality in the West condemns the entire class of woman to a position of inferiority, in African life the recognition of the differences between masculinity and femininity are seen as merely relative.

In Europe, however, especially within the last few years, there is an awareness of the fact that woman had for too long been deprived of some natural rights and opportunities for self-development. For example, women were denied the right to education, they were dis-enfranchized and could not be represented in any seat of government. And even creative artists from Western Europe took male pseudonyms to secure for themselves recognition in their societies. The Yoruba, like several other Africans, did not specifically make rules which retard the progress of women. At times the African society even creates bridges across "natural" barriers to assist both male and female citizens to attain the good life.

CONCLUSION

A few points of importance come into focus in this essay. Contrary to a conventional belief, acts of discrimination engaged in for the purpose of classification are rational and defensible. The traditional failure of the human mind or fancy is that at times it wrongly regards such otherwise purely value-neutral distinctions as canons for assessing the worth of humans or objects so classified.

Furthermore, negative acts of discrimination (against women, for instance) can be understood as wrong appreciation of brute force or mere abuse of power. In human judgment, strength is usually preferred to weakness. But in several "civilized" cultures of the world, both strength and weakness have their intrinsic merits. That the woman is different from man has been accepted as true. But, as many have observed, "difference is not inferiority." It is only in a state of nature, something like that described by Thomas Hobbes, that strength becomes the greatest asset in a community where everybody is against everybody else in the fight for survival. PrÈsumably, human society has moved far away from that situation which can justify the axiom that might is right. For even at the so-called "primitive" level of people such as Africans, there is still the awareness of the complementarity of male and female. It may therefore be reasonably argued that man has witnessed a post-Hobbesian movement from the eulogy of brute force to the recognition that "*Ogbón ju agbára*" (Wisdom is more important than physical strength). This no doubt is a reliable proof of cultural advancement in time and place.

The incidence of women's oppression by man is undeniable, as instances of this abound in modern life as well as in antiquity. But to equate fortuitous acts of physical torture with injustices based on woman's essential inferiority is to take an irrational and indefensible step in arriving at the correct understanding of the African's life and experience. A physically weak human being may be, and oftentimes is, psychologically strong and vice-versa. The African's recognition of this fact is illustrated in a saying from Zambia:

> See, my grandchild, they are not stupid.
> Nothing in the world is cleverer than the
> female sex. Know this: if you are as other men
> you are not as intelligent as a woman ...
> I tell you a woman is clever (Chinweizu:123)

We know of course what has led to the gender crisis of the present age, that is, the notorious act of pigeonholing with an aim not only of using group characteristics for description but also for qualitative judgement. In short, whenever African women were oppressed by their men, the action may not have necessarily been directed at the entire class of womanhood. And when the men of those days did, they misbehaved in acting contrary to their cultural heritage. The African village was never really synonymous with the state of nature. Most acts of oppression in African society today are rÈsults of the imposition of so-called "modern civilization," which in this case is nothing but retrogression.

Only a few of the traditional Christian Church denominations have leading roles for women. Some are still caught in the web of an argument that a woman cannot be a priest. For example, the decision of the Presbyterian Church to ordain women as ministers in 1975 was overturned in 1991 by the National General Assembly by a two to one majority vote (Awake 1992:7). This same campaign to integrate women into the Anglican Church has also failed woefully in Great Britain. Female priests among Yoruba people, on the other hand, was a common phenomenon (Mba 1982:4).

A first step in the right direction to avoid charges of oppression against women seems to be the recognition that individual failures of men and women do not constitute a gender prejudice and need not justify class or gender isolation. Once this is well realized, the other problem of assessing individuals on their own merit (i.e., in terms of levels of achievements rather than in terms of commonly shared characteristics) becomes easier than before to define and solve.

Understanding the nature of gender crisis in Nigeria and Africa as a whole can be difficult if the journey back to traditional culture is not made attractive enough to the moderns. The sun of today cannot go back to yesterday, but human thought and civilization can surely benefit from one thousand years of experience. This is why, in the light of this exposé, scholars of the feminist school may seriously wish to look once again at the whole argument about women's progress in the world.

In Africa today it appears as if gender discrimination against women is fundamentally similar to the oppression of women in the West. For although it is unlikely to have racial discrimination among the women from black Africa, ethnic and negative prejudice by the elitist female are just as real as those by white women against the blacks (hooks 1982). Ethnic discrimination has replaced racial discrimination to a level where some women in Nigeria can be regarded as "stateless," most especially in matters of appointment to public office. The woman who is married to a man from another state is regarded as a foreigner in her own nation.

The history of the development of Western philosophy and the mode of evaluation of masculine energy makes the notion of the Madonna's excellence anomalous within a culture that identifies womanhood with the whore. As noted earlier on, in Shakespeare's "Hamlet" the treatment of Gertrude by her intellectual son is not accidental to the age of Queen Elizabeth I. For the Yoruba people, among whom female virtue in a mother, sister, etc. is distinguished from vice or natural propensity for anti-social behavior, neither goodness nor frailty is associated with one particular gender. Hence a woman can be good or bad, but she is never seen as determined by nature to be inferior.

REFERENCES

Abimbola, Wande. *IFÁ: An Exposition of Ifá Literary Corpus*. Ibadan: Oxford University Press, 1976.

Abimbola, Wande. *Oju Odù Merindinlogun*. Ibadan: Oxford Univ. Press, 1977.

Abimbola, Wande. *Ijinlé Ohùn Enu Ifá*. Glasgow: Collins, 1968.

Awake. Magazine of the Jehovah Witnesses, 1992.

Barrow, Robin. *Injustice, Inequality and Ethics*. Norfolk: Barnes and Noble Books, 1982.

Césair, Aimé. *Discourse sur le Colonialism*. Paris: Présence Africaine, 1955.

Chinweizu, N.B. *Anatomy of Female Power*. London: Sundoor

Diop, Cheikh Anta. *The Cultural Unity of Negro Africa*. Chicago: Third World Press, 1978

Ezeigbo, Theodora Akachi. "Traditional Women's Institutions in Igbo Society: Implications for the Igbo Female Writer," *African Language and Cultures*, Vol. 3, No. 2 (1990).

Grimshaw, Jean. *Feminist Philosophers*. Brigthon: Wheatsheaf Books, 1986.

hooks, bell. *Ain't I A Woman*. Boston: South End Press, 1981.

Johnson, S. *The History of the Yorubas from the Earliest Times to the Beginning of the British Protectorate*. (1921.) Lagos: C.M.S. Bookshops, 1966.

234

Rowland Abiodun and Ulli Beier on Yoruba Women

UB: Throughout my life in Nigeria I was always impressed by the independence and power of Yoruba women. And yet, there are still many writers, even knowledgeable ones,- who see Yoruba society as highly patriarchal, where women are being dominated and exploited by men. How does this misconception arise?

RA: The fact is that foreign religions have reduced the position of women in Yorubaland in recent years; and Western values and education, Islam and Christianity have modified Yoruba concepts ... they have put a new layer of values on top of Yoruba values.

U: This is true. But even those who experienced Yoruba society three or four decades ago, when Islam and Christianity had not yet undermined Yoruba religion to this extent, were often fooled by the demonstrative show of male dignity in Yoruba society: they see the head of the household, pompously enthroned in his embroidered *agbádá*, his wives kneeling to greet him in the morning, while he casually hands a few shillings to the children to buy school books.

Yet the image is deceptive, because it does not reflect the real power relationship between the husband and the wives. The women are economically independent: they pursue their own craft or their own trade, they feed themselves and their children. Thus they can be economically independent of their husbands in many respects. They may rise to high positions in the cults of the *òrìsà*, they may be leaders in their trade unions (say, the cloth-sellers union or the yam-sellers union) and they can even achieve important chieftaincy titles in the city—like *Iyálóde* (the head of the markets). In fact, they pursue independent personal careers and may carry more respect in the town than their husbands.

R: Another factor may be that men are reluctant to talk about the power of women. They feel a little uneasy about the spiritual power of women ... so researchers who talk only to men do not get a true picture of the situation. How much do we know, for example about *Lobun* (the female ruler) in Ondo?

She surely was a powerful figure politically, economically, and possessed much spiritual power.

U: Maybe we should talk about this spiritual power. . . .

R: If you look deeper into Yoruba thought, you will find a lot of references to this power. For example, the greeting for every new year is: *odún áyabo*, which means: May the year turn out to be female.

U: Meaning peaceful ... productive ... harmonious ... and successful.

R: Yes! It would be a curse to say: may the new year turn out to be male! Nobody wants to hear that. So if women are not important, why should we invoke them at the beginning of every festival? Because we are invoking the power of "our mothers"—who wielded a considerable spiritual power and influence!

U: Immediately it comes to mind that there are so many *òrìsà* who are female, like *Òsun* or *Òtin*, who create order in the society, who bring peace and health, and who are responsible for the perpetuation of the society.

R: In Owò there is Oronsen, an ancient queen, who married *Oba* Renrengenjen. She was very beautiful and she had the power to make the Olówò rich. She was not his first wife, the Olówò had married many other wives before she came to Owò. I have the feeling, too, that Oronsen, who was a mysterious woman, had married one or two kings before she married Renrengenjen. He got all kinds of good things as a r*Èsùlt* of marrying her; but, of course, the other wives got very jealous and they decided to make sure that he would send her out of the palace.

They knew her taboos: no one was to cut okra in her presence; if women brought back firewood on their heads from the farm, no one must unload it in her presence; and, finally, nobody must spill water in front of her.

One day, the co-wives conspired to do all these three things to provoke her, and immediately she packed her things and left.

When the king discovered that his favorite wife had gone, he summoned the chiefs and the hunters and he asked them to pursue her. Finally they discovered her in a place called Ugbo Lajá, which means literally: the bush of the head gear!

They called out: Please stop! But she refused. They tried to grab her, but she eluded them. She sank into the ground and only her head gear remained in their hands. That is why the place was named Ugbo Lajá.

Before she disappeared, the *Oba* asked her what they could do to be safe, because while she had been in Owó all neighboring cities had been powerless against them. Then she said: "If you want to enjoy peace, you must pray to me every year and you must sacrifice 200 birds, 200 snails, 200 yams, 200 kolanuts, and so on. . . ."

And it is very interesting: the place where she disappeared is the very area where the Nigerian archeologist Ekpo Eyo has made all those wonderful discoveries of terracotta sculptures.

U: So Oronsen is the protectress of Owò, much in the same way in which *Òsun* is the protectress of Osogbo and *Otin* is the protectress of Okuku.

R: Yes. And every year there is a big festival: we call it the *Igogo* festival. During this festival the men plait their hair like women and they dress in those big skirts like crinolines. They put on blouses like women, in fact they acknowledge the power of women! Even the *Oba* will sit down for hours, to have his hair plaited!

U: Thirty-five years ago I witnessed an *Igogo* festival in Owò and I was shocked to see the *Oba* expose his plaited head! Because for an *Oba* to show the crown of his head is normally unheard of. It is considered extremely dangerous for any one to look at his head!

R: Yes, but I think this is an exceptional circumstance. It also shows how much the *Oba* and the other people respect and acknowledge Oronsen's powers. And for the *Igogo* festival lots of potent protective medicines are applied onto the Olówò's head before he wears the long white Okin feather and three red parrot feathers in his hair. That is how he dances round the town on the last day of the festival.

U: It seems to me that this is an awesome symbol! For it must signify that the mysterious power of women can neutralize the dangerous magic of the *Oba* 's head. I do remember an incident when the *Alaafin* of Oyo cursed a Lagos lawyer by lifting up his crown and exposing his head to him—and the man went mad and died two years later.

R: Yes, at the *Igogo* festival the women really assert their strength. All the Chiefs must plait their hair, too, and they must go and sacrifice at the grove of Oronsen.

Then the women dance around the town. They plait their hair elaborately in a very high dome and they wear literally thousands of red parrot feathers. The feathers of *Ayékòótó* have great magical qualities; that is why one is not allowed to bring them into a blacksmith's forge: because they can change the chemical composition of the metal!

The women dance through the town chanting and they accompany themselves on *Agogo*, on iron bells. Five or six of them usually go into trance. And I can tell you that this music is so powerful that it will grab you, if you stay near there for too long: I think that is why one is usually warned not to go near those women. If you stay near them for even 15 minutes you will feel the music in your intestines and your heartbeat starts responding to it—it adjusts to the beat ... some people also say, that if you stay too near them, you will become impotent!

On this day you will see thousands of young women dancing through the town: they are bare-breasted, they are dressed only in beads, and they carry a red sash around their chest. Nobody would touch them, because it is in fact frightening! This day is the assertion of women's power.

U: You mention the fact that the men plait their hair like women on this day and that they wear skirts. No doubt it's a way of paying homage to women. But at the same time it is also part of a much wider phenomenon in Yoruba culture: namely, that though there are male and female roles being played out in society, these roles are frequently blurred or even reversed. I think it has to do with the basic Yoruba concept that nothing is absolute: that all boundaries are flexible, all the truths ambivalent.

Sàngó is one of the most male òrìsà: extrovert, warlike, boisterous, full of bravado, an òrìsà who loves spectacular entries, who revels in dramatic performances; and yet his priests, too, plait their hair like women, they wear skirts and earrings, whereas the priestesses do not kneel before him (as women do) but they prostrate like men! In fact there are towns in Western Yorubaland where Sàngó is worshipped as a woman, where "he" is the wife of an ancient thunder god called Jakuta!

R: Even Esu, who is generally considered male, also has female attributes.

U: It lies at the very core of his personality! Esu questions every kind of conventional thinking, he disturbs all complacency in men and constantly forces us to re-think. It is natural that he should also challenge conventional concepts of gender.

R: In English we translate "Oba" as "king," but the Yoruba word does not imply gender. It simply means "ruler," whether male or female.

U: There have been female Obas in Yoruba history: there were female Oonis in Ife; the founder of Ondo was a queen!

R: You know the very ancient crown in Idanre, which is said to be the actual crown of Oduduwa. It is more or less a predecessor of the nineteenth century beaded Yoruba crown with which we are familiar. It has a conical head.

But do you know that in Ilesa today, the priestess of Owari wears a crown, called ade-aforisokun, that is almost identical to this ancient crown from Idanre? Owari was an early Owa of Ilesa, a powerful, temperamental ruler, who is now worshipped as an Òrìsà. This suggests to me: if a woman can wear a crown that is identical to the crown of Oduduwa, does it not indicate that women used to wield great political power, and that Oduduwa even could have been a woman?

And take a look at Yoruba art. There is a famous bronze pair of figures excavated by Frank Willett at Ile-Ife.

U: You mean the couple with the interlocking legs ... found at Ita Yemoo?

R: Yes, they are regal figures! There is no doubt that the shorter one is a woman. She wears a wrapper, covering her breasts. The taller one is a man but there is no difference in status. No one is inferior, they both wear the same type of crown, the same diagonal sash across their shoulders. . . .

U: Almost reminiscent of the *Igogo* festival in Owo! And the playful interlocking legs indicate a relaxed, playful relationship. . . .

If this was thirteenth or fourteenth century, what happened between then and now? I am almost certain that the change in the status of women happened with the coming of the new religions and colonialism.

U: If you go back further to the terracotta heads of eleventh and twelfth centuries, you find women with the same regal look, the same splendid dignity. . . .

R: Look at their hairstyles: there is a hairstyle called *Owewe* (which means "finely crafted"). It is very regal, obviously reserved for very powerful people: priestessess, almost goddesses. And it had been preserved right into the nineteenth/twentieth centuries. *Owewe* appears on the *Epa* masks of *Alaye*.

U: Maybe we should look at Yoruba attitudes preserved in the language itself in sayings and proverbs and *Ifá* divination verses.

R: Yes, if you look at Yoruba proverbs you realize that the Yoruba people thought that a man's life did not really start until he was married and parents would get extremely upset if a man was late in marrying. An *Ifá* verse says:

> *Having no wife calls for positive action,*
> *to keep quiet is to invite*
> *trouble and inconvenience.*
> *Having a wife is as different*
> *as having none;*
> *One without a wife should weep publicly*
> *in the marketplace.*
> *It is neither an extreme action,*
> *nor an over-reaction.*

U: When I lived in Ede and Ilobu in the fifties, a girl could not be forced to marry a man she did not want.

R: O no!

U.   People ·would put pressure on her, but she could not be forced. Moreover, I found that women did not find it hard to leave their husbands; a

239

woman could always run to her father's house, or even to a new husband, and have the case "settled" later. But it was not as easy the other way round: a husband could not easily send away a wife, because usually his mother and other senior female relatives would interfere. I don't know what happened in earlier times, but in those days women seemed to have the upper hand. They often toyed with men. I remember one situation in Ilobu where a young girl was to be married to an important old man. She secretly loved a young school teacher, but she realized that her lover did not have the money to give her an elaborate *Iyàwó* ceremony. So she married the old man, and got herself decked out in expensive clothes, beads, and jewelry; she hired drummers and danced through the town in a triumphant manner. But within a few days she ran away from her new husband and went to live with her school teacher. This kind of thing was rather the exception, of course, but it does show what a girl could get away with!

R: That reminds me of the story of Òsun, descending from heaven with the 16 major Òrìsà. This is a story from the *Ifá* Oracle. After the creation of the land the 16 major òrìsà settled on earth. They were doing their work and all went well—only they paid no respect to Òsun. They did not know who she was; they thought she was unimportant because she was plaiting people's hair.

> Òsun sèngènsén
> olóòya iyùn
> Òsun the exquisitely beautiful woman
> the expert hairdresser with the largest comb

So they neglected her, until one day she decided to show them who she was. They did not know that when they were corning down from heaven the creator had given her all the Ase, the magic power, to make things come to pass. So all of a sudden plants would not produce fruit, disease could not be cured, men could not produce semen, and when rain fell chickens just picked it up and ate it. Many strange things happened. The whole world was turned upside down.

Then the male divinities held a meeting—again without Òsun—and they decided to go back to the creator, to tell him that the world was not going well. Things had been good at first, but suddenly everything had gone sour ... The creator asked them why they had come back to him. When they explained what had happened, he said to them: "I see sixteen of you. Where is the seventeenth? If you do not return and reconcile with the seventeenth, your problem cannot be solved!"

So they returned to earth and they tried to woo Òsun. They said to her: "Aaah, Òsun, you are our mother, you are everything to us. We are sorry we ignored you, we did not mean to do so. But please: the creator said we should make up our differences!"

But *Òsun* did not listen to them: "Look I'm not interested in your talk." They started begging her, they begged from morning to evening. She was just looking at them: "You think you have the power? Go ahead. We'll see how far you can get." She didn't even ask them what their problem was: but she knew, because she was the cause of it all.

After some time she felt sorry for them and she said: "I will consider your request. You see I am pregnant now; I am expecting a baby. If the baby I am carrying will be a girl, then I will have nothing to do with you any more. But if it will be a boy, he will join you: and this is how your problems will be solved!"

So they were all praying and making sacrifices that the child should become a boy! She gave birth and it was a boy. She called him *Osetura*. So *Osetura* became the bridge between men and women. Now I have done some other work on this which convinces me that *Osetura* is *Èsù*!

U: That makes sense! Because *Èsù* is the boundary-crosser; so he is the natural mediator, the link between men and women. He is the one who carries the sacrifice: he mediates between men and *Òrìsà* as well as between the different *òrìsà*!

R: And another thing: in the *Ifá* ritual, you have the sixteen Ikin, the palmnuts of *Ifá*, but there is always a seventeenth, a small conical ivory head who is called Olori Ikin, the chief of the Ikin. It is this Olori Ikin who always receives the sacrifice for the *Babaláwo*. Now I believe that this *Olori Ikin* is *Òsun*!

U: So that although the men are practioners of the *Ifá* oracle, and although they hold the power of the oracle, they can't do any of it unless they get the sanction of the female power behind it!

R: So when you are talking about women sacking men, but men finding it hard to sack women, I thought you were right! Because *Òsun* sacked the men, but the men could not sack her!

U: I think we should look at the role of sexual relationships in Yoruba society, because in Europe people associate polygamy with a seraglio type of male indulgence: a harem filled with ravishing odalisques waiting for their master's pleasure. But the reality was not so at all. A man may have had several wives, but the sexual act was not considered to be an "independent art form," as we try to make it now in Europe, or as it was developed, say, among the upper cast of classical India.

The sexual act served the production of children, and as soon as a woman was pregnant, she could not be touched by the husband until the child was weaned, which amounts to three years! So that even a man with four wives would live a relatively abstemious life in traditional Yoruba society.

R: And there was virtually no extra-marital sex or adultery in the older days.

U: I believe there was a very serious reason for this. A Yoruba woman could never hide the identity of the father of her child: because whoever buries the afterbirth of the child *becomes the father.* No matter who was the biological father of the child, it becomes part of his lineage. So if a woman allows her husband to bury the afterbirth of her lover's child, she is depriving that other family of life. This means that the equilibrium between clans, the harmony of society is seriously disturbed: a much graver situation than our concept of the "sin" of adultery.

R: The husband was actually a bit left out in the polygamous society. He was rather alone!

U: He was certainly alone, because although the children legally "belonged" to him and the woman is said to bear the children "for him," they were in fact mother-oriented and the father played a lesser role in their lives. Each woman lived in her own rooms with her children, and the children relied on their mother and on the co-wives for their needs.

In the early days of the extra-mural department, we were given a university car and an official driver to take us round the country. And I remember that each one of these drivers would suddenly stop when we were driving through some town and ask to introduce me to his mother. None of them ever took me to see his father.

And in a bigger context: when the Olokuku feasts his crowns, he must lead a procession, in which all eighty crowns are carried by his wives' daughters to the cemetery to pay homage to his mother.

R: Yes, that is right. Women, and mothers in particular, are held in awe. A woman is the vehicle for some awesome magical power. Even in ordinary children's riddles, *àló*, the vagina is referred to as:

> *A cup that is turned upside down*
> *never spills its contents.*

It's magic and it's sacred. It is also called:

> *The road that leads to/from heaven*

That is, a passage, a sacred passage through which we came-from heaven and through whose power, if directed against you, you must return to heaven.

If a woman is provoked to extreme anger and she suddenly exposes her private part to the man while she is cursing him, the man will run away interor.

U: It's similar to the *Oba* exposing his head, because the *àse* is there!

R: When a woman undresses in the context of a serious argument, it is an explosive situation! A man will not be sexually aroused by suddenly seeing the woman naked, he will be terrified. The vagina is sacred and power concealed. That's why another name for vagina is *Eégún*, because it covers a mystery. So being exposed to the vagina is rather like someone trying to lift the mask of an *Egúngún* in order to see the eye of the dancer... it is an absolute taboo.

U: So now we see why women have lost their status and their power in recent decades, because Christianity and Islam have deprived them of their magic. Once a woman loses her *òrìsà*, she loses her power. She has become profane.

R: Look at another aspect: the woman kneeling down and holding her breasts. . . .

U: As you see on carved *Sàngó* dance staffs for example. . . .

R: Many would think it was erotic, maybe ... but it is not, it is the most sacred position. For a woman to kneel down, naked, and hold her breasts is the most sacred, powerful thing on earth she can do. Because in that position she can speak to the *òrìsà* and the *òrìsà* will listen to her. Anything she says in that state has the potential of coming to pass. In other words, these women possess their own *àse*.

U: In that position, women pull together the highest powers that no man can withstand: it's like an exercise in concentration that allows all her powers to converge.

R: It is a power that is linked with:

   ikúnlè abiyamo

that is the pain of childbirth. This is again linked with the saying:

   That which is received kneeling down
   that is your destiny

U: So you could say that in this kneeling position, the woman has the power to confront her *orí*, her destiny. Just as every human being kneels down to receive his destiny before coming to earth, so she now has the power to confront her *orí* again and to change her destiny or even the destiny of others.

R: In this gesture women can disarm the òrìsà, so that they have to listen to them. That's why women are supposed to possess owó èrò, the hand that makes things easy, the hand that softens life, that softens the hardest people, softens Sàngó , softens Ògún. . . .

U: So the female figure that kneels on the osé Sàngó , proffering her breasts, is cooling Sàngó 's temper, softening his power. Just like Òsun heals a disease with cool water.

R: In Yoruba, healing always has to do with the attributes of water: it is smooth, soft, and gentle. There is an association between èrò (soft) and èrò (medicine).

U: The water of Òsun softens and heals. The brass fan of Òsun cools. These are symbols of her power. That is why every shrine in Osogbo has a pot of water from the river Òsun, which is sprinkled over the obì (kolanut) before it is broken and used in divination. The issue that is being confronted through divination is thus calmed in advance; the tension is diffused. . . .

R.   *When the fire is raging really high*
        it is water we use to quench it
        When the weather is blazing hot
        it is the fan we use to beg it.

        There is a competition between fire and water.
        Fire chases water.
        Fire continues to chase water
        and refuses to turn back.
        A blazing fire
        If fire pursues water
        and does not turn back
        propitiation is the answer.
        Fire cannot maintain it's glow
        beyond the water
        No matter how powerful fire is
        when it gets to the water
        it must die.

U: That is a wonderful image of male and female power.

R: You know if somebody is mentally ill and the Babaláwo has tried everything in vain, he will usually ask a last question: "Is the patient's mother still alive?" If the answer is no he will say: "This is going to be a most difficult case." But if yes, he will say: "There is one last solution." Then he prepares a concoction and rubs it onto the mother's breast. And the patient, even if he is seventy years old, must suck it. That is the most powerful cure.

U: The healing power of woman's breast is a very basic concept in Yoruba. Sucking a breast is not simply a matter of being fed. In a society where husbands and wives largely pursue their own separate ways in life, marriage is something akin to a loose federation.

So it is not surprising that in most women's lives the child has the preference over the husband and tenderness and even eroticism are directed more towards the child than the man. For the child, too, the mother's breast is a source of reassurance. Children suckle their mother's breast affectionately, long after they have begun to eat solid food. Even when the mother is suckling her new baby, the older child, of three or four years, may seek reassurance and peace by briefly sucking the mother's breast. Even grandmothers allow children to suck their breasts, and in certain circumstances even older women begin to lactate again.

R: That is amazing. Is that proved?

U: Yes, it was observed by doctors at the University College Hospital in Ibadan in the fifties.

R: Perhaps this orientation towards the mother explains why in every important Yoruba ritual, there are some women in the background. Even the *egúngún* must ask the blessings of some old women in the cult before they can come out and perform their energetic dances in the street.

U: The *Gèlèdé* masquerade is really all about the placation of women's power.

R: Though charged with political and important judicial functions, the *Ògbóni* society I believe also helps to maintain the balance between mother earth, the producer, sustainer of life, and man as the user and/or beneficiary of the new wealth of *ilè* (the earth).

U: And even in the installation of a king: after the kingmakers have had their say and the *Ifá* oracle has confirmed the choice, the installation cannot proceed unless the head of the palace women will perform the most important installation rites and ceremonies.

R: So we come back to the beginning: the sixteen *Òrìsà* descended from heaven to rule the world, but everything went wrong, until they remembered to placate *Òsun*. Because she holds the ase.

U: In the end it is only the *Ifá* oracle that enables men to live with this magic power of women. *Ifá* teaches them to live with patience and coolness. It teaches them how to soften the world and placate the powers of the universe.

Yoruba Values
A Conversation Between Rowland Abiodun and Ulli Beier

U: I want to talk to you about your childhood in Owo. About the education you received from your parents, and the type of "cultural baggage" you have carried through life with you. Because you are one of the few people I know who have had a very traditional Yoruba upbringing and at the same time you have reached the pinnacle of your profession in the Western world. You have gone through the whole complicated process without loss of identity. That is very rare. You have been lucky to grow up the way you did. But we must recognize that, compared to your own period, millions of Yorubas now grow up in a cultural desert. When Georgina ran a textile workshop at Nike's place a couple of years ago, she took the students to see an Agbegijo dance performance at Erin Òsun and it was the first time that any of them had seen such a performance, even though they live only a couple of miles away from the home town of these dancers and musicians.

Now you must ask yourself: how will these young people cope with Western values, if they have no values of their own to use as a yardstick to evaluate them? Where will they get the sense of security from, that enables them to understand a foreign culture?

When I first came to Nigeria in 1950 I experienced the reverse situation. Discovering the excitement of Yoruba drumming did not make me abandon my interest in classical European music. On the contrary: the more I understood about Yoruba music, the more I began to understand about my own musical tradition.

Those colonialists who had no deep understanding of their own music thought Yoruba drumming was nothing but a lot of noise. The tragedy is that those people educated a whole generation of Nigerians who thought that rejecting their own culture was an integral part of acquiring Western skills. Abandoning their own cultural base, they had no means of interpreting European culture, and they were left with the grotesque substitute of British colonial rituals. This is how we got the sad phenomenon of what villagers soon labeled *oyinbo dudu*—the black white man.

R: I think you are perfectly right.

U: So what I want from you is really very simple: what were the particular Yoruba values that you got from your parents and that have enabled you
to cope with Europe in the way you have? In the light of what I said, you will
agree this is an important thing to do.

R: Owò was a town that never had it's culture overrun or tampered with,
even though it was situated between those two powerful kingdoms of Ife and
Benin. When I grew up the culture was still very powerful and all the traditional festivals were still being celebrated: the *Igogo* festival the *Egungun*
masquerade, the *Ogun*, festival and the *Upabi*—the splitting of the kolanut.
That was like a harvest festival, a celebration for the new kolanut crop.

      From 1946 on I was becoming aware of what was happening around
me. My parents were both Christians and they were very prominent and
respected members of the Anglican church. But I had an aunt who was doing
the *merindinlogun* (the oracle thrown with 16 cowries) and my paternal grandmother knew a lot about herbs and she was helping many women in childbirth.

In my family many members of the extended family took chieftaincy titles,
and I followed them when they danced around the town. We lived in a traditional house: a large rectangular building situated round an open courtyard.

U: With thick mud walls. And courtyards leading into courtyards.
Everything facing inside.

R: Exactly. I was interested in this compound structure. Of course, I
wasn't looking at it as architecture then. I was looking at it as a place that
brought security.

      One place that attracted me was the *Ojomo*'s palace. *Ojomo* is the
most important chief after the *Olowo*. His palace was said to be as big as that
of the *Olowo*. It is undoubtedly one of the finest palaces in Yorubaland: thick
mud walls. Polished red mud. The walls, even in our house, were annually
painted with a slip of red mud and the floors were painted with cow dung.
These houses were cool and we collected rainwater, like an impluvium. I
often ran away from home to go to the *Ojomo*'s palace. I loved the sacrifices
there, the meetings of the chiefs, the court sessions. . . in fact, they used to
tease me at home about it. They would say: "He'll grow up to take a chieftaincy title in the *Ojomo*'s palace."

U.   You have already pinpointed a very important aspect of Yoruba culture: accessibility of the chiefs. The *Ojomo*'s palace, even the king's palace,
were open to anybody, not exclusive domains of an elite. Yoruba culture was
very democratic.

R: Exactly! And they always loved me when I came. They enjoyed my interest. There were always sacrifices. Women were officiating. And then the *Ojomo* in his regalia! I was overwhelmed. I loved it. The whiteness! He came out in these white robes, and the calm and the dignity with which he moved!

U: There was a stateliness about Yoruba ceremonies. A cool sincerity. But however dignified the king, however holy he was, he always remained accessible. He could never say: "And who are you? What are you doing here?"

R: Never! If you were a stranger he would have to give you kolanuts. You know, in the *Ojomo*'s palace they had a set of huge drums, standing on three legs. In the morning there was drumming, in the evening there was drumming. Everything was enchanting and there was a special courtyard, which I liked to enter, which was where the *Ojomo* would talk privately to his chiefs and supporters. I was never barred from it; and when you sat on the *Ojomo*'s right hand, you were overlooking a collection of images: some were *sigidi* moulded from clay, some were carved in wood like the *Osanmasinmi*, others were cast bronze heads. Sometimes there was fresh blood from a sacrifice on the altar. To me that man was indestructable!

The man who was installed the *Ojomo* in 1948 had been my headmaster. He had always impressed me at school because he spoke beautiful English. But then, when be became the *Ojomo*, we discovered that his command of our own language was wonderful and he seldom used the English language again. I would always follow him during the *Igogo* festival. He would come out the day before the *Olowo*'s *Igogo* festival. He had to dance from house to house, from street to street, through the entire town. I am telling you, he had unbelievable strength. I don't know where he got it from, but I think he must have been possessed during that period. He must have had some special medicine to sustain him.

Then at harvest time, when the *egungun* came out, I would follow them again. I would wait at the edge of the sacred grove for them to appear in a blaze of color. And as I watched them coming out from the darkness of the forest, it was as if my own life was being renewed, not just the life of the town.

U: In many Yoruba towns, the church actively campaigned against all traditional festivals, and clergymen would condemn children from the pulpit who were seen to follow the ancestral masquerades. Did such a situation exist in Owo?

R: Nooooo! Not at all! Not when I was young. Prominent church members attended these festivals. Nobody had anything against it at all. It was much later, maybe in the early seventies, that the churches started grumbling. But when I was a child, they thought that was stupid. They said: how can you abandon your traditional obligations? Christianity does not stipulate that you should abandon your traditional duties. Oh no! There were several festivals every month: burials and chieftaincy installations. People coming out in their regalia and many kinds of music being played and I would follow them around in the street and I would be one of thousands!

When I finally went to Government College Ibadan I kept on rehearsing this dream! I sustained myself by reliving it all again. I visualized these festivals in all their details: the movement, the dance, and the color of it! This was really necessary because we learnt Latin and French, we learned the History of the British empire, we learned about America and Australia. I knew the geography of Tasmania! But we learned nothing—nothing at all!—about our own people. Their very existence was denied. We were even forbidden to speak our language! And anybody who was caught speaking the language would be fined and sometimes those caught three times would be caned and those who were caned for the third time could be sent out of the school.

But there was a very interesting occasion, when a boy was reported by the prefect for speaking "vernacular" and the house master decided that he would have to be caned. The boy agreed he had been speaking Yoruba but he said he wanted to make a point before being punished. The house master agreed to listen. Then the boy said that it was true that he had spoken Yoruba but the prefect had also laughed in Yoruba! The house master said: "How do you laugh in English?" The boy demonstrated a polite chuckle, whereupon the house master broke into loud Yoruba laughter and the boy was let off.

The only way I could express my own feelings in this environment was through art. I was doing a lot of artistic work then; I won many medals in the Western Region

Festival of Arts. Dr. Olúmbe Bassir and his wife Constance encouraged me a lot.

There was a time when I thought there was no need to study any further, because I

was going to become a practicing artist.

U: Let us return to your childhood in Owò. I want to know: how was a child brought up? How was the child treated? In Europe we regulate the lives of children a great deal: they are expected to eat at certain times, they are expected to finish their meal. They must go to bed at a fixed hour. We relegate the responsibility for their education to institutions—even from a very early age; because there are usually no aunts and no grandmothers around to share the burden.

On the other hand, Yoruba children moved around freely. They wander from compound to compound. They eat when they are hungry, they go to sleep when they are too tired to stay awake, and they participate in all grown-up activities. No child is ever sent out of the room or is told "you are too young to understand." At the same time children also participate in the work of adults.

R: O yes. I went to farm—only once a week, because I went to school. But even when I was quite small I followed my grandfather. You would trek about eight miles; you would carry something on your head. We would make a few yam heaps, we would also play a little. You would learn how to roast yams on the farm, how to hunt little animals. My parents really had less influence on my traditional education than my grandparents.

U: That is very common in Yoruba country. What was this influence?

R: I acquired their attitude towards work. I would learn the way they thought, because they told me stories. I followed my grandfather when he went hunting. I followed him to meetings. I wouldn't say a word. I sat there and listened and I saw how elderly people resolved issues. You marveled at the language they spoke, the proverbs they used. It was fantastic. And you started learning.

U: Learning without actually being taught.

R: Yes, my mother talked to us with her eyes. *Omo tó m'ojú*—the child that knows the eye, that is a great compliment. The child that can take it's cue from the eye is a well-behaved child.

U: Were you ever beaten?

R: No! No, no, no, never! And you know there is one thing called *ìfara-balè*, which is control. To have control over your physical body and your mind. This is very important to Yorubas. You know that Yoruba would say: Ah, *Tunji omo tíí farabalè ni*. You know when I saw Tunji playing in the Opera House, what came to my mind was: *omo naa ni ìfárabalè*—he was totally in control.

So everybody strives to achieve this control. I think it has to do with *àló* (riddles) and story-telling in the evening, because in those days there was no television. When there was moonlight, everybody would gather outside the house. All the children would sit there, absolutely quiet. Then one of the older men or women would be telling a story. It could start with a song and then lead to the real *ìtàn*. In one year I must have listened to at least eight hundred stories ... that trains you to listen.

U: It trains you to concentrate.

R: It trains your imagination.

U: But then how do you learn such attitudes? Because your parents don't wag their fingers at you all the time, saying: "Don't do this, don't do that."

R: It has to do with a number of concepts. One is *ilutí* (good hearing), that is the ability to listen, the ability to respond, to carry out instructions. Another is *omolúwàbí*.

U: Chief Delano has defined *Omolúwàbí* as a person who embodies all the good qualities appreciated by Yoruba people: a man who is good at his profession (whatever it happens to be), a man who shows respect to his elders, who works well in a team—whether it is a hunting party or a court session—a man who is respected by the community around, or one who is, as the popular phrase goes, "known to two hundred people."

R: Good character (*ìwà*) is continuously quoted as the basis of a successful life in the *Ifá* oracle, and children hear such verses quoted—not just when they happen to be present at a divination, but also because many of these phrases have entered everyday language.

U: For example:

> *The man who marries a woman without good character*
> *has married another man's wife.*
> *The man who has a child without a good character*
> *has another man's son.*

But the main question then remains: how does one acquire good character in Yoruba society? How is this transmitted?

R: *Sùúrù*—patience! *Sùúrù baba iwà*—patience is the father of good character, that means you can listen, you can learn many things, you can take many shocks, you can reason, you respond to situations.

People love that! People watch that from youth. You get rewarded for exhibiting such qualities. You receive praise. Even in the profession of a woodcarver, you cannot be a great artist unless you have *ifárabalè*—total control, total concentration. Nor can you be an artist without having *sùúrù*. Without *sùúrù* you cannot absorb the wisdom your father or grandfather has to impart. Only *sùúrú* enables you to learn the skills of a great master craftsman. There are different kinds of individual *ìwà* and people respect that. But if you want to be respected as a king, as a priest, as a diviner, then you have to have *sùúrú*."

U: *Sùúrú* is not to be mistaken for passivity.

R: No! It is what I would call "calculated patience!"

> *It is with calculated patience*
> *that one kills the sandfly*
> *that lands on a man's scrotum!*

U: *Sùúrú* is a form of pragmatism.

R: That's right. If you take a big stick to kill the sandfly...Yoruba restraint is not the oriental type. You do not deny yourself

U: On the contrary. The Yoruba live out everything... but they know when and how!

R: *Sùúrú* means that you have the conviction that the world goes on. It takes it's course and your opportunity will come. Just hold it. . . .

U: Don't hassle.

R: No! Hassling, being over-ambitious, being pushy-these are considered to be the worst qualities in a man. An *Ifá* verse says:

> *Somebody who carries a basket of eggs on his head*
> *has need of a composed gait*

U: And, life being what it is, we are all carrying baskets full of eggs on our head, and every time you feel irritated, every time you lose your patience—you are breaking some eggs in your life.

R: *It is with grace and dignity*
        that the child from an important family walks

U: One thing I loved most about living in Yoruba country was this. An old man comes to visit you. Maybe a priest. He greets you: '*E kuleo, Iyàwó nkó, omodé nko?*' and so on. He sits down. You offer him kolanuts. Maybe a drink. He has not come because he has something to say. He has not come to report some crisis ... there is a wonderful Yoruba greeting: "I hope nothing?" He hasn't come because he needs money or because he wants to chat. He wants to be with you. He sits down quietly. Nothing is said. There is no need for it. No small talk. You may even go on doing what you were doing. He will be there for ten minutes or half an hour. You are not even aware how long it is. . . .

R: Exactly!

U: Finally he says: "*Mo ti rii yin*" (I have seen you), and leaves. Nothing has "happened," but you feel refreshed, even elated, because you were in his presence. There is a radiation, a strong magnetic field that charges your spirit. And I am sure it is this *Sùúrú*, this inner calm.

R: Yes, it is, it is.

U: It's a quality you cannot find in the West.

R: It has been lost. We felt this very much, when we came to America.
        It seemed unnatural, the speed with which people deal with you. "Yes? What do you want?" And they just snap off and move to the next thing. Many people avoid communication. As bad as Nigeria was when we left, people would still just come like that. We would have four or five visitors a day. "Ah, it's a long time since I have seen you"—and they just sit

down.

U: Even children can do that!

R: Yes, because they are sent to call on older people! My grandfather sent me on such "greeting errands" countless times a week: I could be sent ten times to greet somebody! So I will go there, to that elder person:

> Bàbá mi ní kí n kíi yín
> Aaah, o sé o, o sé o
> Inú mi dùn púpò.

After about five minutes of silence he will say: ah *pèlé*...A long time we sit and don't say anything. During this period, he will be thinking how loved he is, that somebody sent his child to come and greet him! Then, when I am leaving, I pay homage, prostrate, and go. I will come back to my grandfather and say:

> Mo ti kí won,
> àlàáfía ni wón wà
> wón ni ki n kii yin
> *I have greeted him very well,*
> *I have asked for his health*
> *he told me to salute you*

My grandfather says:

> o káre-*Well done, I am proud of you*
> omo ni ó-*You are a real child*

Maybe the following morning my grandfather will say:

> *Ah, that woman near the market,*
> *go and greet her for me*
> *tell her, I am greeting her*

So I go there, and again:

> *My father says I should greet you*
> *I hope you are well*
> *Thank you, I am well*

I won't say that my father is not feeling very well at first. After some time she will ask: Why have you come to see me?

> *I have come to see you*
> *because my father's body is not very well*

Eeeh, it is fever

She may go into the house and bring some small medicine and wrap it: I am giving that to him. I would not ask what is inside. When my father receives the parcel he will say: *Aah, o káre* (Aah, thank you). Then he will call my grandmother to see what I have brought back. You see maybe in the first place my grandfather wanted to ask for that medicine but he didn't tell me to get the medicine, and I didn't know his intention. It was a very subtle message. He didn't ask for it, but he got it through this means.

U: At the same time you were receiving a subtle education!

R: I was learning all the time on these errands. On another occasion my grandfather will say again:

U: This was the finest education you could ever have. You learned manners. You learned composure. You learned diplomacy: You had to know what to say, you had to sense when the right moment came to leave, you had to be able to convey the spirit of the message, not just the words. You had a great responsibility: a clumsily delivered message could lead to a rift between adults. Because everything here depended on subtlety and balance. So this is how you learn how to become a man, a reliable, secure, well mannered person.

R: And I enjoyed listening very much. Just sitting. When my grandfather was very old,

he couldn't move much. He just sat in one place for hours. He just sat down. He had this long pipe: a long bamboo stick with a clay piece at the end. Do you know what discipline it was for me to stay by him for about six hours? I would remove the old tobacco when he had finished his smoke, then I would get some glowing embers to rekindle the pipe. Then I would sit and wait ... I wouldn't be able to doze off.

U: But this is again the presence, the magic of just being together, being attuned to the *ìwà* of the other person.

U: It is authority emanating from an undisturbed calm. From a perfect balance of mind.

R: It is this peace that I got from my grandfather that helped me throughout my life, helped me in my work, my research. Most things that I achieved in the world happened through the utilization of those values.

U: You were not interested to participate in a rat race.

R: Exactly. In fact I remember my grandfather used to tell me:

> *The water you are meant to drink*
> *will never flow past you.*

It teaches you not to join the rat race. When it is your turn, you will get it. If you grab it too soon, you will lose it.

U: The little phrase *Sùúrù baba ìwà* seems to explain the very core of the Yoruba attitude to life. It would be totally absurd for the *Babaláwo* (the oracle priest) to be ambitious or greedy! He simply could not function! His reputation and his effectiveness rest on his modesty, his calm and his composure. And an *Oba* with personal ambitions would be a disaster for his town. Remember the saying:

> *You are an Oba*
> *and now you want to become rich.*
> *Do you intend to become Olodumare?*

R: *Sùúrù* makes it possible for you to appreciate at all times who you are, irrespective of whether you are a cleaner, a night-watchman, or a town crier. People were proud of whatever they were doing.

U: Muraina Oyelami told me about a man in Iragbiji whose job it was to get the hay for the king's horse. He was highly respected in the community because he did the job well.

R: Of course! This is something I learned as a small boy. You are respected, not for what you do, but for how well you do it. I learned many things through proverbs and *Ifá* verses. And even now, these sayings just come to me when the need arises. The other day I was trying to settle a case between two friends. One had offended the other, but he took it rather lightly, saying that since they had been friends for a long time, the other need not take it seriously: But I told him:

> *He who shits may forget;*
> *the person who cleans it up*
> *is not likely to forget it soon.*

You hurt a person, you may say let's forget the whole thing, but the other one's hurt still gnaws at him ... it does not work that simply.

U: Your traditional Yoruba education has prepared you for almost any human situation, you have learned how to manage a crisis, how to maintain a calm perspective in a conflict. You can place an individual situation into a wider human context that takes the sting of bitterness out of it. That way you don't have to panic! You know it has happened before and it has been dealt with and it can be resolved.

R: One thing I have learned from my grandfather is that there is a reason for everything. You don't trust people who claim to have no motivation. If you would show my grandfather a canvas, which I have painted white on white he would ask me: "Why are you doing it?" And if I told him: "No reason, I just felt like it," he would bluntly call me a liar. "You are a liar. There is a reason for it." And he would back it up with a saying:

> *If you see a man running in the forest*
> *and you ask him why he is running,*
> *and the man say: I just like to run,*
> *don't believe him.*
> *He is either running after something*
> *or something is running after him.*

U: That is a very good example, because there is an everyday Yoruba wisdom which applies to the situation in your profession that your grandfather could never have imagined in his life. Your upbringing actually helps you to take a critical look at modern art and I think that must have helped you to live through a eurocentric institution like the Art School at Zaria.

R: Exactly. It was this kind of traditional wisdom that made me question everything. I

was not prepared to analyze African art by simply dissecting it into shapes and proportions. The study of African art must go beyond that, because Africans themselves never thought of it in those terms. It's alright for Western art historians to look at African art like that, but for us—it is absolutely empty.

U: It's like a grammarian looks at language. They pull it to pieces, to discover the rules. But the great writers are not aware of rules—they just write! In my experience, Yoruba people have never really talked about proportions or outward aesthetic qualities of carvings, even though the artists clearly worked according to certain criteria. But just as the greatest compliment you can pay a man is to simply say, "*okùnrin ni*" (he is a man), so priests, when they have installed a new sacred carving in a shrine and they have performed the ritual for it, will simply say, "*ère ni*" (it is a sacred image).

Okùnrin ni means, yes you are a man, you take your full place in society, so *ère ni* means that you recognize it's presence, it's force, you acknowledge it's *ìwà*.

R: Of course, many things in Yoruba are understood, although they remain unsaid. The small child learns how to interpret the mother's look. Similarly we say:

> *You only speak half a word to an Omolúàbí;*
> *It becomes whole when it gets inside him.*

It is only to an insensitive person, an uncivilized person, that you have to spell out everything to. Even as a child, I instinctively understood unspoken messages.

U: I think the essential difference between the way Europeans and Yoruba treat their children, is that Europeans never give the child any responsibility. They underestimate their children! That is why they seldom listen to their children. They make all the decisions for them, whereas Yoruba children are given the opportunity to determine their own lives.

If a child goes to an uncle or aunt and says "I want to live with you," the elders have no choice! If a child decides he wants to apprentice himself to a wood carver, even although he does not come from a carvers' family, the master carver cannot refuse him.

When I allowed Tunji to leave school at 15, because he wanted to become a drummer, my European friends thought I was extremely irresponsible. But somehow I felt that he had made a responsible decision and I had to respect it.

R: Yorubas would say that it was what his *orí* had chosen.

U: Aha! You see, in Europe they do not respect the *orí* of a child!

R: In fact they kill it, they wipe it out totally. Then later in life they tell him to start looking for his identity.

U: After killing people's identity, they make a research project out of it! But Yoruba parents are sensitive to those idiosyncrasies of the child through which the *orí* manifests itself.

R: It starts from birth. When the child is born you take it to the *Babaláwo*. There is a ceremony called *imorí*-the knowing of the inner head. The *Babaláwo* may tell you who the child is. He may point out certain food taboos that he should keep. He may tell you that the child has a particularly strong *orí* which you must respect.

When I was young I used to disappear from the house and go to an uncle who was a blacksmith and a carver: he was carving *Akó* (funeral) figures. He was said to be the finest *Akó* carver of all times. My father used to say that his *orí* and mine had come together. He accepted my artistic inclinations. I would rather be drawing than do school work. Rather than arithmetic I would be lying under a jacked up car in a mechanics workshop. They knew I was close to *Ogun*.

So when, at Government College, I decided to become an artist, my father said: I'm not surprised. Even though we would have liked you to become a doctor or a lawyer, nobody can stop what your *orí* has chosen. Go ahead and do it.

U: The really wonderful thing about the concept of *orí* is that it makes society respect the individual. The individual has a wonderful sanction for doing what he wants to do. After all, he brought this gift, this inclination from heaven, and he must live it out.

R: Even the *Òrìsà* respect your *orí*. No *Òrìsà* can come to your aid without first taking permission from your *orí*. They have to get clearance from it! So how could the parents try to ignore it. It is foolish and dangerous for somebody to try and ignore somebody else's *orí*. It might be better to kill the person than to tamper with his *orí*! I think, in the wider world, those who have "made it" are those who have followed their *orí*.

U: Only those can do it whose *orí* is strong.

R: And you have to make sacrifices to allow your *ori* to function. There is a ceremony called *orí wíwè*, the ritual washing of *orí*. They wash the *orí* with a specially prepared medicinal black soap, so that one's destiny can shine. In practical terms it means: you beg the world not to interfere with the function of your *orí*.

U: I think the sacrifice is also a symbol. Because if you want to live according to your *orí*, you must also be prepared to sacrifice other, lesser interests to it. You must give direction to your life and become single-minded, up to a point.

R: Of course. That's why I was not at all surprised when I heard about Tunji leaving school even though other people were saying: What's happened, what's happened! I said: he is doing what he has come into the world to do. It's what we call:

> *Àkúnlèyàn—that which we have chosen kneeling down*
> or
> *àkúnlègbà—that which we received kneeling down*
> or
> *àdáyébá—that which is already part of us, when we come into the world*

U: Once a person has understood that, he can go through a lot in life without losing direction. And here, I think, we have the answer to my original question: remembering "what you have received kneeling down" enabled you to travel the long road to Western institutions, without losing your identity. Whether in Government College Ibadan or Ahmadu Bello University Zaria or the University in Toronto, you could absorb any foreign ideas, as long as they were compatible with your *orí*.

R: The whole essence in life is just to know who you are and to fulfil your destiny accordingly. And this is exactly what a traditional Yoruba education helps you to do.

U: I believe that all this throws some light on another important issue. Many perceptive observers of Yoruba culture—including a man like Pierre Verger—have said that Yoruba culture is amoral.

R: Oh no!

U: Well, you can see how it arises, because there is no "ten commandments" in Yoruba in which everything is neatly laid out. Moral values are being conveyed in a more subtle form. But if you apply the concepts of *ori*, *iwa* and *sùúrú*, it becomes clear that a successful life—and therefore a good one—is a life in which a person fulfills his destiny by living out his potential to the fullest. An unsuccessful life—and therefore a bad or wasted one—is a life in which the person has been diverted from his original path. He has ignored his *ori* and wasted the assets he brought down from heaven.

What I am trying to say is that the person who has acquired the patience and the inner peace that are derived from a life in accordance with one's *orí* does not need the ten commandments, because greed and theft and jealousy and all the human failings and offenses that arise from them have become irrelevant.

R: That's true. The single-minded person simply finds these things meaningless. What a shame it is we have failed to build these ancient values into our modern education system.

Iconography of Order and Disorder
Femi Abodunrin in Conversation with
Ulli Beier

FA: May I start this conversation by quoting rather extensively from
R.H. Stone's book *In Africa's Forest and Jungle: Or Six Years Among the
Yorubans*, published in 1899:

> What I saw (of the city of Abeokuta) disabused my mind of the many
> errors in regard to Africa. The city extends along the Ogun for nearly
> six miles and has a population approximately 200,000...instead of
> being lazy, naked savages, living on the spontaneous productions of
> the earth, they were dressed and were industrious...(providing) every-
> thing that their physical comfort required. The men were builders,
> blacksmiths, iron-smelters, carpenters, calabash-carvers, weavers,
> basket-makers, hat-makers, traders, barbers, tanners, tailors, farm-
> ers, and workers in leather and morocco...they made razors, swords,
> knives, hoes, billhooks, axes, arrow-heads, stirrups...women...most
> diligently follow the pursuits which custom has allotted to them.
> They spin, weave, trade, cook, and dye cotton fabrics. They also
> make soap, dyes, palm oil, nut-oil, all the native earthware, and many
> other things used in the country.

Was this the sort of setting that you found in Yoruba cities and towns when
you arrived there in the 1950s? If not, what had changed?
UB: When I came to Nigeria in 1950, I found a very similar situation. All
the crafts Stone listed were very active. Yoruba towns were industrious. They
were bursting with activities.
       In Oshogbo I lived opposite a blacksmith's workshop. All day long
half a dozen craftsmen were busy producing hoes, cutlasses, and other farm
tools. They were even forging the pellets for shot guns by hand! They tended
to beat in a steady rhythm, like musicians creating a "groove." From time to

time they interrupted their work for a brief spell to recite *oríki* on what you might call a "talking anvil." Then you knew that some important man was walking down Ibokun road.

Looking down into the Abolubode compound from my back verandah, I could see a woman weaving *aso oke* on a vertical loom. Within five minutes' walk I came to an *alaro*'s compound, with huge dyeing pots standing in an open courtyard. Yarn, *kijipa* or *adire* were hanging up to dry in the sun. There were many *alaros* and many *aladires* in Oshogbo and the cloth market was a feast for the eye. A large variety of *aso oke* and *adire* was on sale. A specialty of Oshogbo women weavers was the heavy men's sleeping cloth: a kind of large Toga in stripes of different shades of Indigo—woven, of course, from thick handspun cotton. I still have some of these clothes in my possession: after forty years they have neither faded nor worn thin! *Adire Eleko* was so common that you thought nothing of cutting up the most refined "*Ibadan dun*" or "*Eyepe*" pattern to make yourself a shirt. Intellectually one knew, even then, that these crafts could not survive the onslaught of Western industrial products. But you could not really imagine such a situation, because these arts were still so alive.

There was leather work and refined embroidery, there was even a brass caster, Jinadu Oladepo, who lived down the road. Only the great Yoruba tradition of woodcarving had ceased to exist. *Obas* and chiefs no longer commissioned carved pillars, and the *Olórìsà* were too poor to commission ere. Many of the old carvers had become carpenters, and they now made wonderfully inventive and elaborate chairs for the *Obas*: a new art form!

Another new art form was cement sculpture: lions, elephants, and occasionally soldiers placed on the balconies or arched gates of "Brazilian" houses. In many respects Oshogbo, Ede, Ilobu, Ifon, Erin-Osun were fairly traditional towns. Of course there were inroads into the culture: each town had its motor park with its noise and, if you like, "vulgarity," and its new professions or tout, *mekaniki*, and vulcanizer. But even the motor parks had their own culture: the tail boards of lorries were usually painted with proverbs and images ("*Iwalewa*" could often be read at the back of a truck!)

In those days the truck drivers would cleverly manipulate their motor horns (rubber balls at the end of a shiny trumpet shaped horn) in order to address potential customers. They could actually "talk" on these new instruments and inform people that they were about to depart for Lagos or Ibadan. Often enough, when I lived in Ede in 1952, they woke me up at three or four o'clock in the morning. People liked night travelling in those days, because the roads were absolutely safe and one could reach Lagos in time for a full day's business activity.

To cater to the travelers, clusters of restaurants grew up around the motor parks. A "modern" development, because in a traditional town there was obviously no need for a restaurant. But these little restaurants were wonderful places: you could eat pounded yam with *egusi* or okro and bush meat—superbly cooked. The women would compete with each other. You sat in a simple wooden shack, with a corrugated iron roof. The tables in those days were scrubbed until the wood became white and exposed its markings. The women entrepreneurs would also sell palm wine or, if you preferred, sent out for star beer. Some motor parks had a nationwide reputation for the quality of their cuisine and the availability of bush meat. Travelling to Benin or further East, I would invariably stop at Igbara Oke for a meal.

Even architecturally, Yoruba towns in the fifties would not have been all that different from the Abeokuta the reverend R.H. Stone saw a hundred years earlier. He would have seen a fair sprinkling of Brazilians houses, blending harmoniously into the townscape of sprawling mud compounds.

F: Many people have talked about these Brazilian buildings. Could you please talk about how this type of architecture came to Nigeria?

U: A Yoruba town used to be a maze of large rectangular mud compounds. The size of these compounds depended on the terrain: in the landscape of Oyo province they tended to be huge. In the hilly areas of Ekiti, they were more compact.

These mud buildings had virtually no windows to the outside. Facing inwards the doors of the different rooms would open onto a wide verandah. Short square mud pillars supported the roof that gave ample shade to the people working in this space. In the palaces of *Obas* or Chiefs the low roof would be supported by carved, wooden pillars. (In the palace of Old Oyo the pillars in the *Alaafin*'s palace were made of brass. What a sight that must have been!)

The rooms were mostly sleeping rooms. Social life and activities took place on the verandah. That's where people would sit and eat. That's where a woman might have her upright loom against the wall. Some of the slightly larger rooms might serve as shrines. The shrines of Yoruba *Orìsà* were extremely modest: a mud bench served as an altar. Some pots with sacred water; a calabash containing kola-nuts, maybe a couple of wooden carvings, and sometimes a carved door. They were no bigger than was necessary for three or four priests to officiate in it. The bulk of the worshippers would sit in the verandah. When it came to dancing they would simply step out into the open courtyard or onto a space in front of the house.

The mud walls were repaired with a mud slip after every rainy season and then polished with a stone, so that the red laterite soil would shine like marble. In the fifties the majority of houses in Oshogbo were still of this

263

traditional type. Only the thatched roofs had been replaced by corrugated iron. In most Yoruba towns the council had made this a law, because of the danger of fire. Undoubtedly, pressure was also exercised because some British firms made a lot of money selling this highly unsuitable material in Nigeria. The roofs were quite beautiful to look at, once they were rusty-almost the color of laterite.

Yoruba builders created attractive roofs with little gables jutting out and with decorative cut shapes along the corners. But of course, they made the houses uncomfortably hot. Many of these beautiful mud compounds were in a neglected state in the fifties, with deep cracks in the walls and the parallel building layers exposed to the eye. The owners were saving money for cement and considered it a waste of time to work on the old buildings (for an "upstair" house). The "upstair" house (*petesi* in neo-Yoruba) was a country version of the so-called Brazilian mansion.

Brazilian architecture was introduced by liberated slaves from Brazil in the middle of the nineteenth century. Brazil had experienced a number of slave revolts in the 1820s, all these had been organized by slaves of Hausa or, in any case, Muslim extraction. In the early 1830s the Yoruba slaves revolted. The government was alarmed at the size and vehemence of the uprising. (It was said that there were twice as many slaves in Brazil as Portuguese "masters.")

When the uprising was finally put down, the ringleaders were killed, but the liberated slaves who had supported the revolt were repatriated to West Africa. Lome, Ilu Ajase (Porto Novo), and Lagos were the major sites for resettlement. These Brazilian Yoruba soon became an elite, because they were literate and were competent in several modern crafts, such as building. They built beautiful houses with pillars, balustrades, balconies, and archways, and often with heraldic lions demurely resting their paws on a shield, sitting over the gate. Stucco decorations were imitated in cement.

The center of Lagos, the triangle between Broad Street, Martin Street, and what later on became Nnamdi Azikwe were full of such beautiful houses. The British administration destroyed most of these houses in 1959 in what was absurdly called the "Lagos slum clearance scheme," and they replaced it with a concrete jungle and set the stage for the permanent traffic jam that Lagos has since become. A few houses are still left to give an indication of the former charm. In Independence Square Olaiya House is still standing, and most important: No. 10 Elias Street has been declared a national monument. Its a remarkable house with a cast iron revolving staircase inside, and with blue Delft tiles covering the walls of the first floor on the outside. (The Dutch had occupied Salvador, the capital of the state of Bahia, for only two years, but they left this tradition of blue tiles behind!) Even some of the early mosques show the influence of that style! Upcountry it took a great deal longer for this new architecture to become fashionable.

In the town of Erin-Osun, six kilometers from Oshogbo, the first corrugated iron roof was constructed in 1924 and the first "upstair" house was built in 1935. It is a small building erected in thick walls that taper inwards. It has few windows, but both the windows and the front door are surrounded by elaborate mouldings carried out in cement. When I last saw it, it was painted in a pale pink. People did not bother to apprentice themselves to a professional builder. They looked at the Lagos houses, then went home and did it. I asked the builder of this Erin house who had taught him to do this.

He laughed and said: *Ogbón Orí*!

The great days of Brazilian architecture were the forties. In Ikole Ekiti, the *Oba* built a palace that had five stories, in mud! It was incredible. As the style became fashionable upcountry it became more baroque and more extravagant. These buildings were full of fantasy. And the classical Brazilian sculpture, these demure heralding lions, evolved into a fantastic new form of cement sculpture: lions, elephants, soldiers, snakes in relief! The illiterate Yoruba builders used all these different style elements quite freely; they played with them. Oshogbo still has some wonderful houses dating back to the forties. You may know Olaiya's house right next to the *Oba*'s palace. A four-storey mansion! It is linked to the smaller buildings set further back from the road through a balcony that is supported on pillars. An amazing device. The cemented open space in front of these two buildings has been used for the last forty years as a second-hand bottle market. (Nobody had to go and teach Nigerians about "recycling"!)

These houses were built by an Ibadan man called Kadri. He also designed the house I lived in, on Ibokun road. But whereas the houses on King's Market were built in brick, mine was built in stone. Kadri was another self-taught builder. I went to visit him in Ibadan and he told me that he wanted to build himself a house, so he simply went and watched the construction of another house. I was told that when he built 41 Ibokun Road, he would sit under a little shade tree in the blacksmith compound opposite and draw with his finger in the sand. Then would instruct his builders: put three windows here, put the door there! There was no plan, but the statics of the house are perfect: no sinking foundations, no cracks in the wall, no leakages, no damp. The building became quite famous and variations on it were later constructed by Kadri in Ikirun, Okuku, and elsewhere.

These Brazilian houses were prestige objects. People didn't really like living in them. Old people certainly did not like to live high off the ground! It seemed unnatural to them. They were status symbols of a new bourgeoisie: cocoa farmers, "transport magnates," contractors. Of course, the traditional

265

status holders—*Oba*s, Chiefs—had to compete. Still, if you compare these houses to the concrete monsters the nouveau riche of today are building for themselves, they were really modest. And they were works of art. Moreover, they seemed to grow organically out of the lower mud compounds, they did not fight their surroundings. The builders were capable of producing new ideas, yet respecting what had been there before. At that time one could feel optimistic about Yoruba culture: it seemed capable of absorbing a wide range of foreign influences without giving up its identity.

The Yoruba lifestyle was not destroyed by these wealthy traders in the forties. It was the lawyers and doctors and accountants who returned after years of study in the U.K. who built themselves "modern" bungalows: concrete houses with glass louvres and sitting on a separate "plot." These ugly houses were anti-social—they emphasized the owners' elitist status, they sometimes were grouped in "housing estates" that were aping the British "Government Residential Area." Like the colonial housing estates these were elitist ghettos. I was happy that, when I changed over from the English department to the Extra-Mural department, I could move out of the University campus, which was also a ghetto. I could live in a town of my choice and pick a beautiful Brazilian house. Since many of them were empty or almost empty, they were cheap to rent. You could have a beautiful two-storey mansion for (10 a month and what is more, you could live right in the middle of town where all the life was and where drummers would come past your house in procession virtually every day.

F: So there was the influence of the "Brazilians been-to's," then that of those who had gone to Britain to study

U: Yes, you know that in the fifties and sixties many Nigerian academics and intellectuals thought of me as some kind of crank. Tony Enahoro, at one stage was the only African member of the "European Club" in Ibadan. There were others who aspired to become honorary whites. No wonder the man in the street began to call them "*oyinbo dudu*." A lot of "progressive" jargon was in the air in those days and few Yoruba people had the courage to stand up for their own conviction.

The been-to's displayed British mannerisms and many of them became remote from their own society. Chief Awolowo himself speaks in derogatory terms about Yoruba culture in his book AWO. He had no interest in Yoruba art or music, and he despised Yoruba religion. He would not even eat pepper! The been-to's created an "elitist" class in Yoruba society. You could say that is the beginning of the disorder you are talking about!

I still experienced Yoruba towns as classless societies. Of course, they were highly structured, innumerable chiefs and priests all with specific duties and functions assigned to them. But titles were not passed on from father to son (though many of them ran in families). They were open to competition. Moreover political power could not automatically be translated into wealth-as it happens today. The *Oba* was a man through whom a great deal of wealth circulated, but he was not meant to accumulate it. He was not even meant to build a house for his children while in office. The *Oba* had almost unlimited social responsibilities: if a woman had triplets, he became automatically responsible for the upbringing of one of the children; if a woman could not find a husband, perhaps because she was unable to produce children, he would have to marry her; when a woman gave birth and there was neither husband or father or any close relative to bury the afterbirth, the *Oba* had to do it—which meant that he became the father of the child.

In the fifties, all the *Oba* s I knew, literate or not, had to spend much of their time farming in order to meet their social responsibilities. After all, there was no religious ceremony to which he was not obliged to contribute food.

F: And all this did not fascinate the new African elite as something they wanted to carry on?

U: No, there was this obsession with "progress" which I found really painful at the time, because I could see where it would lead. The society was very well balanced at the time and it was also fairly well off. No one suffered real hardship. There was no poverty. With communal land ownership administered by the *Oba* , no one could go hungry. And the extended family, the compound created a social security net that worked better than the Western system.

F: The welfare state?

U: It works better than the welfare state on several grounds. First of all: in European society there are many people who fall through the "social security net." Even in this small provincial town (Bayreuth) we have an increasing number of beggars on the street. Secondly, the system is becoming absurdly expensive. I know a single, self-employed woman who has to pay 700 Marks a month for her health insurance. In the end you work your guts out, just to pay insurance and tax. What it means is you can't live a simple life any more. You spend an increasing proportion of your life dealing with bureaucracy.

Thirdly: Western society considers old people useless. They are looked after in a home, maybe with a fair amount of comfort, but they are removed from families and they feel that they are a burden. In Yoruba society there were some tasks reserved for old women: for example, the collection of *èlú* leaves (indigo) or the preparation of ashes for the *alaro*. These were essential services for the dyeing industry and an old woman would remain active....

F: In other words, there was no unemployment.

U: In Yoruba society everybody contributed, however little. Even children. And your dignity did not depend on the type of job you did. You would be respected, as long as you did your work well, whatever it was.

F: You had your freedom, but with responsibility.

U: Exactly.

F: Many scholars have blamed the "collapse" of Yoruba traditional culture on the slave trade, civil wars, and modernization. Which among these experiential factors has done the most damage?

U: I don't think anybody could measure the share any of these three evils had in corrupting Yoruba society. The slave trade was certainly the beginning of the disintegration of Yoruba society and other West African societies for that matter. It is not just the brutality of European or Arab slave traders-it is above all the fact that there were enough Yoruba willing to hunt for slaves and sell slaves in order to supply the new "market." Some Yoruba succumbed to this pressure or this temptation. The tolerance, the respect for human dignity and individuality were abandoned because of greed. The damage to the society must have been irreparable. You could say that there is a contemporary variant of the slave trade today. About a year ago, one of Georgina's students from the Nike Center was asked by a car dealer to drive a white Mercedes to a customer in Ede. On the road he was waylaid and robbed of the car. The young man went to the police to report the incident. And you know the Yoruba custom: on serious business you don't go alone. So he picked up three friends at the gallery to accompany him. The police jailed all four of them and demanded a heavy ransom. This happens all the time, nowadays. People are imprisoned for no good reason and their relatives or friends have to buy their freedom.

The intertribal wars which Samuel Johnson describes so vividly must have had an equally disastrous effect on Yoruba society. Not merely because of the many deaths and the displacements and the suffering, but above all because of the loss of values. The brutalities of war have to be justified and it is this false morality, this "doublethink" that does more harm that the war itself. Let me give you an example. Johnson reports that the *Olowu* of Owu was captured by an Ibadan warrior when the city fell. He carried him to Ibadan and delivered him to the Olubadan. The Olubadan, however, was horrified. How could he, an ordinary *Baale* keep a sacred *Oba* , a descendant of Oduduwa as a common prisoner in his palace? He feared the curse of the *Oba* and his traditional Yoruba world-view was sufficiently intact for him to realize that this was sacrilege.

He wanted him out of his palace as quickly as possible, and he would have preferred to see him dead rather than alive, but who would dare to lay hands on an *Oba*? In the end he came up with a ruse: he told the *Olowu* that he was too big an *Oba* to be held at Ibadan and that the only *Oba* who could look after him was the *Ooni* of Ife. One of his chiefs was detailed to lead the *Oba* to Ife. The chief hired an Hausa slave to kill the *Olowu*. In return for this he promised him his freedom. The arrangement was that that slave would always walk behind the *Olowu* and, as they were going to pass a bend in the river, the chief would give a sign and the Hausa man would kill the *Oba*, whose dead body should then be thrown in the river. The Hausaman kept his side of the bargain, but the moment the deed was done the chief killed the Hausa slave, and then prayed to the spirit of the *Oba* : "*Kabiyesi*, you see that I have avenged your death! Do not punish me for the crime that this worthless slave has committed." This, to me, is the symbol of the perversion of cultural values. People pay lip service to traditional values, while they have in fact succumbed to the uninhibited lure of power, violence, and greed.

In spite of the disruptive effect of both the slave trade and the fratricidal wars on Yoruba society, the Yoruba people showed considerable resilience and surprising ability to restructure their society. When I first came into Yorubaland in 1950 there was a sense of order and stability. Many traditional Yoruba values were very much alive. Religious festivals were being celebrated with vigor.

We have to acknowledge here the fact that the situation was helped by the Pax Britannica. The British presence put an end to the war. Not that they really had the military force to suppress all the fighting, but probably the Yoruba kingdoms were tired of wars and were glad to accept this unexpected arbitration. But it must also be admitted that the British Colonial administration did not interfere very much with the daily lives of the citizens. They had brought the concept of "indirect rule" with them from India; and it meant that they ruled through the existing chieftaincy structures—not, of course, because they had any real respect for Yoruba culture, but because it made it possible for them to rule the country with a minimum of personnel. In order to rule through the *Oba*s they had to leave intact all those traditional structures that propped up his authority. They could not interfere with the chieftaincy structure, the *Ogbóni* society, or any other aspect of Yoruba religion. Otherwise they would have undermined the *Oba*'s authority. It is true that they outlawed the *Sònpònná* cult, but it was a Nigerian doctor who started the rumor that the *Sònpònná* cult spread the disease in order to make money (a case of vicious libel!) However, having banned the cult officially, they made little effort to effectively suppress it. In fact, in the 1950s *Sònpònná* shrines existed in all Yoruba cities I was familiar with, and I attended the *òsè* of *Sònpònná* in Erin-Osun regularly, while I was living in Ilobu. . . .

F: So the sort of thing Soyinka dramatizes in *Death and the King's*

Horseman is an isolated incident?

U: It was a major interference and a tragic one; but the district officer simply lacked the knowledge to realize the implications of his action. As far as he could see he was trying to save a man's life.

F: So it was a case of ignorance rather than oppression.

U: Absolutely. But of course, a lot of harm is done through ignorance. The late K.C. Murray used to point out that the Colonial Education Ordinance started with the sentence: "Education is an instrument of change." The implication is clear. Education was not a means of widening people's horizon. It was not attempting to build on what was there already. It was a matter of discarding everything you had, suspending any belief you ever held, disowning every kind of wisdom you ever held, and embracing wholesale and without adaptation somebody else's lifestyle. So it was the education system that deliberately helped to destroy the fabric of Yoruba society.

Many of the school teachers and clerks who attended my extra-mural classes, and who were also personal friends of mine, could not understand why I spent so much time with *Sàngó* worshippers. They could not see the beauty of the dances or the poetry of the music. They could not read the beauty in the faces of these magnificent people. They simply said: "*Sàngó* does not exist." I said: "why not?" "Because you can't prove it." I said: "Can you prove the existence of the Christian God?" To them one was "superstition," the other "truth." They measured both with a different yardstick. Biblical mythology was taught as "fact." Yoruba mythology was denounced as some backward, heathenish, even evil superstition.

I once spent a couple of months as a school inspector for the Education Department in Ondo province. It was a very revealing experience. Nobody among the teachers ever explained the difference between "truth" and "fact." Nobody ever attempted to find common ground between the religions. I told a class that the Yoruba people had their own version of the Biblical myth of "Paradise Lost." Every single child knew the Yoruba myth that said: once upon a time the sky was very low down, and when people were hungry they could simply cut off a piece of sky and eat it. For a long time everybody obeyed this rule, until one day a greedy woman cut off a huge piece of sky. She could not finish it, and even her husband and her children and all the relatives could not finish it. The entire village ate of this huge piece of sky. When they could not finish it, the woman had to throw the remains on the rubbish heap. The sky felt deeply hurt and removed itself from human reach. Since then, human beings must plant to eat.

The teacher felt offended. He thought I was undermining his authority and putting funny ideas into the children's heads. The children, who had younger minds and were less prejudiced, responded with curiosity and enthusiasm. I pointed out that the Yoruba story in some respects compares favorably with the Biblical one. The basic idea of course, is the same. That once life was better and easier. That man was closer to God. But through man's own fault, and disobedience, hardship was brought into life. The difference lies in the image of God. The Biblical God is all powerful, cantankerous, and self-righteous. He is in fact taking revenge. In the Yoruba story, God is vulnerable. He can be hurt. The vice that has brought the misfortune upon mankind is not so much disobedience but greed. The story is perfectly applicable to Yoruba society today. It is above all greed that has created even greater distance to God and that has ultimately destroyed Yoruba society.

Yoruba religion was designed to overcome this distance between man and god, and they developed a technique of breaking it—if only for brief moments. Through trance the *Sàngó* worshipper could be united with *Sàngó* and the *Sònpònná* worshipper become one with *Sònpònná*, and they could come back from this excursion into the supernatural world with renewed strength, understanding, and wisdom.

It would have been easy to relate Christian mythology to Yoruba mythology: the creation of man; the flood; the sacrifice of the only son are all myths that are partly related to Yoruba traditions, but in each case the Yoruba God is less self-righteous, less perfect, more human than the Biblical one. It was sad for me to see how readily the Yoruba intellectuals succumbed to the cultural brainwashing of the European mentors. The cultural arrogance of the British was extraordinary, as I have described in a little essay called "In a Colonial University." The first professor of History at the University of Ibadan said: "There is no such thing as African history—only the history of the British in Africa..." and everybody accepted it. Of course, we soon had people like Dike and Biobaku who proved him wrong. But when it came to religion, people were inhibited.

But I think that the most damaging influence on Yoruba culture was Western materialism; I suppose that is what "modernism" mostly boils down to. People were dazzled by the opulence of the life-style of people who returned from Europe—the lawyers and the doctors and the engineers.

I remember that Dr. Dike, when he became a lecturer in history at the University of Ibadan, sent nine nephews and nieces to secondary schools! And even the first generation of politicians believed in circulating money. Many of them tried to upstage the local *Oba*, by making bigger donations to the local school or church or sports club, demonstrating through lavish spending that they were the new elite and that they had a legitimate role to play in the running of the community.

F: According to Robert Farris Thompson, it is believed that *Ifá* encompasses the whole of the wisdom of the ancestors, the whole of the deities, and thus safeguards "everything that is considered memorable in Yoruba culture throughout the ages." Do you see the total absence of this "all encompassing wisdom" in the syllabi of colonial and neocolonial educational systems as the primary factor accounting for the precarious Nigerian/African present?

U: Yes! The *Ifá* oracle is a great source of wisdom; and something that our modern wisdom can be measured against. It could indeed fulfil the same role in Yoruba society that the Bible fulfils in Europe. Not many people in Germany or England really know the Bible; but everyone knows and sometimes lives certain ideas, and people justify their general conduct and set moral standards with the help of certain catchphrases like "love your neighbor as yourself." I only have a very superficial knowledge of the *Ifá* oracle, but even from the little I have learned from Timi Laoye or Wande Abimbola, I have adopted certain lines that have clarified ideas in my mind and actually serve as guidelines for my life. For example:

Anybody who meets beauty
and does not look at it
will soon be poor!

Anybody who lives by that saying will be immune to the corruption of materialism. But nobody wants to know about the *Ifá* oracle, or about *Sàngó Pípè* or *Ìjálà* or *Ewì*, because they are associated with "paganism." At the core of the disaster is the missionary concept of "conversion." In order to become a Christian (or a Muslim for that matter) you must publicly denounce every aspect of your forefathers' culture and wisdom and religion. In the old days this even involved public burning of images.

The problem is: you cannot wipe out the past or your personal experience. You cannot eradicate them from your mind, you can only suppress them. Sigmund Freud, the founder of modern psychiatry, proved that most neuroses can be traced back to experiences from early childhood which have been suppressed. And unless you bring this back to the patient's awareness from his subconscious, he will not be able to cope with that situation.

Every culture in the world has been "multicultural": conquering peoples usually absorb much of the culture of the aboriginal inhabitants. Babylonian culture was superimposed on the culture of Sumer and Akkad. The Assyrians in turn conquered the Babylonians but at the same time they picked up many of the cultural achievements of the conquered people: their writing for example.

The Yoruba people and most other African societies respected the people they superseded politically: they absorbed the cultures that were there before them and integrated them into their own. Only the monotheistic religions refused to tolerate any other ideas, other wisdoms, other beauties beside their own. This purism must warp the mind of the "converts," must give them all kinds of inhibitions—even in some cases an inferiority complex. How can you feel confident, if you have actually been taught to despise your father? Some Europeans saw me as a convert. A European "gone native" as the phrase used to be. In their eyes that meant: a human being who has dropped all his standards, who has gone "to seed," become mentally derelict. I was the object of much European prejudice in the fifties. That didn't bother me, but it was sad that there were even a few Africans who felt the same! But for me the Nigerian experience and the Yoruba experience in particular was not a case of exchanging one set of values for another. It was a case of widening my horizon, of having a new yardstick to evaluate my own culture; of being more sensitive. I learned what was really relevant in my own background to my life and what was not. I became a better judge of classical European music after having been exposed to the experience of Yoruba music. I still listen to Bach and Beethoven passionately, but also more critically. I am more aware of what is mere technical perfection and routine, and what is organic and alive. In Africa you learn what spontaneity is, what improvisation is, and you become more sensitive to the weaknesses in many European performances.

I believe that Yoruba religion is much more flexible than the monotheistic religions with their claims of absolute universal truth. And this has affected every aspect of Yoruba life. Take the position of women, for example. In Christianity and Islam the position of women is quite clearly defined as being inferior to men. In Islam the position of women has never changed; and even in Europe, in spite of the feminist movement, deep Christian prejudice towards women has not been eradicated in people's minds, even if the law has made them equal.

Look at Yoruba society by comparison: the roles of men and women are in some sense clearly defined. Both men and women have monopolies on certain professions: men are drummers, wood carvers, brass casters. They are weavers, but can only use a certain type of loom. Women hold monopolies on pottery, indigo dyeing, batik, tie-dye, and weaving on the vertical loom. They are also in charge of oil and soap production.

In the worship of the different *Orìsà*, women can hold the most senior positions. Men basically run the government, but women have strong representation through the *Iyalode* and they can exercise various veto powers. Women dominate the market, which gives them financial independence from their husbands. On the whole their position was infinitely stronger than the position of European women up to the Second World War. In spite of these formal divisions between men and women, and these clearly demarcated

273

spheres of influence, the male and female roles are not as rigidly defined in Yoruba society as in Europe.

The sex of many *Orìsà* is changeable: Oduduwa is sometimes the creator of the earth, a male god who descended from heaven; sometimes he appears as mother earth herself! *Èsù*, the ever-changing, ever paradoxical deity, can (surprisingly) appear as a woman. Even *Sàngó* , the most masculine, extrovert, boisterous of all the gods is worshipped as a woman (wife of *Jakuta!*) in Ketu and other Western Yoruba towns. The fiery priests of the thunder god wear a woman's hairstyle, an earring, and their dance costume resembles a woman's wrapper. The priestesses of *Sàngó* adopt certain male mannerism; for example, they prostrate to the *Orìsà* like men, rather than kneel like women.

F: Reflecting on similarities and parallels between Japan and Africa, and praising the former for having learnt so much from its turbulent past, in a recent article, Nigerian poet and academic Niyi Osundare surmises that the apparent technological ingenuity of the Japanese people underscores a view of the world that is authentically Japanese in nature. How much of the rush to be accepted universally, without acquiring a relative expertise in the ABC of their cultural mooring, has blurred the worldview of the emergent sociocultural and political elite in Africa?

U: This is a very relevant question. The Japanese, with all the mastery of Western technology, still show a great deal of respect for their tradition. They have been helped greatly by the fact that they have never succumbed in any large numbers to Western missionaries. Until today, their traditional religions, Shintoism and Buddhism, are intact. All their great theater traditions-No, Kabuki and Bunraki—are still immensely popular with the Japanese public. The government honors its great actors, artists, and craftsmen by declaring them to be "living national treasures." This assures them a life free of material worries and they can devote their entire time to perfecting their art.

Can you imagine a Nigerian government conferring a comparable honor on the leader of a troupe of traditional masqueraders? Has the *Kwaghir* masquerade in Tiv ever received any real support from the government? Look at Atanda Oyeyemi, the head of the *Alarinjo* group from Erin-Osun. It is the only *Alarinjo* company surviving in *Òsun* state. And it is due to the giant effort of this one man who trained his family relentlessly in the arts of singing, dancing, acrobatics and theater. Yet he was jailed three times by his relatives in an effort to force him to become a muslim and give up his profession. The only support he received came from overseas, not from Nigeria. The Japanese have been unusually successful in mastering Western technologies and even Western culture-think of the prominence of Japanese performers in classical European music-because they are being educated to become Japanese first. With all their Westernization they could not dream of making English the language of instruction in their schools.

Yoruba educationists have underestimated the potential of their language. A typical case in hand is the late S.O. Awokoya, the first minister of education in Western Nigeria. He was a very brilliant man and the first Yoruba friend I ever had! He showed me, then, that he had worked out a complete Yoruba vocabulary for the study of Chemistry. He explained that the Yoruba language had the capacity of creating new words out of clusters of nouns, very much like German; and he gave me the German example: Hydrogen had been translated by German scholars in Wasserstoff, which is made up of Wasser (water) and Stoff (matter).

I saw a lot of Awokoya in my early years. I enjoyed his company and his brilliant mind. But when he became Minister of Education, he did not implement his ideas. Chemistry was being studied in English, and so was Physics and Mathematics, History and Geography! He had demonstrated the capacity of Yoruba to go through a process of modernization, but he lacked the conviction or the political clout to implement his idea. I remember telling him about the introduction of Hebrew as the official language of Israel. Long before the state of Israel was created, in the early thirties, nationalists in Palestine rejected both German and Yiddish or English as possible official languages. They were not deterred by the fact that Hebrew had not been a spoken language for 2000 years. They worked on this fossilized language until it became a modern tool, in which you could study atomic physics if you wished. It required a certain fanaticism, even violence, to get it accepted!

In Nigeria educators were overawed by the English language. In 1956 Awokoya introduced the famous free universal education scheme. ("First in Africa," as the Action Group proclaimed it). I said to him: "You are embarking on a very dangerous project: you have a school system devised by the British and it has been set up to alienate children from their society. As you can see, it has already created a deep rift within Yoruba society. Should you not first give some thought to the context of education, before you subject everybody to it? Nobody has asked: what kind of citizen do we want and how do we go about educating him towards this end? What must he know about his own language, history, religion? What must he know about Nigeria? The diversity of its people? The concept of the nation state?"

Awokoya's answer to this was: "the rift in Yoruba society has come about because the educated class consider themselves superior to the illiterates. Once everybody can read and write there will be nothing special about it any more."

It was a good argument on the surface and he felt that a reform of the school syllabus could come later. In retrospect I wonder whether he was not under pressure from the Action Group. Because you cannot get much political mileage out of reforms in the school syllabus. That kind of thing is a quiet revolution. And in this case, Awolowo would not have believed in Yoruba Studies or Nigerian Studies in local schools. The way for Africans to become equal to Europeans was to become like them. George Orwell understood this whole syndrome when he said in his novel 1984: "You become what fight." Conversely, the introduction of free universal education gave the Action Group the image of being the most progressive party in Nigeria; of "forging ahead," of turning the Western Region of Nigeria into the first modern state in Africa, whereas everybody else was lagging behind and remained "backward."

Needless to say, it didn't work like this. The free universal education scheme merely helped to ingrain British education further, and it invariably lowered the standard. It was one thing to build thousands of new classrooms within two years-a fantastic achievement, no doubt. But it was not possible to train sufficient teachers in that short a time. The massive introduction of "pupil teachers" (standard VI leavers who had received a 6 week crash course); meant that standards dropped disastrously. The old Standard VI leavers had been employable as junior clerks or sanitary inspectors. Now they were unemployable because they had not acquired sufficient literacy skills. They were unemployable. Being "literate," most of them no longer wanted to work on the farm. The education scheme contributed to the drift into the cities.

Four decades later, one can observe another disturbing development in the big cities, particularly Lagos. What is happening to the Yoruba language? Is what taxi drivers, touts, and "area boys" speak still Yoruba? They speak it very fast; the rhythm of the language is lost; the tone levels are somehow flattened: Yoruba used to be called the "missing link between music and speech"; but the music seems to have gone out of the language altogether! There are not many people left who still have that sonorous quality in their speech: who still take their time over it.

F: And that supports your point about modernization having done the greatest damage. First, we were encouraged not to speak the language the way an *ará-oko* would speak it; then in school we were punished for speaking it at all.

U: That's criminal! This is one of the things that contributed towards the twisting of people's minds. On the other hand you must admit that there were quite a number of people who survived it all. Look at people like Biodun Jeyifo or Kole Omotoso, or Sophie Oluwole or Wole Soyinka. They had to go through all this, but refused to be alienated from their culture, while availing themselves of the opportunities the foreign language and the foreign education offered them.

Wole Soyinka must be the most international figure among Nigerian intellectuals, yet who but a Yoruba could have written *Death and the King's Horseman*?

F: Yes, and with sufficient feeling for the language to have translated *Ogboju Ode Ninu Igbo Irunmole*!

U: Exactly, in spite of his very wide horizon, he has remained a thoroughly Yoruba person. In a way you could say that I went a similar way— except in the opposite direction. My background was THOROUGHLY EUROPEAN—highly "civilized"—but also very middle-class, and a bit stifling. It was the experience of Yoruba society that widened my horizon, that gave me an international perspective, that offered me an entirely new angle from which to view my own culture.

In all those years I spent in Nigeria, I kept reading German poetry and drama. I had virtually no opportunity to speak the language, but I kept reading it. I even translated several radio plays by Gunther Eich for WNBS and they were produced in English by Segun Olusola. We even produced a radio play by Friedrich Durrenmatt ("Der Doppelganger") in Yoruba with the Duro Ladipo company. I adopted two other Durrenmatt radio plays for stage ("Evening in Latre autumn" and "Conversation at Night"). They became part of the repertoire of "Theatre Express" starring both Segun Olusola and Segun Sofowote. I have always believed that cultural boundaries are there to be crossed and that any culture that tries to seal itself hermetically from the rest of the world will quickly become stale.

F: In Cuba, Brazil, and among other New World Yoruba, the cult of Roman Catholic saints was not merely introduced but their attributes were learnt, and series of parallelism linking Christian figures and powers to the forces of ancient (Yoruba) deities; the smallpox deity (*Sònpònnâ*), for example, was equated with saint Lazarus because of the latter's wounds illustrated in chromolithographs; the Virgin Mary was equated with the sweet and gentle aspects of the multifaceted goddess of the river, Oshun; *Sàngó*, the Yoruba god of thunder, was equated with Saint Barbara, etc.: why has such a creative reorganization or syncretization of traditional religion with the imperial religions eluded the Yoruba in the homeland?

U: Conditions in Brazil were unique. African slaves outnumbered the white population two to one! They therefore constituted a potential threat to the "masters." Plantation owners encouraged their slaves to hold traditional dances after Church on Sundays so that they would retain loyalty to their respective "nations." It was hoped that in this way the slaves would not unite. The policy was successful. Some of the early slave revolts were staged by Hausa slaves, but the biggest and most dangerous of all in the early 1830s was a Yoruba revolt, in which the Hausa slaves did not participate.

On the other hand, it gave the slaves the opportunity to practice their traditional religion. To satisfy the Church, the Yorubas would always have the statue of a Saint placed at the door of the "candomble." If a priest came to ask what they were doing they could say: "we are praying to Saint Peter," when in fact they were worshipping Ògún. The famous Brazilian syncretism started as a form of camouflage. The identification between Saint and Òrìsà was on the most superficial level:

Saint Peter was identified with *Ògún* because he cut off a soldier's ear! Saint Barbara was identified with *Sàngó* , because she is symbolized by a tower of alternating red and white bricks, and *Sàngó* has a necklace of alternating red and white beads. *Yemanja*, goddess of the ocean was identified more logically with the Virgin Mary in her specific role as protector of sailors. Yoruba slaves had carried their belief system to the new world intact. Since they did not become literate in Portuguese for some time, they saw Catholic Saints like some additional *Òrìsà* to be incorporated into their pantheon or like manifestations of existing ones. In the same way in which they could recognize *Obàtálá, Òrìsà Ògìyán*,and *Ajàgemo* as different manifestations of the same *Òrìsà*, they could now embrace Catholicism on their own terms. The Catholic Church has always had the policy of allowing elements of traditional religion to be absorbed into Christianity: the Christmas Tree and Easter eggs are ancient European pagan rituals absorbed and trivialized by the Church. With the *Olórìsà* in Brazil, however, the policy backfired. The Yoruba would not allow their rituals to be trivialized.

There is a famous incident, observed by Verger, when the Yoruba went to worship *Yemanja*. They led a candlelight procession along the bay of Copacabana in Rio de Janeiro and when they reached a certain sacred spot, they turned to the sea and brought a sacrifice to *Yemanja*. On this occasion the Church had become worried about the persistence of "pagan" rituals. So they decided to stage a counter procession. When the Christians arrived at the beach carrying the image of the Virgin Mary, the Yoruba turned around happily and said: "The Virgin has come to greet *Yemanja*." They prayed to the Virgin, then faced the sea again and continued the ritual unperturbed!

Another interesting thing that happened in Brazil is that while Yoruba religion identified (to a point) with Catholicism, other African religions identified with Yoruba. I once hit upon a ritual in Bahia which I could not interpret, and which was conducted in a language I had never heard before. When I asked them whom they were worshipping, they said: "This is *Ogun Angola*." Yoruba religion has such a prestige in Brazil, that other African religions now identify with it. In the meantime, you can also find many white people worshipping in the *candomble*, and, unlike Nigeria, the *Òrìsà* hold a strong appeal to people from all walks of life. I encountered police officers, even lawyers in the *candomble*; and of course, many artists and writers feel drawn to it. In Brazil a successful balance was achieved between Yoruba values and a more modern life style. In Nigeria, on the other hand, I had to watch the painful process of disintegration of a culture. The educational system managed to create a rift between the *Olórìsà* and the "educated" Christians, not to speak of the Muslims. On top of it all we experienced the oil boom and all the corruption it brought in its wake. I witnessed a generation of priests, who were aware that they would be the last exponents of a great and noble way of life and who would nevertheless carry the burden of that huge responsibility without compromise.

At the core of any *Òrìsà* ritual was the trance: the *Òrìsà* must be present amongst the worshippers for the ritual to be concluded successfully. And the only way in which he can manifest his presence is to "mount" somebody's head. During the weekly *òsè* on *Jakuta* day, *Sàngó* would mount any one of those present: the worshippers dance in a circle to a monotonous *bata* rhythm. Suddenly a slight tremor goes through the body of one of the women, her eyes are glazed, and she is gently led aside into a cool recess of the shrine where she will rest until the ceremony is over. Then the senior priests will gather around her and she will prophesy. The *Òrìsà*'s manifestation is so discreet in such a case, that a stranger happening on such a scene does not usually realize the drama that is played out in front of his eyes.

There are other situations, however, when the god manifests himself in a spectacular manner. During the annual *ebo*, in front of the *Oba*'s palace, *Sàngó* will manifest himself in his full force and only a powerful priest who has been subtly prepared can carry the weight of such a manifestation on his head. He has to be *Sàngó* in public: he must walk like *Sàngó*, roar like *Sàngó* , speak like *Sàngó* and dance like *Sàngó* . He is wild, fierce, awesome, yet again gentle and witty, a great performer, who entertains the public not only with demonstrations of supernatural strength, but also with humorous conjuring tricks and sleights of hand!

F: Every culture perceives the world ultimately through its mythological allusions. How would you describe the mythological pantheon of the Yoruba?

U: A major difference between the Yoruba world view and the monotheistic religions is that Yoruba does not insist on a declaration of faith. In Christianity, faith has become the ultimate virtue. Remember the medieval play *Everyman*, which is about a successful rich man who is suddenly confronted by death. He has led a ruthless life and doesn't know how to confront his creator. He begs his friends to accompany him and plead for him, but they all desert him. He asks his good deeds to go with him, but they are too weak to make the journey. In the end he is saved by his faith alone. In some fundamentalist Christian sects, and in Islam, the ultimate Evil is to renege on your faith and it is punishable by death.

In Yoruba, this notion does not exist. A Christian may find himself morally obliged to believe something that his reason tells him is wrong. Yoruba people don't draw this rigid line between physical reality and the realities of the mind. An *Obàtálá* priest in Ilobu was taunted by his grandson: "You and your *Obàtálá*—the teacher said *Obàtálá* does not exist." Whereupon the old man answered: "Only that for which we have no name does not exist."

Reality is not a set of scientific data: reality is the interpretation we impose upon the world in order to make sense out of it. This reality is flexible, changing, and it exists in the context of other parallel realities. The Christian single-mindedness appears naive, if not slightly absurd from a Yoruba point of view. Hence the Yoruba term for a Christian is *onígbàgbó* (a " believer").

F: Which among the many *Òrìsà* exercises the most fundamental influence in every or any area of experience or entity, and what are the fundamental dichotomies in their functions either within the cultural framework or body of mythological presuppositions?

U: Strictly speaking, this question makes no sense in Yoruba terms, because for every human being it is his own *Òrìsà* who will exercise the most profound influence on his life. An *Obàtálá* worshipper is not normally concerned with the power of *Sàngó* or *Ògún*—it is the relationship he can create between himself and *Obàtálá* that will shape his life

That is not all: there are different manifestations of *Obàtálá*: *Òrìsànlá*, *Òrìsà Ògìyán*, *Ajàgemo*, and so on. They are all closely related, they regard themselves as one, attend each other's festivals, but they emphasize different aspects of the *Òrìsà*'s personality, so that from the *Olórìsà*'s point of view they are not interchangeable!

On the other hand there is a philosophical framework within which these personal interactions between *Òrìsà* and man take place. And here we have a body of mythology that is widely shared, even though different variants of the same myth may be told in different cult groups. There is a body of shared knowledge that informs people's attitudes to the world.

There is the well-known myth about Oduduwa, the creator of the land. Oduduwa descends from heaven with the mission of creating the land, because at the beginning there was only water. He carries a snail shell full of earth, some pieces of iron, and a cock. He places the iron on the water, pours the earth over it, then places the cock onto the earth. The cock starts to scratch and thus he scatters the earth over the water. Oduduwa calls the sixteen major *Òrìsà* from heaven and they settle on the earth and found the holy city of Ife. The political significance of this myth is: Oduduwa is the creator and therefore the owner of the earth. Therefore all other *Oba* owe allegiance to his descendant, the *Ooni* of Ife. But there is a second, equally well-known myth about Oduduwa. Here he is represented as a warlord who leads his people across the river Niger, subdues the Aboriginal population in the Ife area, and forces them to settle within the walls of the city of Ife which he has founded. Unlike the oriental despotic rulers who tended to wipe out the descendants of a defeated king to the last baby, Oduduwa integrates the conquered people by giving their king a chieftaincy title within the hierarchy of Ife.

As you well know, this whole episode is being commemorated annually in the *Edì* festival in Ife, where the original owners of the land are recognized and paid homage to, before the status quo is restored and the *Ooni*, descendant of Oduduwa, rules for another year. To the European mind these two myths are contradictory and an historian might be tempted to say that if one is the true story the other must be wrong. But it is this very capacity of the Yoruba mind to accept these two apparently contradictory accounts as alternative truths that enables them also to recognize the conquered culture as of equal worth. Therefore they could accommodate the coexistence of these cultures within the walls of the same city.

Ife was the first multicultural city. And it is not hard to see why Muslims and Christians (or even different Muslim sects or different Christian sects) cannot easily live harmoniously together: the very fact that each claims to be in sole possession of the truth makes coexistence extremely difficult. On the other hand, the Yoruba who liken God to a swarm of bees-a conglomeration of many *Òrìsà* who all represent specific aspects of the divinity-makes a harmonious society imperative, because society as a whole cannot exist unless all segments of the community (that is all the different groups of *Olórìsà*) put their insight and their wisdom and their ritual techniques together, for the benefit of the community.

But there is another aspect to that story: Oduduwa did not descend from Heaven alone. In fact the mission to create the land had been entrusted to his senior brother *Obàtálá*, and Oduduwa was only accompanying him. Then, as they were resting on the way, *Obàtálá* drank too much palmwine and fell asleep. Oduduwa usurped his brother's privilege and went ahead to create the land. Here is another very important element: even gods are human. They have virtues and vices. They are strong and weak. They are generous and vindictive, loveable and fearsome-all at the same time. The *Òrìsà* reflect the world as it is-they are not perfect.

This divine fallibility features prominently in the second creation myth: *Obàtálá* creates human beings out of clay, not in a single act of creation but continuously. He shapes every new baby in the mother's womb! But here again: occasionally the *Òrìsà* is drunk on palmwine and then he creates albinos, hunchbacks, and all kinds of deformed people and lunatics. In other words: he takes full responsibility for all his creatures; unlike the Biblical god who is perfect. To explain imperfection and evil in the world Christianity had to invent the devil. The Yoruba myth on the other hand encourages a very tolerant attitude. If *Obàtálá* is responsible for deformed people then we must respect his spirit in them and we must pay them a certain respect. *Obàtálá* shrines gave very special positions to albinos and hunchbacks in their ritual; and all lunatics were treated with extreme respect and tolerance by Yoruba society. As long as a person was not violent, he had the right to wander about naked, to let his hair grow into dreadlocks and to sleep on the market place. Everyone had a moral obligation to feed such people or clothe them, if they accepted clothes. In the early sixties, I knew a couple, a man and a woman, who wandered about together and they had a child that was born in the market place and was brought up by them. But when the child was about six years old, Duro Ladipo went to them and said: "Look, I think it would be better for your child, if you allowed me to bring her up for you." They did and the child grew up in Duro's home, led a normal life, married and had children.

F: Incredible!

U: The French artist Jean Dubouffet said: "Lunacy is the extreme form of individualism." One could say that Yoruba people feel that way too and they treat them accordingly. In a European society, that is not easy. There is a modern trend now to open up psychiatric hospitals and send the patients back into the community, but people in Europe find it hard to deal with them. They have neither the tolerance nor the patience.

F: You're saying that every *Òrìsà* embodies one aspect of a specific way of looking at the world?

U: You know the story that explains the multiplicity of gods. At the beginning there was *Òrìsà*. He is depicted in this myth as an old man who lived under a steep cliff. He had one servant, who secretly hated him. One day when *Òrìsà* returned home in the evening, the servant was waiting on top of the cliff and rolled a huge rock down onto the hut. *Òrìsà* was crushed and hundreds of splinters were scattered throughout the world. *Òrúnmìlà*, the first oracle priest, collected as many pieces as he could find and deposited them in a calabash in a shrine in Ife and called it *Òrìsànlá*—the big *Òrìsà*. But many of the splinters are still in trees and rocks and rivers and animals and human beings. So there is some spark of the divine essence everywhere, even within ourselves. We have to discover it and try to be in harmony with it.

So it is not like the Biblical concept: God on one side and the world on the other. And God telling man to make the earth and everything in it his subject. The Yoruba saw themselves as part of a divine environment. They believed in balance. Balance between gods and men, between animals and men, between plants and men. It would not occur to them to cut down huge stretches of forest to create a plantation. Their farms, even in the fifties were small patches that were integrated into the forest. It is only since they have lost their religion that the Yoruba began to destroy their environment.

It is a curious thing that many intellectual Yoruba, even those who try to come to terms with their culture, still can't face the "stigma" of polytheism. They dodge the question, or they concoct a scientific myth according to which the Yoruba were good monotheists, but somewhere along the line they degenerated into Òrìsà worship; or else they try to see the Òrìsà as a mere mediator between god and men-as something separate from and essentially different from god. The Yoruba world-view is more subtle than that.

But to return to the concept of the scattering of the divine essence. Since every person has some of this divine spark within him, it is his duty to identify the nature of it. Unless you know who you are and what your human potential is, you cannot establish the right relationship with an Òrìsà. You can only worship the Òrìsà that befits you, not just any divinity.

Graphically, this is depicted as follows: before you enter this world, you are led into a "garden of heads." You are made to pick your own head, your inner head (*orí inú*), that is, your destiny. This is what you bring down from heaven and this is what you have to live with. But it is not to be confused with a fatalistic world-view. On the contrary, what you bring down from heaven is your capital and you must make it work. Your *orí* sets your limitations but it also determines your potential, and you must make sure that you develop this potential to the fullest! To enable you to do so, you must identify your Òrìsà, the one that is congenial to you; the one whose personality is closest to your own. Because only with that Òrìsà will you be able to achieve that interaction and harmony that will enable you to develop your personality to its fullest extent. Yoruba religion and Yoruba philosophy place the utmost importance on the development of individuality-there is no regimentation in this culture even though you have to develop your personality within a certain framework. You have to work at yourself all the time; you have to work at your relationship with the Òrìsà continuously and relentlessly. It is a religion that places a lot of responsibility on the individual.

This is why, contrary to the prejudice that was long held by Yoruba scholars, Yoruba art was anything but anonymous. We have since learned to distinguish easily between the styles of say Bamgboye, Areogun, and Olowe of Ise. And even within the oeuvre of a single artist you always find some unique pieces! Some little joke, some quirk of the imagination which the artist produced only once. That is why when you look at the vast collections of Yoruba art that are found in Europe and America, there are always pieces which you can't classify; which don't seem to fit any of the laid-down criteria. The Yoruba were too flexible for that. They wouldn't allow their imagination to be regimented.

The Yoruba, as we have said before, conceive of the divine essence as something infinitely complex, so that no individual—and not even an ancient hierarchy of priests—can grasp it all. People can only understand aspects of it. And according to the nature of our *orí*, we can become specialists in dealing with certain aspects of supernatural powers. For example: the *Egúngún* masqueraders are specialists in communicating with the dead. *Sàngó* worshippers know how to communicate with another aspect of the divine essence. It is naive to say "*Sàngó* is the god of thunder." Of course, thunder is one of his symbols, but it does not describe him. To understand the complexity of his being, we must listen to his *oríkì* instead of transferring the shallow terminology of latter-day Greek mythology to Yoruba *Òrìsà*.

Sònpònná has to do with suffering. The *Sònpònná* priests can teach you how to live and cope with suffering; for example, with a serious disease like smallpox or any other disease, in particular the "hot" diseases or fevers. The *Sònpònná* priests teach us that the reverses of life can turn out to be positive, provided we know how to live with them and how to interpret them. You don't simply fight the disease (even though the *Sònpònná* priests have treatments). You are made to see that the *Òrìsà* has something to tell you, that he wants to draw you into his orbit, and that he uses this harsh method of letting you know. You will lead a much more meaningful and purposeful life, once you have understood the message and draw the consequences.

If you read the *oríkì* of *Sònpònná* or *Obalúayé* or *Alájíire*—the various manifestations of the god-you will find a lot of tenderness in them. Such tenderness could never be engendered by a cult that consists of exploitative charlatans, as some missionaries tried to tell us. These vicious tales are absurd. First of all, if they were true why were the *Sònpònná* priests not rich? They were as poor as all other *Olórìsà* because material wealth didn't even enter it!

Secondly: look at the faces of the *Sònpònná* priests I photographed in the 1950s. How do they get such sad, wise, compassionate faces? You don't put on a face like a mask. Your face is the result of your life; it is the result of your spiritual life. It cannot lie. Again, it was the personalities of the people that attracted me to *Sònpònná*. Their *òsè* was not boisterous and witty like *Jakuta*, the weekly *Sàngó* ceremony. But I found these people very moving. *Sònpònná* is a very beautiful, a poetic *Òrìsà*.

Òrìsà worship is not about good and evil in the Christian sense. Nor is it about following rules and regulations and commandments. It is about fulfilling yourself. About living out your *orí*, about becoming what you are meant to become. Only closeness to the *Òrìsà* can help you do this.

F: According to Hans Witte, "in contrast to the Òrìsà and earthspirits, who attract worshippers on the basis of family tradition, profession, special vocation, Orunmila and Èsù are venerated by every traditional Yoruba. The cosmic system would fall apart without the integrating activity of the oracle and the trickster." What is so extraordinary about these two deities?

U: The Òrìsà all have a very distinct historical personality and their cults are particularly virile in places where this connection is strong There are some religious institutions, though, that cut across Yorubaland and they even play a politically unifying role. The Ogbóni society is one of these. If you are an Ogbóni, you can go to any town in Yorubaland, go to the Ilédì, make yourself known through a series of passwords and participate in their rituals, and contribute to all their deliberations. The Ogbóni society has been used, historically, as a peacemaker between warring parties, because this cult cuts across national boundaries. All Yoruba people live on the earth and they must take care not to offend the earth spirit. The Ogbónis therefore have a lot of political influence, beyond the walls of their own city.

In a very different way the Ifá oracle transcends all boundaries. Information about one's Òrìsà is simply absorbed from childhood. You learn the oríkì simply by hearing the drummers or chanters at the big festivals. You are not made to sit down and learn a catechism. The Ifá oracle, on the other hand, is a code of knowledge. It was not written and not fixed—new Odu were always invented and added, but it was a body of knowledge that had to be learned and interpreted by professionals. The study took at least seven years, and a real Babaláwo would extend his knowledge at every major festival when he heard other great priests recite their versions of the Odu.

The Ifá oracle created a structure, a framework in which the wild and the ever changing interaction between different Òrìsà and conflicting mythologies could take place. It imposed some kind of order onto the multi-faceted world-view of the Yoruba, though you must not think of the rigidity of European or middle Eastern Belief systems when you hear the word "order." When you come to the Babaláwo with a problem there is no clear-cut answer. He does not consult a law book. There are any number of Odu verses he can quote and interpret, and it depends on the degree of his sensitivity and his ability to grasp the personality of his client. Now your question about order and disorder. Èsù has always been called the principle of disorder. Superficially that is true. But remember, there is a new branch of physics that is called "chaos research." It is based on the assumption that what we perceive as chaos is simply based on a different kind of order.

Now take the myth I recited before, about Òrìsànlá being crushed by his servant who rolled a rock onto him. Here somebody creates chaos—or apparently so.

But when I tell you that the servant was really Èsù in disguise (as is said in some versions of this myth), then there is an entirely different significance to it. It becomes a case of divine intervention, and what looks like chaos is in reality a new kind of order: instead of a single, monolithic god we now have a divine substance spread throughout the world. A new world order. No longer god vis-a-vis the world, but the god and the world being inseparably interwoven.

And this is the function of Èsù—to create a new order by challenging the old. The Yoruba have always understood that routine is the death of creativity and that complacency is the death of a spiritually alert life. Therefore Èsù systematically upsets our plans, provokes us with the unexpected, and keeps us wide awake. Èsù reminds us every minute of the day that we cannot take anything for granted, that we have to live responsibly all the time, and that we must work at our relationships with gods and men.

If you look at modern life in Europe, how our thinking is dominated and shaped by the media, by advertising, commerce, and politics, I feel that we badly need Èsù in the modern world: our youngsters often turn into zombies. The concentration span becomes shorter and shorter-we badly need the provocation of the trickster god.

F: Well, if Ifá, as we are often told, consists of the sacred texts of the Yoruba people as does the Bible for Christians, and Èsù is the path to Ifá (and his image often appears at the center of the upper perimeter of the Ifá divining board), could one say that the literal translation of Èsù as the biblical equivalent of Satan or devil is more than an accident? That the translation was in fact "meant" to sound the death-knell of this view of the world?

U: I am convinced it was a deliberate attempt to discredit, to demonize Yoruba religion. The Church has a long history of that. They have done the same thing in Europe.

They have a real difficulty in grasping the complexity of Yoruba culture. In Christianity there is this rigid division of the world into good and evil. They could never understand a concept like àjé, for example. Àjé represents the magical power of women, particularly of the powerful female spirits whom even the Orìsà must fear. But their power is not necessarily evil. It can equally be creative. There was the concept that some old women could become vehicles for destructive magic forces. They could-quite unwittingly at times-be responsible for the death of children in the compound. It was usually the Egúngún masqueraders who could identify such a person. But she was not killed! Unlike medieval Europe, where "witches" were burnt alive, Yoruba society was content to identify the destructive force and through exposure render it impotent. It was not a question of crime and punishment, but rather a question of the restoration of balance and social harmony.

F: If I could use Obotunde Ijimere's The Imprisonment of Obatala as a guide, would you say that epistemologically speaking, the abiding metaphor of Yoruba philosophy or mythology reposes on tragedy rather than comedy? U: This is difficult to answer, because you are now imposing foreign criteria on the culture. It is true that every *Òrìsà* lived a tragic life, that it was disappointment with the world-a disillusionment with the small-mindedness of human beings-that made them remove themselves to another sphere where they could really become themselves. Either through suicide, like *Sàngó*, or through a metamorphosis, like *Òtin*, the transformation of a human being into a river or a rock is merely a mythological metaphor for suicide.

F: And if you move from the domain of *Òrìsà*, as you've said earlier on, Yorubas believe in intensive living—the abiding atmosphere of the motor park, for example, is boisterous, comical, lively, but equally serious.

U: In Yoruba life, tragedy and comedy are not separated. Look at *Sàngó* : the most tragic of *Òrìsà* is also the greatest joker. Think of the entertaining performance of the *Bàbá Elégùn* at the *Sàngó* festival: the delightful mixture of physical prowess and slight of hand!

Think of the *Egúngún* masqueraders: the awe-inspiring ancestral masks, so holy that the public have to be protected from their touch by groups of young men who lash around wildly with whips; yet these same *Egúngún* produced the *Alárìnjó* theater—sometimes during the same festival—which lampoons all the village characters as well as other tribes and Europeans! They even make fun of *Sàngó* and don't stop short of the ancestral masks themselves! Tragedy and comedy live closely together in Yorubaland. They are seen as two sides of the same coin.

VI.
MUSIC

The Music of Yoruba Gods
Akin Euba

The Yoruba have through the ages consistently promoted religion through music, and some of the best examples of Yoruba music are those connected with religion. The Yoruba in traditional culture are ardent cultivators of music and, since religion is of high importance, it is reasonable to expect that they would excel themselves in the creation of music for the gods.

It is not only in traditional culture, however, that the Yoruba exhibit a deep sense of religion through music. In modern culture, some of the most exciting new types of Yoruba music are those used in the African Churches, such as the Cherubim and Seraphim Church, the Christ Apostolic Church, and the Celestial Church of Christ.

There is also a considerable degree of creativity in the music generated by Islamic culture. In consonance with Islamic tradition all over the world, there is no liturgical music inside Yoruba mosques, but outside the mosques and in connection with the Moslem religious festivals, music is used extensively (see Euba 1971 for a fuller discusiion). Moreover, Islamic culture has influenced the development of new types of secular music, such as *sákárà, wáká, àpàlà,* and *fújì,* which rank among the most popular types of modern Yoruba music.

I have referred to the musical achievements of Yoruba Christians and Moslems simply to demonstrate the consistency of religious musical inventiveness and it is not my intention to dwell on these matters. In this essay, I am concerned more specifically with the role of music in traditional religious culture.

The Importance of Religion in Yoruba Society

Religion plays a very important part in Yoruba society; according to Ìdòwú, it is the keynote of life. The divinities are held responsible for all affairs of life, and for practically every important activity (such as the birth of a child, betrothal, marriage, taking up a career) the Yoruba would consult the oracle, in order to determine what the future holds. Religion is so dominant that it forms the theme of songs and topics for minstrelsy, myths, folktales, and proverbs. Yoruba philosophy is also based on religion (Idowu 1962:5)

Who are the Divinities?

Among the Yoruba, gods and goddesses are referred to individually and collectively as *òrìsà*. There is a great proliferation of divinities in Yorubaland and some authorities believe that there are over 400 in number.

The Yoruba believe in the concept of a Supreme God, Olódùmarè, but this God is thought to be too important to be approached directly. He must therefore be solicited through his assistants and these are the *òrìsà*. The perception of Olódùmarè is like that of a Prime Minister, for whom the various divinities act as Ministers, each having a specific portfolio. Most of the divinities have shrines and cults of devotees, but there is no shrine or cult of Olódùmarè as such.

Of the over 400 divinities in Yorubaland, the vast majority are local divinities, known and worshipped in specific towns or regions, while only a few are universal divinities known throughout Yorubaland. There are male as well as female divinities, whose functions are fairly well defined.

The universal or widely known divinities include Obatala, the god of creation; Orunmila, god of divination and controller of the *Ifa* oracle; Ogun, god of war and iron implements; Sango, the god of thunder and lightning; Osun, goddess of the River that flows through the town of Osogbo; Oya, also a river goddess, her domain being the Niger River; Osanyin, the god of medicinal herbs; *Orisa*-nla, god of the forest; *Orisa* Oko, the special god of farming; Esu, god of fate, described by some authorities as the trickster; and Sonpona, the god of small-pox.

Examples of minor divinities, whose influence is localized, are Olosunta, who is peculiar to Ikere-Ekiti, and Osara, a river goddess worshipped in Ile-Ife. In some places, the universal divinities are given local names. In Ile-Ife, for example, Ogun is also known as Olojo. Obatala has many different manifestations. In Ile-Ife alone, he is known as *Orisa* Ideta, *Orisa* Akire, and *Orisa* Ijugbe (Idowu 1962:68-69). In Oyo, he is called Irawe; in Ede, *Orisa* Oja; in Ifon, *Orisa* Olufon; and in Ijaye, *Orisa* Ijaye. The names *Orisa* Ogiyan and *Orisa*nla (the big god) also refer to Obatala. Jakuta and Oramfe are manifestations of Sango. Although Jakuta pre-dates Sango, the characteristics of Jakuta were assumed by Sango, and Sango now dominates the concept which embodies these characteristics. Jakuta continues to be worshipped, but in a minor way. There is a ceremony in Oyo, known as *Jimo Oloyin*, which occurs every time the traditional ceremony for Jakuta falls on a Friday (*Jimo* or *Jumaat*).

Yoruba divinities may be categorized in terms of their temperament. There are the peaceful divinities, such as Obatala, Osun, Orunmila, and Osanyin, and there are the potentially destructive divinities such as Ogun, Sango, Sanponna, and Esu. The latter need to be constantly propitiated in order that they may not unleash their terror against humanity.

Let me further explain the characteristics of the divinities. Obatala is conceptualized as the giver of children. The Yoruba rationalize deformities in children (for example, the hunched back) through a myth that says that the first deformed child was created on a day when Obatala was drunk with palm wine and this is why the devotees of Obatala today abstain from palm wine. Deformed children are regarded as the special creatures of Obatala and such status prevents people from looking down on them.

Orunmila is the patron god of all diviners. All persons wishing to know their destiny or to seek solutions to problems consult the *Ifa* priest. By chanting appropriate texts from the vast corpus of *Ifa* poetry and looking at the configurations that emerge from his working of the divining board, the priest is able to advise his client.

Esu, the god of fate, is in a position to adversely affect a person's destiny. For this reason, people planning major undertakings consider it wise to propitiate Esu before pursuing such undertakings. I once watched a demonstration of this at Ede, during a masquerade festival. I was at the time observing the practice of one of the major masquerades in Ede and was among the crowd waiting to accompany the masquerade to the market place, for the ceremonial congregation of all the town's masquerades. As the masquerade emerged from the family compound, together with his drummers, the first thing that he did was to go before a stone rooted in the ground. A short ceremony, consisting of the pouring of palm oil and reciting of prayers, was performed in front of the stone. This was a ceremony to Esu so that he would not interfere with the performance of the masquerade on that day, the most important day of the masquerade festival. Orunmila, the knower of destiny, and Esu, the controller of destiny, both have a parallel channel of activity, even though they work in opposite directions. For this reason, symbols of Esu and Orunmila are sometimes juxtaposed.

The devotees of Ogun include all persons whose work is connected with metal objects, such as hunters and blacksmiths. In modern times, even lorry drivers see the need to propitiate Ogun in order to avoid accidents.

Sango, when angry, uses thunder to destroy, while Sonponna inflicts punishment by spreading small-pox. Whenever there is an epidemic of small-pox, the Yoruba believe that all efforts to combat it through medical means would be futile unless offerings were made to Sonponna. Sonponna is believed to dwell in the earth and, when there is a small-pox epidemic, people avoid saying directly that Sonponna is angry. Instead, the situation is described as *ile gbona* ("the ground is hot"). It is also in recognition of Sonponna as an earth-god that Yoruba acrobats, when giving a performance, would invariably begin by chanting an *ijuba* (in which the powers of the earth are acknowledged) so that there might be no accidents (Idowu 1962:96).

The Yoruba people's conception of the divine status permits them to view gods and goddesses in almost human terms and this is partly manifested in the kinds of offerings that are made to the divinities. Offerings to Esu are usually placed in bowls at crossroads (where he is supposed to dwell often) and such offerings invariably include his favorite palm oil, and may also have other edible objects and sometimes coins of money.

The humanization of the divinities is no doubt related to the fact that the divinities are people who once lived on earth and were elevated after their death to the divine status as a mark of their achievements on earth. Ogun was a great warrior whose hometown was Ire in the Ekiti section of Ondo State; this is why his praise poetry includes the phrase *Ogun Onire* ("Ogun, owner of Ire town"). Sonponna is believed to have come to Yorubaland from the northern parts of Nigeria and his praise poetry refers to him as a northerner.

Sango was a powerful king who ruled in Oyo in the fifteenth century. He was said to have been a great magician who could breathe fire from his mouth and cause lightning to occur. Sango encouraged his warrior-chiefs to subjugate other Yoruba towns and these chiefs eventually became so unruly that Sango could no longer control them. Sango therefore sought to get rid of his two most powerful chiefs, Gboonkaa and Timi, by setting them against each other, hoping that they would destroy each other. As things turned out, Gboonkaa was victorious over Timi and afterwards pursued Sango himself, driving the king into exile, where he committed suicide by hanging. Some of the people in Oyo remained loyal to Sango and refused to believe that he was dead. As they contemplated their dilemma, Sango suddenly spoke to them through a display of lightning and the people shouted in delight, *Oba ko so* ("the king did not hang"). To this day, one of the praise names of Sango is *Oba ko so* (also the title of the Yoruba folk opera by Duro Ladipo that vividly dramatizes Sango's reign).

The Divinities and the Origin of Music

Some divinities are credited with the invention or promotion of certain types of music. According to the former King of Ede, His Highness Oba Adetoyese Laoye I, who was an authority on Yoruba music, when Obatala lived on earth he had four wives and whenever he wished to dance, his wives supplied music by clapping their hands. In course of time, Obatala got bored with hand clapping and decided to make four drums for his wives to play.

The drums were named after the wives, *Iyanla, Iya Agan, Keke*, and *Afeere* and they are the drums which form the *Igbin* ensemble that is used up to this day by the devotees of Obatala. An analysis of this story reveals some interesting information. Why did Obatala need to create drums and make his wives act as drummers rather than engage professional drummers (as someone of his eminence would do today)? Perhaps the answer is that neither drums nor drummers existed in Yorubaland in Obatala's time. Beier (1960:35) has suggested that Obatala predates Oduduwa who led the first wave of migrations of the Yoruba to Ile-Ife. Historians put the date of this first migration at around the seventh century. This implies then that *Igbin* (singleheaded, fixed-pitch drums) were already in use in the area that became the new home of the Yoruba. In my doctoral dissertation (Euba 1974:32-33) I suggested that the double-headed hourglass tension drum, which is believed to originate from somewhere in the northeast, did not reach Yorubaland until after the Oduduwa migration. All this leads to the conclusion that the *Igbin* existed in Yorubaland before the double-headed hourglass tension drum, and this view is supported by Sachs' theory that single-headed drums pre-date double-headed drums (Sachs 1940:33).

Sango, too, made an important contribution to the development of Yoruba music. *Bata* drums were selected during his reign as the special drums for Sango and continue to be used today by his devotees. Incidentally, the river goddess, Oya, was in her lifetime a wife of Sango, and the music and other artistic symbols used by her devotees are similar to those of Sango.

The creativity of Ogun has been acknowledged by Soyinka (1976:27) and there is ample evidence of continued creativity among his contemporary devotees. Yoruba hunters specialize in *ijala*, one of the most popular forms of Yoruba chant and according to Babalola (1966) it is possible that Ogun himself may have invented *Ijala* when he was alive in human form.

The patron god of drumming in Yorubaland is Ayan and, although there is neither shrine nor cult of priests for Ayan, individual drummers now and then make sacrificial offerings to him. According to Oba Laoye (1959), Ayan once lived on earth and came to Yorubaland from Saworo in

Ibaribaland. (Saworo was almost certainly located in the region of Borgu in Kwara State, where the Bariba people live today.) Oba Laoye further mentioned that Ayan was the first drummer in Yorubaland and that he taught the Yoruba the art of drumming.

We may note in passing that the connection of Ayan with Ibaribaland is consistent with other evidence suggesting a northeastern origin for the Yoruba tension drum.

By the custom of the Yoruba, drumming is a family craft and one is permitted to take up the art of drumming only if one belongs to a drumming family. Every drummer inherited the art from his father and is expected to pass it on to his male children. As the first Yoruba drummer, Ayan may be regarded as the ultimate ancestor of all drummers. Drummers believe that Ayan is the spirit which resides in the drum and that everything that they play on the drum is dictated by this spirit. It is because of this spirit that a drummer is able to recall poetry and other drum texts which he did not even know existed in his memory. One of the praise names of Ayan is *Ayanagalu, asoro 'gi* ("Ayan of Agalu, one that speaks through the medium of wood"). All drummers have personal drumming names, prefixed by the word Ayan, such as Ayantunji, Ayandele, Ayankolade.

In a series of interviews which I recorded with Laisi Ayansola, a brilliant exponent of the *dundun* tension drum tradition, Ayansola (now deceased) gave an extended eulogy of Ayanagalu, describing the god not simply as the source of musical talent, but as the provider of all benefits for the drummer. The drummer's house and other worldly belongings are all acquired through the benevolence of Ayan. Moreover, Ayan is the power that gives the drummer the necessary confidence to enter an assembly of dignitaries and perform his music.

Ensembles Used for Various Divinities

We know from the foregoing that the favorite instruments of Sango are the *bata* drums. These are a set of conically shaped, double-headed, fixed-pitch membrane drums usually consisting of four instruments. The drums are *Iyaalu, Omele abo, kudi,* and *Omele ako* and they are played by three musicians, since the last named couple of drums are joined together. *Bata* drums are not restricted to Sango but are played for some other divinities and for certain masquerades. These drums are carried in performance and are therefore convenient when performers have to move about from place to place.

In some cases, divinities have instruments which are ritually dedicated to them. Such instruments are usually housed within the shrine and played therein; they are seldom, if ever, played outside the shrine. A good example of ritually dedicated drums are the *igbin* ensemble played for Obatala. In view of the importance of these drums in Obatala ceremonies, their wooden resonators are often decorated with carvings and sometimes bear the marks of ritual symbols and offerings. Shrine drums are cumbersome and heavy and do not allow for easy mobility. There are instruments which are preferences of certain divinities but are not necessarily dedicated or exclusive to them. In addition to drums, the devotees of Orunmila also use an ensemble of iron bells, *agogo Ifa.* As far as I know, these bells are not played together with drums.

The special drums of Orunmila are called *ipese.* The devotees of Ogun also have a special set of single-membrane, fixed-pitch drums known as *agere.* I have heard and read about these drums but can recall having actually heard them played only once, and this was at a festival for Osun in Osogbo. (It is not unusual for devotees of other *orisa* to be involved in such a major celebration as the annual Osun festival in Osogbo.) Also comparatively rare are the *apiti* drums, a set of two or three single-membrane drums accompanied by an iron bell. These drums, too, were familiar to me from the writing of Oba Laoye (1959) but it was many years later that I got a chance to see and hear them played. This was at a performance which I specially commissioned and recorded at Okinni, a village located about six kilometers outside Osogbo. During the recording session the musicians played a variety of secular and religious pieces. The most commonly used ensemble in the performance of music for the divinities is the *dundun*, a set of double-headed hourglass tension drums which, because of their popularity, have come to characterize Yoruba drumming in general. At the height of the Oyo Empire, the capital city, Oyo, not only had political control over most of Yorubaland but also had a cultural influence that extended beyond the city and adjacent regions. Whatever was fashionable in Oyo quickly spread to other parts of Yorubaland and it was in this way that the tension drum became universal among all Yoruba people.

The tension drum has many physical advantages over other types of drums. It has a wide tonal range, an important asset for a people who use a tone language and are much addicted to talking with musical instruments. Moreover, the tension drum is exceedingly mobile and is totally free of contextual restrictions. It is no surprise, therefore, that it has tended over the years to dominate not only secular music but also religious music. Even in cases where divinities have their own special drums, the *dundun* ensemble is substituted more often than not, particularly in performances that take place outside the shrines.

There is a general principle guiding the use of drums for the divinities. Readers familiar with the music of tension drums in Yorubaland would know that these drums are either played by themselves or together with the large gourd rattle (*sekere* or *aje*) and/or a pair of metallophones (*aro*). The common practice among the central Yoruba (that is, the Oyo-Yoruba) is that whenever tension drums are used for the divinities, the ensemble excludes other types of instruments. The *orisa* apparently prefer the sounds of pure drumming and this is further illustrated by the composition of the *bata* and *Igbin* ensembles, both of which are exclusively drums. It is interesting to note that the ensemble of bells played for Orunmila also excludes other types of instruments and the only time that I have heard drums mixed with a bell in the performance of religious music in central Yorubaland was during the performance of the *apinti* ensemble mentioned above. But this was merely a recording featuring secular as well as religious pieces and the musicians might well exclude the bell when playing at actual religious ceremonies.

I ought to explain that when I refer to central or Oyo Yoruba, I mean such towns as Oyo, Osogbo, Ede, Ogbomoso, Ikire, Ikirun, Ibadan, and so forth. Outside central Yoruba (for example in Ekiti, Ijebu, Ondo, Owo, Okitipupa, Egbado, and so on) local types of ensembles (and probably also the tension-drum ensemble) used in religious music combine drums with other instruments. Musical practice in central Yorubaland differs in other respects from that of the western, southern, and eastern Yoruba, but this is not the place to dwell on these differences.

Ceremonies for the *Orisa*

The devotees of the *orisa* observe three kinds of ceremonies. The most frequent is the *ose*, which is performed once every five days. Next comes the *itadogun*, observed once every 17 days. The *ose* and *itadogun* are minor ceremonies which usually involve the priests and devotees alone. Minor ceremonies are single-day events and all of the music is supplied by the devotees themselves.

The third and most important type of ceremony is the *odun*, which takes place once a year. Elaborate preparations are made for the *odun* and the events are spread over several days. While the *ose* and *itadogun* involve the devotees only, an *odun* is publicized to the town in general and non-devotees are welcome to participate in the general merriment, if not in the actual rituals. Some of the rituals are, however, made public and watched by non-devotees.

The *odun* (at least those performed for the major divinities) are identical with what Nketia (1963:119) describes as state events and the king of the town must be officially notified about the proceedings as soon as the dates of a festival have been determined by the priests, after consultation with the *Ifa* oracle. In view of the fact that the *odun* is an occasion when the priests invoke the benevolence of a divinity, not only for his or her devotees but for the town in general, the involvement of the king and his subjects in essential.

The Music

Music for the *orisa* is realized in various forms. There are the vocal forms and the instrumental forms, but all forms have one thing in common and this is that the principal focus and a substantial proportion of the musical content are the *oriki* of the divinities. *Oriki* are a form of eulogy comprising poems in which the attributes, status, characteristics, personality, ancestry, importance, and so forth of the subject of an *oriki* are emphasized. *Oriki* exist not only for people but for towns, lineages, animals, and inanimate or consumable objects. For example, palm wine has an *oriki* (*emu ogidi ponbe*) which describes the delicious taste of fresh palm wine.

The *oriki* of a person refers not only to his/her personal attributes and characteristics but to those of his or her ancestors as well. A person of sufficient standing in the community would usually have specific *oriki* created for him or her by musicians but he/she also inherits the ancestral *oriki* and musicians would regularly include this in the repertoire of his/her *oriki*.

The *oriki* of an *orisa* then, is a poetical and stylized description of his/her attributes, characteristics, temperament, and supernatural powers. *Oriki* are not only spoken, chanted, and sung, but are also played on musical instruments. Since Yoruba is a tone language, musicians have been able to develop a highly sophisticated use of musical instruments as speech surrogates. When playing in the *oriki* mode, the leading drum in an ensemble talks incessantly and there is extensive variety in its speech. One of the most important forms of music for the *orisa* is the invocation, usually referred to as *pipe orisa* ("calling of the divinities"). This may be chanted or played on the drums. During the minor ceremonies of *ose* and *itadogun*, the invocational chants are sung by the female devotees in unison. Although they are not professional musicians (in the sense that they do not perform for monetary gain or outside the context of ceremonies for their specific divinity), the group of female devotees would normally include a few people who specialize in the poetry of their *orisa* and it is these experts who lead the other women (who have varying degrees of expertise) in the rendering of the chants. These vocal invocations comprise *oriki*, exceptionally rich and complex, recited in heightened speech. The chants are in free rhythm and are unaccompanied. Once in a while, as is customary with Yoruba chanting in general, the women may initiate a song, which is performed in strict rhythm with instrumental accompaniment and which allows for responsorial vocal participation as well as dancing by the general assembly. The Yoruba distinguish between chant (something that you *sun*, that is "cry") and song (described as *orin*). Nowhere was this distinction between the non-danced, non-accompanied, free-rhythm chant and the danced, accompanied, strict-rhythm song made more clear to me than during an annual ceremony for Obatala (*Orisa Oja*) which I watched at Ede. In the course of a session of praise chanting by female devotees, the Chief Priest of Obatala, Ajagemo (who obviously wanted to dance), asked the women to start a song. The progression from chant to song went as follows.

AJAGEMO (in speech mode, interrupted chanting)
E ba n darin/ Please start a song for me.

CHANTERS (in speech mode)
Iru orin wo/ What kind of song?

AJAGEMO
Eyikeyi to ba wu yin/ Any kind that you wish

CHANTERS (in chant mode)
Baba iwo lo ran mi/ Father, it was you that sent me (that is, I am performing the duties that you assigned to me)
Orisa Ajagemo o/ O god of Ajagemo

AJAGEMO (in speech mode)
Ko ni hun o/ may you never be incapable

CHANTERS
iwo lo ran mi/ It was you that sent me

(The transition from chant mode to song mode took place in the course of the next line. The chanters changed to strict rhythm vocalization at the beginning of the line and the drums entered at the end of the line.)

Iku i pojise o/ Death does not ever kill the messenger (that is, "A messenger can never be at fault simply by performing a master's duties")

CHORUS (other participants, on-lookers in general)
Iwo lo ran mi

CHANTERS

Iku i pojise o
CHORUS
Iwo lo ran mi

(Singing was abandoned somewhere around this point and general dancing began.)

It is interesting to note that, in order to initiate dancing, the Ajagemo did not address the drummers (who would eventually play a major role in the dance) but rather requested a song from the chanters. In this sense, a song may be regarded as being synonymous with dance or at least something that automatically leads to dance.

At the minor ceremonies of *ose* and *itadogun* the instrumental music is played by the male devotees. As with the women singers, the male devotees include people who specialize in the drumming techniques, music, and poetry of the relevant divinity and it is these specialists who take charge of the instruments. It is customary to use only the shrine drums at such minor ceremonies. During the annual festivals, the devotees not only supply their own music at the shrines but engage professional musicians, usually *dundun* or *bata* players, who are not necessarily devotees themselves. Most of the professional drummers in Yorubaland are in fact Moslems. Yoruba professional drummers routinely include in their repertoire music and poetry appropriate to practically all of the various occasions for which a drummer might be required to supply music. Every drummer, for example, would know something (however limited) about the music of Ogun or Sango, or of a specific masquerade, household, or king in his community.

Since the knowledge of most drummers would tend to be generalized, it is the practice of kings and chiefs, as well as important households, organizations, religious and secular societies, and occupational groups to patronize specific drumming families which specialize in the specific types of music and poetry of their clients. A cult group, then, would not engage professional musicians arbitrarily but would patronize a specific family of drummers. In view of the fact that most professional drummers among the Yoruba are Moslems, it is of some interest that followers of Islam are able to specialize in the music of the *olorisa* ("worshippers of *orisa*"). I once asked a drummer in Ede how it is possible for Moslem drummers to play cult music without reproach from the Imams. He replied that such a problem had never come up in Ede before. He said that since music is their profession, the Imams never question the right of drummers to practice the profession in whatever way is profitable.

It is not only the musicians within a cult group that perform invocations; professional musicians, too, often do this. On the first day of an annual festival, for example, it would be in character for the drum ensemble engaged by a cult group to stand before the shrine house or the dwelling of the chief priest and play, for as long as one hour, non-danceable ensemble music in which the master drummer declaims the *oriki* of the divinity in question.

Since the actual shrine music is supplied by the devotees themselves, the main duties of the professional group is to provide music for events outside the shrine. For example, they would play processional music for the devotees as they move about the streets, and also music for dancing whenever the devotees stop processing in order to dance at some points on their processional route.

We may identify at least three main types of religious drumming, namely (a) praise drumming, (b) processional drumming, and (c) dance drumming. The three types are not markedly different from one another and they are distinguishable by the placement of greater or lesser emphasis on certain elements. In praise drumming, the musicians concentrate on *oriki*. The musicians are static, there are no dancers, and the arena of performance is fixed. In processional drumming, the texts played by the *Iyaalu* drummer (being relatively unimportant) are repetitive. The other participants move along in a kind of shuffling/dancing movements and the arena of performance is a shifting one. Dance drumming, also, makes minimal use of speech texts; the *Iyaalu* drummer is more concerned with playing *ijalu* (non-textual, rhythmical motifs to which the dancers must synchronize certain movements). During dance drumming, the procession halts and the arena of performance becomes fixed. The dancers expand their movements and create more artistic variety.

African religious ritual has a theatrical orientation and the music of Yoruba religious ceremonies (particularly that performed during the annual festivals) is synonymous with music theater. Annual rituals for the *orisa* frequently include reenactment ceremonies which are highly dramatic and in which music plays a central role. A good example of this is the dramatization of the myth of the imprisonment of Obatala, which is one of the highlights of the annual festival of Obatala in Ede. The central figures in this dramatization are the Ajagemo and the Oluwin, the two principal priests of Obatala in Ede.

Summary

The music performed today for a given divinity probably existed at the time when he/she lived on earth and could be the kind of music that he/she loved. According to Idowu (1962:9), the liturgies of the *orisa* have been preserved without change because the Yoruba believe that the efficacy of worship depends on whether or not the liturgies are performed correctly. For this reason, the music of the *orisa* is one of the oldest types of traditional music.

Music fulfils various functions during religious rituals. First of all, it helps to publicize and announce the event and to draw the community together. The Yoruba believe that any ceremony that does not include music would be poorly attended and unsuccessful and, for this reason, most people engage musicians as a way of attracting participants and audience to various social ceremonies, religious or secular.

Secondly, the music performed during religious events creates an atmosphere that is conducive to spirituality and facilitates communion between worshippers and the *orisa*. Thirdly, the divinities are pleased when they hear their favorite music and when eulogies are heaped upon them. Music, then, is like a sacrificial offering that induces the benevolence of the divinities. Fourthly, the richer and more elaborate the musical display mounted for an occasion, the higher will be the perception (in the community at large) of the importance of the divinity whose rites are being celebrated.

Lastly, as the tempo and mood of the music become more and more intense, the probability that the divinity will descend from the spiritual world to mount one or more of the devotees increases. Music, therefore, is a means of inducing trance states among the devotees.

REFERENCES

Babalola, S.A. *The Content and Form of Yoruba Ijala.* Oxford: Oxford University Press (1966).

Beier, Ulli. "Obatala: Five Myths About the Yoruba Creator God." *Black Orpheus 7* (1960).

Euba, Akin. "Islamic Musical Culture Among the Yoruba." *Essays on Music and History in Africa.* Ed., Klaus P. Wachsmann. Evanston, Illinois: Northwestern University Press, 1971.

——————. *Dundun Music of the Yoruba.* Ph.D. Dissertation, University of Ghana, Legon, 1974.

Idowu, Bolaji. *Olodumare: God in Yoruba Belief.* London: Longmans, 1962.

Ladipo, Duro. *Oba Ko So.* Transcribed and translated by R.G. Armstrong, Robert L. Awujoola & Val Olayemi from a tape recording by R. Curt Wittig. Ibadan: Institute of African Studies, University of Ibadan, 1972.

Laoye I, Timi of Ede. "Yoruba Drums." *Odu 7* (1959).

Nketia, J.H. *Drumming in Akan Communitites of Ghana.* Legon and London: University Of

Ghana and Thomas Nelson, 1963.

Sachs, Curt. *The History of Musical Instruments.* New York: W.W. Norton, 1940.

Soyinka, Wole. *Myth, Literature and the African World.* Cambridge: Cambridge University Press, 1976.

OTHER RELEVANT STUDIES

Euba, Akin. "Ilu Esu/Drumming for Esu: Analysis of a *Dundun* Performance." *Essays for a Humanist,* New York: The Town House Press, 1977.

King, Anthony.   *Yoruba Sacred Music from Ekiti.* Ibadan: Ibadan University Press, 1961.

Nketia, J.H. Kwabena. "African Gods and Music." *Universitas* 4, 1 (1959).

A Gift of the Gods:
The Story of the Invention of the "ODU" Gongs and the Rediscovery of the Ancient Lithophone
Ademola Onibonokuta

MY INSPIRATION

In music, an ounce of practice is better than tons of theory.

Our forefathers were natural technologists. They invented things which are of great use to us today. They worked freely without the constraints of formal education, yet what they left behind is invaluable to our present attempts to achieve a cultural reorientation.

I, too, might call myself a natural musical technologist; my musical training was solely achieved through the songs, the folklore, and the rituals my forefathers passed on to me and through the cultural plays in which I took part when I was young.

My creativity and my inventiveness cannot be called accidental. When I was a child I had wonderful dreams of God's creativity. I had visions of heaven which were a great inspiration to me. At the same time I also pondered over the wonderful creative ability of our past generations: their intricate designs on mud walls, drums, carvings, clothes; all these things are a major source of inspiration to me in my endeavor to create new things in music; as a child I always wished that, in some distant future, I might be referred to as one of those inventive ancestors, who left something behind for future generations.

In 1966 I was a member of the Nigerian contingent to the First Negro Arts Festival in Dakar. There I met and saw many world-famous artists and numerous musical instruments and I began to ask myself a series of questions, some of which were: Do you want to immortalize your name through your art? Do you want to become a legend in your life time or after death? Do you want to be referred to as one of the ancestors who left something behind for future generations? How would you raise money to do all this? Would you accept criticism and act on it and would you accept defeat when it comes? These and many other questions passed through my mind from time to time.

In 1968 a postgraduate student of the University of Ibadan came to interview me, because he wanted to write about my artistic work so far. Later he told me that because of what he wrote about me and others, he was now a Doctor. I was glad about this, but I felt he could have written a better book, had I done something really new in the field of art.

People I have met and worked with have also proved an inspiration to me. First among these was Ulli Beier. What I liked about him was the way he lived in that Yoruba house at Ibokun road in Oshogbo; everything was new about him, he was different from any other White Man we had seen; he would come to Mbari Mbayo Club in his native attire; he would eat our food and drink our palmwine; he would always greet you warmly. And I said to myself: if he did not do so many new things, the people would not like him; and I told myself, I must do new things too, to have the same glory as Ulli Beier.

I am equally inspired by the late Duro Ladipo, who made history in Nigerian drama. Often I looked at him and burst into laughter. Why? Because he was different from any other Nigerian I knew, and many people didn't even understand what he was doing! I remember that an old man once told him: "Big as you are, you are still playing about like a child, up and down the road, as far as Ibadan!" He could not understand, that it was not child's play that Duro was playing, but serious drama plays!

Wole Soyinka, Segun Olusola, Wale Ogunyemi, Dapo Adelugba, and other great men in our theater also motivated me. And here I must not forget my mother's wish for me to become something good in life and her constant support. When I told her I will travel with Duro Ladipo's company to Western Germany to perform *Oba Ko so*, she was glad that her son was the first person in her compound who went abroad.

In the play *Oba Ko so* I played the leading part of Gbonka and at the time many people called me: "Gbonka the Great". But even though many people told me, "You are wonderful in your part, especially in the witches scene," I was not satisfied with it. Because I thought: Why should people not cry in the witches scene? I was hurt, because I could not move them, but I summoned courage and I invented a new style, a sonorous voice for the witches scene; and at a later performance the audience were captured and some were even crying during the witches scene. I was glad that Duro Ladipo and Ulli Beier were happy too with the new style of performance.

It was during this period that I learned to accept criticism. Criticism helps one to develop, if only one has a strong mind and is willing to accept the reality of the game.

It was a joyful occasion for me to travel to the United States with Wole Soyinka in 1970, to participate at the Drama Workshop in Connecticut State. After one of our performances of Wole's new play *Madmen and Specialists,* there was a discussion during which a member of the audience said to him: We know that you are very good and that you have a fine command of the English language, but why can't you write in your native language; perhaps then people might enjoy you more. I cannot remember what Wole Soyinka's answer to this question was, but ever since then I said to myself, that when I get back home I will produce an authentic musical group. I will not use foreign instruments and I will use local materials to invent instruments of my own.

Many are the people I met, who became well known using our forefathers traditional instruments like *Dundun, Bata, Agere,* and others; like the late Oba Adetoyese Laoye, the Timi of Ede, from whom I first learnt the art of *Dundun* drumming in 1963. A traditional King who traveled far and wide with his talking drum, he became widely known inside and outside his domain. And again the late Lasisi Ayansola of Oshogbo, who was employed as chief-drummer in the Department of music in the University of Ife at level 08, even though he had never gone to school.

When I returned to Nigeria from the United States in 1970, I spoke to one of my good friends about my intention of creating a new awareness in African music. I told him I wanted to create new musical instruments and that I wanted other generations to see the trace of my hand. My friend laughed and said to me: "You now want to travel to an unknown land, where nobody has gone and returned." He told me that it would involve much money and I would make my family suffer. Secondly, that if I was not successful, I might run mad. He urged me to abandon this funny idea of mine and also said that it would be possible only if I went to Europe to learn about it. I asked him: "Did our forefathers go to Europe before they created so much?" He said: "You see, our forefathers had cleaner minds than we have. They could endure more than we today. They were not worried about material wealth, as we are today." He went further to say that to make any invention, one would first have to become a witch or wizard, and that even Europeans employed witchcraft before they invented their machines. They would fast and pray for several days first, then mould the object in clay and finally use their psychic power to conjure up the object.

My friend's talk did great harm to my mind, as it paralyzed all ideas of creation for a while. At that time I had been thinking of several things I wanted to invent, like a machine that will grind gari and a machine that will help mothers with their children in the kitchen: a machine that will play with their babies while they work. I had also heard a story from my father, that there was a Yoruba medicine in those days that would allow a man to watch the events on the battlefield by looking into a bowl of water. I thought that I would develop that into a kind of television. I had thought of dozens of ideas I could try my hand on. But determination refused to stay with me, because of my friend's story. I did not want to become a witch or wizard. So for a while I abandoned the idea of inventing machines that will play with babies and so on.

The Origin of Music in Yoruba Land

In April 1971 I determined to find out the history and background of music, song, and dance. I therefore set out on the journey to the unknown, as my friend had put it, and I went to several of our elders to collect their stories.

My first visit was to Mr. Salawu of Ile Bioku Agbagi of Oshogbo, who told me that birds were the first beings that used musical instruments. His story goes thus: when the earth was created by Olodumare, he created all sorts of beings, but they could not communicate with each other. The earth was dull, very quiet and each creature walked about in its own direction without saying anything. Then the Coucal, whose job it was to dye the clothes for all the other birds, decided to go to Olodumare and report to him the situation on earth—that it was not worth living in. By this time the Woodcock too had become worried about the dullness of the earth, and he too decided to tell Olodumare about it. The Coucal left the earth for Olodumare; and the Woodcock, after finishing his job in hand, did likewise. At *Ibode Orun*, the gate of heaven, the gatekeeper refused them entry, and the Coucal and the Woodcock, with much annoyance, returned to the world. A few kilometers from the earth, they both saw that their house had been badly damaged by rain. Then the Coucal started to cry: *Ileemi oo, Ileemi oo,* meaning: "Oh my house, my house!" Then the Woodcock decided at once not to return to his house but to live in the forest instead, and he started to cry: *O d'odan jidun-jidun,* meaning: "I will now head for the thick forest." But the Coucal cried: *O dile ko-ko-ko,* meaning: "I am heading for my house, by all means."

The crying of the birds was heard by everyone on earth. They were trembling and each one was trying to say or shout something or other. And thus the cries of the Coucal and the Woodcock were turned into music!

Then came a story from my father. He told me that the first people in ancient times who invented music were those known as Lakuta. They had no permanent abode, but they wandered from place to place. Their major work was hunting and the only instrument they used were stones. The breaking and sharpening of stones for tools became their music—their speech became their song, and their walk became their dance. As they discovered the joy that is in music, they developed it more and more. And every time they killed an animal, they would make music on their hunting instruments—the stones. In my quest for more knowledge about the origin of music, I also went to a place called Okua, near Inisha. There I was told about a man who was said to be one hundred and seventy years old: Baba Awoyinfa of Ilee Bale. He was glad to see me, and we became very good friends. From him I learned many things to do with Yoruba medicines, the history of tribal wars, some of the less common *Odu Ifa* poems, and above all he taught me the *Aasan Oba Ogun* (Aasan the King of Medicines). These are very powerful incantations; they are like the very ancient history one has to recite, but there are very strict rules as to where and when they can be spoken: some must not be said in front of a pregnant woman, others can't be pronounced in the city, but only in the forest, and so on. I asked Baba what he knew about the introduction of music into our world. He told me that man did hot bring the gift of music with him into the world when he was first created but that he invented it here. In the early days, in the morning of the world, everything was quiet and dull, but people began to create things for their use. One of these was music— which was discovered by accident. People communicated with Olodumare through images, but it was their practice never to say anything in the shrine. They would enter the shrine and just sit there, looking at each other and at the images. One day a woman, whose husband's house was on fire, rushed to the shrine to report the incident and she clapped her hands wildly and jumped up and down and shouted: *Ile njo, ile njo*, meaning: "The house is on fire, the house is on fire!" They all rushed out to put out the fire. Then they returned to the shrine to report the situation to their gods and they all started to say: *ile njo, ile njo* imitating the woman. From these three things—clapping,, jumping, and shouting—the people developed music (drum), dancing, and singing.

He said that beating one's chest and stomach was probably man's first musical instrument, but that later stones were developed and later still, wooden musical instruments. He said that stones were much loved by the deities at Ife.

With all these stories I began to have more interest in developing musical instruments from whatever material that can produce sound.

The Invention of the "Odu" Instrument

I finally decided to go into musical instrument building in January 1971. I began by collecting different kinds of local instruments, like *Sekere, Koso, Dundun,* and so on. My main objective was to arrange them in a tonal scale, so one could sing with them. I started with Sekere, but that did not work. I tried the skin drums; this was successful, except that they tend to change their tone with time and weather and so I gave up the idea. Next I built up an instrument out of coconut shells. I found this very interesting, because they produced a good sound and a very unusual one too. The problem here was, that they tended to crack within a fairly short time, and I didn't find a solution to that until a very much later date.

In March 1971 I went to Oshogbo to attend an *Ifa* Festival held by a friend who is a *babalawo* (oracle priest). There I saw them playing the *agogo* bells, the forged iron gongs. There were ten people who beat one gong each. I could notice that the whole ten bells produced only three tones or pitches: the low tone, the middle, tone and the high tone—corresponding to Yoruba speech tones. I was highly interested in this and thought these gongs might be a very good starting point for me. I asked my friend the *babalawo* whether he would sell the gongs to me, but he told me quickly, that they were sacred gongs and that he could not sell them for any amount I could offer.

I was determined to turn the *agogo* into a new instrument and, as the tradition of our people will have it, I first went and made sacrifice to Ogun, because he is the god of iron. Then I consulted the *babalawo* and the oracle said that I would be successful. Finally I made another offering called *etutu* to our gods, asking them to guide me through.

I went to the market and bought about two hundred different kinds of gongs in the hope of creating a good keyboard-type instrument. But to my astonishment, the over two hundred gongs that I had bought, could not produce more than four tones between them! For many days I locked myself into my room and I would not allow my wife to see me, except when she came to bring my food. But after two weeks, when I had not produced anything worthwhile, I came out of my self-exile and went to the market again to purchase more gongs, from different parts of Nigeria.

During this time I invited about twenty-five people to test their voices and record them, so I could produce an instrument that would sing like African people would sing. As I failed repeatedly, I nearly broke down and might have ended it all in an asylum, but the timely intervention of my wife saved me. She came to me and said: "Rest a while, and later, I am sure, you will do it." I rested for a week and then remembered Georgina Beier's word of encouragement: "Continue to try more," which was all the time tapping me on the back.

When I took up the project again in December 1971, I tried to retune the gongs. I made holes in some of them, I cut off others, I did different things to them, but alas, it did not work out the way I wanted it.

Then I decided that the only way to succeed was to learn black-smithing, with special emphasis on iron gongs. I went to Agbede adodo, which is the headquarters of the blacksmiths' workshops in Ibadan. I met a blacksmith and told him my plight. I was told that I would have to pay N60.10 and that I would serve under him for three years. I was immediately given the rules of the blacksmiths. I only remember one portion of it, where it says: you must obey your seniors in the profession, even if they are younger than you in years. I didn't mind at all obeying all the rules—but where would I find N60.10? And my other problem was time: how could I spend three years with him? Because at that time I was working for the University of Ibadan. I refused to go back to him.

Luckily I met another blacksmith, Mr Akomolafe, an Ijesha man, who was living very close to my arts shop near the University of Ibadan. He was ready to help me, when I narrated my story to him. He was highly interested in me. He said that he would not be able to pay me more than one shilling a day (10 kobo), but that any day he made big money he would give me two shillings. He didn't charge me anything, like the man at Agbede adodo, but said I could be sure of receiving a shilling a day.

I told my wife: "Tomorrow I will become an apprentice of Mr Akomolafe, the blacksmith." She was surprised and wondered if by now I had actually gone mad. Her parents called on me, and I told them my mission. They finally approved. I went to the University and told Professor Armstrong that I wanted to learn the art of blacsmithing. He was glad, but was confused when I told him that I no longer wanted to work at the Institute of African Studies. I quit my job with bad feelings, but it was my desire to face my job squarely. I did not tell my wife immediately that I had given up my job. I wasn't going to tell her until I had mastered my new job.

I served under Mr. Akomolafe for only six months. I met a senior apprentice with the master who was younger than I, but I did take instructions from and usually went on errands for him too. When we finished in the workshop in the evening, I went to fetch water for my master and my senior to bathe. This indeed aroused the interest of my master, and he showed me several techniques of making things.

During the first two months I did little but poke a fire with the *ewiri*, but at the end of that time my master allowed me to make some gongs myself. I studied closely the types of metal to be used, the time the metal remained in the fire, as well as length and width of the gongs. The most important thing to know are the different kinds of iron to be used.

I worked out the three major tones of our language. Then I began to subdivide each tone into three parts: low before low; low; low after low; the mid and high tones were equally graded.

By September 1972, I came out with the first completed musical instrument. At the 1973 National Festival I stole the show when I sang the

National Anthem on it before a crowd of sixty thousand people at Liberty Stadium, Ibadan. Soon after, it became a popular instrument and was copied by many musicians in and outside Nigeria, though they could not arrive at the Point where I was then. They all had the same problems as I had when I started. I made an instrument for the Apola King Idowu Animashaun at a cost of N600. I had spent over N2000 to produce the first "Odu" instrument. Currently I am working on a more elaborate version of the "Odu" which consists of 48 tones and which I hoped to finish by the end of April 1984.

The Stone Lithophone: A Gift of the Gods

I have had a great love for stones from my youth days. I cherish them and communicate with them. I discovered that they can be friendly, if you love them. I picked up stones on the way that attracted my interest and talked to them. I found much joy and desired happiness in them as a child, and I collected hundreds in different sizes and shapes.

Stones have a great influence on the lives of each and every one of us. They are the oldest solid things on our planet, the earth. They were in existence before human beings were ever dreamed of or nightmared, they will even exist long after we have gone and they will live to be forever.

Some people may see stones as a collection of molecules wobbling around in their solid shape; others may see them as chemical compositions. But in fact stones have strong vibrations; they are like radio transmitters or television boxes, transmitting their messages to you for good or bad, at all times. Stones have life in them.

A Yoruba proverb says: *Ile ti a ko tii ko, yoo dara ju eyi ti a ti ko lo*, meaning: "The house that is not yet built will be better than the house that is already built." After the completion of the Odu musical instrument, my inner thoughts returned to instrument building. I kept thinking of one idea after another. I tried the coconut shells again, and this time I managed to scale them; but I wasn't sure whether people could widely accept this instrument, so I just reserved it for my personal enjoyment.

The instrument through which I became most widely known within and without Nigeria, the stone lithophone, was indeed a gift of the gods. For I did not make it, nor did I shape it, after I had dug it out with a team of laborers in 1972.

I remember very well the conversation I had with my mother the day before she died. On her sick bed, I sat beside her and asked her a question. "Mother, did I offend you so much, that you cannot get well today?" She answered: "My dear son, even if you offended me, I would forgive you. But you have not offended me at all." I asked her another question: "Mother, do you want me to continue my artistic life with the Duro Ladipo Theater group?" She smiled and said: "That is your way, my son, and through your chosen career you will become known." As I began to think over her remark, I fell asleep. I could not know at that time that it would be my last discussion with my mother. Early the next morning my father woke me up. It was about 5 a.m. He said: "Ademola, go to your mother's brother, and return here with him." But I was so upset, I did not know what I was doing. Instead of going where I was sent, I found my way to Ulli Beier's house. I woke him up by all possible means. He was furious at first but I told him I had lost my mother. He then came down and comforted me and he said, be calm, all will be well. I started crying and left his house, but he called me back and gave me 2.10. By the time I got back home my mother's death was announced and people were crying. As they were preparing her grave on the cemetery, I was preparing another one for her in her room, with some of my friends, but I was disturbed by the relatives.

The day before her remembrance feast was held, I searched all the corners of her room, to see if I could find any money or jewelry. I could not find anything. I knew very well that she had been a very rich woman, though I thought that some relatives had packed everything. I went back to Ulli Beier, who gave me 12.10 for the feast.

When the feast was over, something directed my mind to continue digging the place where I had wanted to bury her. I started again with some of my friends and I found a pot containing some money and beads including gold jewelry. That was the first excavation which was carried out by me in 1964. A man once called me a "natural archeologist" but I don't know if there is such a word in the dictionary.

My mother has been the leader of a singing group from our compound. My father is a well known traditionalist and a brave hunter. He taught me to shoot very well, when I was fifteen, but he always worried, that whenever I shot an animal I hit in the head. He performed some rites for me several times because of this, but I continued to shoot animals in the head with my gun. I could not read any meaning into his worries over this and I continued to be a hunter like him, though he warned me not to shoot again.

On many occasions, when I killed an animal I would send some parts to him from Ibadan or I would go to him with the meat, when I could. He was glad to give me a pat on the back, especially on the day I killed a buffalo. I will never forget that day, for it was the first time my father revealed to me the secrets of seven medicines which he had received from his own father. He also gave me several incantations.

My father would not give me the secret of any particular medicine that I asked him for, unless I killed an animal first. This really encouraged me more to be a hunter like him. One day I went to him and asked him, what kind of medicine I could use, if I met a demon in the bush, so that he would not harm me. He said: *Bi ode ba r'oko, bi ode ba ro ise ro iya, bo ba dele, ko ni fun enikan ninu eran ti o pa*, meaning: "If a hunter went to the bush, and if he remembered all his hardships and punishments on coming home, he would not give anybody else a share of the meat!" I agreed that this was true. Then he told me: "You will have to suffer in the bush first, meet a demon, fight with him and try your power. If then you fail, come back to me for the medicine." I said: "And what if the demon kills me? Will you be happy to lose me?" My father laughed and said: "No, you will come home," and quoted another Yoruba proverb: *Eniti a se oogun aiku fun, ti o so wipe oogun koje, nje o tii ku na?* meaning, "If we give a person a medicine to prevent him from dying and he comes back to complain that it was a fake medicine, has he died yet?"

I told him that if he refused to give me that medicine I would stop coming to his house for a whole year, so he would know that I was not happy. He said: "O.K., but you will have to give me something for it. I cannot, just because you are my son, give it to you for free, because you will never appreciate it." Then I said: "All right Sir, how much do you want me to give you for it? But I want you to be sincere with me: how much money did you pay your own father when he gave you the medicine?" He laughed again at this: "I see your point, son, but this is between me and my father; and again, I was fifty years old when my father gave it to me. You are very young now—do you see the difference?" "Well, since you want some money from me, how much exactly do you want me to pay?" "Give me only 5.10 and I will give it to you right now. Also you will give me a bottle of dry gin." "Will you accept my promise? Because I only have 10 shillings here and I will pay the rest in installments." My father laughed and said: "Alright bring the 10 shillings". I gave it to him and he also asked me, if I would accept his promise too, because he would give me the secret of the medicine in installments. "I will give you only two leaves today, the value of your money." I thought he was joking, but he was serious. He mentioned only two leaves. I strongly demanded my money back, but he told me to pray to the gods of our ancestors to remove the names of the two leaves from my brain, but he warned me that I might lose everything I have in my brain! When I returned to Ibadan, I sent him the balance of the money and the gin. He wrote a letter to me in which everything was mentioned. I later went to Oshogbo to verify whether the medicine was true. I was glad to learn from other hunters that he had given me the full secret; because many people who give you a medicine, will not mention all the ingredients to you.

At Ibadan, many of my friends were hunters and we often went on expeditions together. In January 1972 I told my wife that I would not return that day, as I wished to see a friend of mine at Keeda village in Ibadan. I told her I might return the third day, as I wanted to follow a group that was going to hunt an elephant. My wife was afraid about this, but I had no doubt that the new medicine would help me in the bush. However, I did not go straight to Baba Keeda, I entered the forest at Majeroku at Olorogun village near the Iraye stream. The previous night I had seen a deer and I was lying in ambush for it. It was a thick forest and almost in the middle of it, I sat under an Iroko tree. In a few minutes I was fast asleep. I dreamt that I unearthed my mother, who had died on the 10th July 1964, a few weeks before I left Nigeria for Germany with the late Duro Ladipo's theater troupe, to participate in the Berlin Theater Festival. In my dream my mother revealed to me the location of an ancient musical instrument that lay buried some fifty meters to the right from where I sat. She said that it would be the beginning of "a new thing in music." Then I woke up. I was afraid and I was cold. I left my gun there and I returned home immediately.

I decided to go and work on the site. I had in mind that I would find a big pot of treasure there. I went to a friend who lived in the area, who was vast in our culture and knew a lot of Yoruba medicines. He told me not to do anything on the land, as it was once used as a house of the gods. I asked him how long ago people had been living there. He said about eight hundred years ago according to the stories he had heard from his father, some warriors were living there. I told him of my intention to follow the instruction of my mother. He warned me seriously not to do so for fear of losing me. I asked him who was the owner of the land and he took me to the family and I paid a token fee to them, so that I could work on the site, but they refused to follow me there. The following week I started digging after I had performed some rituals on the site.

I measured a portion about ten by ten meters but decided to dig out only a circular area in the center with a diameter of about 4 meters. I employed eight laborers from 10 am to 3 p.m. daily. On the fourth day we were about seven feet deep and I was discouraged that we hadn't found anything yet, except one small bead and a few broken pots. I stopped working for a while, but on the third week we returned to work on the site, and on the fifth day the laborers ran out of the pit, when they hit upon some earth of an unusually bright red color. I jumped in and spoke some incantations and then we performed some more rituals. I now worked alone and at exactly thirteen feet deep I struck something hard and began to work more slowly and more carefully. Finally I unearthed a pot, covered by a stone. At the bottom of it there was a big stone that obviously had been carved by human hand and that might have been used as a seat. Other stones of different sizes and shapes were neatly packed around this big stone.

After removing the stones from the pit, I handed them to the elders who quickly made offerings to the gods of our ancestors. After consulting the oracle and performing further rituals we took the stones home, thinking it now quite safe to handle them, but a terrible thing happened a few days later. Two of my children went into the room where the stones were kept. Nobody noticed them while they took out a stone each—probably they wanted to play with them. We found them after they had fainted with the stones in their hands and all efforts made by the doctors failed to bring them back to consciousness. They died the same day. I now became very much afraid. I called my personal oracle priest, Chief Babalola Fatoogun of Ilobu and after consultation with the oracle, we performed some further rituals over the stones. Since this time I have had no further problems with the stones, and I soon became very familiar with them.

My first idea, however, was to sell them off and took them to the Head of the Department of Archeology, University of Ibadabn, who said that they were not man-made and that they had probably been shaped by erosion.

I kept the stones in my room and I slept with them. One night I was drunk and I returned home very late and as I entered my room, I stumbled against the stones and I heard a very strange sound. I ran out quickly, as I thought there were perhaps spirits in the room.

The following day I used the medicine my father had given me against spirits and I entered the room and struck the stones one by one. To my amazement I found out for the first time that they produced musical notes.

I now took the stones to Chief Ulli Beier in Ife, who was very excited about them. He said that he was convinced that some of them had been shaped by human beings and that they were an ancient lithophone. He advised me strongly never to sell the stones. I was glad about all this and I began to work out different ways of playing the stones.

Some people think that I have changed my name to Onibonokuta ("Owner of the ringing stones") after I discovered this instrument. But this is not true. My grandfather was called Onibonokuta because he was in charge of the Odun-Okuta festival which was celebrated in our family before Islam and Christianity destroyed the tradition. The Okuta festival was held for a very ancient stone that our forefathers used to grind medicine leaves. When I became interested again in our Yoruba traditions, I changed my name from Lamidi Gbadamosi, which is a foreign Muslim name, to Ademola Onibonokuta, which is my real Yoruba name.

I had played the stones before Kings, Chiefs, Governors, Heads of States, and, in 1980, I received a standing ovation when I played them in the United States of America.

And the more I want to stop playing them, the more I receive invitations to play the stones, both within and outside Nigeria. So in spite of the suffering that the stones have brought me I have accepted them as a gift of the gods.

A Career in Music & Theater
Muraina Oyelami

I grew up between the three religions. In my family we only had Muslims and *Orisha* worshippers, but at school I came in contact with Christianity. I played in the Church orchestra and since I could read Yoruba well, I was often asked to read the lesson in Church. I attended Bible studies, but, to be frank, I can only remember that there were ten commandments, but I couldn't remember the order in which they follow.

I enjoyed the music in the church, but the Bible made no sense to me, because of the manner of its translation in Yoruba. The Yoruba Bible is so proverbial, so confusing, you don't know what they actually mean. I could read the books of J.F. Odunjo perfectly well, and understood D.O. Fagunwa's novels, but the language of the Bible is quite different. I didn't care about the tunes in the church either—they were pure English tunes—but I did enjoy playing the drums. My teacher thought I did so well reading the lesson, he thought I should be converted. He tried to convert me along with some others, but I never took that step. I never became a good Muslim either. My father never attempted to take me to the mosque. He just gave me that name and left me alone. But I did go to the mosque sometimes with my age group, particularly during Ramadan, because that's when a lot of people go. Or sometimes for the funeral of a well-known Muslim elder. They usually bring food to the mosque and we always tried to be there for that.

I learned some Arabic prayer like *Al Hamdullilah*—you know, the standard phrase. Everybody knows that, or murmurs it. And when the leader of the congregation says *Fatia*, everybody will be humming something like "mmmmmmmmmmmmmmmm." So every time we just hum along, without actually saying anything. This *Fatia* is like the ending chapter in the Koran and the congregation would recite this *Al Hamdullilah*. But I was a very irregular mosque goer and I would never get up and pray when the Imam called, as I was never a serious Muslim. The few things I did, I did in company of others. For example, I joined my mates in their fast, simply to be with them. But when I grew up I asked myself: "Why do I have to pray in Arabic?" I can also pray in Yoruba and I don't have to go to the mosque.

I can't change the Moslem name I was given, because I like the sound of it and also because it's known; it's found in books. I would have liked to change it really, but by the time I realized, it was too late. I might have preferred to use my other beautiful Yoruba names, like Sangodare or Adebisi. Today I would say that I am sympathetic to the Yoruba religion. I do not have an *orisha*; I am not initiated. But I want to be identified with Yoruba religion. What appeals to me most about Yoruba religion is its tolerance. Sango priests see Yorubas become Muslims, yet they do not complain. They may merely make fun of them, like the song they used to sing:

> Níbo lóní ngbé Sàngó mi sío
> Abunú Lémómu t'óní nwá sè'mòle
> Níbo lóní ngbé Sàngó mi sí o.

> Where does he want me to put my Sango?
> The stupid Imam, who says I should abandon my *orisha*
> Where does he want me to put my Sango?

And all these *orisha* worshippers, they are not enemies of one another. They recognize the difference in human beings. And so that is the reason why I prefer Yoruba religion. To me it is the best religion in the world. It doesn't have the aggressiveness of Christianity and Islam. And secondly, it is Yoruba religion; and I am Yoruba. The African is being assaulted by all these other cultures: the culture of dress, the culture of language, the culture of food. One discovers that one's own religion is a useful shelter from this assault. This is why I am now ready to participate in the revival of the Yoruba religion, especially as a motivator.

It is in pursuit of this goal that I, in 1981, created my own *Egungun* mask. It comes out during every *Egungun* festival. It is named after the sacred tree, *peregun*. *Peregun* symbolizes eternity. The *Egungun* is now well-known and I hope, like its name, it will not die.

Prior to the creation of *Peregun*, I used to celebrate the *Egungun* festival with my friends. The well-known band leader, Lamidi Ayankunle, will bring his *bata* drummers from Erin-Osun and with them, we will feast, dance, and chant *oriki* to *peregun* who is yet to come out:

> Awa ni pèrègún etí odò
> bó bá d'àmódún
> ewá á wò wá

> We are like the peregun plant by the river-side
> in another year
> come and celebrate with us

In 1982 I had just returned from Bayreuth in Germany and I had little time for preparation. So we had to hire a man who had an *Egungun* costume because they said I would have to have an *Egungun* if I wanted to celebrate the festival. Finally, by 1983, we made our own costume. For example, the appliqué cloth I made in Bayreuth, I hung on the back of the *Egungun*.

Before I made this *Egungun*, I went around the houses of the *Egungun Agba*, the elders of the masquerade society, and I told them what I wanted to do. Tunji (Ulli Beier's son) was with me at that time. And one particular man, who is the head of the *Egungun*, said: "Whatever you want to do, you can do, because we like you. You do not behave like an educated man." And of course I also go and play the *bata* with them. I do whatever I can to encourage them and help them.

Now my *Egungun* is an established thing. People travel from other towns to celebrate with me. And some people, who would be shy to come out and be seen with *Egungun*, when they see me, they come out and dance. So seeing me participate gives many people the courage to come out in their true colors; and if children are told by their teachers that it is bad to follow *Egungun*, then they can say: "But don't you see this man who is working at the university?" So how can they say it is a bad thing? So I hope in years to come people will follow me and establish their own *Egungun*.

I myself readily identify as an Oyo Yoruba, because that is the language we speak. Even then, Iragbiji is situated very close to the Ijesha area; and you can see that we use *Épa* masks, similar to the ones found in Ijesha and Ekiti. (Though we don't call them *Épa* masks; we call them *ère*.) Our language is a modified Oyo dialect. It has been influenced by Ijesha dialect. It is not dissimilar to Oshogbo, which is also a mixture of Oyo and Ijesha dialects. But then again there is a difference between the language of Iragbiji and Oshogbo: even between Ikirun and Oshogbo.

So every few kilometers you can find a dialectal variation in parts of Yoruba country. And yet, the idea of all of us being children of Oduduwa, the legendary ancestor, has grown stronger in recent years. The political entity of Nigeria has forced us Yorubas to regard ourselves as one. Because we cannot survive in the Federation until we have that sense of unity. The older generation may stick to their tribal loyalties. As when an Ijesha may not want to marry his daughter to an Oyo man. But the younger people do not find such differences important anymore. Teachers or public servants get posted to different areas and they may marry there, even without the consent of their parents.

Education has been another important unifying factor. Now the language we write is one, we don't write in Ijesha or Ijebu dialect. There is a standardized written language and our great writers, like Odunjo or Fagunwa, don't write in their own dialects.

Of course, I also happen to be a Nigerian, because I am called a Nigerian. But my approach to life is that of a Yoruba. Maybe there are people who think of themselves as Nigerian, rather than Yoruba, Igbo, or Hausa, but I haven't come across one. I know that my passport says Nigeria, and I know that this Nigeria has been created for us by non-Nigerians; and I have also grown to think that it is a good idea to have a Nigeria. Potentially it is a wonderful idea to have this large country that offers so many opportunities: so many cultures that can all interact with each other. How wonderful it would be, if I could go to the North and be accepted there by the people as one of them; and for a Northerner to come down South and become part of us. But unfortunately it is not possible, because of the politics. Politics has not encouraged unity. Even if you have good intentions of being a Nigerian, you are not encouraged to do so, because all the power is concentrated in one place.

I will use my artistic medium to promote unity, to assert the authenticity of my culture, and that's all I can do. That's what I call being patriotic. I have not been seriously influenced by other musical cultures in Nigeria. I hear Hausa or Igbo music on the radio, but I don't have that appreciation of it. Only when I traveled, saw them perform, saw them react, saw how they produce a certain kind of sound, then I begin to respect them more. Then I can fall in love with their music.

Because of my work in theater, I have had perhaps better opportunities than many other Nigerians of understanding and liking different forms of Nigerian music. Gradually you begin to realize that there are some concepts of good and evil, of beauty and ugliness, of conflict and harmony, which are expressed in all cultures. And funnily enough—though I may not know the names of some Western composers—I do like classical music. Why? Because when I listen to it, I can imagine something and most of the time what I imagine is what the composer was thinking: sadness, happiness, contemplation, an adventurous mood—I can hear these things in the music and I enjoy it.

I bought my first classical music in 1967, when I was working at the museum. I cannot remember now what made me do it, or even who the composer was. It had a violin in it and I then liked violin a lot. Come to think of it though, it must be from Ulli Beier's house that I first heard classical music. I remember that sometimes Ulli would close the door and withdraw with his music, and I could listen to it in my room downstairs. Years later when Peggy

Harper was packing and she threw out some records, she said: "You can pick anything from there, if you like." So I got some classical records, I listened more and more to it and I read the line notes on the sleeve. But I think I like Mozart more than any other composer and I visited his birthplace in Salzburg. There was a music teacher at the Ife University called Michael Strumpf, who actually taught me how to play the clarinet. He went on leave and bought me a second clarinet, and I started playing.

The first time I became really interested in non-Yoruba music was when we performed *Moremi* and Ulli Beier brought down the Agbor dancers to perform with us. I got along very well with them as I really enjoyed their slit gongs and horns. They too enjoyed our music; and probably it was through this play, too, that they first learned to appreciate Yoruba music. And then, again, years later, during FESTAC ("World Black and African Festival of Arts and Culture"), which took place in Lagos in 1977, I was in charge of some instrumentalists and I had to rehearse them. And there I saw these old men orchestrate—it's something I can never forget. These old men from the North Eastern part of the country—the rhythms they produced and the power of their music! Up till today the music is still ringing in my head. As a matter of fact, the other day I was trying to play it. I might not have appreciated them, if I had merely heard them over the radio. But meeting them, seeing their costumes, watching how they went about it made me appreciate the music they were making. The visual contact was very important.

My first experience of what you might call "cross cultural music" was at Ulli Beier's house, when he gave a party for the Peter Brook Company. There was a composer called Swados who played a Spanish guitar. I picked up my *dundun* drum, and spontaneously began to improvise with her. I enjoyed that experience very much and it opened a whole new horizon for me. I understood that Yoruba music was flexible enough to be played outside its cultural context, and that it could be used to contribute to new musical inventions. I had not even heard of the term "fusion" music at that time. A year later, I think, Ulli Beier brought out a black American painter and musician to the Ife Festival, Lloyd McNeil. He was a jazz flutist. I remember one day Ulli brought him to Ori Olokun and introduced him to me and said: "Look, Lloyd is a flute player and he would like to give a concert at the festival, but we need a group to back him. Can you come up with something?" Then Ulli left him there to work out a cross cultural music, which we did. When I listened to the delicate sound of his instrument, I decided not to use either *dundun* or *bata* drums, I used a small *agidigbo* (thumb piano) and a wooden xylophone. I had never played with a jazz musician before, but we got on so well that by the time Ulli returned to Ori Olokun an hour later, we had already worked out three numbers.

Come to think of it, the most important breakthrough in my musical career was my meeting with Akin Euba in 1967. Ulli Beier had left Nigeria in December 1966 and was living temporarily in London, before taking up an appointment in Papua New Guinea. He had invited me to come to London on visit. After I cabled him to give him my arrival date, he sent a cable asking me to delay my departure for two weeks so I could rehearse with Akin Euba. I had never met Akin before and Ulli's suggestion came as a total surprise to me. Akin was going to accompany the "Theater Express" with Segun Olusola, Segun Sofowote, and Segun Akinbola, at the Traverse Theater where they were going to give an evening, that included Ulli's translation of Durrenmatt's "Evening in Late Autumn" and his sketch "The Suitcase." They were also going to stage a dance drama, "Morning, Noon and Night," for a solo dancer (Segun Sofowote) for which Akin was composing the music.

This was an entirely new experience for me. Akin was an experimental composer. He used African instruments freely and in a very novel way. He played a xylophone and a variety of other drums and I had to improvise on the *dundun*. We got on so well together that from then on, Akin sent for me whenever he had a major production.

Mostly there was no money in these productions but I did not mind. Sometimes I traveled from Oshogbo to Ife or even to Lagos at my own expense. But I always came, because I knew I was learning a whole new approach to music and I was really grateful for the opportunities given to me to participate. I played for Akin in many important productions at the University of Lagos. I was in his production of "Chaka" in Ife and Dakar. I went to the cultural Olympics in Munich with him; we went to the World Theater Festival in Nancy where we performed "Purakapali" and "Alatangana." I actually wrote the music for those productions, but the master put the finishing touches to it.

Through Akin I gained a lot of experience and confidence. Working with Akin also gave me the opportunity to work closely with Ayansola, the powerful drummer from Oshogbo. In "Obaluaye," a dance drama written by Wale Ogunyemi, much of the music was purely traditional, and was led by Ayansola. However, there were sections of entirely free composition by Akin, and that's where I played the lead. I performed again with Ayansola at the Horizonte Festival in Berlin in 1979. Akin did not actually come with us, but he had rehearsed the production.

I still play with Akin a lot, and I always enjoy doing it. In recent years I have become much more independent. I have become a known *dundun* player and composer and some people have called me "the successor to the Timi of Ede," in the sense that I have travelled through the world demonstrating and explaining the Yoruba talking drums, its technique, its function, and its poetry.

The first time I ever did that was in Sydney, when I came to visit Ulli Beier in January 1981. My first lecture demonstration was at the Festival of Sydney in Hyde Park and then at the Annandale Neighbourhood Centre. In November 1981 I went to Bayreuth to become artist-in-residence at Iwalewa-Haus and that was the time when I perfected the technique, lecturing even in the Music Department of the University of Cologne and other tertiary institutions.

Music, Art, and Theater

I do not come from a drummers' family. As a school boy I played music in church and in several bands, but ordinarily I would not have had the opportunity to learn any of the classical Yoruba drums, like *dundun* or *bata.*

One of the greatest things the *Mbari Mbayo* did for me was that it introduced me to traditional Yoruba music. My first teacher was none other than the famous Timi Laoye of Ede. It came as a great surprise to me that an *Oba* could stoop so low as to travel from Ede to Oshogbo twice a week and teach youngsters like us. This in itself was like a blessing already.

Timi introduced the drum to us as a singing drum. He started his first lesson with a song about himself:

> Mo b'Ólúgbón je
> Mo sì b'Àrèsà je
> N o bá Láoyè je
> Láoyè akorobítí
>
> Àyà re ò pé méjì
> N bá fì'kan f'ómo ojo

The song says: "I have eaten with the Olugbon, I have eaten with Aresa; now I will eat with Laoye, Laoye Akorobiti. What a pity, you haven't got two hearts - if you had two hearts, I would ask you to give one to the coward." This song praises the Timi and mocks his rival, who contested the chieftaincy title against him.

The Timi played the song on the drum, and sang along with it. He never came with the big *Iyaalu*, he always played on the *Adamo*. He demonstrated to us how he manipulated the strings, and we would copy him. I was really keen. My concentration was high and soon I could play what he taught us.

325

Later Duro employed a professional drummer: Lasisi Gbadamosi. Lasisi had an *Apala* group and they used to come and perform at Mbari. But Lasisi joined the theater company for performances of *Oba Koso* and he traveled to Berlin with us in 1964. He was always in charge of the music, and though he did not teach us directly, as the Timi did, we learned by listening to him.

In order to learn and understand more about the talking drum, I spent much of my spare time following different drummers through the town. I accompanied them, listening to their music. Even before I came to Oshogbo I used to do that for many years. This was how I learned the poetry and got the music into my ear. I didn't really know then why I was doing it; maybe subconsciously I wanted to become a drummer even then, but I did not know it.

Actually, how I ever learned to play the talking drum is still a miracle to me! But my morale was really boosted by being with somebody like the Timi of Ede. I can say that he really changed my life, because he made me seriously involved in drumming. I decided to be musician then, even though I am not from a drummers family and though drumming was not considered to be a very respectable or desirable career. Few of the so-called "educated" people would have respected a drummer in those days. The Timi began to change all that: a drumming *Oba* was something absolutely unheard of.

I was lucky, too, because I always had the support of my parents. My parents never ever disturbed me. If they were curious about something they would ask me; but whatever I told them they would accept. Now I can sit back and say: if not for their co-operation, I could have become something different. But they were never demanding or restrictive like other parents.

After I resigned from the museum, I had no intention of ever leaving Oshogbo. But then there was this letter from Akin Euba, asking me to apply for a position in the newly created Music Department at the University of Ife. I decided to move to Ife, because of the respect I had for Akin and because I knew I would be able to work in harmony with him. I was interviewed on the same day that Ayansola was interviewed and we were both offered positions. We started work in September 1976 and a few months later I was sent on secondment to Lagos, to help Akin in the preparation of FESTAC. After the Festival I returned to Ife. However, by that time Akin had got a job at the University of Lagos, where he was made a professor. I was very disappointed. I had left Oshogbo because of him, and now he couldn't even consider my own position! I was going to back out. I was going to leave immediately. He asked me whether I wanted to come to Lagos; I said: "Look, Ife is far enough from my home town. I can't even go any further." Besides, I said to myself, if I go to Lagos with him, then the next thing he will do is go overseas. Finally, I decided to stay in Ife and give it a try. I said to myself: if I leave now, people will say that I cannot function without Akin. Let me stay and find out the myth behind this university business. Let me find out what they are really up to in these institutions.

The saddest thing about University work is that you will be working hard for the benefits of the students; but ninety percent of them are not ready to learn. Most of them take drumming as an elective study, just to have their credit units together. There we have very few students who are really dedicated. In fact there has been only one student whom I have taken right through from part 1 to part 4. He will be the first student to graduate in drumming: and that is my greatest reward.

When we started the course, Ayansola was the master drummer, but then he could not teach. However, since he learned his art from early childhood, he was able to analyze it in the way that makes it comprehensible to an adult student who has not grown up with the tradition. Ayansola was like the demonstrator. I had never been taught a teaching method either, and it took me some time before I devised a system.

Now I have devised a system. The first course I teach is called "Elementary Performance in *Dundun.*" Here, students learn the basic rhythmic patterns. They are also exposed to the *Agogo* ensemble, the *Igbin* ensemble, and the *bata* ensemble. The students learn the basic patterns of *omele dundun,* and the *gudugudu,* which is fairly difficult. They also learn the *omele* of *bata,* then towards the end of the second semester they are introduced to the very basic phrases of *Iyaalu.*

During the next course, proverbs and some poetry are introduced and taught. In the third year the student would have decided which instrument he wants to specialize on: *dundun* or *bata.* In the final year the student will have to present a thirty-minute concert on his chosen instrument to the public.

Over the years, I have perfected this and because I am the only one in the department who is a practitioner of Yoruba music, they had to allow me to use my own imagination to construct the system. So I was lucky to be given enough freedom.

Later on, we designed another program for people who wanted to improve their proficiency in performance. It was a one-year proficiency program. There I also supervised a class called "Introduction to African Dance." I bring in dancers who give the instructions, but I draw up the sequence for the course. We also have a class called "African Music Workshop," where we actually teach the students to work in an ensemble. That class has to stage occasional concerts for the department. Up till now this is still the only drumming course offered in any Nigerian university. I am proud that this is largely my creation.

One of the most exciting and decisive periods in my development as a musician was my time as an artist-in-residence at Iwalewa-Haus in Bayreuth (Germany). My first strange dialogue was with Professor Helmut Bieler, who is a composer and pianist in the Music Department of the University. We were to give a concert together for the sixth anniversary celebration of the University of Bayreuth. In the first half of the concert I was playing Yoruba music with Tunji Beier. In the second half I played *dundun*, while Tunji played drum-kit and Bieler played the piano. It was a totally improvised session—there was no pre-arranged structure to it. Bieler used the piano in a very eccentric way: he was hitting it with an hammer, dipping both hands into the belly of the piano, pulling at the strings. I must say it was difficult at first to react to it. Although we came from very opposite ends of cultural experience, we respected each other. And so our grouping resulted in music that actually impressed the audience. It must have been a strange and difficult experience for Tunji, too, but he gave a remarkable vigorous and imaginative performance on his kit.

Then of course there was the encounter with "Embryo." I never had any problem playing with them, because they were a group that was very open to music from other cultures. They have been taking an interest in Indian and Turkish music and they were ready to absorb new ideas. Even at the very first concert in the University Hall in Bayreuth, I found it easy to improvise the *dundun* to their music, they also gave me a spot to play Yoruba music with Tunji, to which, in return, they began to improvise.

I met many interesting musicians through "Embryo," like Christian Burchard, who is the leader of the group. Edgar Hoffmann, their flutist, and Roman Bunka, their oud player. I also met that remarkable Persian drummer Nemat Daman. I remember that on one occasion I could put together a complete Yoruba *dundun* orchestra at Iwalewa-Haus: Myself *Iyaalu*, Tunji on *gudugudu* and Christian Burchard and Neman Damat on *Kanango* and *Isaju*.

The most important encounter I had through "Embryo," however, was with Ramesh Shotan. The opportunity to play with Ramesh was wonderful. We had many things in common and we could play for a whole day and still we would be in harmony with each other. Two of my greatest performances ever were the two duos I played with Ramesh: one at the Alabama Halle in Munich, the other at the Opera House in Bayreuth.

I find it easier to improvise with Ramesh than with most European musicians, perhaps we both come from a strong tradition. Once the improvisations become too loose, we can both retreat into traditional patterns for a while, then we have firm ground under our feet and then we can break out again.

One wonderful exception was Daniel Blatt, the cellist to whom Ulli

Beier introduced me in Sydney. That was remarkable. I had never played with a cellist before. I had hardly ever listened to a cello consciously. The spontaneity of that performance was fantastic and now, when I listen to the tape, I still like it. In fact, the more it ages the better I like it. I would love to meet that musician again, but I am told that he has gone to Israel. It's a great pleasure when these encounters succeed. Another one was with the South Indian drummer Krishna Murti in Singapore. That was a great encounter; it was recorded on television, but I have never succeeded in getting a video of it.

Not all such musical encounters can work. I tried to play with an Aboriginal *didgeridoo* player in Munich. He was so traditional, he wasn't interested in what I was doing; I tried to run after him, but it didn't work. I remember another occasion in Berkeley, California: they invited me to have a jam session there. There was a very beautiful sax player there, with a whole group of percussionists. I said to them: "Look, just start something, and when I find an opening, I will come in and play." But then, as soon as I tried to come in, everybody started to become individual. Everybody just played for himself, not minding what anybody else was doing. So they were producing just noise, like delinquent kids, not like mature adults.

On other occasions, I would invite different traditional musicians to come and perform during the Oshun festival. Later on, I had an experimental piece that I produced together with Franz Peter Goebel: "Song of Lawino." We set Okot P'Bitek's poem to music. I composed some of the music and Franz Peter composed some, introducing European instruments. But I did the casting and looked after the dramatic side. We performed in Lagos, at Ibadan University, in Ife, and we even performed it at Oshogbo grammar school. This was about 1970.

Then during the 1974 National Arts Festival I was asked to select and produce a group of traditional Yoruba musicians. I selected musicians from Erin, from Okinni, from Oshogbo, playing different instruments. I tried to weld them together into one big orchestra. This was a major production. We had *dundun, bata, apinti, sekere, aro*—there were about sixteen musicians in the group and they really performed well together.

Finally, in 1983 I formed the "Oyelami Performing Troupe," with financial assistance from Kola Ogunwale and his friends. Our first production was "*Oya Koko.*" It was a dance drama, which dealt with the conflict between Shango and Ogun, when Shango took away Ogun's wife Oya. In this production I used the myth really as an interesting story line. I was not interested in doing research into Yoruba mythology to produce an authentic version. My main interest was to enrich the production with a great variety of music and dance. I even had some Efik dancers, I had an Urhobo dance and

I had an *Egungun Agbegijo* dance. I changed the story to suit this purpose. I ended the play with the other *orisas* coming to settle the rift and compensated Ogun for the loss of Oya with the gift of Orebe, a much younger and more beautiful maiden. So both went away happily. The Shango people went away with the *bata* drummers and the Ogun people went away with the *dundun* drummers.

I rehearsed them vigorously. I was so busy with direction, that I could not play the drum myself. We were rehearsing in the Oshun grove, behind Iyamapo shrine. There we had no disturbance and the atmosphere was conducive to what we were doing.

The next production—which we took to Germany—was a purely musical production, with different Yoruba musical performances and dances. We had masks and acrobats, a great variety of performances. There were no stories, only the miniature sketches of the *Agbegijo* masqueraders, like the corrupt policeman, the prostitute, the European couple, and the kolanut seller.

The Making of a Multicultural Musician Tunji Beier in Conversation with Wole Ogundele & Femi Obodunrin

INTRODUCTION

At the age of twenty six, Olatunji Akanmu Beier has already gained a reputation as an unusually gifted and inventive musician. He can already look back on sixteen years of professional musicianship! He has performed with some of the greatest American jazz giants like Bill Cobham, Charlie Mariano, and Randy Weston. He is equally at home with musicians of a classical European background like the trumpeter Markus Stockhausen or the cellist Anup Kumar Biswas.

In Nigeria he has performed with both *dundun* and *bata* ensembles at the installation of *obas* and chiefs, and during funeral ceremonies. He has also been musician to *Alarinjo* masqueraders. In India he accompanied some of the greatest singers like Ramamani, performed in temples and concert halls all over South India with the famous Karnataka College of Percussion. In Australia he was a member of "Theater of Sound." Tunji Beier's musical friendships, like his father's, extend all over the five continents.

One of his greatest gifts is the ability to bring musicians from the most varied background together: he initiated the famous OKUTA PERCUSSION, which started out in Australia as a trio combining and integrating Afiican, Indonesian, and Indian percussions into an organic fusion that transcended the limitations of each of the three traditions. In a second group, BASSAMA, he brought together a Sudanese Oud player (Wafir Sheikh el Din), and a Spanish Flamenco guitarist (Jaume Bosser) who also plays the Indian bamboo flute with his own multicultural percussion. In another formation, GANPATI, Tunji played with the Hungarian violinist Zoltan Lantos who spent nine years in India. Tunji Akanmu has also formed numerous duos with: the Australian percussionist Greg Sheehan; the Egyptian flutist

Mohammed el Toukhi; the English saxophonist Iain Ballamy; the German organist Volker Jaeckel; and the Norwegian drummer Terge Isungset.

Tunji's ability to play in so many different combinations arises not only from his unusual musical background and the flexibility of his mind, but also from his modesty as a musician. On stage he impresses with his quiet concentration and total alertness. He has no star mannerisms whatsoever—if anything, his appearance is somewhat shy. He wants to communicate with his audience purely through his music and so avoids the chitchat, banter, and jokes with which many musicians woo their audiences.

Of Tunji Beier, Barbara Wrenger, the music critic of the *West Deutscher Rundfunk* (West German Radio, Cologne) has said: "he is the multicultural musician *per se* because he grew up with musical traditions which to *us* (Germans) are very strange." Indeed, Tunji's success derives from the fact that he adjusted early to his father's nomadic life—constantly moving between Nigeria, New Guinea, Australia and Germany—and above all, because he managed to absorb the contradictory influences of African and Indian music seamlessly into his own make-up as a musician.

Undoubtedly it was his experience of Yoruba drumming as a small child that determined the entire direction of his future life. Particularly, the powerful *dundun* drummer Ayansola from Osogbo made an enormous impression on him. This musician was outstanding even among the greatest Yoruba performers. It was said of Ayansola that when he played an *oriki*, the articulation was so strong and clearly defined that the music "stood in space like a piece of stone sculpture." When Tunji was about eighteen months old, Ayansola played in his parents' house at Ile-Ife and the child danced all night—danced himself into a trance-like state. Of course, Tunji has forgotten this incident, but from that time on he always knew that he wanted to be a musician and nothing else in life. He left school on his fifteenth birthday (the earliest legally permissible day) because he felt that to continue in school would merely divert him from his real purpose in life.

In a career already full of great achievements and with greater ones to come, Tunji's greatest achievement so far is the creation of the concept *Grenzuberschreitungen* (Bordercrossings): a series of concerts and festivals in which musicians from different parts of the world come together to live, eat, argue, and work to create new music between them. It is not an easy thing to achieve, because it needs patience, curiosity, modesty, open-mindedness, and a great deal of hard, intensive work. No single musician, culture, or genre of music must dominate. The concert series that Tunji Beier has put together in the baroque Opera House in Bayreuth has now become a legendary annual event in Germany, drawing people from as far away as Hamburg, Cologne, and Munich.

The annual festival which takes place in Bayreuth in autumn makes even heavier demands on the musicians. Six groups, each in itself already multicultural, are invited from all over the world. During the first two or three days each ensemble presents its own repertoire. Simultaneously they spend the days exchanging ideas and experimenting with new music, forming new compositions. On the final day they surprise the audience—and themselves—with the new creations!

Grenzuberschreitungen has already moved on into several other cities, mainly in eastern Germany: Leipzig, Erfurt, Chemnitz, Zwickau, and Plauen. In a new CD series started by FARAO in Munich, a wider audience will soon become acquainted with this new development.

In the following pages, Tunji Akanmu Beier talks—a little reluctantly—with Wole Ogundele and Femi Abodunrin. Never a great talker, he prefers to convey whatever it is he has to say through his drums. Even while the short conversation was going on, his restless fingers did more talking.

My music education began in Nigeria. Although I was born in Port Moresby, Papua New Guinea in 1970, I spent the crucial period from one to five years of age in Nigeria, hearing a lot of percussion music going on around the house and at festivals. I cannot remember much of it, but I know from my parents that I was always interested in the drummers and used to follow them around. Ayansola, the great *dundun* drummer was a friend of my father's who came regularly to our house on the campus (of the University of Ife) to play. There are pictures of me as a baby playing a *dundun*. Obviously, growing up in Nigeria with that sort of childhood experience and interest was very crucial to my later development as a musician.

Then we moved to Papua New Guinea, where the drumming is not nearly as interesting as in Yoruba society. There the concept of drumming is very different. There can be fifty drummers, all of whom are playing at almost the same time and beat. The aim is to make drumming sound like a waterfall. It is tremendous, but not quite it for me. I actually got some bongos as a present once, but as you could not do much with a bongo really, it was not the right thing for me either. "This is not a *dundun* drum," my parents remember me saying, rather emphatically. I also remember one minor incident in this house of this lady Gaby Duigu, a German Jewish lady married to a New Guinean. She had worked in Ondo for four years and brought back a *dundun* drum. We went to visit her and, once, she opened the cupboard where the drum was kept. I saw it and was instantly drawn to it; I lit up.

When we moved to Australia I became more interested in drumming when I heard Abdullah Ibrahim's (Dollar Brand) jazz quintet. The group's drummer, Andre Strobert, played the normal trap set and he really sparked me off. My father tells me that I insisted on being taken to every one of the group's performances until I finally got introduced to the drummer! Then I learned how to play jazz drums for about a year or a year and a half. I also performed with some groups who played just the conventional Western drums and, again, I was not satisfied at all—both the training and the playing were too stiff, tight, and technical. It did not allow you to express yourself.

Seeing my frustration at such an early age (I was about 9 or 10), my father wrote to Muraina Oyelami, then teaching Yoruba percussion at the University of Ife, but frustrated and unhappy, to come and spend some time with us so as to teach me Yoruba drumming. Muraina came and we started with *gudugudu*. Thirty minutes or so into the very first lesson, he exclaimed: "Tunji is born to be a drummer!" By the second week, we had started playing together in public. We played traditional Yoruba music as well as a multicultural piece in the Sydney Open Air Festival of that year. There were thousands of people present and it was my first big concert. It was very successful. I remember that when we finished playing, an old woman who liked it so much came up to me and gave me $A20.00 I felt so embarrassed and refused, but she made me take it. We also went on radio. When Muraina had to return home I followed him to Nigeria. I was not quite eleven yet, but for three months I was with him and we played on several public occasions and in various parts of Yorubaland. I cannot remember most of them, but the one that I do remember clearly was during the installation of the *oba (Olufi)* of Gbongan.

Twins Seven-Seven came to Australia in 1984 and I teamed up with him quite a bit. It was a different kind of experience and good, for Twins is such a great showman. I was also playing with Colin Offord. He has a strange way of behaving on stage, but he is a very, very good musician. In a way, he turned me into a professional before I knew it: he respected me and integrated me fully into his group when we played at a festival in Adelaide. He gave me my first pay as a professional musician. Not long after that, Ademola Onibonokuta also came to Sydney. A group was formed comprising Greg Sheehan, Ademola and me. We called the group OKUTA PERCUSSION because of Ademola's stones. (These archaeological stones are musical instruments, producing sounds like the *balafon*—Eds.)

Then, later, in 1986, 1 went to the University of Ife to attend courses in African drumming. Incidentally, I had to get a special permission for that, because I had not attained the minimum age for university entrance! I spent an interesting time at Ife, but the music program itself was not very good. Something was missing: there was no life in it and even the teacher himself could not put much into it because of the students. They were neither demanding nor terribly interested, and did not think much about learning African (Yoruba) instruments as part of their music education. The teacher therefore responded to them in a very lukewarm manner. But otherwise the six months I spent in Nigeria were quite good: just being alone, all by myself, at the age of fifteen, was a good experience. Outside the university program, I played at some festivals and ceremonies with Muraina himself, and that was great. I still remember the charged atmosphere, the crowds, the energy, and the people. That environment has had a permanent input on my subsequent development as a musician. The Yoruba environment has given me the most important thing for my music: the life of playing percussion with energy and intensity, plus the intimate rapport between musician and audience.

I went directly from Nigeria to India. Actually, I had met Ramesh Shotham earlier in Germany, when he gave me my first lessons in South Indian percussion, in 1983 or '84. He said if I was really serious and interested in the music I had better go to his teacher in Bangalore. I myself had actually met this man, Mr. T.A.S. Mani, before. The first time was in 1982 when Muraina took me to the Singapore Arts Festival. We played for an *Alarinjo* masqueraders group, so I had to get some special lessons in *Omele Bata* before we went. After the festival Muraina and I were invited by the Goethe Institute in India to give several concerts of Yoruba music. It was during this tour that we met Mr. Mani in his Karnataka College of Percussion, Bangalore. The second time was maybe a year later when Mr. Mani came to perform in the Bayreuth Opera House in a big concert called "Classical African and Indian Percussion." I performed with the African group (of Muraina, Lamidi Ayankunle and others), but Mr. Mani invited me to join the Indian group for one piece. Shortly after that concert, my family returned to Australia. We stopped for a week briefly in Bangalore and I got a few lessons from Mr. Mani. I knew then that he was the person I wanted to learn from. I had met many other famous percussionists in Madras, but it was Mr. Mani who really inspired me.

I spent three very intensive years in India, studying percussion. It was a very rigorous training, though also very monotonous. There was an initial, slight problem of getting up in the morning. Mr. T.A.S. Mani woke me up at six every morning and this took time getting used to for me, but I did soon enough. I practiced ten hours a day! I would get up at six in the morning and by six-thirty start practicing with a young singer in his house, for one hour. From there it was straight to Mr. Mani's house to practice for two hours. Then I would have breakfast, immediately after which I went to Shashi Kumar who would teach me Thavil. This went on till midday. Then back to Mr. Mani's house for lunch, followed by some more lessons till 3 o'clock. A three-hour break followed. By six or seven in the evening I would be at Ashok's (another singer) house to practice till ten in the night. Then I would go home to bed and be up at six the next morning again. This schedule was unvaried and so gruelling for me because I had to pack into three years what should normally stretch out into eight. However, at the end of it all, I emerged the best student in the state examination conducted for all the students in South India. This examination consisted of theories and practicals. The theories were not so good, but the practicals were outstanding.

I got into real difficulties at one point in a long practical session. This was the Mukhtaim, which has a very complicated calculation. In it you are supposed to invent a very complex improvisation on the spur of the moment: the examiner prescibes a number, say 47 or 73, and you must calculate your improvised piece in such a way that after 47 or 73 beats, or whatever number has been prescribed, you slide back into the basic rhythm. Because of the complexity of the Mukhtaim, another drummer is always present to clap the basic rhythm for you while you are doing it, otherwise you get lost. Many experienced musicians have in fact gotten lost. Now, when my examiner was clapping for me, he made a mistake! Was it deliberate so as to trap me or genuine? As I could not very well tell him that he had made a mistake, I had to recalculate my entire improvisation while performing. It was tough, but I was rewarded with "First Rank," meaning that I was the best student of the *aresar* in South India. Another student of Mr. Mani's, who had been with him long before me, came second. My earlier experiences did not help much in India. Indian percussion is very mental and has very difficult techniques. You just have to practice these extremely complicated techniques on a regular basis, and also learn to play very fast.

On the whole my experience in India was very good. I stayed with the Manis and was like a son to the two of them. Their son, who is about ten years younger than me, also became my brother. The relationship has continued on that note ever since. Mr. and Mrs. Mani love playing together with me and, between my leaving India and now, we must have played together at least twenty times. It might even have been more if we were not so far away from each other. I communicate with them fairly regularly and they always express the wish that I could come on a playing tour of India with them. I suppose that is a testimony of their pride in their former student. In the Indian tradition, anyway, the relationship between a teacher and his former student is permanent, but Mr. Mani also respects me in my own right as an accomplished and professional musician.

My parents are open-minded. When I became interested in percussion music, they were quite happy and very supportive. They both really like Nigeria, so they readily agreed to my going there all on my own, at the age of *ten*! Perhaps if they had stood in my way the music talent might just have died in me. I think a lot of my music talent is inherited. My grandfather was a musician, my mother is an artist. What I find interesting is that my brother took the scientific side of our grandfather (he was a medical doctor by profession) while I took the artistic side. I have no doubt that he would have approved of my type of music. Unfortunately I met him only once, when I was about five. He was almost as great a guy as my father but he did not have the opportunities of bringing out all that he had.

Apart from my trainings in Yoruba and South Indian percussions, I have also been influenced by a few other musicians. In fact, the initial, serious influence came from Dollar Brand, whose jazz combines African and European elements, though more of the former than the latter. I also like the South African type of choral singing. I listen a lot to Philip Tabane, the old South African guitar player. There is Billy Cobham from the USA, who has an incredible technique as a drummer. I looked up to him very much in my early days. I have since performed with him on several occasions, the first one being in 1989. Though theirs are not the kinds of music that I play, I also do listen to a lot of African popular music and it is good that musicians like King Sunny Ade, Youssou N'dour, Salif Keita and others have come out and are very big on the international pop stage now. What is especially good about them is that they keep some aspects of traditional percussion going. A lot of people feel strongly about South American percussion music, whose distant origin is Africa anyway. But I find African music much deeper; so if you have one you do not really need the other. I don't have the feelings for it: so many rhythms going on at once and all fancy. I don't get what they are saying and the music does not move me at all.

When I returned from India in 1989, the first thing I did was to organize a little tour with Greg Sheehan and Rabiu Ayandokun, the Yoruba percussionist. I had met Rabiu the year before when I came to Germany. Lamidi Ayankunle, another wonderful Yoruba drummer, had brought him along, for the first time on a European tour and, even then, Rabiu was already quite impressive and versatile. So in 1989, when I returned, we decided to try him out. We sent for him, and Greg Sheehan came over from Australia. So this new group was composed of Rabiu, Greg and myself . This was the first full OKUTA PERCUSSION group (so named on account of Ademola's stones), although its beginning was in Australia. We played in many places in what were then West and East Germany and the reception was good all over. We also played a lot for the radio. In 1992 we also produced a CD titled OKUTA, which won the German Music Critics Prize.

The composition of OKUTA PERCUSSION has changed because the music we produce is always growing. When it gets to a crucial point, a member no longer fits in, is no longer right. The group then needs a new influence. This is because every member brings in his own expertise or talent to influence the direction of our compositions and performances.

337

We have had quite a string of engagements in the recent past. One of the big ones was the performance at the Opera House in 1995, at which the great AfiicanAmerican jazz pianist, Randy Weston, played, and a Mexican group. Our group had not played before either with Randy Weston or the Mexican group. In fact we met the group only a week earlier and played together for the first time at the Erfurt concert. So we had only that week to get to know each other and know what each could do, what we could all do together. On the whole, the experience of playing with Randy, Iain Ballamy from England, Terje Isaugset from Norway, and the Mexicans that night at the Opera House was great. We also brought out a CD last April, which has been favorably received. The main comment people have made about it is that they have never heard anything like that before. Another comment is that it is more complete music than just a mere percussion arrangement. It is something you can listen to and get all the full range of a musical composition. What this means is that we play percussions as complete music, not just the rhythmic background to something else. The present composition of OKUTA PERCUSSION has depth to it, perhaps that is why its performance and music have that ritual or spiritual atmosphere to them. We did not set out to deliberately create it.

We had another great concert during the *Grenzuberschreitungen* festival at Das Zentrum here in Bayreuth, where the main idea was to make all the musicians from various places come together, so the last piece really achieved that aim. In most concerts or festivals, musicians come from different parts of the world, do their separate bit, and leave; no chance to meet other musicians. On such occasions, a musician or group should watch others perform and possibly get a chance to participate with others. Then new ideas can arise, one gets an incentive to experiment with new sounds and move forward. I am always open to new ideas, ready to experiment with others, with other types of music and even instruments.

OKUTA PERCUSSION has done some recordings too and our latest CD has moved fairly well. I regularly get a list from GEMA, an organization that keeps track of where your music has been distributed and is being played. That list shows that the CD is virtually all over the world. Of course, we don't make much money on it. I have also done another CD with Zoltan Lantos, the Hungarian violinist (he too trained in India) but it has not yet come out.

I also have another group we have called BASSAMA. It is made up of an English saxophonist, a Spanish guitarist who also plays Indian flute, and a Sudanese lute player. The group does not perform regularly because the guitarist is an instrument-maker and cannot take off more than two weeks in the year to play. We are trying to do a recording, however. We have just put together another combination: Iain Ballamy (English saxophonist), Zoltan Lantos (Hungarian violinist), Giovanni Parricelli (English guitarist), and myself. It is a new group. We have not had our first tour—we don't even have a name yet—but we are already doing very exciting things, musically.

In none of the groups that I belong to do we play by first composing. Rather, we start by just sitting together, basically, and playing whatever comes to us. When we have done this for a while, we decide which piece is good and which not. We forget the bad ones and try to improve on the good ones. It is by this slow method that we arrive at our compositions. I think this improvisational method is natural, it is the way music is made. We play "jazzy" things, but we are definitely not jazz musicians. However, our technique of composition (improvisation) and non-rigid format of performance are similar to those of jazz. We are free and open, nothing is rigid or fixed before we go on stage.

I think I personally took that positive and open approach from my early experience and little training in Yoruba music. I play with the audience as primary consideration, but also I play by instinct. I want to bring out what is inside me, which I don't know precisely until it comes out. So I lay myself open to all kinds of influences, let them go inside, and also allow whatever it is in me to come out. Sometimes what comes out is as much a surprise to me as it is to my audience. When that happens, I am extremely happy.

I have not deliberately chosen the direction of multicultural or intercultural music. But having grown up in different parts of the world, and moved around a bit, multiculturalism in music is natural with me. It was part of my growing up and music training.

It is very hard to be definite about my identity, although I have no problem with who I am. I feel very close to Yoruba culture and people, I have two Yoruba names, the other is Akanmu. I was named Olatunji in the full Yoruba tradition of naming: first, I resemble my grandfather very much; second, a Yoruba naming ceremony was performed for me, in far away Port Moresby where I was born, by Dr. Lucas, a Yoruba medical doctor then on a WHO mission in Papua New Guinea. I carry an Australian passport, my mother is English, my father is many things. Perhaps I am the true, living embodiment of multiculturalism, a citizen of the world in the true sense of that word. So, apart from that which my parents have given me, I should say that I define, or identify myself, mainly through my music.

If I should find myself staying in Nigeria for a long period, I would explore all the range and types of drumming within the culture. I would not go near the university at all, either to teach or learn more music. That is the wrong place. One should go back to the roots and among the people who practice and use the music. The university cannot give the music any form of respectability. Respect for it can only come when people see its popularity outside the continent, especially now that traditional musicians cannot make a living out of the profession at home.

Performance in Africa is different from performance in the West, and both are normal in their respective contexts. In the African type of performance, there is an intense relationship between the musician and the audience and there is hardly any gap between the stage and audience. In Europe the gap is strictly adhered to. The African mode generates the kind of relationship that pushes the musician to greater heights. Last year at the burgherfest here in Bayreuth, we had that kind of audience interaction. I just asked Ademola and Taju if they felt like playing. They said yes and we went out there and simply played, parading the city for about four hours nonstop. We were followed all the way by a huge crowd of about sixty people, dancing. It had a big impact. That was the first time such a thing happened here in Bayreuth: it was all so spontaneous and exciting. Afterwards, the pub owners claimed credit for it, saying that they had organized it. This, of course, is a big lie. But both the performance and the lie show how the African mode of performance is beginning to have an impact here in Germany at least.

I would not want to change the quality of the music I play with my groups, even though we might modify the mode of performance to move nearer the audience. In fact, we are this evening going to play at a concert part of which will be among the audience. Many groups are also doing this in Europe now. I saw a group from Holland the other day which played among the audience, using wireless microphones. One of the players actually had himself suspended about twenty meters up in the air, right above the audience.

I hope my music never stops growing. I am no longer as good as I used to be as an Indian musician, but that really is no loss, for I don't want to be just an Indian musician. I should think that I have grown musically, become more complete and versatile. On the other hand I have no fear of leaving the Yoruba background behind, especially as I will always play with Yoruba musicians. It would be lovely to go and play in Nigeria and I hope someday soon it will happen. But right now, it is a pretty difficult thing to even think about.

VII.
COLONIALISM

Wole Soyinka on "Identity"
From a conversation With Ulli Beier

Ulli Beier: Recently a famous commentator on African life and literature referred to you as "the man between," and in his article he expounds that eternal cliché of the African intellectual "between two worlds," between two languages, two cultures. But it seems to me that Europeans worry far more about the "identity problems" of Africans, than Africans do themselves. I have known you now for over thirty years and you have never struck me as somebody who is constantly aware of oscillating between two worlds. Or have you ever thought of yourself as living in a situation of conflict?

Wole Soyinka: It is a strange but certainly deeply ingrained attitude that certain commentators hold, and of course it is a very Eurocentric thing. It does not occur to me, for instance, to consider you, Ulli Beier, as a "man between." It does not occur to me that you suffer from a conflict: you come to Nigeria, and you are immediately at home. You can sit in a Shango shrine or follow the Agbegijo masqueraders: you are just at home. And there are some other Europeans like that: Susanne Wenger has stayed in Oshogbo for decades, she has become a priestess of Obatala. It has never occurred to me to consider her a woman between—she is a deeply spiritual person, and an artist, who creates where she has put down her roots.

I look at Gerd Meuer—he is at home one moment here and one moment there. Right now he is in Addis Ababa. It has never occurred to me that there is a problem, or that there is something special about anybody striving towards two or three or four multiple worlds. It is a very Eurocentric thing.

U: It's European, but it is especially German. In this country people still talk about "die Bewąltigung der Vergangenheit." They still wrestle with their Nazi past and those who weren't even alive at the time torture themselves by examining their father's role in those years. There is a spate of books on that subject. Very different kinds of books from your own reminiscences of your father.

Germans have a problem with their identity because they are very theoretical people—they don't trust their gut reaction—they have to argue an issue to the end, before they know how to react.

W: There is another aspect to this: I think that Europeans still marvel at the ex-colonial—somebody at the lower scale of civilization as far as they are concerned—being able to respond in a very natural and intelligent way to another civilization. I think that this, lurking underneath it, is the notion.

U: Of course Europeans have long felt that they have to export their culture in order to lift other peoples to a higher level of civilization. In the early days of the University of Ibadan there was just this attitude. There was no curiosity about Nigeria at all. The notion that there could be some kind of exchange, some mutual enrichment was quite foreign to them.

They used a formula to justify any absurdity in the curriculum which they imposed on Nigerian students. If you asked them why they thought it necessary to teach Anglo-Saxon in Nigeria at a time when no African language was taught and when there was not even a second European language, the answer was: "We have to maintain British standards." Africans were only acceptable to Europeans if they could perform on their terms and live up to "British standards." On the other hand I feel that certain kinds of early African literature has also contributed to this. . . .

W: Indeed, I was going to refer to that. The early African intellectuals accepted this perspective themselves; and, as I wrote somewhere, enjoyed the "angst" which was created for them through the notion of having to transcend one culture and having to link up with a superior one. The early poetry.

U: Well, Senghor. He is certainly somebody who moves very smoothly between the cultures; but on the other hand he talks too much about it, doesn't he?

W: He wanted to intellectualize it. To create "problematique" and then analyze it; and poetize it also because he used both approaches, the creative and the intellectual. Of course, he was a magnificent poet, and therefore his influence was more deleterious than, let us say, Mabel Imoukhuede. You know the kind of poetry we are talking about. But the interesting thing is that Mabel and others soon gave up on that line. There wasn't too much yardage.

U: No, at least in Nigeria such notions were abandoned fairly quickly. But to come back to the European image of Wole Soyinka—"the man between." There are certain assumptions: your British education, your high achievement in that culture and your exceptional command of the English language, these things now stand, allegedly, between you and your own culture. The English language separates you, so the legend goes, from Yoruba culture. It's like saying you've been converted: he who was a pagan and has now become a Muslim, he who was a Protestant has converted to Catholicism. You have given up one thing to attain another.

W: This is a problem that arises out of analytical attitudes. The very principle of analyzers is that an object or a subject is not interesting until you have created many analytical angles and made the subject as complex as possible—never mind whether the various angles are interesting or not. Once you can create multiple approaches towards the understanding of a subject, then of course you can play games with the entire analytical nexus. And that applies very much when the subject is a writer or an intellectual or a creative person. The more complex you can make the subject, the more intriguing, the greater the amount of conversation and discourse you can weave around it. I think that is exactly what happens: whether it is truthful or not, people no longer bother about that. Because it is more interesting to propose, let us say, that because one has had a particular kind of education and because one has had a certain amount of success in operating within other cultural measures, therefore something must have happened to that person.

U: Some twist to his character, some uneasiness in the mind.

W: And yet you have lots of people who leave their society completely and take up residence somewhere else, even in their formative years.

U: Joseph Conrad. . . .

W: Yes, and nobody bothers about this alleged "problem."

U: Nobody asks, what about his Polish soul.

W: That's right, it's only when it gets to this ex-colonial, and unfortunately some of our own intellectuals, they have their own axes to grind. Then they come and say: he is a success only because he had danced to their cultural tune. Some of them are even more overt—cruder—about it. Oh yes, he is completely alienated. They love him, because his opinions coincide with theirs.

U: The Nobel Prize controversy. . . .

W: That's right. You should never get the Nobel prize, that's the ultimate proof. . . .

U: That you're a traitor to your culture.

W: But some of these people who write these things—they can't stand in their own societies, the way I can go back to my village and be immediately recognized and absorbed ... they cannot. The contrast would be too shaming for them. So it's a myth that has been created for different kinds of motivations. Then common interest makes them all speak with one voice.

U: Maybe this is cynical of me. But you said that people create complicated arguments for their own sakes, but is it not also a case of people creating an academic career for themselves, creating a "subject"?

W: Of course, that's right.

U: Think of the Professor of English at the University of Ibadan who once said: "Wole Soyinka teaching English literature? Over my dead body. Only an Englishman can teach English literature." And that other gentleman who proclaimed: "if we were to teach the works of Wole Soyinka in the University of Ibadan, who are we going to drop—Milton or Shakespeare?" Now both of them are the big African literature experts!

W: They have to find new angles to replace the original resistance.

U: So they can talk endlessly about the agony of Wole Soyinka standing between two worlds.

W: I've said that many times: there is so much attention being paid to the sociology of the writer, and not to his writing!

W: Aha! So it is high time we paid some attention to the sociology of the critic. That is important, and when you look into sociology of the critic or analyst, you'll find self-interest, opportunism, often intellectual dishonesty; you will find phantasizing over and above the level of a fiction writer. You'll find the polemicist's tendency, which has to be fulfilled, and it does not matter what the subject is. Before you come down to mundane issues like, is he or she married, white or black, or from another race: I mean all those various things that are foisted on the artist, it's about time we directed them at the critics themselves! And I am telling you—the results! I have done it in one or two instances and the results are fascinating. For example, one of those people I call Neo-Tarzanists—digging into his sociology, I found that he had fled Biafra during the war, so he is suffering from that immense guilt complex. He suffers from the adulation I received from his compatriots for the role I played in that war, while he was busy collecting money for the Biafran cause—much of which never arrived in Biafra. Little things like that. So it's about time to examine them and see what they eat, what they drink, what sort of clothes they are wearing, who they move with, whose approbation they seek, what sort of conferences they go to, on what circuit of conferences they are constantly to be found. It's about time we turned this blade around. The results are most fascinating. . . .

U: I think this should be applied on the widest basis. When this research scheme on "Problems of Identity" in Africa first started in Bayreuth a decade ago, I said that "if you think you are entitled to go into any part of Africa to solve their identity problems, at least you should have a parallel scheme of African scholars coming here to solve your identity problems. Because in my mind you have the bigger problem!"

W: The scholars who are into "what makes the African tick," the sociologists and the literary sociologists, they far outnumber and outweigh the creative material that is coming out of Africa today.

U: Easily!

W: So I think it's about time we moved in and studied the identity problems of the European scholars!

U: Another thing is this compartmentalized thinking. When that Professor of English literature said: "Wole Soyinka can't teach English literature," the implication was "he *ought* not to teach English literature." Just as there are still people who feel that someone like Akin Euba ought not to play Mozart. People want to protect their cultural preserves. No African could be sensitive enough to really understand our classical music. And when they say "classical," they take it for granted that they talk about European tradition. No other culture can have produced a classical form of it's own.

A famous "ethnomusicologist" in Berlin issued a series of LP's on African and Asian music under the title "Musical source material," as if entire cultures had merely evolved to provide "source material" for his scholarly work. In the same way African literature is merely "source material" for some of the scholars. They may not even enjoy reading it.

W: They're using it for their careers.

U: A related issue concerns the English language. Some commentators, both European and Nigerian, have argued that using English as a vehicle for creative work is a sign of elitism—an argument that has been used especially against you. It's curious, but in a different context, those same people talk about "World Culture" and the "Global Village" and all that and yet they want you to write in a language that will drastically limit your readership to a very local audience. I suspect, when travelling around the world to their different conferences, the same people are quite grateful to find that English is spoken almost everywhere.

W: I know, it is very curious. It's a non-existent debate that falls into two parts. Let's take the language aspect first. You will find that the African critics who are making this complaint, are not making it in their own language. One would expect their commitment to be so total that they would turn their back on English and French altogether and write in, say, Efik, and say: Anybody who can read me, good! Anybody who can't: let him read Wole Soyinka. For me, that would be the first mark of integrity. If that is missing, it is difficult to take them seriously.

The other thing is this: am I, Yoruba-speaking Wole Soyinka, am I to be cut off from Chinua Achebe? From the works of Taban Lo Lyong, Ngugi wa Thiong'o, Denis Brutus? If South African writers followed this precept and wrote in their own languages, am I to be cut off from the political struggle in South Africa? It's an argument I have never really understood.

I come now to the second part. I too lament that in Africa, which I regard as my larger community, we don't have a language that binds us all together outside the European languages, the colonial languages. After all, even the European language fragments. I have to study Portuguese to read Dos Santos.

I study French to read Senghor.

I'm on record as having seriously promoted the use of Swahili, and in the inaugural congress of the "Union of Writers of the African People" we took the decision that we should set up a cooperative publishing house and undertake the mammoth task of translating all works—all new works to begin with—into Kiswahili. Beginning with all new works. And we encouraged all African writers to reserve their rights to this cooperative publishing cooperation. I haven't seen any practical steps taken by the people who had been screaming their heads off about African languages. For me the two things go side by side. We should all admit that we need a single literature, which makes economic sense. We also asked that all schools should eliminate one useless subject and substitute Kiswahili so that we build up a generation of Kiswahili speakers. The two ideas coincide, I see no problem in this at all. I want to continue writing in English and, more importantly, reading my fellow Nigerians, my fellow Africans, in English and, of course, the literature of the entire English-speaking world. I insist on keeping the facility to do this. Many people oversimplify the word criticism. They don't understand that criticism also means exposition: exposition of the work and the life. They feel they have not engaged in literary criticism if they are not "criticizing"

U: In the sense of "finding fault."

W: Precisely. They have to be negative. They make a fetish of it. And ultimately, which is nauseating, they profit from it. And they communicate this in the very language they condemn. How ridiculous can you get? That contradiction never occurs to them.

U: Even Europeans have talked about elitism along the lines of "More people can understand *Death and the King's Horseman* in New York than in Nigeria," which is not true at all. In fact, from the reports I read, the people of New York were quite baffled by the play. They couldn't penetrate it at all.

W: Yes. That is true.

U: I don't think that any critic has the right to prescribe a particular language to a writer anymore than he can prescribe the contents of a book or the mood or the intellectual level on which the ideas are to be developed. The irony is that those who constantly nag Wole Soyinka about his elitism forget that, though you may have written some rather cerebral stuff, you have also operated on a very popular level. I can't think of another African writer who produced anything as popular as the LP, *Unlimited Liability Company*. To communicate on that level you even had to use Pidgin English.

W: I used Pidgin, I used Yoruba, I used mime, I used song, dance. I feel a total—if you like elitist—indifference to those kinds of critics. I consider them quite ignorant. When I read a statement like: "Nobody reads Wole

Soyinka outside Nigeria," I ask myself, what do these people talk about. If they said: This particular work is not read in Nigeria, we could begin to discuss that. But when they make a statement like "in Nigeria Wole Soyinka is far more popular for his political position than for his creative work," I say, I don't know what they are talking about. Unfortunately some of them are Nigerians!

U: Most of them!

W: We do our political sketches, we take them to the market place!

U: *Before the Blackout!*

W: Yes, you remember *Before the Blackout* from the sixties. And again during the last civilian regime, with all the scandals going on. We took the theater to the museum kitchen at Onikan and from there moved to the street in front of the House of Assembly. We did a series of sketches there and then jumped into the vehicles and ran away before the police could seize our vehicles.

There are various ways of communicating a work to the public. I use all of them, including, as you remarked, a record. We are bringing out a video shortly which has emerged from the latest equivalent of *Before the Blackout.* We call it *Before the Deluge.* They came out of a theatre workshop in Abeokuta and some of the sketches we performed in open places. I reach the public in a way—and I am not being immodest—that few people do. Yet I am the one who gets all this nonsense about "Nobody reads Wole Soyinka in his own country."

U: I remember some very potent poems of yours appearing in Nigerian newspapers. For example, the one about the pathetic death of a Yoruba *Oba* during the 1966 crisis in the West. Everybody would have understood that. Of course, I too may find some of your poems baffling, but few things could be more popular than 'Telephone Conversation"?

W: Of course there are always works that are more accessible than others.

U: Again this brings up the alleged identity conflict! There are two Wole Soyinkas, so the theory goes: one is the lofty intellectual who despises his readers, the other is the political agitator, the gang leader, who doesn't mind throwing out the occasional doggerel rhyme, another simplification, another variant of the "man between." They don't seem to see that different situations require different responses from the writer.

W: Yes, I believe that the armory of creativity that is at your disposal is so vast that one would be a fool not to use whatever corresponds to the theme one wishes to use at the moment.

U: I think we have agreed that most Nigerians cope fairly effortlessly with the alleged conflict between their own culture and the Western values that have been imposed on them. They don't worry about it and there is no intellectual equivalent to the *négritude* writers. But at the same time there has been little interaction between the various Nigerian cultures themselves. What attempts have there been made to find common denominators between, say, Igbo, Yoruba, Efik, and Angas cultures? Do people consider it irrelevant or even undesirable?

Remember what we tried to do in Duro Ladipo's play *Moremi*. Because the play deals with the conflict between the Ifes and aboriginal population, I recruited a group of Agbor dancers for the production: so Duro had two languages, two musical traditions, and two dance styles at his disposal. It enriched his play enormously and the final scene was spectacular. The Yoruba *dundun* drums were playing simultaneously with the Igbo slit gongs and horns. Duro made all the musicians orientate themselves towards a strong simple beat that was played by Rufus Ogundele on a huge Conga drum. It was a very successful piece of "fusion music," even though we did not know the term in those days. I rather hoped it would lead others to develop this idea further, but it wasn't taken up. What a missed opportunity. Imagine a Nigerian orchestra, involving *Dundun, Bata, Bembe*, slit gongs, xylophones from the Plateau, horns from Ekiti and Igbo country, and *kakaki* trumpets from the North. You could create sounds that would make a European symphony orchestra sound grey.

W: It's interesting you should say that. Just yesterday when we were rehearsing the poetry with OKUTA PERCUSSION and Tunji played that Indian gatham, my mind went straight to the Igbo pot drum. And you are right, there has not been that fusion of music. I have felt the need for this myself and, you remember, when I produced *A Dance of the Forest* for Nigerian independence, I brought the Atilogu dancers from the East! And since then, most of my productions have integrated, wherever possible, a wide range of music. My mind goes immediately to whatever is available within my entire cultural milieu.

No, in case of music, you are right. A lot of this is missing. If you have a choir like Steve Rhodes Voices or, say, an Efik-based choir, you'll find that they make a point of including at least some songs from other parts of Nigeria in their repertoire. But it is there on an itemized level, not integrated. When I made my record, *Unlimited Liability Company,* one side and that is acknowledged on the cover ...

U: ... is based on Njemanze!

W: Yes. I have always had this idea of cross-fertilization, but the composers, the real composers, don't seem to use it.

U: There has also been an unfortunate influence, I think. The various state "Art Councils" in Nigeria have promoted a kind of folklore.

W: That's right. You know after the oil boom, there came a time when culture became culture with capital "C," and folklore became folklore with a capital 'F' for "Folklorism." When there was money for the states to set up individual arts councils and when all these national competitions were organized each state went it's own way with a sense of creative rivalry. This has affected thinking till today. And has impoverished the range of creative possibilities.

U: There was another very negative aspect to those Arts Council competitions. It's an absurdity to have a group of Shango priests, who are performing "*Sango Pipe*" compete against Alarinjo singing "*Iwi*" or *Babalawo* chanting "Odu." What criterion is there to judge it? And usually it involved the humiliation of the performers. Some pompous cultural bureaucrat herding them on stage, then after ten minutes he would get on the stage and say "O. K. that's enough! Obatala priests next, please."

W: It's still going on.

U: And then the crude attempts to "choreograph" what to, the people concerned, is a ritual, not a theatrical performance! I suspect that the unfortunate model for all these developments was Keita Fodeba's "*Ballets Africaines.*"

W: Oh yes, the beginning of African folklore, cut to European taste. But at least they moved on from there. Whereas there has been no such evolution here. From the videos I have seen of the Nigerian "*National Troupe*," I gather that there has been no mandate for it to get a modern choreographer and produce a synthesis. It was a question of getting troupes from different areas and each doing their own thing. There has been, shall I say, a lack of progressive cultural policy. But the answer never lies in government policies. For example: Peter Badejo went to the North, to Ahmadu Bello University and created a really marvelous form of choreography, utilizing material from all over Nigeria with very impressive results. From small beginnings—he went there to take a diploma—he proved himself an imaginative choreographer. Recently he did the choreography for *Death and the King's Horseman* in Manchester. Nigeria is very rich and there are many idioms of creativity which really beg to be welded together. For me it is not a principle: it's just that the material is there. The possibility is there. Why isn't it used?

U: Some Nigerians have come to think that there are incompatible elements in the various Nigerian cultures. This belief has expressed itself in a great deal of political strife, even in violence and civil war. Thirty years after independence, have we come any nearer to any Nigerian identity or have we moved further away from it? Has Nigeria been no more than a colonial conception? What does it mean, being a Nigerian today?

W: That is a question which has been given very high profile in recent times. Consequent on the civil war, consequent on the rise of Islamic assertion (which has taken it's toll on the Nigerian psyche, with sudden violent flashes, eating into the university system, with fundamentalists organizing themselves and laying down the law for the rest of the university), the question, I am afraid, is on everybody's minds and lips.

It is a very real problem and it demands that a national debate should take place on the national question. Because certain parts of the country feel that other sections are dictating *their* idea of Nigeria, not a national concept –simply their own attempt to impose what they consider the ethics of their locale, whether it's religion, or region, or whatever. Certainly it is a very large question. What form it will take, I don't know.

U: The only hope for the country to become a genuinely organic unit is for it to be allowed to grow, isn't it? You cannot prescribe national unity, it can only evolve.

W: Yes, that is correct.

U: Is it not then the creative people who. . . .

W: Oh, no, I don't accept any extra burden for creative people. It is as much the responsibility of the politicians, the bureaucrats, because we are talking about quite prosaic things like the resentment of certain states over the apportionment of revenue. That kind of thing is listed as part and parcel of the need to discuss the national identity. It is being suggested that certain areas are being consistently privileged over and above others.

But, you see, when the writer comes in and tells the truth about a situation like this, he is then charged with fanning ethnic tensions. In other words, he can add to the problem, while he tries to reduce it. It all depends. There is a joint responsibility. The artists can't be expected to take a leading role in it.

U: Well, of course, if it comes to solving such issues, the artist is only another citizen. But I was in fact referring to something quite different. How does the image of Nigeria evolve? Who defines Nigerian identity? Does it not happen through the kind of creative activity of a Peter Badejo that you have just described?

W: I am afraid it is very idealistic and romantic to think that fifty or a hundred Peter Badejos are going to create that national fusion which he achieved on stage.

There was a former student of mine, who was caught in the recent Kano riots. Jimmy Sodimu, a very marvellous actor. He was one of those who went independent, who formed their own little troupes. He was in the North doing a one man show and he had an interpreter. His interpreter was beheaded right next to him! And he himself received severe machete cuts. Are you ever going to persuade that person to go on any cultural fusion mission? Ever again in his life? No way!

U: This happened recently?

W: Recently. This was the very latest riot that was triggered off by that German evangelist. That riot! There are lots and lots of cases like that. Everybody knows somebody who has been traumatized in that way as a result of the national question. So people are asking: does it mean that I cannot go anywhere in this country, on whatever is my mission, my business? There was somebody driving a delivery truck. He'd done it for donkey years, around Bauchi. When the riot started, this man was taken out of his lorry, the vehicle was set on fire, and he was burnt. Just an ordinary worker, a driver. Just because he was driving a truck load of beer and delivering it to all the shops. This is no problem for the artist. The artist will create his own work and fulfill his mission, but it's on a different level. . . .

U: Is it a situation, then, of which we can't know where it is going?

W: No, I cannot. I believe that successive governments have underrated, have underestimated this question. Even people like myself—we have always assumed that we have a nation. Or at least, as you rightly said, that if things were just left, progressively, a nation would evolve. So it's not a question that we have tackled.

When the whole debate began, I was cornered several times. Let's say, I give a lecture. Somebody is bound to get up and say: "Excuse me, Professor Soyinka, what do you say to the national question?" And I would pretend that I don't know what he is talking bout. I know damn well what he is talking about, and I know that whatever I say can be taken the wrong way. So I would say something like this: "Listen, I can be in Enugu or in Kano or in Jos or wherever—as long as I have my typewriter with me, that's where my nation is at the moment." But I know that's not satisfactory and the questioner is not satisfied. He wants Wole Soyinka to pronounce, and from the way he asks the question I know what he wants me to say. And he will be satisfied with nothing less than what he wants me to say and that would be misunderstood. The next day there would be twenty headlines and as many twists in the newspapers. Words would be put in my mouth and I could not debate it. So I would say: "Listen, if you see me afterwards, we can sit down and talk." I am not going to be drawn into that debate in public because I know what will happen.

U: But beyond this issue of the "national question" there is also that natural sense of obligation that a person like you has towards Africa at large. . . .

.W: Precisely. I keep reminding people that I have a very large constituency which extends well beyond the Nigerian borders: I tend to see even Nigerian problems in the context of my vision of Africa. This has been with me for a long time, ever since my student days, when I was so focused on South Africa, that my early play dealt with apartheid.

And even in practical terms: if I get an invitation from Angola or Cape Verde, the passion with which my presence is solicited is much stronger than what I could get from Nigeria; there I am taken for granted. So I make an extra special effort to fulfill those requests whenever I can. This also creates extra problems. If I go away for a couple of weeks, there may have been some new event, something that has outraged public opinion. And they think: Oh yes, Wole Soyinka has stopped speaking. He doesn't comment any more. He doesn't criticize the government. I am supposed to be in Nigeria for 365 days a year giving running commentary on the government's activities. It's an absurd existence, and I ask people: What did you do? What exactly did you do? By the time you have arrived from overseas, this thing is no longer news, it is no longer on the front page. You move to act in a quiet, strong, and often successful way. But it doesn't hit the papers. The next thing is you get flak from these lazy, idle, very comfortable armchair critics, whose mission in life is not to participate in nation building, in trying to enforce corrective measures—their mission in life is to point the finger and say: Oh, he's no longer doing anything, he's said nothing.

U: Not unlike those literary critics.

W: Yes, they don't even know what else you've written and how it's been received, but they will say: Yes, he's elitist now, he's removed from the people. It's boring, it's one huge bore! They don't even know that they've said it all before and that they've been proved wrong; it makes no difference.

U: There is a whole level of society that expects you—and maybe Tai Solarin—to take on the burden of pulling the government to heel, of being the consciousness of the nation. Mind you, I remember very well the time of the first real crisis we went through, the time of the massacres that preceded the civil war. Who else was speaking then? The fact is that everybody remained silent, and that was the most frightening aspect of it. There is no country in the world, that does not experience violent convulsions, as parts of Europe do now. But when everybody is suddenly on the winning side. . .

.W: Yes, it was one of the worst periods, the exhibition of collective compromise! Acquiescence! A kind of surrender and therefore moving from surrender to aggressive association with the side that inflicted a very serious wound on the national psyche.

U: Do you think that a lot of politicians still blame colonialism for the country's problems and for their own shortcomings?

W: No, not the politicians, but the intellectual commentators. They still do that to some extent, but that has been diminished over the years, as they have seen the capacity for economic depravation. They finally couldn't close their eyes to internal oppression in their own societies any longer.

U: What about the new debate on compensation for slavery. Isn't that a revival of the argument that colonialism is solely responsible for what's gone wrong in Africa? Of course I am fully aware that colonialism hasn't ceased to exist after independence. On the contrary: the exploitation of Africa by the West is far worse now than it has ever been.

W: Oh yes!

U: But on the other hand foreign firms could not exploit Nigeria without the cooperation of some Nigerians. That's why we have all those industrial white elephants, those vast factories that produce next to nothing.

W: It's huge! Bottomless-stomached elephants! Yes, they're all over the place! But nevertheless, I found the reparations theme very fascinating. First of all, it's such a wild idea! That I find attractive. Also it could have a concrete result. If, for instance the whole industrial world, the former colonial powers, the former slaving powers suddenly say: O.K. we forgive all your debts. That's your reparation. From now on we are entering a new relationship. Now we wipe the past clean: a totally new economic relationship. We are going to be strict. It's going to be *quid pro quo*: You have, I want, you sell, I pay. It's a curious thing, but a wild idea like this could just. . . .

U: Maybe that's the way to finally get rid to these eternally strangulating loans.

W: Thank you. For that reason I don't dismiss it outright. But I agree, it's a debatable notion, a very controversial notion.

U: Well, to begin with, you can't just isolate the slave trade as the one big crime of the West. What about the Aztecs, or the Incas, or the Australian Aboriginals. They would have to compensate the whole world! If they tried that, there would be nothing left of the West! That might not even be a bad thing, but it is simply not feasible!

W: And then how to work it out—it's very complex.

U: And in fairness to the West, you have to admit that they have had no monopoly on genocide! What about Idi Amin! Bokassa! What about the long catalogue of atrocities carried out by Africans against Africans?

W: O yes! And then we would have to talk about the Arab slave trade which was every bit as atrocious as the European one. I have always said: there must be no double standards! No double standards! If we're going to have reparations, it's very dangerous—a two-edged weapon. But if it can be handled in such a way that the West will get tired of the noise and if they will say: O.K., take your debts, go away, we are all starting all over again, a new relationship—that would be a very interesting development.

U: An utopia!

W: But it's a fascinating exercise!

The Making of a Philosopher
Ulli Beier talks to Sophie Oluwole

U: There are not many people who have tried to study and define Yoruba philosophy. This is surprising, because you might say that those of us who study the art, the literature, the religion of the Yoruba people are studying various manifestations, symptoms perhaps, of the basic Yoruba interpretation of life.

And yet philosophy was introduced rather late into Nigerian universities and most Nigerian philosophers seem more interested in Greek or British philosophy than in African philosophy.

I am curious, therefore, to hear from you how you became interested in the subject and what problems you faced on the long road towards becoming a leading authority in Yoruba philosophy. First tell me something about your background.

S: Well, I was born in Igbara-Oke, a town that lies on the border between Ilesha and Ondo.

U: I know the place well. In the fifties and early sixties it was a favorite stopover for truck drivers on the way to Benin city. The roadside restaurants sold the best pounded yam and the best bush meat in the whole of Nigeria. I enjoyed many wonderful meals there.

S: Yes, that is true. Unfortunately our people lost that trade, when the shorter Lagos-Benin road was built further south. Nowadays that market has almost disappeared.

U: What did your father do?

S: He was a trader. He first went down to Lagos in 1910, buying clothes. Then, in 1912 he established his trade in Igbara-Oke and he would walk to Onitsha. . . .

U: . . . walk all the way to Onitsha?

S: Yes, in those days there were no trucks. Traders used to trek with a group of carriers. So for many years he would walk between Igbara-Oke and Onitsha, which was even then the largest market in West Africa.

My mother was trading on the market of Igbara-Oke, but she was also a dyer and a weaver. She must be close to a hundred years old now, because her first child was born in 1918. She had eight children altogether. Four of them died and four of us remain. I am her last born.

My mother was a very short woman, that is why she married rather late. She still looked like a child when her age group was getting married. She told me that she married about four years later than the others.

U: Did you still know your grandparents?

S: Yes, my grandfather came from Benin. My father was born in Igbara-Oke, but my grandfather came from Benin in about 1850. He was already a married man then, with about five wives. He had been a high-ranking official in the *Oba*'s palace in Benin. Igbara-Oke was part of the Benin empire then; in fact it belonged to the *Oba*'s mother, because the *Oba* divided the empire among members of the family. So when there were reports that Ogedengbe was raiding Igbara-Oke. . . .

U: ...you mean Ogedengbe, the famous Ijesa warrior?

S: Yes ... and so it became necessary to send somebody to keep-watch...somebody to act as a kind of resident or governor looking after the interests of the *Oba*. In those days the Chief of Igbara-Oke could not make any decision without consulting my grandfather.

U: What about your father's mother. Was she a Yoruba woman?

S: No. As a matter of fact, she was the daughter of another Benin "governor" who resided in Ogotun, a few kilometers away, because the *Oba* of Benin had these residents all over the place. My father married the daughter of a man who had come with my grandfather from Benin. Only my maternal grandmother was Yoruba. So actually I am an Edo woman, except that I was born and bred in Igbara-Oke.

U: Did your father speak Yoruba or Edo?

S: My father grew up speaking Yoruba, but he made sure that he went back to Benin to learn Edo. My mother could not really speak Edo. She was a very shy woman. She could understand it but did not speak it.

U: Did you consider yourself Yoruba or Edo as a child? Or didn't you really think about that?

S: I did. I thought of myself as an Edo girl. Because until I left primary school, the *Oba* of Benin used to stop in Igbara-Oke, whenever he traveled to Ibadan. You remember that Benin was part of the Western Region of Nigeria then, and the Oba of Benin had to attend the House of Chiefs in Ibadan. So whenever he was to travel on that road he sent a message some days ahead to my father, and as from seven o'clock in the morning all the Edo people in Igbara-Oke would wait on the road side, drumming and dancing, with a banner, saying: "Welcome, *Oba* of Benin!" There were about ten Edo

families in the town and the local people referred to us as *Ado Igbara.*
U: Ado meaning Edo?
S: Yes, that's how they pronounced it. And even the local people would
come and gather on that day, because we had different drumming and different dancing. . . . . So many of them were curious and they would not go to
the farm that day.
U: Were you singing in Edo?
S: No, we were singing in Yoruba. The *Oba* would not leave his car. He
would remain seated and talk to my father and then drive away. He did not
stop in Igbara-Oke on the way back. Only once he appeared mysteriously on
his return, under very strange circumstances. I remember that one night, I was
still a small girl, we were sitting in our house and we suddenly saw the *Oba*
entering our house. I was frightened because I had never seen him leaving the
car and he had not announced his visit. My father immediately took him into
his private room and told us to keep away.

What happened, apparently, was that the *Oba*'s car had an accident
on the way back from Ibadan. His car overturned about five kilometers away
from Igbara-Oke. But mysteriously he suddenly appeared in our house.
U: Was that Akenzua II?
S: Yes, it was Akenzua. My father then arranged for a mechanic to go
to the site of the accident with him and repair the car. He found the driver in
great desperation, because he had been looking for the *Oba* everywhere and
could not find him. He was so relieved to hear that the *Oba* was safe, but, of
course, as soon as he got back to Benin he resigned his position.

So I was calling myself an Edo girl when I was small, but I never
learned the language. I can hear a little, but I cannot speak it. My sisters speak
Edo very well and my only brother who was a very well known journalist with
the *Daily Times* in Lagos has now retired in Benin. You must know him—
Ebenezer Williams.
U: What names were you given by your parents? What does the initial
"B" stand for? Is it a Yoruba name or a Bini name?
S: It is Yoruba: Bosede—"a girl born on a Sunday." And I was also
named Olayemi, which is Yoruba again, meaning: "I feel comfortable with
dignity."
U: And how did you get Sophie? It is unusual in Yoruba country.
S: My parents didn't think of such a name, of course. But we had a
headmaster then, who was a friend of the family. I suppose he came to the
house often because there were several beautiful young girls and he was
unmarried.

I was very tiny then. He liked me, he gave me biscuits and I followed
him around everywhere. I ended up living with him at the age of eight. It was

after I had started school that I was to be baptized and he told my father that he should name me Sophia. My father didn't know what it meant. But the headmaster thought that I was a clever girl. It is funny, but many years later my supervisor for my PhD thesis at the University of Ibadan said to me: "Why should you call yourself Sophia, just because you have decided to become a philosopher?" And I said to him: "I was given that name long before I knew what it meant." We used to even write it with an "f" like the capital of Bulgaria.

U: What kind of naming ceremony would you have had? Was it like the Yoruba one, where you give the baby various things to taste—kola nut to teach him that life can be bitter, pepper to teach him that life can hurt, and honey to teach him that sweetness always follows pain in life?

S: It would have been similar; only some of the items would have been different. For example, in Benin we can hardly do anything without coconut or snails. Snails are for peace. The snail moves slowly. It is soft. It doesn't fight, it doesn't harm. And when you break the shell there is that beautiful blue water. The snail is harmony.

There used to be plenty of snails in Benin. In the olden days, when you cooked food and the meat was not enough, you would just go behind the house and pick a dozen snails. They would be everywhere. But today they have gone. The Binis buy snails from the Yoruba.

U: So you were not given any Edo names?

S: No, my brothers were given Edo names. By that time there was a nostalgia to go back to Benin. All my father's grandchildren were given Edo names. All of them. At that time he would have loved to go home, because he was not fully accepted in Igbara-Oke. He reminded them of the "colonial" rule of Benin. There was an incident that nearly forced my father to leave the town. My brother went to Government College Ibadan and during the first term, when he was asked, he said that he was a Benin boy. The people in Igbara-Oke got angry and said: "Why should he call himself a Benin boy? Was he not born and bred in Igbara-Oke and was not his father born here also?"

U: I gather that your parents were both Christians.

S: Yes, they were Anglicans. My father was baptized in 1912, my mother in 1915, just before they got married. In fact, you could say that Igbara-Oke was a Christian town.

U: That means, I suppose, that you grew up without knowing anything about Yoruba religion.

S: Since my grandfather had come from Benin, we had Olokun in our compound and all the traditional dances were still being performed for him. And the worshippers of the other *Orisha* would come and celebrate with us. For us children it was very, very interesting; and in the evening, when nobody was watching, we would imitate them. We would dramatize the ritual with all the songs and dances. But my father was always worrying us not to go and watch the "pagan" ceremonies. As Christians we were supposed to stay clear of all that. To him it was like worshipping the devil. We would be sneaking out whenever there was an *Orisha* ceremony somewhere, but when we came home we would deny we had been there.

One morning during our prayer session my father said to us that he had warned us several times not to worship *Orisha*, but we had refused to listen to him. He was not going to warn us anymore. But we would have to remember that on the day of judgement, God and the devil would pick their children among all the human beings. Then some of us would say that we were the children of God, but the devil would say: "No, you are mine." Then there would be an argument. God would say: "They are my children" and the devil would say: "They belong to me." And then the devil would have to prove his case.

Then my father said: "Do you know that each time you are watching the *Olorisha* the devil is there with his camera, taking the picture of all the worshippers ... and on judgement day, when there is an argument, all the devil will have to do is to bring out his pictures. When they have identified you on the photographs, you will be asked: was it a ceremony for God or for the devil? And you will have to answer: it was for the devil."

From that day on, we never went to see the *Orisha* dancers again, and for years after that I was so afraid. And at night I wondered how I could recapture those photographs from the devil, because although I had stopped going to the ceremonies, but of the pictures he had taken before?

U: Did you go to school in Igbara-Oke?

S: Yes, I finished my primary school—Standard VI. Then I went to Ile-Ife to what was known as a "Girls School." It was only a two-year course, but it was so intensive that you could come out with a Class IV certificate. In those days the full secondary school was six years. But you could leave with a Class IV certificate and find a job fairly easily. Or you could go back to school and work for your Class VI. I went on to Ilesha to the Women Training College. It had been set up by the British when they were on their way out of Nigeria. It was wholly financed by the British government and thirteen out of fifteen teachers were British. Every single thing we used in that school was imported from Britain: biros, paper—everything. Even our uniforms. I trained as a teacher and began to teach first at Ogotun then later at Ibadan.

U: But your teaching career didn't last that long. When did you go to university?

S: I went to Moscow in 1963.

U: You went to Moscow to study philosophy?

361

S: No, no. My husband got a scholarship and I went with him. I wanted to study economics, but at first I had to do a year of preparatory classes. Mainly Russian language, but also some other subjects. But after one year my husband decided to leave the Soviet Union, so I never had a chance to do the proper course.

U: Why didn't he like it? Was it the life style? The politics?

S: He found the language too hard. He wasn't a language man. As for me I could pick it up quickly.

U: What was life like in Moscow on campus? Did you have Russian friends?

S: We lived in what they called Cheriomushky: a whole house full of foreign students. Maybe I was biased coming from a completely free country, but I found everything terribly regimented. You could not, for instance, freely listen to the BBC. If you wanted to visit somebody, you had to deposit your passport with the porter of the house. You had to tell him which room you were going to and whom you were going to see. They recorded the time you entered and the time you left.

Another fundamental problem was food. Rice was a rare commodity. Sometimes you saw people queuing in front of a supermarket. They told you that rice was going to be sold. After queueing for three or four hours, somebody would come out of the shop and say: "What are you waiting for?". . . "We are waiting for rice." Then he would say: "But I don't have rice!" and everybody would go away without saying anything.

In 1964 I went to the Studienkolleg in Cologne while my husband went to the United States to continue his studies. I didn't have A levels so I couldn't enter a German university straight. I had to do another preparatory year. It was more or less like what I had to do in Moscow, except that this time I studied German. I did well, but I didn't enter a German university, where I had been offered a full scholarship in philology; I went to the US instead. But after three months I decided to return home, because all my children were at home. I already had three children then. I had made sure I gained admission to the University of Lagos, before I returned home.

U: You went on a long Odyssey abroad, that in the end didn't get you anywhere. But I suppose that it was all to the good: if you had stuck it out overseas and completed one of those courses, you would never have become a philosopher.

S: That's right. And when I returned home I was still not thinking about philosophy. I had been admitted for a BA Education and my main subject was to be English. But in those days the University was very relaxed about things: as long as you had a letter of admission you could go around and shop for subjects. You could do anything, as long as the Department was willing to have you. I did not really want to get back into school teaching. I first decided to do English, but some of the students said to me: "Madam, you better be careful. Because if you want to do English you may never end up with a degree from this university." I said: "Why?" They said that Wole Soyinka was their teacher and he had passed only two students that year! So I ran away. I didn't want to waste my time, because I already had three children.

I was looking around for subjects I could do. I had O levels in history and geography and I needed a third subject. Philosophy was the only department that was willing to take me, because they were the only ones who had no prerequisites. The system was that after the first year you dropped one subject and carried on with two. Then you did "Combined Honours" in the remaning two subjects. Or, if you did very well in one subject, you could even end up with "Single Honours."

I had intended to drop philosophy. But at the end of the first year my worst subject was history. I discovered that I didn't have the retentive memory that an historian needs. So I dropped history and decided I would try to aim at "Single Honours" in Geography. If you could score more than 60% in one subject, you would be allowed to do "Single Honours" in it.

At the end of the second year I qualified to do geography, but I also qualified to do philosophy. I got 62% in geography, and 64% in philosophy. It was difficult for me to make a choice: geography was willing to take me. At that stage I had already discovered my love for philosophy, but the problem was that they had only three lecturers and the professor said they couldn't accept a "Single Honours" student until they got another lecturer. But the new member of staff wasn't expected for some months.

So I decided I was going to run two "Single Honours" courses concurrently. I went to geography and I went to philosophy. But as soon as the fourth lecturer arrived in the Philosophy Department I dropped geography. It became very embarrassing, because the geography professor said: "She is my student!"

U: So you got into philosophy almost by accident. Or was it Eshu blocking all the other roads on which you attempted to travel, until you hit upon the right one? What finally attracted you to philosophy?

S: It was my nature. I found it so easy. I wasn't good at learning facts. But I could look at critical issues. I could take a sentence and pull it to pieces. So I was at home. I was comfortable. . . .

U: What kind of philosophy did they teach you at the University of Lagos? I suppose it wasn't African philosophy.

S: No, no. The first year we did Greek philosophy: starting with Thales and down to Plato and Aristotle. The second year we did British philosophy: Hume, Locke, Hobbes, all of them. In the final year we did British philosophy again with the one exception our English head could not ignore: Immanuel Kant. That was the only German philosopher we studied. I came out top of the class: Second Class Upper Division, which was the best you could hope for in any Honours class those days.

U: What could you do with a philosophy degree in Nigeria then?

S: I had to get a teaching job. I asked to be posted to Igbara-Oke, because I hadn't been home for many years. I wanted to spend time with my parents, who were getting old.

I taught geography and history in the local High School. But then a telegram came from my head of Department in Lagos, asking me to come and see him. He showed me an advert in the *Daily Times* asking students who had passed out with an Upper Second Honours degree to apply for a scholarship. I hadn't seen this advert at home and it was past the dead line; but Mr. A.G. Elgood had spoken to the registrar and he agreed to accept my late application. Four months later I became a university scholar. As a graduate assistant in those days I was a senior staff member of the university immediately. That was in 1972. Unfortunately Mr. Elgood, who had been so nice to me, had gone. I had to wait for a new supervisor to come, before I could register for my Masters Degree. Fortunately for me Dr. J.B. Danquah, Jr. joined the staff and he supervised my MA, the topic of which was *Trans.formational Grammar and Philosophical Analysis.*

U: You will have to explain to a layman like me what that means.

S: Noam Chomsky who tried to show that grammar and philosophical analysis were identical. He tried to break away from traditional grammar and he created a new grammar which he called "Transformational Grammar." This means that in a language there is a surface structure, which does not actually give you the true meaning of a sentence. The true meaning is the deep structure. So he said that trying to distinguish between the grammatical form and the logical form of a sentence was really a philosophical process. For Chomsky, grammar and philosophical analysis are the same thing, if it is properly done.

I wanted to refute that. That was the theme of my thesis. Up to a point he is right, yes. But when it comes to metaphysical issues, the grammarian has nothing to say. For example, take the word "shadow." For Chomsky it is something you can analyze. Shadow is a noun. It is referring to an object. But the point is: is it a physical object or is it abstract? You can see the shadow, but it is not a concrete object. So what is the true nature of shadow? And when we move to the area of the mind, for example, what is the mind? Physical? Non-physical? Spiritual? You are really talking metaphysics. That is not grammar. So I tried to show that we might actually start from identical notes, because the philosopher actually talks of the grammatical forms as being misleading.

Gilbert Ryle tried to show that some grammatical forms are systematically misleading as to their true meaning. He wrote a paper called *Systematically Misleading Expressions.* But his most popular work was *The Concept of the Mind,* where he tried to show that we may try to say something—but the intention is different from the meaning received by somebody else. For example, if I say: "Punctuality is worthy of praise," you may make the mistake of thinking that "Punctuality" is the name of a person.

I finished my Masters in 1974. But then I had to wait a long time for my Ph.D. because there was nobody to supervise. In 1976 a new Head came from the United States: Prof. G. Chatallian. He came with all the arrogance of a foreigner, with preconceived ideas, and he told us that he was going to make the Philosophy Department of the University of Lagos the best in the world. The way he thought to achieve that was to remove all African lecturers from the department. He said this publicly and in the first year he sacked Dr. Danquah. And when Dr. Danquah had left he held a staff meeting and said to us (we were all Nigerian) that we shouldn't be too happy that we were still remaining, because actually his recommendation to the University had been that we should all be sacked! But the university had said that he could not sack all lecturers at the same time. He should do it gradually. Next one on the list was Dr. Idoniboye, who was from the Rivers State and the most senior member of staff.

I was the most junior, but I just had to ask him: "Why are you sacking us? Is it because we lack competence?" And the answer was: "No. There are many competent people in the world, but I want the best." Then I said: "Who determines who are the best?" He said, he would, by virtue of his position. Then I said, that if I were the head of the department I would say that he was incompetent. He said I should wait until I became the head of department before I could take that position. I asked him what he expected us to do when we lost our jobs, because we were all married with children. He said, we should not worry, because he would give us all letters of recommendation to the new State Universities that were developing everywhere in those days. Then I said: "Yes, that is a good one. I can just imagine what you are going to write: Mrs. Oluwole was so good that I fired her!" It became a big tussle and I had to go to the people in authority. And this was the man who was to supervise my Ph.D.!

I had first wanted to write on witchcraft and he said I would need somebody to supervise the thesis who could read Yoruba. I went to Wande Abimbola and enlisted his support.

Then I handed in my proposal to Prof. Chatallian. A year later he called me and said that I would have noticed that he had not been looking at my papers. I said: "Yes, but why?" He said that I was too rude! And he said that was why he felt he was not going to look at my papers.

U: What—all because of that earlier incident?

S: No, every day! We were always coming up against each other. For example: there was a time when we were going to reorganize the syllabus. Prof. Chatallian said he was going to teach a course on the philosophy of non-violence. I said I was going to teach the philosophy of violence. He objected, he said: "Nigeria does not need violence." I said: "Who determines that? And secondly: you are a philosopher. You are not supposed to be dogmatic. We should give the students the option to choose. I have nothing against your teaching the philosophy of non-violence, but you must allow me to teach the philosophy of violence." He said there is nothing like that. I went to my office and picked out a book, the title was *The Philosophy of Violence*. So we were always having conflicts.

There came a time when he stopped responding to my greetings. But I continued to greet him. It's a subtle way of being rude. After a while he became uncomfortable. He called me to the office and said: "Mrs. Oluwole, why are you so stubborn?" I said: "What do you mean?" He said: "For the past six weeks you have been greeting me and I refused to answer you, but you continue to greet me." Then I said: "Oh, I am sorry, I didn't notice that you were not answering me." Then he said: "I am telling you: I shall not answer you, because you are so rude. So you should stop greeting me." I said: "That is interfering with my personal freedom. I will not interfere with your freedom. I give you the option to answer or not to answer. But it is my decision whether I want to greet you or not; and I am not asking you to answer." The next day he answered me.

But the problem was that he was the only person in the department who could supervise my Ph.D., because he was the only professor. So I had to look elsewhere and I went to Ibadan. Dr. P. Bodunrin there told me that he would accept me. So I registered to do "The Rational Basis of Yoruba Ethics." But he said there was no way I could do a Ph.D. on anything to do with African philosophy under his supervision. I was forced to look for a new topic. I looked at the work of Professor R.M. Hare. He has a strange theory which is similar to Kant's. But he denied that he did exactly the same thing as Kant. He believed that he arrived at exactly the same conclusion through pure logical construction of moral terms. He said that if you take some moral terms and see how they function in human language, and you examine the logic of the function, then you have two principles of understanding, which will now serve as logical principles and which will define the language of morals. Hence his first book had been *The Language of Morals*. His next book had been *Freedom and Reason*. That was actually the basis of his thesis: that every human being is free to do whatever he likes in moral matters, but that reason tells you there should be consensus. But then how do you reconcile the freedom and the reason which determine consensus?

So I called my thesis *Meta-Ethics and the Golden Rule.* And my conclusion was that all formulations of moral principles which, like Kant's, claim a position of universality, are formulations of the golden rule. The golden rule is usually defined as "do unto others, what you want others to do unto you." People have always defined it as the supreme moral principle. But in my own analysis I tried to show that it was not a law. It was an attempt to define what morality was all about. And if you regard it like that, you don't have to use it to find out whether an action is right or wrong.

Because actually it is not a canon of moral action, it is a definition of rational endeavor. Morality to me is a discipline, it is something you can describe purely in descriptive terms. When I think of salt——of its chemical properties—or of water, I am talking about an object. But whether my own personality as a subject comes into it is another thing. At least my aim is to look at water and to know what it is.

But when you talk about morality you have to assume the existence of at least two human beings and their relationship. So it is purely a classifying definition. I am not giving a law. I am merely letting you know when you are involved in moral matters and when you are involved in scientific matters. I am not telling you how to behave.

I am merely telling you that morality is about human actions and human relations. And that if you want to study human relations, in most cases the golden rule will fall into place. So that was my PhD thesis in 1984.

U: I hear that you got into conflict with your supervisor at Ibadan also.

S: Well, I had a lot to do with Prof. Bodunrin, even outside my thesis. I had started the Philosophy Students Association of Nigeria in Lagos and I had been its first president. The Association had spread to all the universities that taught philosophy and we organized an annual Philosophy Week. So I was always meeting Prof. Bodunrin for discussions on this and that. But we hardly ever agreed on anything. Even when he was supervising my thesis, he could see that I was revolting silently, because I was writing his thesis not my thesis. I wrote it merely to satisfy him. So when I had the oral examination, he was there with Prof. Wiredu of Ghana and Professor Sodipo. When they had finished examining me I had to go out, so that they could discuss whether I had been successful or not. After 45 minutes I was invited back into the hall and my supervisor said: "Well, congratulations, Mrs. Oluwole. You have done very well indeed. And I think that now we are giving you the authority to say all the nonsense you have been willing to say, because with a Ph.D. people will have to take you seriously."

U: Well, I guess the man was honest at least. But now that you have told me how you cut your path through the university jungle to obtain your Ph.D. I want to know: how did you get interested in Yoruba philosophy and how could you finally devote yourself to the study of it, after so many detours and side issues?

S: It was Dr. Danquah who first got me interested in African philosophy. But he was on that Egyptology thing, trying to trace the origin of African philosophy to Egyptian religion.

U: Another detour!

S: Yes. Although his father had written *The Akan Concept of God,* he had not actually stressed that point. The grand old man was not interested in proving to the West that Thales had borrowed the concept of God or mathematics or whatever from Egypt.

U: It is still fashionable. Cheikh Anta Diop and so many others still claim that there was a West African civilization from which the Greeks derived their ideas.

S: Yes, but I had a feeling right from the start: if it is true that the Greeks came and stole African philosophy, what happened to the Africans? You can steal my ideas, but you can't steal the brain from my head. Forget the borrowings. I don't mind what they took. But do we have anything left *today,* which I can show?

So my first concern was to find records of Yoruba thought. I went to the Yoruba Department and asked them whether I could have access to records of Yoruba thought before colonialism. There was an Egba poet called Sòbò Aròbíodu. I had heard about him even as a small girl. My father had been quoting his poems and his proverbs. I was excited to find that Prof S.A. Babalola and Moses Lijadu had recorded him and that I could listen to this material. But I was so disappointed to discover that he had been a Christian! He was talking about Jesus! He was hardly a Yoruba thinker! But the Yoruba Department told me they had no other records predating him. So I decided to look into the *Ifá* oracle texts.

To be honest, I had no hope of finding philosophy there. But at least I knew that these texts predated Christianity. At first I even found it difficult to read it properly. The language is not the common everyday language and I had not been trained to read it. It took me hours to figure out the first lines. But when I had worked out the meaning of the first poem, I was thoroughly surprised: there was nothing religious, supernatural or ritual, purely secular argument! There was a verse, for example, about the relationship between an adult and a child.

U: *Ifa* uses the famous image: the arm of a child is too short to reach the shelf under the rafters, but the hand of the adult is too large to fit into the neck of the calabash.

S: That's right. So it explains with simple logic that adults and children are interdependent. That none is superior to the other. That each has his own value.

U: Which is a philosophical statement.

S: Yes, but I realized immediately that I would have an uphill task. If I called *Ifa* philosophy, I would meet a lot of criticism. People would say that oral literature did not qualify as philosophy, because there is no author. They would say it was not a vehicle for philosophy. They claim there is no room for criticism or argument in oral traditions and poetry. They all agree that oral traditions can not develop intellectually. They said that Africans sometimes say things that were philosophical, but they did not have a tradition of philosophy. Some of them are not even as articulate as that. They simply say: "Philosophy is scientific, and Africans are not scientific." I have to use *Ifa* to debunk all that. The more I look at *Ifa* the more I see that all those things which, according to them, cannot be found in African thought are *there*. In *Ifa* we find arguments, we find criticism; *Ifa* is open. . . . . You can do many things with that poetry.

U: They will probably tell us that Africans had no system!

S: I was coming to that. Do you know the work of Allan Wood? He was a young man who wanted to write on the development of Bertrand Russell's philosophy. But he died so young. He had only written about ten pages or so. But this beginning was a masterpiece. And Russell himself later included them into his own book: *My Philosophical Development.* Allan Wood showed that Russell had a good understanding of the way the Western mind worked. He knew that they are lovers of systems. They like to create systems. But the only system they like is the hypothetical deductive one. Which means that you start from basic axioms and then you go deductively to arrive at conclusions. They think that anybody who presents a philosophy and cannot show that it is derived deductively from basic axioms is not writing philosophy. That is a widespread belief in the West, but Russell also said it was a fiction of the mind. That thinking does not have to start with an axiom and end with a proposition and that you cannot demand that your axioms be accepted as certainties. These philosophers who have been brought up in this Western System, they don't realize that they have been trapped by it. They always start to ask: what are the facts?

When you put up a piece of oral tradition they will ask: what are the facts? Do you move from premise one to premise two? You must prove things logically and draw your conclusion from the premise. This is an approach that is very fine for mathematics, but it is not even adequate for science. Scientific theorems are not absolute; no fact of experience logically entails a theory. Sentences that express causal relationships do not have to be logically related to one another. David Hume actually taught us that in science there is no logical relationship. When we say: "Fire causes heat," heat is not logically deduced from fire. It is just a matter of experience.

So this is not applicable to science, but it is what the philosophers want to do. Apart from saying that it is a questionable method for philosophy, I wish to maintain that even if the West wants to do it that way, others might want to do it differently. From what I have found, Africans are not looking for deductive systems.

U: Now tell me one thing: are you still the only one trying to establish Yoruba thought as a philosophy? Are there others now working in this field, or do you still come up against a lot of opposition?

S: There are now quite a number of lecturers and students who want to establish African philosophy. But the fundamental difference is: what is the basis for their claims? If you look at my book *Witchcraft, Reincarnation and the God-Head,* my claims are based on what people are saying in the street. How they describe a witch or what reincarnation means to them. But one must always be very careful; we can never be sure what recent ideas—for example Christian ideas—have influenced peoples thinking. People are not even aware of such influences.

For example, there is a current belief among Yoruba theologians, that you cannot become an ancestor unless you have lived a good life. Prof. Awolalu at Ibadan said so in his book. My question is: in what sense does he use the word ancestor? Because in the Yoruba conception, your father and your mother are your ancestors. Once you have lived to an old age, you become an ancestor. And when you have problems you can always go and pray to your ancestors. The conception of a holy life has nothing to do with it. Whatever one's father was in his earthly life—an armed robber or whatever—he is still one's ancestor. I cannot imagine that a Yoruba will say: "My father died in prison, therefore I will pray to another man's father who is holy."

These theologians are confusing ancestors with sainthood. But to declare that you cannot be deified unless you are a saint is a distortion of the facts. Was Ogun the best man in the world?

U: None of the *Orisha* could be described as "holy." On the contrary: they were all too human. Some were violent, all committed serious faults during their earthly existence, before their metamorphosis.

S: Exactly. So where did this idea of "holiness" come from, if it is not an infiltration of Christian ideas on Yoruba thought? But even the opposite can happen. There was another argument, when the government considered cremating dead bodies in Lagos, because of shortage of land. The first people to protest were the bishops. They said cremation was against the Bible. I had to go on televison with some of them and ask them: "Just where does it

370

say in the Bible that cremation is an offence? I am not denying it, but where is it written?" The argument was that when you cremate a dead body, you are destroying God's handwork. My answer to that was: "Who is destroying God's handwork? Is it God who allows me to die, or is it the one who burns my body? Because you are not burning a living person. And if I die and you bury me, am I not being destroyed?" I tried to let them see that the problem with the Lagos bishops was that they were transporting their Yoruba beliefs into Christianity. Because as an African I cannot allow you to burn my father. It is not possible. Because I know I have to pray to him.

What I am saying is that when you have a source that is dependable, because it records what people said a long time ago, then we are on a much firmer ground on which to base the claim of an authentic African philosophy before the advent of colonial education. *Ifa* is the most ancient and reliable source we have. I have found that many times the *Ifa* verses contradict what we have been accepting as Yoruba belief. We assume that the Yoruba associate age with wisdom. The *Ifa* oracle states very clearly that a young boy can at times be wise. So it is not the prerogative of the elders to be the only wise ones in the society.

Then there is the popular belief that masqueraders are ancestors who have returned. This worried me: I thought, can my people be so stupid, that they don't know that there are human beings in the masks? I was so relieved to find that the *Ifa* oracle tells a very elaborate story about the origin of the *Egungun* masquerade, which makes it very clear that there are human beings carrying the masks.

U: I think that the myth of the naivety of the Yoruba women and children who are terrorized by the masks is a missionary invention. Yoruba women have always known that the masks have human carriers; but of course, during the ritual the performer may become the ancestor and the ancestor may speak through him, in the same way in which the *Orisha* can speak through the priest who is possessed by him. Yorubas have a great sensibility for the powers of the supernatural, but they are certainly not naive.

S: There is a proverb which says:

> *A masquerade has died in the street.*
> *The news has been hidden from his family.*
> *But even though you say he is a heavenly being*
> *His parents must enquire about*
> *Their child's whereabouts at sundown.*

U: That is right. The Yoruba are very sophisticated people. They are neither hoodwinked nor are they intimidated by a fraudulent class of priests, which is a favorite defamation of Yoruba religion spread by missionaries. They are not fundamentalists. They understand the meaning of symbols and they have a great deal of common sense.

S: Yes. There is another proverb which says:

> *If you are being chased by a masquerade keep running.*
> *Just as human beings feel exhaustion*
> *so the heavenly beings get exhausted too.*

What I am trying to say is: there are a lot of people working on African philosophy. But what they are actually doing is to take some western concepts—God, society, woman, whatever—and then look for it in Yoruba thought. They go into various customs and proverbs and look for ways of justifying the existence of these ideas in African thought.

U: Archdeacon Lucas and Dr. Idowu come to mind.

S: Well, I don't mind them. But my own approach is different. I say: Let us examine what is there. Let us see what the oracle says, let us look at the style, let us look at their methodology. Let us look at their philosophy.

I want to look at the aims of the traditional intellectual Yoruba artist, at the intricacies of Yoruba language, I want to look at the forms. If you try to study African thought you may be tempted to use the Western principles, which have been taught. But if you do that, you are not going on a journey of discovery, you are going on a journey of invention.

But I don't want to *invent*—I want to *discover*—African philosophy.